THE
DYNAMICS OF
SUPERVISION

THE
DYNAMICS OF
SUPERVISION

MICHAEL E. ROCK

DRYDEN

A Division of Holt, Rinehart and Winston of Canada, Limited

Toronto Montreal Orlando Fort Worth San Diego Philadelphia London Sydney Tokyo

Requests for permission to make copies of any part of the work should be mailed to: Permissions, College Division, Holt, Rinehart and Winston of Canada, Limited, 55 Horner Avenue, Toronto, Ontario M8Z 4X6.

Every reasonable effort has been made to acquire permission for copyright material used in this text, and to acknowledge all such indebtedness accurately. Any errors and omissions called to the publisher's attention will be corrected in future printings.

Canadian Cataloguing in Publication Data
Rock, Michael, 1942–
        The dynamics of supervision

Includes index.
ISBN 0-03-922920-3

1. Supervision of employees. I. Title.

HF5549.12.R63 1994   658.3'02   C93-093258-7

Publisher: Scott Duncan
Editor and Marketing Manager: Donna Muirhead
Developmental Editor: Yolanta Cwik
Director of Publishing Services: Jean Lancee
Editorial Manager: Marcel Chiera
Production Manager: Sue-Ann Becker
Manufacturing Co-ordinator: Denise Wake
Cover Design: Dave Peters
Interior Design: Michael E. Rock
Typesetting and Assembly: Michael E. Rock
Printing and Binding: Best Gagné Book Manufacturers

♾ This book was printed in Canada on acid-free paper.
1 2 3 4 5   98 97 96 95 94

TO

Julianna Kathleen,
the promise of newness

PREFACE

The teacher, particularly the teacher dedicated to liberal education, must constantly try to look forward toward the goal of human completeness and back at the natures of ... students here and now, ever seeking to understand the former and to assess the capacities of the latter to approach it. Attention to the young, knowing what their hungers are and what they can digest, is the essence of the craft. One must spy and elicit those hungers. For there is no real education that does not respond to felt need ...[1]

M ost students have had the experience of being supervised. Ideas of being controlled, managed, perhaps manipulated or cared for may come to mind. Take a few minutes now to jot down the ideas or images that come to mind when you read or hear the word *supervision*.

1. _____

2. _____

3. _____

4. _____

5. _____

Most probably what has emerged from your list is a "push-pull" dynamic: what *you* wanted and were prepared to offer -- what Allan Bloom calls your "capacities" -- and what your *supervisor* (be he/she your parent, teacher, or actual supervisor) wanted for you. A good supervisor, as we shall see, assesses the capacities of his/her employees, knows what their "hungers" are and what they can "digest," and goes about fulfilling those goals. These skills apply, not only to the "craft" of teaching, but also to the craft of supervising.

The Dynamics of Supervision is a special book, written with the student's "hungers" in mind:

> *Relevancy*
> *Clarity*
> *Knowledge*
> *Application*

The book is (1) *relevant* because one of the great needs in business today is for effective supervision, (2) *clear* because unnecessary jargon and complicated theories have been eliminated or made simple, (3) *knowledge-based* because current ideas and practices in supervision are addressed, and (4) *applicable* because the text is experiential -- students *use* it in their learning.

The future of business and of the economy is intimately tied up with the *global marketplace*. We need a new paradigm or model of how we live and relate to the rest of the world. Globalization, or the conscious reality that each of us is interrelated with all other people on the planet, is " 'opening' Canada to the world, whether we like it or not."[2] The words "competitive," "service," and "people skills" are the real currency in today's supervisory practices because the competitive edge begins in managing both internal and external customers.[3] It is at this "moment of truth"[4] that the real winners[5] shine forth. The supervisor is the key person in this dynamic for he/she is the most immediate influence on the strategic and cultural success[6] of the business to making those moments the best they can be.

Supervisors are the first-level of management. While it is true that more senior management make policies and strategies for the business, supervisors carry them into action with the their front-line employees. In that respect supervision may be the most critical role within the company because of its strategic alliance with organizational goals and the practical day-to-day experience with and motivation of employees to carry out those goals successfully. The supervisor *bridges* those two worlds.

The Dynamics of Supervision is divided into four parts. *Part One, "Supervisory and Administrative Dynamics,"* addresses the technical topics of what supervisors do, the total quality ethical philosophy that needs to be promoted, how people are organized and priorities set, how problems are addressed and solved and decisions made, and the special concerns of supervisors: time management and how to conduct effective meetings.

Part Two, "Personal, Interpersonal, and Group Dynamics," addresses the personal development topics of understanding individual behaviour, the communication skills of speaking and listening, how to motivate and empower employees for productivity, providing leadership and championing groups that work effectively, and the special skills involved in conflict resolution and negotiating.

Part Three, "Human Resource Development Dynamics," addresses the important work topics and issues of how to select and keep employees, job performance evaluation, working with the union, promoting health and safety and dealing with stress, acknowledging women and equity issues, and the whole area of addiction and problem employees.

Throughout the text every effort has been made to keep a "how to" focus for the student. The most basic question an employer is going to ask a new employee is: "Can you help me with *this* problem?" The student/new employee will need to know *how to apply* what he/she has learned. The theories and content knowledge base will help steer the problem-solving process in the workplace, but what will matter is the answer to the following question: "Can I apply what I know?" *The Dynamics of Supervision* prepares you, the student, with an affirmative answer. You will not be entering the work world *cold*, so to speak, but with an experientially based preparation.

Throughout this text there are many references to companies, organizations, and business people. While all of these deserve recognition, one particular organization, Valhalla Inn Markham, a family-owned Canadian company, opened in 1990, has been used consistently throughout to highlight different themes. Valhalla Inn Markham was chosen because of its outstanding contribution to the customer and to business practices under the leadership of general manager Graham Willsher.

There is a special *Endnotes* section at the back of the book. Every effort was made to have the text flow smoothly, without too many visual interruptions by way of footnotes on the page. Material is amply researched, and for those students who want to pursue further reading, or to have references for projects, papers, etc., the endnotes will be of great help.

Within fifteen months of opening its doors, the Valhalla Inn Markham was recognized by prominent business organizations for its commitment to quality performance. The 650-member Markham Board of Trade provided the hotel with its Award for Overall Business Excellence followed in 1992 by the Award for Excellence in Community Relations and Cultural Environment. *FoodService & Hospitality* magazine and Ecolab presented the hotel with the Clean Kitchen Award (Hotel Sector), for the cleanest hotel kitchen in Canada; and the AAA/CAA travel organization presented the hotel with its prestigious Four Diamond Award, a recognition afforded to only twenty-eight hotels in Ontario in 1992.

An *Instructor's Manual*, with teaching notes, answers to end-of-chapter discussion questions, true-false and multiple-choice questions, and overheads, is available to those who adopt this text as a course requirement.

This Canadian text has been possible only with the support of Donna Muirhead, Acquisitions Editor, and reached completion with the support of Yolanta Cwik, Developmental Editor, who provided oustanding assistance in its production. I also thank the following reviewers, who helped keep the material on track through their suggestions and feedback: John Brierley, Seneca College; Dorothy Derkse, Red River Community College; Charlie Miller, S.A.I.T. and Miller Management Consulting; John Miteff, Seneca College; Stuart Morton, Delta Faucet Canada (professional review); Clifford Pitts, Centennial College; John Redston, Red River Community College; and Patrick Webb, Lethbridge Community College.

My final words of thanks go to my wife, Janice, who could have said, "He's always on the computer!" but instead, gave me the time and emotional support to keep going, in spite of the busy schedules we both have. Thank you, Janice.

Special Note: Art Work

"Clipart Images from CorelDraw 3.0 were used in the preparation of this manual."

Special thanks are also owed to the following for their art work contributions: Adrienne M.L. Rock, Ross C.K. Rock, and D. Paul Sinden.

A Note from the Publisher

Thank you for selecting *The Dynamics of Supervision* by Michael Rock. The author and publisher have devoted considerable time to the careful development of this book. We appreciate your recognition of this effort and accomplishment.

We want to hear what you think about *The Dynamics of Supervision*. Please take a few minutes to fill in the stamped reply card at the back of the book. Your comments and suggestions will be valuable to us as we prepare new editions and other books.

CONTENTS

PART ONE:

SUPERVISORY
AND ADMINISTRATIVE DYNAMICS

Executive Summary

All supervisors need to be skilled in the technical matters of their work. Unlike more senior levels of management, supervisors, being first-level management, must know the "nuts and bolts" of the job.

Typically a supervisor has come up from the shop floor, not just by being promoted or appointed, but through merit and with adequate training.

To be effective, a supervisor must understand the supervisory role (ch. 1), in other words, what supervisors actually do. A major part of supervising well is to put into practice a total quality ethical philosophy, a philosophy that says, "Do it right the first time."[1] It is a philosophy geared to excellence, ethical conduct, and a quality service or product from the very beginning (ch. 2). To do this, supervisors need to organize their employees well and set realistic objectives (ch. 3). These objectives must be for the company, but also benefit the company in relation to the global, or world, marketplace.[2] No longer can supervisors see their role only in relation to their immediate surroundings. The global marketplace is not just a pretty phrase. It is a reality that managers of all firms, large and small, must face every day. " 'Those Canadian firms that are going to succeed will be the ones that are successful in international markets,' says Jim Parr, who heads the executive search practice for management consultants Peat Marwick Stevenson & Kellogg of Toronto.' "[3] Each and every day supervisors are confronted with problems; they have to solve these problems and often make decisions regarding them (ch. 4). Finally, as part of their technical commitment, supervisors must often attend and run meetings. Doing that part of the job well is more and more crucial.

CHAPTER ONE

UNDERSTANDING WHAT SUPERVISORS DO

> Supervisors are, so to speak, the ligaments, the tendons and sinews, of an organization. They provide the articulation. Without them, no joint can move.
>
> -- Peter F. Drucker[4]

LEARNING OBJECTIVES

At the end of this chapter, students will be able to:

- Define the key terms in this chapter
- Explain the supervisor's changing environment
- Specify the role and importance of supervision to the organization.
- Outline the key work functions of supervisory success
- Identify the three management skills supervisors must practice
- Detail the significance of managing the boss
- Describe the "big picture" of supervision as a process

Opening scenario

*B*eing a supervisor today is both challenging and somewhat painful. Many of the old ways of doing things have disappeared, and, for older supervisors, that condition may be quite distressful. Like many things that are changing in our society in this information age, some supervisors feel the loss of what could be called their *trusted meanings*, or what they have relied on up to this point in their lives. No longer are the skills they came into the workforce with needed or useful. They face obsolescence, or not being useful any more to their company. Complicating this loss are first-hand accounts, from newspapers and colleagues, of those who have been laid off or of those who will have to assume a larger workload of responsibilities to make up for those who were dehired when the company downsized or restructured.

On the other hand there are existing supervisors, and would-be supervisors, who are happy with the changes in our society today and the overflow effects these changes have on the working environment. Because of the women's movement, for instance, a more egalitarian, or equally balanced and managed, workplace is in some companies an actuality, in others a distinct possibility. Both federal and provincial legislation against discrimination in the workplace have begun to make their impact. Treating employees with dignity and respect is a value and a workplace ethic that may not be systemically evident in every company, but it is certainly a welcome challenge for many supervisors today. They realize that employees want to be challenged, but in a positive and motivational manner. Gone are the days when fear and belligerence were the norms by which supervisors got what they wanted done. The challenge now, as Winston Churchill pointed out years ago, is how to get people to do what *you* want them to do so that *they* want to do it. This leadership role, of course, assumes that what you want employees to do is both ethical and legal.

The discriminating supervisor will acknowledge what is valuable and needed in the workplace, and will begin addressing the important issues and implementing strategies to enhance workplace effectiveness.

What would *you* do if you were the one called in and given the supervisory promotion? What would be going through your mind if you heard the words: *You are being promoted to supervisor?*

Reflective Exercise

Think of some of the hopes and concerns that you might have if you were given the promotion.

Hopes

_____

_____

_____

_____

Concerns

_____

_____

_____

_____

Like most people you would probably feel excited as well as somewhat apprehensive. Your excitement would be because of the new opportunity, your apprehension would concern whether you were capable of handling the new role and responsibilities.

This book is set up to help you to know about, anticipate, and practice some of the supervisory skills you will need in order to be successful. All too often someone "on the line" is promoted to supervisor and expected to be successful, even without training. Being a good worker does not necessarily mean that you will be a good supervisor. Supervision is a skill, and like all skills it can be learned and mastered.

THE SUPERVISOR'S CHANGING ENVIRONMENT

dy•nam•ic
Gk. *dynamikos* powerful
fr. *dynamis* power

su•per•vis•ion
a critical watching and directing

Today's world is a different world from even that of the early 1980s. There have been so many changes, so much reinterpretation of what we have traditionally taken for granted. As values change, so does society, and so do individuals. Practices and activities that were once thought impossible or "fringe" are acceptable today. It is an understatement to say that the workplace has become a challenge!

It is quite understandable if you panicked somewhat in thinking of yourself as a supervisor. Where do I begin? What should I know? What are the most important things to do? What or who can I depend on? What kinds of challenges will I have to meet and overcome?

Indeed, the challenges are many for today's supervisor. If we were to itemize a list of some of the changes and challenges that are having an impact on society and for which the supervisor must have some awareness, they would probably include many of the following items:

- Canada's diverse workforce and multicultural focus
- heightened awareness of the issue of sexual harassment
- the emphasis on the competitive global marketplace
- the elimination of a lot of the middle management level
- leaner forms of organizational structure
- the aging population and the need for elder-care
- human resource (HR) concerns, such as daycare, flexible working hours, pay and employment equity, wrongful dismissals, inflation, layoffs, organizational restructuring, downsizing
- the free trade agreement (FTA)
- the information technology (IT) explosion
- the information-as-power phenomenon
- *the* critical variable of customer service

- the knowledge *vs.* the industrial employee
- the shortage of skilled labour
- the emphasis on corporate culture, ethics, and people skills
- coping with constant change and computer literacy

For many supervisors, these challenges seem overwhelming, and what was promised as good news with the coming of the technological and information age does not feel that good after all.

However, the good news, according to public policy analyst Stewart Kronberg, is that, in spite of the pain of Canada's recession, a much-needed restructuring and adjustment within the Canadian economy is taking place. What makes the recession as well as the many changes and supervisory challenges so painful to so many is that the adjustment has been compressed into a very tight time frame and not spread over a number of years. The speed of the adjustment is "driven by the free-trade pact, a higher dollar, the discipline of the global economy, changing consumer attitudes and, of course, the recession."[5] Supervisors have to do "catch up" very quickly today because success is more obviously dependent on improving productivity and developing new skills and flexibility. The pain results from some companies not being able to make this adjustment, and hence, not surviving.

> The philosophy of Valhalla Inn Markham is to be a leader in establishing original ideas to attract its clientele, yet at the same time seeking out *role models* in industry from whom it can learn. The hotel acts upon the belief that there is no better way of achieving success in quality service than studying and implementing the ideas and philosophies of those who have conquered the road to success.

THE ROLE AND IMPORTANCE OF SUPERVISION TO THE ORGANIZATION

An argument could be made for the *absolute* strategic importance of supervision in an organization. The argument would run as follows:

> The management hierarchy model of *top management*, *middle management*, and *supervisory (or first-level) management* should be turned on its head. In practical terms this would mean that supervisors should be given more responsibility, pay, latitude,

authority, and recognition. The reason for this "standing-the-management-model-on-its-head" is because supervisors can make or break the organization or company. Why? Because they are the closest to the action, where the company meets its "moment of truth," that is, where front-line employees meet the customer. Front-line employees are who they are to a great extent because of the supervisory environment, philosophy and skills of their actual supervisor. **The supervisor, in that respect, then, is the *ambassador*, or *emissary*, for more senior levels of management and acts as a *linking pin*, or connector, between employees and more senior levels of management.** It's in senior management's best interest to have the finest possible ambassador. On the other hand, management expert Elliott Jacques feels that the traditional hierarchical model is exactly what business needs today. While some would call him "neo-feudal" in his approach, Sunoco Inc. tried his methods and found productivity shot up and moved them, on return on capital, "from near the bottom in the industry to first place in a year," and Jos Wintermans, CEO for Canadian Tire Acceptance Ltd., said Jacques' methods have led to "absolutely fascinating changes," with such spectacular results as 500,000 new credit card accounts in 1989 compared to 135,000 in 1987![6]

Diagrammed below is an example of a customer-driven model:

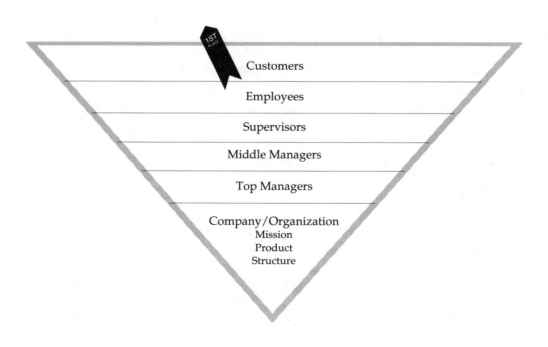

Supervisors are front-line managers! **Management** is often described as getting things done through other people, of trying to influence employees, in this case, to do what needs to be done because *you*, the supervisor, want it done.[7] A contemporary management writer says that management is "the process of achieving desired results through efficient utilization of human and material resources."[8] Since supervision is a front-line, first-level management activity, we can define **supervision** as the process of getting what *you* want done, that is, achieving *your* desired results, through the positive encouragement and efficient utilization of front-line employees and material resources to accomplish organizational goals.

> Moses took Jethro's advice and chose capable men from among all the Israelites. He appointed them as leaders of thousands, hundreds, fifties, and tens. They served as judges for the people on a permanent basis, bringing the difficult cases to Moses but deciding the smaller disputes themselves (Exodus, 18:24-26).[9]

While some might think that supervisory management is a modern reality and activity, all we have to do is look back through history and we find numerous examples of people trying to influence others to get something accomplished. We can pick out examples of early management as far back as humankind itself. Four thousand years ago, the Egyptians used management/supervisory practices to complete the building of their pyramids and run their business affairs. The Hebrews, in the Book of Exodus, make reference to the delegation of authority and responsibility and how Moses supervised his people.

The Greeks and Romans also demonstrated supervisory/management skills in their social and business relations. The Roman army is a classic example of organization, for instance. Throughout the next two thousand years, until the twentieth century, additional examples of management/supervisory practices showed themselves. The Roman Catholic Church and the military are good illustrations of these practices. By the 1800s, around the time of the Industrial Revolution, a greater need for more formal management principles became evident since society and work were becoming more focused around productivity. If it is fair to say that management/supervisory practices to this point were more by "the seat of the pants," we can now say that a more "scientific" approach was becoming necessary.

The more "scientific" approaches that emerged in the nineteenth and twentieth centuries were continuing efforts at formalizing how to get people to do what *you* wanted them to do so that *they* wanted to do it. These approaches have included (1) scientific management,[10] (2) administrative management,[11] (3) bureaucratic management,[12] (4) human relations management,[13] (5) behavioural science management,[14] (6) operations research management,[15] (7) human resources management,[16] and currently, (8) total quality management (TQM).[17]

The main development throughout these approaches in management/ supervisory thought is the following:

> Managers and supervisors have gradually shifted from an approach in which they said, "Jump," and the employee said, "How high?" to one which takes into consideration the employee's contribution, the situational context, and the work that needs to be done. The shift, in other words, has been from a simplistic, and autocratic, understanding of how to get employees to do what you want them to do to one of consensus and relationship, whereby employees want to do what you want them to do because *they* want to do it.

In times past ***industrial employees*** obeyed supervisors because they were told to do something. "Industrial" is a mindset whereby employees were task-oriented and that was what counted -- the "do-what-you're-told" philosophy and approach. The contemporary ***psychological employee*** wants to know what's in it for him/her. This is a mindset whereby employees are more relationship-oriented: their needs, goals, and concerns have to be considered by the supervisor. Some supervisors may not like this reality, but "the dawning of the age of Aquarius" as the song goes brings with it employees who *think*, and not, as before, just *do*. We cannot escape this psychological revolution. Our whole society is "psychological"; our colleges and universities graduate students who are "creatively selfish": these students want to feel autonomous, yet be able to contribute; they do not want to exclude either home or work; and they want to find meaning in their work. These kinds of employees are very different from those of one hundred years ago.

THE SUPERVISOR: A TRUE CATALYST

The supervisor's role, therefore, is one of trying to mediate between what the organization wants -- via middle and top management policies and directives -- and what his/her employees want as modern psychological workers. The supervisor is truly "the middle person" and this can be a very difficult role to fulfil. It requires that the supervisor be mature enough and have attained sufficient personal development and technical skill to navigate through some choppy waters at times.

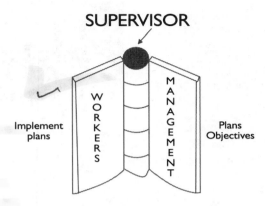

The supervisor's role is accordingly a critical and important one because it is the "hinge" or connector between the organizational goals and the employees who will work to fulfil those goals, and hence make the organization productive and successful. The supervisor is a true **catalyst** here -- a person who makes things happen, from above (with senior management) and from below (with employees). While it is true that the senior management team is ultimately responsible for organizational productivity and success, the supervisor is that part of the management team that is on the front line with the employees and will accomplish these organizational goals. The supervisor's philosophy and approach can make or break this employee task.

THE KEY WORK FUNCTIONS OF SUPERVISORY SUCCESS

Supervisors generally do the same kinds of things as middle and senior managers, but the time they spend on the key work functions differs. What are these functions that all managers do in order to get employees to work effectively and efficiently in accomplishing organizational objectives and goals?[18]

Planning determines *what* needs to be done and the objectives and goals to be accomplished. It involves such activities as forecasting, determining agendas, setting schedules, setting and prioritizing objectives, making budgets, developing strategies, and steps to reach targeted objectives and goals.

Approximate amount of time spent on these functions by supervisors								
Function % of time	5%	10%	15%	20%	25%	30%	35%	40%
PLANNING								
ORGANIZING								
STAFFING								
DIRECTING								
CONTROLLING								

100%

Total "functional" time for supervisor

Organizing determines *how* the needs are to be fulfilled and the goals accomplished. It involves such activities as dividing work into manageable units, arranging duties, responsibilities and tasks for specified employees, establishing an accountability feedback process, making clear the lines of authority, the channels of communication and proper protocol, and the promotion of effective teamwork.

Staffing determines *who* will be able to fulfil the needs and accomplish the goals. It involves such activities as recruiting, selecting, hiring, and training employees to fulfil and accomplish organizational needs and goals, administering pay equity and compensation rates, implementing the appropriate elements of the human resource planning process, transferring employees to any necessary permanent or temporary job postings, and discharging employees through firing or laying off. Usually, if the company is large enough, the more specific technical matters related to hiring and compensation are worked out by the human resources department. However, supervisors need to be aware of these human resource policies, not only for ethical, but also for legal reasons.

Directing determines the *motivational vision and climate* within which the needs are fulfilled and the goals accomplished. It involves such activities as articulating and modelling an ethical and human resources-oriented philosophy of supervision, delegating appropriate work tasks, schedules, duties and responsibilities, communicating effectively to harness employee support and understanding in fulfilling and meeting organizational needs and goals, creating a motivational environment so that employees will *want* to do what *you* want them to do because *they* want to do it, and developing employees to maximize their potential and contributions.

Controlling determines the *measurement of success* and any necessary *corrective steps* in fulfilling the needs and accomplishing the goals. It involves such activities as establishing performance criteria, both human and budgetary, measuring performance against the criteria, appraising/analyzing the results, and taking corrective steps, if necessary, to determine if the original objectives and goals have been met.

MANAGING BY EXCEPTION

Controlling things well the first time so that the supervisor really only has to attend to the *exceptions*, those areas only of responsibility or crisis that demand his/her personal time.

THE THREE MANAGEMENT SKILLS SUPERVISORS MUST PRACTICE

All levels of management are responsible for seeing that the organization meets its needs and accomplishes its goals. The difference between the levels of management -- top, middle, and supervisory -- in applying management skills is one of emphasis. However, there are three management skills that all managers -- including supervisors -- must practice if they are to be successful.

Human Skills - 60% of the time

Technical Skills - 30% of the time

Conceptual Skills - 10% of the time

Human skills incorporate the ability to work well with people on all levels: employee-supervisory, middle management, and senior management. In essence, the supervisor is a genuine *actualizer*:

Actualized supervisors know how they feel, trust those feelings, know what they want -- can say yes or no -- accept their shadow or dark side, enjoy the competitiveness of business, and can be constructively assertive when needed.[19]

Some of the human and personal development skills that supervisors must have include the following:

Self-understanding
Communication
Listening
Giving appropriate feedback
Coping with criticism
Conflict resolution
Giving recognition
Understanding the uniqueness
of individual behaviour
Managing group and team behaviour
Being aware of unconscious or shadow motives
Fostering honesty and openness
Developing harmony
Working well with people[20]

Customer Delight! The Valhalla Inn Markham realized in establishing its criteria for service that customer *satisfaction* was not an acceptable guide. The definition of success would be based on customer *delight*. The theme for a recent convention hosted by a new client to the hotel was "Nobody Does It Better"! The client's congratulatory letter to the hotel after the event indicated that the Valhalla Inn Markham exemplified that slogan through the warm and personalized attention given by its staff.

This list could be intimidating to some would-be or current supervisors. While it is not required that supervisors be psychologists, it is critical, however, that they understand *something* of human behaviour, or, at least, be able to know when there is a problem and get appropriate help.

Aristotle said that the beginning of wisdom is wonder and, for us, in practical terms, it is the wise supervisor who acknowledges his/her "wonder," or puzzlement, about a problem and seeks a solution. It is said that supervision is both an *art* and a *science*. In an age when technology dominates and the belief in knowledge-as-information overshadows the traditional idea of the educated person as the one who makes right judgments, it is good to be reminded by Tolstoy, the Russian novelist, of what real knowledge is, as heard through the words of Mason, in conversation with Pierre: "The highest wisdom is not founded on reason alone ... The highest wisdom is one. The highest wisdom has but one science -- the science of the whole."[21] Mason goes on to say that this real knowledge comes from self-reflection, self-knowledge.

Excelling: the ability to see the "big picture"!

More time has been spent on this particular supervisory skill, not because the others are less important, but rather, the *impact* of this skill *throughout* the supervisory management process is indeed extensive. It can been called **the 90% Factor**, that is, most likely 90% of the time the problems that supervisors will have to confront will be *people*, or *relationship*, issues, and not technical or conceptual ones. When problems occur on the job, it is often more accurate for the supervisor to ask: "*Who* is the problem?" rather than, "*What* is the problem?" Nine times out of ten, the supervisor will be called upon to problem solve around a relationship issue or concern: over resources, time, responsibilities, etc.

Technical skills incorporate *job knowledge* itself, the *what* that needs to be done. This job knowledge may be in the area of service management, accounting, computer programming, manufacturing of x,y,z widgets, etc. Whatever the area, the technical skills will refer to those specialized competencies needed to get the work accomplished. Robert L. Katz, writing in the *Harvard Business Review*, says, "Technical skill involves specialized knowledge, analytical ability within that specialty, and facility in the use of the tools and techniques of the specific discipline."[22]

Supervisors need to establish an *authoritative posture* from the outset. Having an authoritative posture means to be firmly rooted in one's technical discipline, to be firmly rooted in one's inner sense of self, and to be firmly rooted in the commitment to positive human relations.

It is important that supervisors be technically competent because of the *perception* involved on the part of employees. Employees want and expect their supervisor to be technically competent. New supervisors need to establish an *authoritative posture* from the outset. Having an authoritative posture means to be firmly rooted in one's technical discipline, to be firmly rooted in one's inner sense of self, and to be firmly rooted in the commitment to positive human relations. An authoritarian posture uses power to try to accomplish means and ends, and a hands-off posture just doesn't take a stand. Research and experience both indicate that effective supervisors are those who can "pitch in" with employees and do the technical work, if that action is necessary.

Conceptual skills incorporate the ability to understand how the organization works, its policies and procedures, its philosophy and culture, and its interrelationships with its internal and external environments. It is the ability to see "the big picture" and to contribute to the whole, not just the supervisor's particular part. These skills are necessary if a supervisor wants to advance within the organization. In the best sense of the terms, it is also developing "political smarts," appropriate protocol -- gestures, language, behaviour, beliefs, actions -- that contribute to the on-going attainment of organizational needs and goals and reinforce the perception that the supervisor is committed to the *mission* of the company or organization.

Specific things that a supervisor would do in mastering the organizational conceptual skills would be: acknowledging memos and genuinely reading official correspondence to keep up-to-date; investing energy and time in upgrading skills and knowledge through training and development seminars or workshops; volunteering, when appropriate, to be part of company task forces, or planning sessions; projecting an image as a team player, one who will "go the extra distance"; making a conscious effort and commitment to organizational problem solving, anticipating potential problems and contributing to their resolution.

MANAGING THE BOSS /read —

A critical factor in the supervisory experience -- and one which is often overlooked in the preparation of new supervisors -- is the important skill and reality of **managing one's boss**. That expression may sound odd to some because many people think it is the boss's job to manage *me*.

Basic Realities

First, bosses are human too. Second, they have, in their own area of responsibility, similar requirements and constraints that supervisors have, and often more intensely. Third, bosses have generally an even greater demand on their time than employees have. Fourth, bosses usually want good working relations with their subordinates. Fifth, the boss is powerless if he/she is not informed. Sixth, the boss is ultimately responsible.

While that is true, it is equally important to manage *upwards*. Supervisors are responsible to and for their subordinates, to their peers, *but also* to their superiors. To be effective means working with all three levels. Much headache and heartache can be avoided with a little supervisory preventative medicine: taking care of one's relationship with the boss. What does that mean in practice?

> **What Supervisors Can Do To Manage Their Boss**

- Know the boss's world: philosophy, concerns, pressures, hopes, objectives;

- Keep the boss informed about major concerns;

- Promote the boss's visibility and competence in a genuine way;

- Never embarrass the boss;

- Promote new ideas as suggestions tied in with the boss's own goals;

- Give the boss recognition and appreciation;

- Be a dependable, trustworthy friend and colleague;

- Communicate well, acknowledging the boss's style and preferences;

- Seek to secure any loose ends the boss is unaware of; and

- Disagree in private.[23]

SUPERVISION AS A PROCESS

Being a supervisor is never a static activity. There is always something new happening, either in the technical field itself -- such as computer technology -- or in the situations that arise each and every day.

In many ways work is like other areas of our lives, such as home life: each day brings new challenges, problems, solutions, opportunities. We often ask, "How was your day?" Whether it was good or bad, we can predict that it was probably *different* than any other day.

Every day is different. Change is the constant now. People change; technology changes; society changes; organizations change. This is difficult for many people. We will look at change in more detail later (chapter 17).

Supervisors must adapt to this on-going *process* of supervisory management. In many ways being a supervisor is being a *learner* and a *teacher* at the same time. Learning means change; effective learning requires flexibility and sensitivity. The *supervisor-as-learner* knows that there will always be new horizons and challenges to meet and adapt to; the *supervisor-as-teacher* knows that his/her key responsibility is to influence subordinates' opinions, attitudes and work performance in such as way that they will fulfil and accomplish organizational needs and goals because *they* want to.

True supervisory leadership, therefore, is getting employees to do what *you* want them to because *they* want to do it.

SUMMARY

Supervision is a unique challenge in today's modern organizations.

Our world is changing rapidly and Canadians must quickly adapt to the globalization, or world setting, of business or be left out and shunted off to the corner of the international forum.

Supervisors, seasoned individuals as well as novices, work within this "bigger picture" environment, not only in relation to their company, but to the world. The fundamentals, however, of dynamic supervision still remain intact. As a matter of fact, they are even more important and often nuanced differently.

Future organizations will be more responsive to their clients, mainly because the business environment is so *dynamic*, and decision making has to be done much more quickly and at the source, i.e., the customer. Thus, trust and training will need to be important factors in tomorrow's organizations.

The psychological employee demands more human input and meaning from work. Supervisors will thus spend even more time managing the human factor than they have in the past.

Supervisors are involved in the functions of managing: planning, organizing, staffing, directing, and controlling.

Supervisors must also know how to manage their boss. This is a side of supervising that is not mentioned that often. And finally, the supervisor is both a learner and a teacher.

TERMS/CONCEPTS

supervision	management by exception
industrial employee	human skills
psychological worker	technical skills
planning	conceptual skills
organizing	managing the boss
staffing	supervisor-as-learner
directing	supervisor-as-teacher
controlling	

DISCUSSION QUESTIONS

1. No longer can the supervisor see his/her role only in relation to his/her immediate surroundings. Discuss.

2. What are some of the external challenges impacting on the supervisor today?

3. Define *management* and *supervision*. Describe how they are different yet related. *control /direct* *have charge /direct* Pg. 9

4. What is the difference between the psychological employee and the industrial employee?

5. Describe the supervisor's role.

6. Briefly describe the key work functions of supervisory success.

7. What is *the 90% Factor* and why is it important in supervision?
   -people or relationship issues not technical n conceptual
   ^ -confronted c̄   issues-

8. What is *management by exception*?

9. Why is it important to manage the boss?

10. Discuss how supervision is a process?
    -always something new happening
    - new challenges
    -problems
    - solutions
    - opportunities

- People change
- Society changes
- technology
- organizations —

ASSIGNMENT

Think about a supervisory experience that you have had. Describe that experience below.

_____

_____

_____

_____

_____

_____

_____

_____

_____

Identify the skills you practiced and the new understandings that you acquired as a result of that experience.

SKILLS PRACTICED	NEW UNDERSTANDINGS

CHAPTER TWO

DEVELOPING A TOTAL
QUALITY ETHICAL PHILOSOPHY

> We're always standing there with two roads in front of us, every day, every hour, every moment ... We have to make a choice; that's the privilege of being human.
>
> -- Cardinal Leger[1]

LEARNING OBJECTIVES

At the end of this chapter, students will be able to:

- Describe the radically different business environment today
  - Explain the urgency for quality and service
    - Identify the challenge of individualism
    and authenticity for today's supervisor
    - Cite the basic principles and philosophy
    of TQM: **T**otal **Q**uality **M**anagement
- Describe the importance of social responsibility and ethics
  - Identify the main factors in a business ethical philosophy

Opening scenario

*O*n January 1, 1991, employees at IBM Canada got a New Year's welcoming back message from their president and CEO, Bill Etherington. The message said: "Welcome to the first day of the new IBM Canada ... Let's get on with it."[2] "Getting on with it" certainly meant changing philosophy *and* practice from just a few years earlier. For instance, IBM Canada at one time had stated in its correspondence to a Japanese supplier that its "acceptable" defect level was set at 1.5 percent. This was a North American "high standard" at the time. The Japanese didn't quite understand the unusual request, but sent 1.5 percent defective parts in a separate plastic package with a letter that stated, "We don't know why you want 1.5 percent defective parts, but for your convenience we have packaged them separately."[3]

We cannot afford to be sloppy in our work habits any more. Supervisors are the closest "to the action" to prevent this sloppiness and to promote quality products and service. Consumers just vote with their feet as they have been doing with the governmental and fiscal nightmare of cross-border shopping.[12]

Bill Etherington went on to give IBM Canada's strategy for the new business world order. The company just had to produce results. IBM Corp.'s first loss ever in 1991, seeing "its profits dip by 96 per cent to a minuscule $14 million," could not be repeated. What Etherington had in mind was to "go back to the basic principles of how you actually operate that company." Businesses that are not deemed strategic will be dropped. To get to market faster, more "business partners and joint ventures" will happen. For the supervisor, of course, this will mean working in a more co-operative mode, teamwork, planning, commitment, and changing corporate cultures. It will mean facing the challenge of the *individualism* vs. *authenticity* dynamic, that is, the "what's-in-it-only-for-me" philosophy of the *current generation* vs. the *genuine search* that people have to be true to themselves, to find their self-fulfilment, and also to receive "a-good-day's pay-for-a-good-day's work." Says Etherington, "You partner with everybody you compete with. Some of the arrangements involve equity (some don't)." The main point is, though: *IT'S TIME TO GET ON WITH IT!*[5]

BUSINESS RADICALLY DIFFERENT TODAY

The world has radically shifted its priorities. The Soviet Union no longer exists as it was; the Berlin Wall tumbled; a world-wide recession gripped everyone in the beginning of the 1990s.

Reports poured in about companies going bankrupt, employees being laid off, and genuine dissatisfaction with the quality of products and customer service in Canada.

> "Some say customer service is about as bad as it can get in Canada and is appalling not only to consumers, but to employees as well."[6]

We are all more sensitive to the presence or lack of service today. Supervisors will be judged more and more on the basis of how well employees serve the customer.[7] According to some, the lack of quality and service, especially in the retailing services industry, is appalling and needs immediate action.[8]

Reflective Exercise

Assume you are a supervisor now. How do you think you would be expected to mentally shift gears and "get on with it." What would you do?

_____

_____

_____

_____

_____

Japanese quality is so threatening that people resort to Japan-bashing: blaming others for their troubles![9] Prime Minister Brian Mulroney recognized this in the U.S. Honda ruling which forbade Canadian-made cars (with U.S. engines![10]) from entering the United States, when he said, "We are getting sideswiped by American Japan-bashing."[11]

Customer Delight!
"We hope that our cus-
tomers will not just be
pleased, but *delighted* with
our service"
Valhalla Inn Markham

However, the "new wave" in retailing and in business
success for the supervisor will *have* to be customer
service. It is also the most important component in the
Total Quality Management (TQM) strategy.[12] James
Dion, of John C. Williams Consultants Ltd., says that
retail survival alternatives - - for instance, warehousing
- will "put some retailers out of business." He then goes on to add, "But it'll be
the ones with high costs, high margins and no service, and many of them
deserve to go out of business."[13]

*Braun's 10 principles
of good design*
1. Innovative.
2. Useful.
3. Aesthetic.
4. Logically structured.
5. Unobtrusive.
6. Honest.
7. Enduring.
8. Consistent details.
9. Ecologically conscious.
10. Minimal design.[14]

In an effort to rethink and re-examine a new business
environment and future, some even talk about "a
startling agreement between corporate and spiritual
thinking."[15] Anthony Eames, president of Coca-Cola
Canada Ltd., says lack of good quality service is
killing business![16] Donald Cooper, the very successful
entrepreneur of Alive and Well, the unique fashion
warehouse boutique in Markham, Ontario, says, "If
you don't have a passion for serving other humans,
for understanding and meeting their real needs...get
out of the business."[17]

In the automobile industry in North America, the Big Three automakers have
seen the handwriting on the wall, and it reads *teamwork*,[18] rather than "strong
chimneys," or what this author calls **corporate individualism**: "Strong
chimneys [each to his/her own turf] drive decisions without regard for the
customer." Historically, in practice that meant the "functional chimney matrix.
Manufacturing managers reported to one boss, engineers to another." Not
having people work together is still costing the Big Three. This conflict
between "harmony" and "individual expression" has even affected Japanese
management practices here in Canada. While the Japanese stress harmony,
teamwork and conformity, "nothing could be more foreign to the fiercely
independent North American worker, nor to the middle manager groomed in
a corporate star system to personal recognition."[19]

The purpose of this chapter is to look at some of the following key business factors: customer service, total quality management, and an ethical philosophy. Each of these factors is essential for success, "to get on with it" in the nineties and beyond the year 2000.

THE URGENCY FOR QUALITY AND SERVICE

CASE EXPERIENCES

1. Purolator Courier Ltd., Canada's largest courier service is practicing fast and friendly customer response. This service begins from the first phone call to the local office dispatcher, through to the driver. They take time with the customer, call the customer by name, and deal with the details immediately.

2. In an effort to maintain a customer's satisfaction, Mr. Murray Maw, Regional Manager, Service Centre Operations for Sharp Electronics of Canada Ltd., responded quickly in writing: *"Your feedback in this matter and value as a Sharp customer are worth much more."* Sharp pleasantly reimbursed the service fee and Maw concluded, "I hope you feel that this is an equitable action in favour of our effort to achieve your satisfaction as our customer."

3. Ross Laboratories, a Division of Abbott Laboratories, Limited, in Montreal, Quebec, also responded quickly to a customer's inquiry. Key personnel made phone calls, established customer rapport and reassurance, and answered all questions promptly and courteously. Simple. To the point. Immediate. Effective.

Such examples point up one thing: unless productivity (whether an "actual" product or a service) is customer-driven, and of quality, supervisors will not be in business for very long because the company will be out of business! These are the "moments of truth" that Jan Carlzon speaks about. He became the CEO of Scandinavian Airlines (SAS) in 1980 and implemented the philosophy that made his airline so successful. According to *Fortune* magazine, in 1983, SAS became the best airline for business travellers, while *Air Transport World* declared SAS the "airline of the year."[20]

A moment of truth is the encounter of customer and company representative.

Encounters leave impressions. It is the front-line employees who need scope and responsibility to make decisions and keep customers satisfied. And it is for this reason that Carlzon felt the traditional corporate structure needed to be turned upside-down, saying that "a true leader is one who designs the cathedral and then shares the vision that inspires others to build it."[21]

THE CHALLENGE OF INDIVIDUALISM AND AUTHENTICITY FOR TODAY'S SUPERVISOR

MYOPIA!

"Mr. Kissinger summed up one session saying, 'The Americans believe they will be the centre of the New World Order; the Europeans believe they will be the centre of the New World Order; the Japanese know they will be the centre of the New World Order.' " (World Economic Forum, Davos, Switzerland, February 1992)[22]

In chapter 1 we spoke of the psychological worker. While that reality is obvious to anyone who is a supervisor or manager, equally obvious is the challenge of *individualism* and the search for *authenticity* from today's worker. The new supervisor will have to take these realities into account in building a total quality ethical philosophy.

The topics of individualism and authenticity are introduced into this text on supervision because the new supervisor has different challenges from the supervisor of yesteryear. Today's supervisor must come to grips with the clamour of "competing voices, all claiming to be authentic, the true voice ..."[23] As well, Rollo May, the noted psychologist, says that we[24] "cling to the myth of individualism as though it were the only normal way to live, unaware that it was unknown in the Middle Ages (except for hermits) and would have been considered psychotic in classical Greece."[25] May likens this cult of individualism to the Greek mythological figure Narcissus -- from which we get narcissism -- who liked looking at himself in the mirror of the water's reflection! The individualistic or narcissistic worker is difficult to work with since he/she will not have much substance or commitment in relationships. They are too interested in their own causes.

A consequence of this psychology of individualism is the amount of unethical behaviour that is so apparent these years. Greed -- what's in it for me - is rampant and has wreaked havoc in the business world.[26] "A computer search through the outpourings of five months of accumulated reporting ... shows that greed as a private-sector vice has been mentioned 259 times. That is more than one mention a day."[27]

If the cult of individualism tells me that "I only" am the important one, then I can easily act in my own self-interest, and not think of others. We will speak to this issue of ethics below.

AN UNETHICAL LEGACY

The late Robert Maxwell's personal belongings were auctioned off at Sotheby's in London, England, to help pay off some of the enormous debts he left behind. About $1 million was raised, not nearly enough to cover the millions that Maxwell is allegedly accused of taking to cover his expenses and keep his heavily indebted business concerns afloat. Long-time employees were bilked of their pensions; he was known as a very nasty person. Tony Horwitz, of *The Wall Street Journal*, referred to him as "the Al Capone of Fleet Street."[28] Hotelier Shirley Gardner bought his bed for $2,900 to put in her Scandal Suite in her hotel in England. She said, "People can do whatever they want in it and at least they know they are not doing anything worse than the chap who had the bed did."[29]

David Crane, in commenting on the uproar that Japan's former prime minister Noburo Takeshita created with his remarks at the World Economic Summit in Davos, Switzerland, in February 1992, that American workers were not working hard enough, says that we should heed Japan's analysis for we would hear things about ourselves that we need to address, like our *individualism,* for instance.[30] We would hear that, in many ways, we have played "casino capitalism" and that there has been quite a "greed mentality" over the past few years with the relentless individualism, dehumanization, alienation, and innumerable social ills it has spawned. "Harvard economist Robert Reich is persuasive in arguing that the purpose of demonizing the Japanese is to replace the defunct Soviet Union with a new evil empire that binds Americans together against a perceived external threat."[31] However, we must set aside our differences, our rugged individualism, and get on with being productive.[33] We must build

"More than 50% of all workers in inspection-oriented plants spend time fixing other workers' mistakes."[32]

community and appreciate our diversity.[34] This ethic of individualism is taking a terrible toll on our young people in the dulling of social conscience and the worship of materialism.[35]

In tension with this reality of individualism is also the search for *authenticity*. Philosopher Charles Taylor, professor of political science and philosophy at McGill University, in his 1991 Massey Lecture in Toronto, said this search for authenticity -- which obviously shows up in the psychological worker -- is a modern reality and states that each of us has a specific way of being human. We are called upon, by life, to live our lives in *this* way and to imitate no one else's life. We are to be ourselves. Not to follow through with this "contract with myself," because of outside pressures, is to lose the capacity to listen to this very special inner voice. According to Taylor, authenticity is being true to myself and being true to my own originality. It is defining the potential that is properly mine.[36]

If supervisors are going to promote dignity, respect, self-worth, service, synergy,[37] and the need for quality in every employee -- integral ideals to a total quality ethical philosophy -- then they must grapple with promoting the *individual*, not individualism. Teamwork is the natural consequence of this ethical choice, and it is teamwork that will be absolutely necessary to manage business in the future. Example after example comes to mind from the business world supporting this reality of teamwork, even though some would think otherwise.[38]

Teamwork ← The business of the future!

For instance, in the computer world, intragroup communications, teamwork, and partnership relations are essential.[39] In Cambridge, Ontario, Toyota is winning award after award based on its teamwork and quality production of the Corolla car.[40] Digital and Microsoft link up to promote teamwork.[41] KeepRite, the air-conditioning people, "keep their cool" because of teamwork.[42]

Mikhail Gorbachev, while president of the now dissolved Soviet Union, said, "Today the world's nations are interdependent, like mountain climbers on one rope. They can either climb together to the summit or fall together into the abyss."[43] Former Toronto Argonaut coach, Adam Rita calls it going "for the heart."[44] The rugged individualism of yesterday has to give way to co-operation, communication, synergy,[45] and teamwork if we are to survive in a global economy.[46]

"The global economy is a fact," says Allan Taylor, Royal Bank Chairman.[47] We've got to begin to see the bigger picture, i.e., that Canada is part of the global village. Economist David Crane writes, "The world economy collapsed in the 1930s because we had too many politicians tied to special interests and too few statesmen who could understand the big picture. We have a similar problem today, which is one reason the world economy is such a mess."[49] This myopic way of looking at ourselves has historical roots as well. On March 18, 1933, the *Winnipeg Free Press* wrote the following warning about the then government's "obstinate refusal ... to face realities; their painful and tragic tactics of 'passing the buck' ... and ... their childish expectation that providence, or some power external to themselves, would save them from the consequences of their refusal to look into the future, foresee events that loomed black in the sky, plain to be seen, and take such steps as were possible to mitigate the fury of the storm."[50]

Chrysler Corp. president Robert Lutz claims that it is teamwork that cars are all about; MICA Management Resources Inc., of Toronto, says that clients regularly ask for teamwork training. The collaboration of several minds, the amount of new information, and the energy of many people all point to the need of the team concept.[48] International relations, the global economy, and world market realities demand a spirit of co-operation, and a business attitude change on our part.

To be competitive, supervisors will need to establish and promote an ethic of quality based on employee autonomy/authenticity and teamwork. This will be a struggle at times because today's psychological employee comes imbued with both the cult of individualism and the ethic of authenticity. It's an interesting paradox for the supervisor: employees who think only of themselves -- the "what's-in-for-me philosophy (individualism) but also employees who have a need to develop their potential (authenticity).

THE BASIC PRINCIPLES OF TQM:
TOTAL QUALITY MANAGEMENT

At a three-day seminar on Total Quality Management (TQM), the Valhalla Inn Markham's general manager was to hear the same message relayed time and again:
"If you can't measure it, you can't manage it!"

The principle of *managing the process through measurement* -- which is all-encompassing in the TQM philosophy -- is a solid one, particularly in a manufacturing application.

Yet, in a hospitality environment, as in life, the major factor determining success involves *attitude* of service staff, rather than service itself. The Valhalla Inn Markham is committed to the principle of TQM, yet accepts that *managing attitude is difficult to measure.*

Quality through people. Beating the competition. Getting to market faster. Doing it right the first time. Overcoming resistance to change. Global competition in a global environment. Free Trade. Labour with a new face.[51]

The pressures are all around us. We have seen in chapter 1 the key work functions of supervisory success. While planning, organizing, staffing, and directing are essential to quality supervision, the function of *controlling* more aptly contributes to the effectiveness of this quality.

We face the need for control in all facets of our lives, but in the work environment, this attention to quality control will most probably mean the difference between staying in business or not. As a result of IBM Canada's letter from their Japanese supplier - noted above - a 1.5 percent defect standard is not acceptable any more.[52] (Controlling determines the measurement of success that you have in relation to your goals and needs, and any necessary corrective steps you need to take if things are not up to par.[53])

Quality can be defined as "the absence of variance,"[54] and includes five key building blocks:

- Customer-driven quality;
- Commitment to quality by top management;
- Adoption of a continuous improvement philosophy;
- Monitoring extensively with facts, data, and analysis;
- Participation and involvement of employees.[55]

The benefits from TQM have been researched and documented as follows:

- Improved employee relations;
- Improved quality and lower costs;
- Greater customer satisfaction; and
- Improved market share and profitability.[60]

A beginning point for any manager or supervisor is to find out the state of the corporate culture. This is attained in the answer to the question: "Why do people in this company (department) do the things they do?" The answer may highlight functional as well as dysfunctional aspects of the cultural environment. Isadore Sharp, chairman of Four Seasons Hotels, says that the share value of quality service will determine the difference between global winners and losers. He goes on to say that while standards are necessary, they are simply means to an end, not ends in themselves. "Employees cannot be customer-driven and rules-driven at the same time."[61] The manager/supervisor as "mentor" will need to replace the authoritarian/disciplinarian model. He says that at Four Seasons, new hires are already motivated and management's job is to treat employees in the same way Four Seasons wants its customers treated: with respect, appreciation, and integrity.

Excellent companies know that high performance and productivity come by defining, clarifying, and adopting a small set of fundamental values. These values help structure the vision of excellence that the company wants for its employees so that the organization can work towards a common goal. Research shows that organizations that motivate their members through shared values capture more employee support, commitment, and involvement. We

TQM[56]

People unlocking their potential;[57] designing and supporting the corporate culture the supervisor wants to implement by building a climate of trust and a partnership between employees and customers. Ironically, when North American managers are looking to the Japanese for innovative management techniques, they begin to "re-discover" the names William Edward Deming and J.M. Juran, American management professors, adopted by the Japanese and popularized in their *quality circle* application![58] A TQM approach: a spin-off of the Deming - Duran - Japanese foundations, focusing on structural and human forces and values that have profound effects for the organization. "The company is driven by these values. These values draw out the very best from employees."[59]

TQM: The Deming Way
- Consistency of purpose
- Philosophy of excellence
- Build quality
- Reduce costs
- Improve constantly
- Training and more training
- Supervise skillfully
- Eliminate fear
- Create teamwork
- Overhaul the system
- Facilitate workers
- Nurture worker pride
- Develop employees
- Transform through involvement

also now know that excellent companies, companies with shared values orientation and motivation, have high productivity, higher profits, and lower burnout. When a proper balance of shared values exists within an organization, then people will want to do what needs to be done.[62]

Brian Hartien, writing in *Computing Canada*,[63] points outs that TQM "involves aggressively building quality into all phases of a company's business," and says, "Perhaps the most important part of a TQM program is the process of determining what is going on in your business, measuring it, setting goals and monitoring the results." When employees understand *what* it is they are to do and have the needed information and tools to accomplish the job, they simply do a better job.

It's the difference between building a *worthplace* or a *workplace*!

Peter Farwell, director of manufacturing and high technology for Ernst & Young, chartered accountants, underscores this TQM formula for business success. In these recessionary times, what is the difference between companies that are "sailing along nicely" and those that are being successful? Farwell says it is "certainly not by sticking with tried and true techniques" but by focusing on the newest and best in management ideas.[64] His analysis of new and better management techniques includes the following: (1) targeting the global marketplace; (2) use of modern management techniques (TQM); (3) the continuing focus on improving business processes; (4) automation; (5) sound financial planning and corporate organization; (6) investment in innovative products; (7) sensitivity to the environment; and (8) the long-term focus on leadership. "Quality is no longer simply the lack of defects in a product, but involves providing goods and services that meet customers' expectations."[65]

Although implementing a total quality program can be expensive because it usually involves a large amount of money spent on marketing, advertising, and administration to clients, there is evidence that shows a strong connection between corporate quality programs and improved market share and profits. "The bottom line is that quality makes money."[66]

HEADLINE!

"Quality improvement is the fundamental business strategy of the 1990s. No business without it will survive in the global marketplace." So reports Ernst & Young's International Quality Study.[67] National interests don't keep customers loyal. Rather, it is making quality products and services better than anywhere else in the world! *Value through quality --* that's the key element of business strategy *everywhere*! Build products and give services that people want and follow up after the sale.

Selected disciples of quality improvement include Realty World Inc., Burnaby, B.C., and Mustang Industries Inc., Richmond, B.C., Great-West Life Assurance Co. of Winnipeg, AECL, Pinawa, Manitoba, Hewlett-Packard (Canada) Ltd. of Mississauga, Ontario, Northern Telecom Ltd., Ottawa, Ontario BCE Inc. of Montreal, P.Q. Industries Couture Ltée. of Chicoutimi, P.Q., electrical-giant Asea Brown Boveri Inc. of Montreal, P.Q., Apex Machine Works Inc., Moncton, N.B., and Cornerbrook Pulp & Paper Ltd., Cornerbrook, Nfld.

Who's doing *it*?

Northern Telecom Ltd., for example, is making quality the "linchpin of a new corporate culture"[68] as it attempts to make the transition to a global economy. The formation of small work teams are "empowered" with permission and responsibility to do what needs to be done. McDonald's Canada continues to show why it's still "the leader of the pack"[69] with its quality self-liquidating cross-promotion marketing strategy, and reinforces its corporate mission with

Quality, therefore, is the pre-eminent business strategy of the 1990s and the best way to knock out competitors as a result of free trade, deregulation and globalization. Reducing customer defections by only 5 per cent generated 85 per cent more profit for a particular bank branch, 50 per cent more in insurance brokerage, and 30 per cent more in an auto-service chain. "Most of the gurus now define quality as satisfying your customers ... The starting point is outside the company with clients, rather than inside with your products."[66]

it as an "overall value leader in the quick-service restaurant business." And finally, there is Leon's Furniture, the company that sticks to the basics, which includes "the need to control all aspects of the business, the importance of common courtesy and common sense."[70] "In short, there now appears to be considerable evidence that TQM is positively and highly correlated with superior operating and financial performance."[71]

Thus, Total Quality Management, or TQM, is a philosophy of "getting it right the first time." Success is not predicated only on technique, but also on responding to competing demands with balance, ethics, or what Stanford University professor James O'Toole calls "moral symmetry."[72] Lord Weinstock, CEO of General Electric of Great Britain, says, "One doesn't set out just to make money. The thing is to do something right and one hopes to do well out of that."[73] The Quaker Oats Co. of Canada demonstrated this principle of moral symmetry with its shipment of oatmeal to orphans, as a humanitarian gesture.[74] Quaker president Jon Grant said that until the economy sorts itself out, Quaker "must be prepared to assume the social responsibilities of a good citizen in times of need."

One doesn't set out just to make money. The thing is to do something right and one hopes to do well out of that.

The Dayton-Hudson Corporation, a family-owned retail business established in 1902 in Minneapolis, Minnesota, is a corporation committed to a social conscience.[75] In 1932, the founder of DH Corporation, George Draper Dayton, wanted a new *assumption* for his company: to predicate success on the company being useful to and serving society. The DH Constitution reads: "The business of business is serving society, not just making money. Profit is our reward for serving society well. Indeed, profit is the means and the measure of our service -- but not an end in itself."[76]

SOCIAL RESPONSIBILITY AND ETHICS

The major question pertaining to social responsibility is the following: Is a company's main responsibility to make a profit for its shareholders, or does the company also have to take into account other "stakeholders," such as the on-going welfare of its employees, environmental groups, and, in general, the quality of life of the society in which it finds itself? William Dimma, deputy chairman of Royal LePage Ltd., says that the "shareholder does not, must not, win every pot."[77] David Grier says that trust and confidence are not only the essential glue for our society, but "essential ingredients that let our companies operate."[78]

> "The business of business is serving society, not just making money. Profit is our reward for serving society well. Indeed, profit is the means and the measure of our service -- but not an end in itself." -- Dayton Corporation

Values tell us what is good; ethics tell us what is right.[79] Values refer to that interior zone where one's integrity grows; ethics refer to our behaviour, *how* we live out our values. We infer a person's values from his/her actions (behaviour), interests, hopes, aspirations, etc. Wrong, and unethical behaviour, is thus a betrayal of value within oneself. If this betrayal occurs at a deep enough level, we experience severe pain, discomfort, and anxiety. We then aim to minimize this "cognitive dissonance," as psychologists call it, through right action (behaviour). Not to recognize this value-betrayal is to be split and to live a double life. To carry that process to its logical and dysfunctional conclusion is to be dissociated eventually from the core of humanness.

> "Profit is a necessary but not sufficient condition for the continuing conduct of business. It is a handy way of keep score. But to single out profit, rather than productivity or public service, as the central aim of business activity is just asking for trouble."
> -- David Grier, vice-president, Royal Bank of Canada

Milton Friedman, the Nobel Prize winner in economics, says that as long as a company stays within the law, does not break regulations, and makes a proper return on investment for its shareholders, then it is being socially responsible.[80] Others,[81] however, insist that business has to do *more* than just make a profit. Other *stakeholders* are involved. Max Clarkson, Professor Emeritus and former Dean of the Faculty of Management at the University of Toronto, and currently director of the Faculty's Centre for Corporate Social Performance and Ethics, challenges the narrow view of *stakeholder-as-shareholder* by pointing out that the history of the stakeholder concept can be traced back to the 1930s Depression when General Electric Co. "identified four major stakeholder groups: shareholders, employees, customers and the general public."[82] As well, "In 1947, the president of Johnson & Johnson listed the company's 'strictly business' stakeholders as customers, employees, managers and shareholders." And "In 1950, General Robert Wood, who led Sears Roebuck and Co.'s rapid post-war growth, identified the 'four parties to any business in the order of their importance' as 'customers, employees, community and stockholders'." Clarkson goes on to define *stakeholder* as

> any person or group that has or claims ownership, rights or interests in a corporation and its activities, past, present or future. Such claimed rights or interests may be legal or moral, individual or collective. A corporation cannot exist without shareholders, but neither can it exist without customers, employees and the society that provides the market and the necessary infrastructure.[82]

A contemporary view of business and the ethic of social responsibility would say that we can no longer afford to work "only for profits or money." This is deemed "socially irresponsible." Instead, the new supervisor realizes that companies and organizations have "multiple objectives." While "the relationship between social responsibility and profits is not a very clear one,"[83] there is enough agreement to chart a relationship. What is obvious in the relationship is that (1) social responsibility expenditures reduce profits in the short-term *and* in the long term after a certain point, but (2) these same social responsibility expenditures contribute to long-term profits up to this *break-even* point as well.

MAIN FACTORS IN A BUSINESS ETHICAL PHILOSOPHY

Does ethics pay? Union Carbide was fined $1.7 million for price fixing.[84] Beech-Nut, the second largest producer of baby food in the U.S., and its two top executives, received a 470-count indictment in November 1986 when it pleaded guilty to 215 felonies and to wilfully doctoring its product from 1981 to 1983![85] After Walwyn Stodgel Cochran Murray Ltd. in 1987 hired away Tim

Miller, the super-salesman from Wood Gundy and the other 31 employees who later joined Miller, "Walwyn was sued and Wood Gundy received $1 million in cash as well as Walwyn stock options!"[86] Salomon Bros. Inc., the New York investment dealer, "played dirty" with U.S. Treasury bonds. The result? A loss of confidence, persona, and profit to the tune of $30 million for the 1991 fourth quarter![87] Cognos Incorporated, the Ottawa software house, hired Douglas Queen from Calgary in 1983 to join its firm in Ottawa. Estimates for negligent misrepresentation of what Mr. Queen was getting into cost Cognos anywhere between $103,000 and $450,000.[88]

The *Corporate Ethics: A Prime Business Asset* report concludes that corporate ethics programs are not considered primarily "window dressing" but, rather essential to the self-interest of the company in terms of profits and competitiveness. True profits can only be based on sound ethics.

Companies like Boeing, Champion International, General Mills, GTE, Hewlett-Packard, Johnson & Johnson, McDonnell Douglas, Xerox, to name a few, think ethics pays. Top executives from these and other companies were part of study called *Corporate Ethics: A Prime Business Asset.*[89]

What comes out of the research is the following reality: a work environment without a conscious ethical commitment as well as technical competence will destroy the company. The vision of human growth and development certainly has to be the guiding vision and context within which to consider what is ethical or not. There cannot be a question of employing what William A. Dimma, deputy chairman of Royal LePage Ltd., calls MEGO ("My Eyes Glaze Over"[90]), and it's not a question of just being ethical and not worrying about the technical demands, or -- most probably the case -- concentrating on the technical details at the expense of an ethical component. Interestingly, Harvard ethics professor Kenneth E. Goodpaster points out that the Greeks' word for *virtue* referred "to both moral *and* technical excellence."[91] In other words, for the Greeks, the "good person" *was* of moral fibre and *did* something to augment the quality of life, either through a technical or knowledge-based contribution. Goodpaster concludes, "In these terms, the

Virtue, for the Greeks, referred to both moral *and* technical excellence. The "good person" *was* a moral person and *acted* accordingly.

A Business Ethical Philosophy: Key Points

- The determination of key shared values that the company will foster and promote;
- The conscious acknowledgment, promotion, and safeguarding of the dignity, respect, and uniqueness of every employee;
- The articulation of standards of right and wrong applied to business situations for the company, all the while realizing that these "rules" are self-defeating if applied literally, and without the "spirit" involved; *common sense*
- The presence of a working attitude and practice of intelligent social responsibility;
- The acknowledgment and fostering of employment and pay equity within the workplace;
- The valuing and implementation of health and safety standards for all employees;
- The commitment to a clean environment, both inside and outside the company;
- The training and development of all employees, both in personal and in technical matters.

---

corporation as a moral environment requires not only good people, but people who work well." Former IBM Chairman John Akers points out that ethics and competitiveness are inseparable. Stabbing one another in the back or stealing are not ways to be successful. For Akers, they are recipes for a nation becoming wasteful, inefficient and non-competitive.[92]

We urgently need to "pull up our socks" and get on with it, as we have stated. Supervisors are behind the proverbial "8-ball" and must move quickly with a quality management approach and philosophy, especially as the figures show that between 1985 and 1990, productivity only rose 1.2% (compared to 23.8% in the United States) while unit labour costs rose by 24.4% in Canada but fell by 4.1% in the United States, which meant a whopping 45% increase in Canadian unit labour costs during this same time period![93]

Germany and Japan base their economic policies on the economy of the world. Canadians need to make that mindset shift as well. But we are afraid of change; resistance seems to be part of our national psyche.[94] "Weak productivity growth means it will now take 35 years for the real income of Canadians to double, twice as long as two decades ago. ... 'The problem is deeply rooted in Canadian society. We tend to resist change and avoid competition,' said Judith Maxwell, the Economic Council's chairwoman. 'We must see Canadian firms adapting more quickly'."[95] In short, we need a *total* commitment to quality, both in products and in people. ***Let's get on with it!***

SUMMARY

The future of business hinges on ethics, quality, and competitiveness.

In a radically different business environment today, supervisors must adjust not only their sights but also their skills and comprehension. It is urgent that business begin with "doing it right the first time."

The age is past when the one perfect method or product could be invented or produced. Today it is continual improvement; that's what Total Quality Management is all about.

A new emphasis also is the customer as #1. Sheer business survival now depends on that emphasis, attitude, and commitment from business.

Teamwork is also the new order of the day. For the supervisor, this may mean managing the tension between *individualism* and *authenticity* in today's employee. Reared in age where "I" count first, where the "me-generation" feels entitled often to its "rights" without regard for responsibilitites, while at the same time, they are struggling to be themselves, today's employees struggle between the cult of selfishness and the call of authenticity.

We're either going to climb together to the summit, says Mikhail Gorbachev, or fall together into the abyss.

The emphasis in business is on transforming the workplace into a *worthplace*.

To do this well, in addition to total quality management, the organization needs a genuine ethical commitment.

It is not a question of *either* profits *or* ethics: appropriate and acceptable profits assume an ethical base.

The urgency is real: business needs a moral, emotional, product, financial, and competitive turnaround! Supervisors are at the front to lead the way!

TERMS/CONCEPTS

moment of truth
individualism
authenticity
quality

total quality
management
shared values
values

ethics
stakeholder
MEGO

DISCUSSION QUESTIONS

1. What is radically different about the business environment today? Identify some current trends.

2. Why is there an urgency for quality and service?

3. What is the difference between *individualism* and *authenticity*? Give examples to support your explanation.

4. Discuss Mikhail Gorbachev's statment: "Today the world's nations are interdependent, like mountain climbers on one rope. They can either climb together to the summit or fall together into the abyss." Why is this statement an important one for the supervisor?

5. Identify five characteristics of total quality management.

6. Why is ethics the backbone of profits?

7. How can today's supervisor best prepare for the future?

ASSIGNMENT

THE BUSINESS ETHICS PORTFOLIO

List in the "important values" column the values you think are important for today's supervisor. Rank order those values in the shaded "priority" column, with #1 being the most important value for supervisors to build an ethical foundation.

IMPORTANT VALUES	PRIORITY

EXPLAIN WHY YOU CHOSE VALUE #1

CHAPTER THREE

ORGANIZING PEOPLE
AND SETTING OBJECTIVES

Anyone who doubts that the economy is global in scope need only consider the Miata sports car. It was designed in California, originally built in England, assembled in Mexico and Michigan, and built in Japan.

-- John Raymond, *The Globe and Mail*[1]

LEARNING OBJECTIVES

At the end of this chapter, students will be able to:

- Describe the reorganizing
that is happening in companies
- Explain what objectives are
- Define management by objectives (MBO)
- Apply MBO in setting supervisory objectives
- Detail how employees can be organized
- Identify the basic issues in the organizing process

Opening scenario

*T*he 1990s have been tough years for business. It seems as though the whole world is *reorganizing* and *setting new objectives and goals* for itself.[2] The Reichmann family's Olympia & York Developments Ltd., for instance, "watched a $78.6-million investment slide to $39.8-million"[3] on February 19, 1992, in the early days of the reorganization of former Campeau Corp. into Camdev Corp. O & Y are Camdev's largest creditor and now its controlling shareholder.

For some,[4] the post-boom and me-generation[5] had choked on its own consumerism. The shadow[6] side of prosperity had reared its guilty head; the acquisitions of the 1980s seemed so empty; happiness seemed just as far away. Japanese workaholism or "karoshi" -- death from overwork -- had been likened to a "killing field."[7] Economist John Kenneth Galbraith said that we in Canada "shouldn't crow."[8] No doubt we were being forced to return to a simpler life and to basic values. For others,[9] the recession had brought opportunity and positive events,[10] with the belief that the "painful restructuring" -- or "global shakeout"[11] -- would fade by the end of 1992 or the beginning of 1993. Public policy analyst Stewart Kronberg felt that what was happening in the Canadian economy was something "we should have begun much earlier."[12] Economist Allen Sinai said we needed this huge restructuring and adjustment within the Canadian economy, even though it felt like a "mid-life crisis."[13]

This is the new supervisory environment! It is within this environment that supervisors must think of what it means to "organize" and to "set objectives." Peter Drucker, the noted management writer, said that managing in the future will be more akin to conducting an orchestra.[14] If the conductor/supervisor is doing the job well -- that is, if the members of the orchestra (employees) are organized, trained, and conscious of their task (objective) -- then a beautiful symphony will happen. This metaphor of the "orchestra" acknowledges individual members as competent and knowledgeable, and it is the manager/supervisor's job to organize the members to make music. "The supervisor (conductor) knows the organizational plan (the musical score) and has the overview necessary to direct the group toward its final goal."[15]

COMPANIES REORGANIZING

Supervisors sort out what it is they want or need to do to accomplish company or organizational goals on an operational level and organize people to accomplish these objectives. The purpose of this chapter is to understand what is involved in developing objectives and then organizing employees to meet those objectives. To do that well a supervisor needs to meet objectives that are in harmony with organizational goals and, in today's exacting working environment, objectives that also most harmonize the employees' work - home or work - family balance and relationships.[16]

In recessionary times it is easy to understand that the emotional well-being of employees is not business's top priority. But it is a mistake to jeopardize employee loyalty and trust by sacrificing employees on the altar of the bottom line, restructuring, or making things "lean and mean." Organizations have both a practical and an ethical dilemma on their hands today: they may be forced to cut back, lay off, but if they are a paternalistic organization like Imperial Oil, they do it with much agony and distress. They genuinely want to be a humane employer, to have loyal employees, but they also have hard, economic realities to contend with. It is not a fun position to be in for those companies who really do care. With the U.S., in 1992, laying off 2,600 people a *day*,[17] was it any wonder that the threat of being laid off was "the chief cause of [the] corporate morale crisis"? Competitiveness seemed to be the "clarion call" alerting employees to the threat of being laid off.

The restructuring, and consequently reorganizing, that is so prevalent in organizations in the early 1990s means that supervisors face a daunting challenge with the organizing function. For many companies, the best way to

Public policy analyst Stewart Kronberg says we are going through a compressed economic adjustment: everything is happening at once! It is caused by the free trade deal, a volatile Canadian dollar, the impact of the global economy, changing consumer attitudes, and, of course, the recession. This adjustment is forcing companies to cut costs or go out of business, and employees to realize that increased wages are now tied to improved productivity and on-going training and upgrading. The up side of this adjustment is that those firms that make it will be in a better position to compete in the future.[16]

reorganize has been what Thomas Kochan of MIT calls *the slash and burn method* of management. This is insane management! How can a company get competitive, cut costs, be "lean and mean," by believing employees are dispensable during a recession, by treating employees harshly and unsympathetically, and threatening their livelihoods? Economist Edward Neufield, of the Royal Bank of Canada, said, "Competitiveness is linked to job security, not job insecurity, [and to the creation of] rewarding jobs and high

---

*T*reat the customer as God, he says, giving him everything he wants, as fast as possible, at the lowest price you can manage. Don't diversify into things you're no good at. Emphasize teamwork by eradicating the menace of adversarialism both among managers and between management and the rank and file. And above all, play to your greatest strength -- your people. Trite but true.

-- Frederick C. Crawford, founder, TRW Inc.[17]

---

income, not the reverse."[17] Compare this to the order from the Jim Pattison Group in Vancouver, B.C., which stated: "Cut costs -- or else!"[18] And that was after three businesses had already been dumped! Emotion and sentiment were to have no place in the reorganizing. Or the comment made about Mark De Simone from Milan, Italy, that the new 33-year-old Olivetti Canada Ltd. president's operating style involved "rearranging and stripping unproductive operations like a Milanese decorator set loose on a Regina bungalow"![19]

It is readily apparent that today's supervisor has a tough challenge. At a time when work and home must compete for an employee's loyalty because of the high cost of living, the prevalence of more women in the workforce, and the incidence of single and aging parents, the reorganizing going on in our society seems even more cruel and harsh than Edward Neufield of the Royal Bank of Canada describes. For many employees now, "competitiveness [is] a code word for 'lean and mean'."[21]

This is the age of families with two jobs which is "one of the most radical changes in family life in the past 20 years."[22] In addition, "job stresses have been described by the International Labour Organization as 'the end-of-the-century affliction'." For instance, absenteeism costs the Canadian economy $10 billion annually. Employment lawyer Howard Levitt describes it as the major human resource problem for employers in Canada "bar none."[23] In 1992, Ontario alone lost 11.2 million days to absenteeism!

WE'VE REORGANIZED?[20]

"The recession has achieved what it set out to achieve" - Economist Michael McCracken, Ottawa, Informetrica

The recession is "like a boa constrictor swallowing a pig whole and then excreting it at the end of the year" -- Economist Andrew Jackson, Canadian Labour Congress

---

THE FAMILY TRACK?

The trade-offs are just too high!

Robert Half, the world's largest personnel firm in the accounting, finance, and information systems fields, completed a study which showed that executives were just not willing to sacrifice themselves on the altar of the corporate balance sheet at the expense of their families any more.

The *fast track* is out, the *family track* is in!

This family track is a slower career path so that working parents can divide their time more equitably between work and home. For the purposes of this text, this means that supervisors will have to take a more *holistic*, or big picture, view of an employee's contributions, said Max Messmer, chairman of Robert Half International. As well, the management functions of planning, organizing, staffing, directing and controlling, and the corporate culture must be based on recognizing this overall contribution rather than just on how many hours an employee puts in.[24]

It's quite obvious that the new supervisor cannot afford to be without clear objectives and an organized plan[25] of how to accomplish these objectives. Too much is at stake.

Reflective Exercise

Are you an organized person? YES___ NO___

If you said YES, describe below some details about

"MY ORGANIZED SELF"

_____

_____

_____

_____

If you said NO, describe below some details about

"MY EFFORTS TO BE ORGANIZED"

_____

_____

_____

_____

WHAT ARE OBJECTIVES?

Objectives represent what the supervisor wants to accomplish. As the terms "objectives" and "goals" are used within this text, objectives are the stepping-stones to the organizational end results, purposes, or goals.

At a performance evaluation meeting, the front office manager of the Valhalla Inn Markham was asked what her objectives were for her department. Turning to a flip chart located in the room, she wrote down the following words: To run the best Front Desk in Canada!

Objectives, therefore, are concrete, specific, identifiable action steps. Goals are more generic, broader in scope, and ideals to reach. Objectives properly planned by the supervisor will make goal-attainment effective. Poorly prepared or a lack of objectives, will leave the supervisor at the mercy of events, circumstances, and forces.

When Ernst & Young's International Quality Study

indicated that quality improvement was to be the fundamental business strategy of the 1990s and that no business without it would survive in the global marketplace,[26] a company, following this lead, would establish TQM - Total Quality Management - as its *goal*, but then have managers and supervisors strive towards that goal with specific *objectives*. It's all right to have goals, but the objectives get us to those goals. Otherwise, it is "all talk and no action."

WHAT IS MANAGEMENT BY OBJECTIVES (MBO)?[27]

Management by objectives (MBO) is a collaborative process of setting objectives with employees so that organizational needs will be met. MBO in practice says that employees can be trusted, goal-achievement doesn't have to be accidental, and success can happen. Objectives can be established to deal with (1) routine matters: duties and responsibilities as part of an employee's work; (2) problem solving: solving specific, job-related problems; (3) developing innovation: ideas, projects, products, services, etc. (4) personal development: personal, professional and training and development activities; and (5) organizational development: within the organization or specific department.[28]

"Competitive firms survive, increase market share and thrive. Uncompetitive firms do not. ... The ultimate test of a nation's competitive-ness is what is happening to the standard of living of its citizens over time." -- U.S. Federal Reserve Board chairman Alan Greenspan[29]

MBO, in spite of the fact that one writer says it is "like ice cream" and "comes in 29 flavors,"[30] does have some (a) common underlying assumptions, (b) practical steps, and (c) advantages and disadvantages.

MBO: COMMON UNDERLYING ASSUMPTIONS

Besides being a management technique, MBO is also a management philosophy. It makes the following *assumptions*:

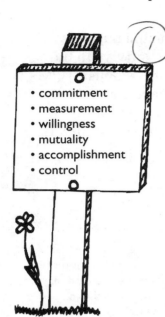

1

- commitment
- measurement
- willingness
- mutuality
- accomplishment
- control

Employees will commit themselves to work and contribute when they have a sense of *control* over their work through dialogue, mutual agreement, and feedback from their supervisor.[31]

Perhaps the core of stress is *not knowing*. When people feel that they have some sense of control, of significance, that their contribution in life and at work matters, then they also feel that their lives have meaning.

MBO sets in motion the process of establishing a working *relationship* with one's supervisor so that employees know where they stand and the organization can count on certain things being accomplished.

PRACTICAL STEPS

5

- Identify the requirements of the job to be done;
- Develop performance objectives to meet those requirements.
- Discuss the objective(s) with the employee(s) involved;
- Determine appropriate standards of acceptable performance;
- Measure the results attained.

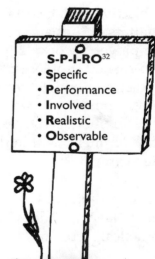

S-P-I-RO[32]
- **S**pecific
- **P**erformance
- **I**nvolved
- **R**ealistic
- **O**bservable

CASE EXAMPLE

Your professor (supervisor) is meeting with you (employee) at the beginning of the semester and will work out an MBO, results-oriented course of study with you. You mention that you want to get an "A" and your professor then shows you a list of performance standards required for that "A." You notice that two of the requirements for an "A" are completion of three (3) case studies of five pages each, one to be submitted each month of the three-month semester, and two (2) project papers of ten pages each, with specific dates for submission. In addition, these papers have to be typed, with no more than five "typos," grammar or spelling errors, and

why it doesn't work.

MBO Benefits

- Forces the supervisor to plan ahead for the future.
- Improves the communication between the supervisor and employee concerning what is expected in terms of job content and its relative importance.
- Makes more effective and efficient use of human and material resources.
- Positions the supervisor - employee relation in a more helpful context.
- Improves employee development and performance.
- Establishes how to measure an employee's performance more objectively and fairly.
- Reduces supervisor - employee conflict by anticipating crises and expectations.
- Increases employee commitment, direction, and teamwork.
- Eliminates duplication of work assignments.

MBO Problems

- May lack senior management support. ①
- Takes time to do and some supervisors may find the paperwork too much. ②
- May contain inadequately developed or thought-out objectives. *NOT CLEAR* ③
- May fail sometimes to link appropriate rewards with attainment of objectives. *results hard to measure not as clear*
- May be unable to modify or change objective(s) because of unanticipated and uncontrollable constraints.
- May be unable to correctly measure realistic and actual results.
- Requires training and time for employees.
- Can become too rigid and structured.

What do you think? [33]

duplicate copies submitted. Your professor then asks you how you want to "personalize" these requirements, and you then begin to set up your own objectives to accomplish them. How would you go about making sure you could get an "A" for yourself? What objectives would you write down to meet the requirements?

APPLYING MBO IN SETTING SUPERVISORY OBJECTIVES

If a supervisor takes the organizational goals and then structures performance objectives, using S-P-I-R-O, for employees, employees will have a clearer direction and a greater sense of accomplishment. While supervisors often need training in the elements of MBO, in reality they can set up a simple chart (below) with their employees. Suppose, for instance, in the XYZ Auto Supply company, senior managers determined that a goal for each department this year would be improving customer service. The supervisor of the parts department could then take that general goal, or desired end-state-of-affairs, and break it down into manageable objectives, or steps, for employees. This exercise could be done at a staff meeting with employees.

A TIDY COMPANY IS A SOUND COMPANY!

Japanese management techniques in Canada stress tidiness[34]

The supervisor would begin by explaining the goal and its importance, and then ask employees for suggestions to reach the goal. These suggestions, in turn, could become the basis and foundation upon which to design performance objectives. The supervisor would remind employees that their objectives will be **specific** ways by which they can each personally contribute. An explanation of S-P-I-R-O would be given as a guideline for their objective writing, some examples given, and after there was general agreement and understanding of the process, the employee would be asked to complete the exercise (often outside of work hours). A time would then be set up for each employee to bring his/her statement of objectives to be reviewed, repositioned, if necessary, and given the stamp of approval by the supervisor. The employee then commits him/herself to a set of objectives that are **specific, performance**-oriented, with his/her interest and **involvement, realistic** and attainable, and **observable** and measurable. With a supervisor who speaks and listens well

Employees want to feel important, part of the company, and that it really can't run without them.

(chapter 7), and gives appropriate feedback, this employee knows where he or she stands. In the example of improving customer service, some of the employee objectives could look like the following:

- To physically go out of my way, at least five times each day, if a customer is searching for some item, and, in a pleasant, friendly manner, ask the customer how best he/she can be served.

- If XYZ does not have the customer's auto part, to phone suppliers each time until the part is located, and to let the customer know when the part will be available.

- To enrol in and be successful in, at "A" grade level, the 10-week customer service course at the local community college by August 11. (The benefit here also, of course, is that some companies encourage and financially support these educational efforts.)

When it comes time for performance review, both employee and supervisor are able to meet and see how well the targeted objective has been met. Of course, supervisors should provide the necessary guidance and encouragement *before* it's time for the actual review. Sometimes, of course, a supervisor has to discipline an employee for unsatisfactory performance. One approach that is recommended is the **HOT-STOVE Rule**: any disciplinary action should be similar to what happens when a person touches a hot stove: with warning, immediate, consistent, and impersonal.[35] Of course, a proactive and "positive orientation"[36] should be maintained.

Many companies do not have an effective performance review process, if they have one at all.[37] Sometimes only lip-service is offered. But in companies where MBO is understood, supervisors are trained, and employees understand the process as an *educational* -- and not a punitive -- one, part of their on-going development and value to the company, then management and employees can both win. Employees want to feel important, part of the company, and that it really can't run without them.[38] They will experience the value and benefits of the MBO process and feel successful because they will know what they have done in relation to what they said they would do.

KNOWING WHERE YOU STAND:
FEEDBACK IN PERFORMANCE ASSESSMENT

As early as 1952, Harry Levinson, the noted American psychologist, wrote that while results of behaviour are emphasized in most companies, "in reality, people are judged as much on HOW they get things done."[39] The system says people are judged on results, but we must not fool ourselves: *how* they get results is just as important. Employees are not often told what *behaviours* are expected of them.

To focus appropriately on an employee's or supervisor's performance or behaviour, an appropriate *feedback* structure needs to be implemented. Research shows that performance is directly related to the amount of feedback received[40] and that the most reliable feedback is from sources closest to the individual.[41] In addition, those closest to us provide not only the most reliable feedback, but the most immediate *perceptions*.

The perceptions we have of ourselves and others evolve from our own interpretations of our social experiences.[42] And how we perceive the facts is the basis upon which we behave.[43] We could say that our perceptions are guesses about the way things are or should be; we all have perceptions. Our behaviour is the acting- and living-out of our personal perceptions about life; our perceptual experiences become our road map for life.[44]

In the work environment, perceptions are also at work. With feedback, a supervisor is able to harness the perceptions of those who know what is going on: the actual employees themselves. In their area of experience and training, they can give invaluable feedback. In turn, employees can obtain essential feedback as well from their colleagues and supervisors. Without feedback we are at the mercy of our perceptions and the perceptions of those around us.

Research also shows that intentions,[45] goals, and resulting behaviour are interrelated. A company or organization that uses a feedback system in relation to objectives, to employee, supervisory and managerial behaviour, and for coaching and development, is harnessing its potential. Feedback tells us where we stand. We need it psychologically and organizationally.

A study by the Irish Management Institute in Eastern Canada "showed a statistically significant correlation between management training and the ratio of earnings to equity in private companies."[46] In short, managers and supervisors who receive feedback and develop objectives and action plans make money for their companies!

An impressive MBO exercise that a supervisor can apply, based on providing feedback and structuring personal setting of objectives for departmental or organizational effectiveness, is the computerized Seneca Needs Assessment Process (SNAP).[47] SNAP is a feedback process for employee and supervisory/ managerial growth, training needs analysis, and career development,[48] and a measurement tool for training effectiveness. How does it work?

- A custom-designed 45- to 50-item questionnaire, reflecting the specific skills important to the department, is constructed. Questions can be categorized in many ways, but typical categories are: communication, performance standards, motivation, objective setting, delegation, decision making, work performance, human relations, leadership, performance feedback, human resource issues, coping with change, etc.

- The employee, or supervisor, completes a "self-rating" questionnaire on how he/she sees his/ her performance on the items, and then has six co-workers (if possible, two superiors, two colleagues, and two subordinates) anonymously complete the same questionnaire and mail it to a designated consultant;[49]

- A computerized analysis is compiled, printed, and presented to the individual employee or supervisor in a workshop setting conducted by the consultant;

- The individual employee or supervisor, using the SNAP Action Plan Booklet, completes, with the help of the consultant, a systematic MBO improvement plan, based on important areas of discrepancy in the printout;

- This MBO Action Plan, with its work objectives, is then included, as the personal development contribution, in the employee's or supervisor's actual performance appraisal portfolio. This is when "the rubber hits the road," so to speak: the objectives become actualized!

An example of an well-constructed MBO objective that meets the S-P-I-R-O criteria, and an Action Plan that is simple and helpful, is detailed on the next page.

Objective #1	Activities and resources for implementing objective	Deadline	Did I accomplish the activity?
By May 1, I will complete a performance review with each employee in my department	• Make a list and timetables for meeting with each employee between April 3 and May 1. • Have each employee complete his/her part of the performance review. • Set a date to meet with each employee. • Develop a format for discussion that builds a positive learning climate. • Research potential problem topics. • Complete each review for signing. • Etc.	March 20 Immediately March 24 March 26 March 29 May 4-5	Accomplished March 20

HOW EMPLOYEES CAN BE ORGANIZED

There are some key structural, or organizational, concerns that the new supervisor needs to be aware of.[50] These are the "contextual" factors for work.

HOW WORK UNITS ARE ORGANIZED

Depending on the size and growth of the company that a supervisor works for, different structures, or organized work units, will already be in place. This does not mean they cannot be changed, but changing organizational structure is a senior management decision.

One way to organize work units is what is called the *primitive structure* or agency form, for instance, a home or cottage human relations adult education business that grows gradually from a one-or-two person operation to perhaps fifteen or twenty people. Each person is an agent, or extension, of the boss who, in essence, manages the company.

A second organizational form is the *functional department*, which develops as a result of the company growing in size and complexity. At this point, managing becomes too much for the one person-owner (in the agency structure) and other employees, with a speciality in their functional area (e.g., finance, marketing, production, etc.), assume a supervisory/managerial responsibility. Organizing functional departments helps the managers and supervisors co-ordinate the activities of certain groups (e.g., production, marketing) so that organizational goals can be met more effectively.

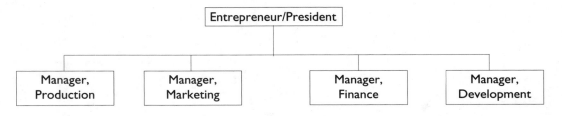

Product departmentalization is a third organizational form. This is necessary when the functional departments become just too big, and further specialization, by product, is necessary. Separate and semi-autonomous divisions, for instance, are then set up to manage the work demands which, in turn, help the company to respond more strategically to, and co-ordinate more efficiently, a larger number of specialized groups.

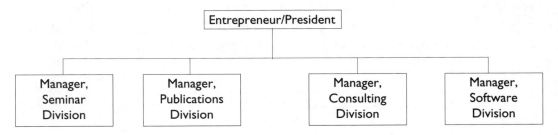

When a business is physically spread out in different places, towns, provinces, etc., a fourth organizational form, called *territorial departmentalization*, can occur, and can be set up, for instance, to meet distance, or political, cultural, legal, and natural concerns. Multinationals with operations in many places of the world, face this challenge continually.

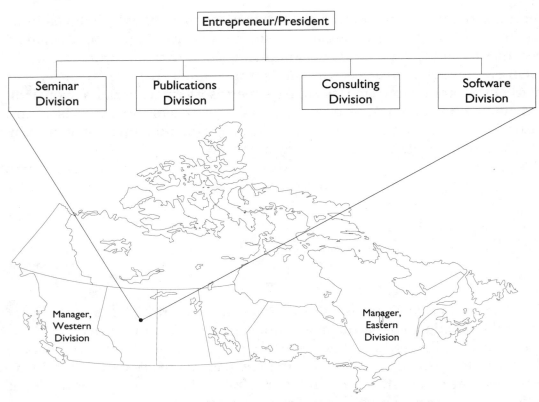

A fifth way that a business can be organized is through *customer departmentalization*. Our hypothetical human relations adult education company might sell products and services to the following clients: single-parent families, customer service agents, dehired executives, and the general public.

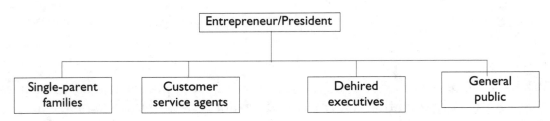

Even though there are benefits and drawbacks to the next form of organizing -- *matrix departmentalization* -- it is crucial when business demands become extremely complex. This organizational form is a combination of functional *and* product departmentation, with the purpose of getting the best, and avoiding the worst, of each. Employees in a matrix organization typically work in two groups: their functional or specialized group (such as marketing or production, for instance) *and also* a product or project group. These two reporting relationships can be in conflict at times, but the great advantage of the matrix form is its spontaneity in response to changing market conditions. Once the project is completed or disbanded, members simply return to their functional departments. Advocates of matrix management say that in complex business undertakings, a simple chain of command is just that: simplistic! The Big Three automakers are realizing this reality now as they try to compete head-on with the Japanese. For too long, they stuck to their "functional chimney matrix. Manufacturing managers reported to one boss, engineers to another," the net result of this individualistic, and simplistic, form being that "the finance staff got what it wanted -- cars that were cheaper to build -- but customers didn't."[51]

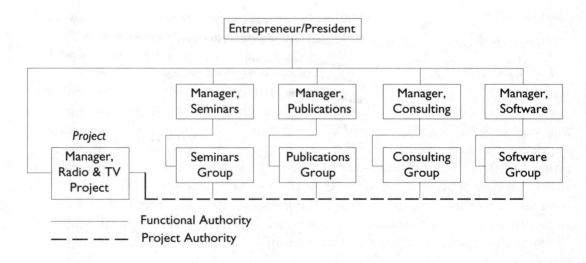

Finally, mention must be made of what is called a *mixed* mode of departmentalization. General Motors is a good example of this mixed mode within a division: product lines (e.g., Buick, Saturn, Pontiac), functional lines (e.g., production, distribution, finance), and geographic lines.

HOW LARGE CAN THE WORK UNITS BE?

To be as effective and efficient as possible, organizations determine what is the largest number of people, or span of control, that a manager or supervisor can manage directly.

The *chain of command* is the line of authority that starts with top management and goes directly down to supervisory management, and reflects the *vertical* structure of an organization. This chain is actualized when one employee is made a subordinate of another. The chain can have different levels. For instance, in the community college system, there is the president, vice-presidents, deans, chair people, and faculty and support staff. Faculty report to a chairperson, who in turn reports to a dean, etc.

The question, "What is the optimal number for a supervisor to supervise?" is answered as follows: "It depends!"

What is called the *span of control*, or the number of people a manager or supervisor can effectively manage or supervise, relates to the *horizontal* structure of an organization or enterprise. The question, "What is the optimal number for a supervisor to supervise?" is answered as follows: "It depends!" If the work is not complex, for instance, a supervisor can oversee a much larger group of employees (possibly 50-150 employees). If the work is highly technical, fast-paced, complex, for instance, a much smaller span of control (7-10 employees) might be wise. Other factors to be taken into consideration include the personality characteristics and capabilities of the supervisor, his/her need for power, the corporate culture, the situation itself, the competencies of employees, how physically dispersed employees are, and how willing employees are to work as a team. Thus, no one span of control fits every situation. In these recessionary times, organizations realize that "small is beautiful," and that fewer levels of management usually increases clarity in communication, as well as possibly making possible substantial savings. It is estimated that *80% of top management communication is distorted by the time it reaches employees at the lower levels!*[52]

MEMORANDUM[53]

FROM: SUPERINTENDENT
TO: ASSISTANT SUPERINTENDENT

Next Thursday at 10:30 A.M., Halley's Comet will appear over this area. This is an event which occurs only once every 75 years. Call the school principals and have them assemble their teachers and classes on the athletic field and explain this phenomenon to them. If it rains, then cancel the day's observation and have the classes meet in the auditorium to see a film about the comet.

FROM: ASSISTANT SUPERINTENDENT
TO: SCHOOL PRINCIPALS

By order of the superintendent of schools, next Thursday at 10:30 Halley's Comet will appear over your athletic field. If it rains, then cancel the day's classes and report to the auditorium with your teachers and students where you will show films, a phenomenal event which occurs every 75 years.

FROM: SCHOOL PRINCIPAL
TO: TEACHERS

By order of the phenomenal superintendent of schools, at 10:30 next Thursday, Halley's Comet will appear in the auditorium. In case of rain over the athletic field, the superintendent will give another order -- something which occurs only every 75 years.

FROM: TEACHERS
TO: STUDENTS

Next Thursday, at 10:30, the superintendent of schools will appear in our school auditorium with Halley's Comet -- an event that occurs every 75 years. If it rains, the superintendent will cancel the comet and order us all out to our phenomenal athletic field.

FROM: STUDENTS
TO: PARENTS

When it rains next Thursday at 10:30 over the school athletic field, the phenomenal 75-year-old superintendent of schools will cancel all classes and appear before the whole school in the auditorium, accompanied by Bill Halley and the Comets.

HOW WORK UNITS ARE INFLUENCED BY TECHNOLOGY AND STRUCTURE

The success of an enterprise is influenced directly by the fit between its technology and structure. We can distinguish between a "goods-producing technology" and a "service-producing technology."[54] "Technology" refers to *how* an organization converts inputs into outputs. Every business, in this sense, has a technology. For instance, at the community college level, the educational "processing" of its students, from the time they register and enrol in courses and programs, to the time they graduate with their diplomas or certificates, is the technology. Because the college has *this* particular technology, it, therefore, through experience, has a structure to match, which is similar to other colleges' structures.

It is similar in a manufacturing business, a goods-producing technological environment. The noted researcher Joan Woodward identified three particular types of technology:[55] (1) unit production, or small quantities, such as a custom-made pair of shoes, (2) mass production, or large quantities, such as assembly lines, and (3) continuous-process production, or on-going production where raw materials are converted into new products, such petroleum products or pharmaceuticals.

In a service-producing technological environment, there can be a (1) mediating technology,[56] such as the exchange between a buyer and a seller, the loaning and borrowing of money process that goes on between Canada Trust, for instance, and a client, and an (2) intensive technology, or the change-producing process that goes on when a client, or student, or patient, or inmate, or seminarian, or IBMer joins the organization. The community college example above illustrates this type of technology.

The conclusion from all this for the supervisor is that the organizing structure for the business will be influenced by the kind of technology used. High performing companies keep a good fit between their structure and technology; low performers do not.[57]

BASIC ISSUES IN THE ORGANIZING PROCESS

 In addition to the structural concerns (above) that are part of every organization and business, supervisors also have *operational concerns*, or the day-to-day decisions that keep a business functioning. These are discussed in the following pages.

1. ASKING THE KEY ORGANIZING QUESTIONS

WHAT work must be done?
(the strategic plan and objectives)

WHO must do the work?
(division of labour)

HOW must the work be done?
(specialization, departmentalization)

WHERE is responsibility for the work assigned?
(chain of command)

WHY is the work successful (or not)?
(monitoring and controlling)

WHEN will the work be done?
(deadlines, measurements, standards)

2. RECOGNIZING THE SIGNIFICANCE OF DELEGATING

For the supervisor the organizing structure for the business will be influenced by the kind of technology used. High performing companies keep a good fit between their structure and technology; low performers do not.

In assigning work, the supervisor is delegating, giving responsibility to others to complete the work. This is an important activity for supervisors, and an important skill to have. Some supervisors don't delegate very well, if at all, possibly because they are afraid of losing control, or fearful that others will not do the job as well as they might themselves. This is understandable because we all take pride in what we think we do well, but, being an supervisor, as in being a parent, is to commit oneself to an educational and teaching role.[58]

This means the parent or supervisor guides a novice (child, new employee, or an employee on a new job) from an unskilled, undeveloped stage, to a more skilled and competent one.

In delegating, supervisors can relieve stress on themselves and promote confidence in their subordinates. Employees will recognize this "vote of confidence" and will demonstrate a greater effort and commitment. For instance, one of the Japanese management practices in Canada refers to employees as "associates,"[59] reinforcing the idea that employees are part of the team, can be trusted, and are competent to do the work. Of course, supervisors have to know *what* to delegate, *to whom*, and what constitutes *acceptable performance* so that subordinates are "playing with a full deck."

3. EXPLAINING AUTHORITY, RESPONSIBILITY, AND ACCOUNTABILITY

Authority is a supervisor's explicit, legitimate, organizational *right* to make decisions that require subordinates to perform or not do certain activities so that departmental objectives and organizational goals can be reached.

In today's more collegial work environment, with its psychological and knowledge workers, in a society which distrusts and resents authority, supervisors have to be more vigilant in its exercise. For instance, smart factories are getting rid of rigid authority structures, utilizing employee involvement, team concepts, quality networks, total quality control and flexible manufacturing techniques.[60] Izzy Sharp, owner and senior executive of the Four Seasons hotel chain, says that participative management is not the same thing as permissive management. Authoritative managers still maintain control, but not in an autocratic manner. Employees look for firm direction, and, according to Sharp, "if we give it to them, and trust them to carry it out, we get the best kind of control: self-control."[61]

The Valhalla Inn Markham never refers to 'categories' of its work force as 'management' and 'staff.' Instead, it classifies its employees as team members. A sign prominently displayed in the staff Communications Corridor reads: **Partners At Work!**

Responsibility is the obligation that supervisors assume to make sure a prescribed work activity is completed. Some authors claim, *"While authority can be delegated, responsibility cannot."*[62] Accordingly, only authority can be delegated, but delegated work activities must be monitored. "You need to pick good people, and you need to kick the tires every once in a while. And if something doesn't feel right, you've got to dig deeper."[63] Others argue that responsibility *can* be delegated, but not fully. "Supervisors can delegate responsibility in the sense of making employees responsible for certain actions. However, this delegation does not make supervisors any less responsible to their bosses."[64] "The buck stops at the boss's desk," says Nova Corp.'s president, J.E. Newall.[65] The supervisor or manager is ultimately responsible and can't pass the blame on to workers or hide beneath the company umbrella.[66]

Accountability is the responsibility involved in the supervisor's accepting legitimate, organizational, delegated authority. Subordinates also assume accountability when they accept, through delegation from their supervisor, the responsibility and authority to complete a work assignment. A supervisor can establish accountability in several ways: personal inspection, written reports or submission of products/

"The buck stops at the boss's desk" says Nova Corp.'s president, J.E. Newall.

materials, feedback from others (such as the SNAP process noted in this chapter), or periodic verbal reporting back to the supervisor. Computer accountability by monitoring telephone operators is done all the time by Bell Canada and customer service agents, for instance, in the courier business. Employees are expected to handle a certain number of calls, in a certain time period, and in a certain manner. While this produces efficiency, it can also produce significant psychosocial stress and a dehumanizing effect in the employee if not managed well.[67]

SUMMARY

The *whole world* is seemingly being reorganized; it is called downsizing, restructuring, reordering of priorities.

How it is done is a critical ethical and supervisory/managerial task.

Competitiveness, productivity and employee loyalty are based on "job security, not job insecurity."

Tomorrow's supervisor will have to contend with the *home - work* dynamic.

Setting objectives and organizing go hand in hand. Goals are broad in scope, ideals to reach; objectives are the stepping-stones to these goals. Management by objectives (MBO) is a collaborative process.

Using the S-P-I-R-O model, a supervisor can set objectives simply and clearly.

Employees can be organized in the following possible ways: agency form, functional, product, territorial, customer and matrix departmentalization. The *chain of command* is the line of authority in a company and *span of control* is the number of employees a supervisor can realistically supervise (it depends!). Work units are influenced by technology and structure. *Operational concerns* in organizing refer to the following: the key organizing questions (*what, who, how, where, why, when*), delegating, authority, responsibility, and accountability.

TERMS/CONCEPTS

restructuring	primitive structure	span of control
objectives	functional department	operational concerns
goals	product department	key questions
MBO	territorial department	delegation
S-P-I-R-O	customer department	authority
contextual factors	matrix department	responsibility
agency form	chain of command	accountability

DISCUSSION QUESTIONS

1. Comment on the following: "The early 1990s have been tough years for business and the world in general. It seems as though the whole world is *reorganizing* and *setting new objectives and goals* for itself."

2. How does the *home - work* challenge affect the supervisor of the 1990s?

3. Explain the difference between *goals* and *objectives*

4. List the benefits and problems associated with the MBO process.

5. Identify how work units are influenced by technology and structure.

6. What are the key organizing questioins? Give an example to illustrate.

7. Why is delegation significant?

8. Explain the difference among authority, responsibility, and accountability.

9. There are arguments *for* and *against* the delegation of responsibility. Take a position a defend it.

ASSIGNMENT

Instructions: Using your personal work experience as the basis, describe one example for each of the following ideas:

IDEA	PERSONAL WORK EXAMPLE
restructuring	
objectives	
goals	
MBO	
functional department	
product department	
territorial department	
customer department	
matrix department	
chain of command	
span of control	
delegation	
authority	
responsibility	
accountability	

CHAPTER FOUR

SOLVING PROBLEMS AND MAKING DECISIONS

What does every group use when it gets together to solve a problem? ... The one thing in common ... is words. Sometimes those words move people along effectively and other times they push people into a brawl.

-- Jane Elizabeth Allen[1]

LEARNING OBJECTIVES

At the end of this chapter, students will be able to:

- Explain the link between problem solving and decision making
- Describe the value of creative problem-solving
- Identify the problem solving steps
- List the steps in decision-making
- Detail the interrelationship among risk taking, groupthink, and office politics in the decision making process
- Describe employee participation in decision making

Opening scenario

*P*ROBLEM #1[2]: The Coopérants Mutual Life Insurance Society's office tower in Montreal used to be the symbol to "towering ambitions," but it has come to symbolize "bigness over soundness." In January 1992, it became the first-ever Canadian life insurance company to collapse under the weight eventually of a $140-million financial debt. "It was a management problem. ... If you give a billion dollars to someone who doesn't manage it properly, you will lose it. It is not because you are big and because you have a lot of money that you are sheltered from problems." The company aimed for growth, not profit, and lost. In their acquisition binge, they stopped "sticking to the knitting,"[3] unlike the BMW Corporation, "probably the best-managed car company in Europe."[4]

PROBLEM #2[5]: "... all is not well ..." with morale problems facing the Ontario government's merger of two court levels, the old High Court of Justice and the District Court. Such simple but troubling problems as knowing where to eat and whether there is a room to sit in are now among the unfinished cutback decisions.

PROBLEM #3[6]: Technological breakthroughs also have a shadow side: their effects on the mind and the community, with loneliness and alienation countered by violence, "made easier by empty streets and anonymity." In trying to identify the core of the problem it makes little sense, according to Hugh Graham -- in spite of the fact that this anonymous society just makes people more lonely, and "lonely men are more prone to violence" -- to blame the problem all on men. He says the "rage of the lost" is not quenched only by feminist fury, women's shelters, and vigilant police. "Taking the cranky and ideological stance that one sex is responsible for the world's problems is comforting and simple, and it dictates simple solutions: get the guilty sex to smarten up, period. It is like the temperance movement, which saw the problem as men and drink, rather than what made men drink." If technology can dehumanize and make us dumb mutes and automatons with no history, as Graham claims, then the solution lies elsewhere than in blame.

The three situations in the opening scenario describe a common theme: problems! All of life contains problems. *The problem is not the problem; it is what we do with the problem that counts.* Some people are proactive or lucky enough to prevent the problem from happening in the first place!

We have the incredible capacity to be dolphin-like!

We are used to saying that we are *homo sapiens* -- people who have developed a mind to distinguish us from the rest of creation. Recent debate suggests we are all potentially *homo sapiens delphinus* -- people with intelligence, yes, but also the incredible capacity to be dolphin-like: tough, charming, intuitive.[7] We are better at problem solving, or at least we're supposed to be, than we think we are.

Perhaps the biggest mistake parents make is developing *obedience skills* in their children rather than problem-solving skills. How many of us when growing up were told, *over and over*, "Don't do this! Stop that! Quit doing that! Put that down! Don't touch it! If you so much as ... !" All threats, and all demanding obedience, submission, and compliance.

Creative Idea #1
Say quickly
every *second*
letter of the alphabet!

But how many of us have been taught problem-solving skills? How many of us, as small children, when we were doing something that we were not supposed to do, were taught how to solve our dilemma, were taken through the problem-solving steps: identifying what the problem was and solving it? How many of us today get frustrated with doing or not doing something only because we have never been taught how to cope with our feelings and solve the problem?

The purpose of this chapter is to discuss the importance of problem solving and decision making for supervisors so that they can act maturely and effectively in their responsibilities.

THE LINK BETWEEN PROBLEM SOLVING AND DECISION MAKING

Problem solving and decision making are connected. Decisions are made as a result of problems. We make decisions because we first have problems. We make decisions because there are problems. There is no sense in making decisions for their own sake; we make decisions because we have a problem to solve. Identifying the issue is the first step in problem solving.

When we are confronted with a conflict, it is important to identify what exactly *is* the problem. Aristotle, the Greek philosopher, felt that identifying the problem was the most important step. If we don't know what we are working on, we'll probably come up with a solution that is irrelevant and doesn't fit! As a result of identifying the problem correctly, we then set in motion a process of choosing which of a set of alternatively proposed solutions will be best. This process is called decision-making. "Thus, decision making refers to an entire process, while problem-solving is one part of the process."[8] While problem-solving and decision making seem similar, there is a difference. A decision is only as good as the identified problem. "Clearly, we ought to spend more time isolating the problem than worrying over the solution."[9]

At the Valhalla Inn Markham, the importance of service and problem solving is exemplified by the commitment of all levels of management, including the general manager, to being highly visible in the public areas of the hotel and to actively participating in the day-to-day operations. Managers and supervisors perform or assist in line duties whenever business demands their involvement.

A problem is the difference, or discrepancy, between your ideal and your actual situation.

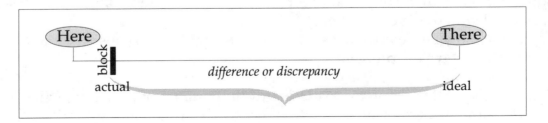

Example: Suppose you want to go to Regina, Saskatchewan, to attend a supervisory business conference. However, you work in Halifax, N.S. The conference is quite important to you and your company; senior management want you to attend. There is also one major problem: your airline is on strike and you have to figure out an alternative. Figuring out the alternatives and choosing one is the decision-making process.

A costly example of refusing to exchange alternatives is the case of Crownx Inc. and its controlling shareholders: they wanted voting shares in return for their preferred shares in order to have more say in the administration of the Crownx board and its managers. "Voting rights would give them the power to change the board." Request refused! No alternatives! Cost and counting? $250 million![10]

Peter Drucker, the noted management writer, has pointed out that in North America we aim for the solution, the answer as quickly as possible while in Japan, emphasis is placed on the question itself and what it implies.[11] Eventually, through a process of consultation, the Japanese make their decision, and, unlike North American managers, don't have to sell it to others for implementation. As early as 1981, Akio Morita, chairman and co-founder of Sony Corporation, stated, in comparing Japanese and American work cultures, that American managers "were too concerned with short-term profits and too little concerned about their workers."[12] The irony is that acceptance of the decision will occur with (1) buying into it and accepting it (the Japanese way) or with (2) selling it and enforcing the sale (the North American way). It is little wonder than when the decision is made, North American managers experience more resistance, fallout, and potential sabotage than their Japanese counterparts.

The problem-solving/decision-making dynamic begins when we meet an impasse and we know we have to deal with the situation. There are two questions: (1) what is the real *PROBLEM*? and (2) what is the appropriate *SOLUTION*? To execute #1, we do *problem analysis* to understand the problem; to

"If you make something the world wants, you will prosper. If you don't, you won't." -- Economist Dian Cohen[13]

achieve #2, we complete a *process of decision making* which, if done well, lets us look at a series of alternative solutions so that we can choose the best one.

THE VALUE OF CREATIVE PROBLEM SOLVING

Nowhere is the multiplicity and openness of life more apparent than in trying to solve problems. We don't have to stay stuck, in other words, in spite of our upbringing or socialization. Studies have shown that by the time a supervisor is 40 years of age, he/she retains roughly 2 percent of the creativity he/she had at age three! [14] We cling to a concept of "mechanized time," often at the expense of a more "timely creative plunge" into creativity.

Creative Idea #2

Say your telephone number to yourself *backwards*!

Creativity is especially important in the decision-making process. When supervisors need to generate alternative courses of action for the problem at hand, the "creative juices" need to flow. Typical blocks to creative problem solving include feeling too tense, not being able to get to the point, fear of criticism, and a climate at work that makes fun of alternative ways of thinking. The best support for creative problem solving is the corporate culture that encourages openness, that trusts people and validates their thoughts and feelings. The movie, *Crazy People*, with Dudley Moore as the psychiatrist who encourages the "crazy people" to be so creative in their advertising slogans, is a good example of the creative problem-solving process, and also an excellent illustration of the shutting-off of the creative juices when fear, mistrust, power, and money become the primary motivators.[15]

The creative supervisor:[16]
- is inquisitive and innovative
- fits new applications to old concepts
- is open-minded and receptive to new ideas
- encourages subordinates to be inquisitive

Appreciating the value of creative problem solving means that a supervisor acknowledges the intuitive approach in addition to the strictly rational approach in solving problems and making decisions. Harvard's Daniel J. Isenberg points out that the higher up a supervisor/manager goes in a company, the more important it is to combine intuition and rational decision making.[17] Intuition is also making inroads in Canadian boardrooms.[18] Stephanie Cox, who operates the Human Potential Institute of Ontario, says, "Organizations are scared. They're failing. They know that they've got to look in different places. They've got all these Harvard MBAs and they're still going down the tubes."[19]

Abitibi-Price, "the beleaguered paper giant,"[20] is keenly aware of this need to come up with alternatives to traditional ways of solving its financial problems. It is survival time for Abitibi-Price, as it is for CP Trucks, which made its mission statement one word, *survival*,[21] because its situation was so desperate. Its "revolution" was to let CP "employees, not managers, run the show." The reason: "Old management came close to sinking the operation." This was a similar situation to that of the now defunct Coopérants Mutual Life Insurance Society in Montreal (mentioned in this chapter's opening scenario). Ronald Aberlander, Abitibi's president and CEO, in spite of a brutal market "out there"[20] in his industry, is trying to turn the balance sheet around. How? His "approach relies less on pure logic than on 'brilliant leaps' of intuition."[22]

Intuition, therefore, is an *experienced hunch*, the result of cumulative experiences over the years which give a supervisor a "gut feel" or "instinct" to do what needs to be done. "Intuition represents a quick apprehension of a decision situation based on past experience but without conscious thought."[23] Many people have said at least once in life, "I should have followed my gut!" or, "I knew better. I should have followed my instinct and intuition." Some supervisors are more "natural" in this intuitive mode of making decisions.

Research has shown that the creative process has four distinct phases. However, one really gets ready and prepares by *expecting* the intuitive insight. Isn't success the combination of perspiration, preparation, and opportunity? Effective supervisors know that. We must also add, they know that both logically *and* intuitively!

THE CREATIVE PROCESS[24]

- "Psyched up" phase
- "Mulling it over" phase
- "Flash of insight" phase
- "Testing of insight" phase

INSIGHT[25]

There are five characteristics to insight:

1. Insight comes to us after we have wrestled with the tension of an inquiry. In other words, the first step towards insight, awareness, consciousness is that we get involved in concrete problems in our lives. Insight assumes that we are searchers.

2. Insight comes suddenly and unexpectedly. What this means is that our efforts are not in vain. ... the old adage of "keep plugging away" is quite apropos here. When insight does come, it is new, it is a gift, and it releases tension. ... It's an "aha" experience.

3. Insight is the result of inner conditions, not external circumstances. You can place all the evidence for proof of something (i.e., the external circumstances), but that doesn't mean that the person will "see," have insight. ... a person can be "staring the obvious right in the face for years" and still not see. ... Inner conditions refer to (1) preparation on our part: we must be prepared to expect something, expect to see; (2) deliberation: taking time to mull over the issue or problem at hand; (3) attentiveness: not giving up, but keeping our eyes on the object of our inquiry; (4) capacity: an ability on our part to be able to pursue this object of inquiry. There are such things as natural limitations! (5) sincerity: an honest desire on our part to be involved in the search for insight.

4. Insight also rests between the concrete world and the abstract world. In searching for awareness, we obviously have to have some tangible problem or issue to be concerned about (i.e., the concrete), but when insight occurs, there is an inner, or abstract, non-concrete experience. Hence, we have the interplay between these two worlds.

5. Finally, when insight occurs, the new insight becomes part of us; it becomes part of our person. It is easy to "see" the point we were struggling over before. In fact, we even wonder why there was a problem in the first place since we now see so clearly! This is especially true if we have to teach this material to someone else. ... Once we become aware, we can't become unaware.

THE PROBLEM-SOLVING STEPS

A problem has occurred. Something is not happening the way it is supposed to. There is a discrepancy between what *should be* and what *is*. This discrepancy has to be cleared up. The "clearing up" process is the problem-solving process.

Problem solving implies that a single correct solution to a situation exists. *Decision making*, conversely, means that one makes a choice among alternatives.[26]

The supervisor has to find the answer to the following question: "What is the problem here?" Of course, the initial responses and considerations may only be *symptoms* for what the real problem is. But the supervisor has to start somewhere. Similarly, in a supervisory situation, the supervisor must determine *what* is the real problem, not just the symptom. The supervisory action of determining the real problem is called problem solving. As in any process, there are certain steps that need to be followed. These steps are listed below.

"Employee ownership alone does not improve productivity or profitability. It must be combined with a practical problem-solving system that includes workers so that managers and employees can built trust." -- Robert Blasi, management professor, Rutgers University, New Jersey[27]

When a problem occurs, the ALARM button should go on for the supervisor. This is the button that tells the supervisor that a discrepancy exists between what *should be* and what *is*. If the problem is a routine discrepancy, the supervisor can easily fix it. But, in the context of today's changing economy and business practices, not all problems are that simple.

Today's supervisor, as seen in chapter 3, has a new problem to deal with: the work - home dilemma. Employees are absent more often now because family responsibilities -- daycare or aging parents, for example -- have to be taken care of. The problem may not be "new" to the supervisor, but it is certainly more pervasive, and in that sense will create more *problematic* situations for the supervisor. A study by Robert Half International, the world's largest personnel firm, found that people were not as willing any more to sacrifice family for work. Those polled in the 1,000-company poll, said they felt companies should foot the bill and be more accommodating to employees when they try to balance family life and work life. "Sixty-eight per cent of people questioned said they believe companies should offer executives [and lower levels employees and supervisors] a 'parent track,' or slower career path, to allow working parents to spend more time with their families."[29]

"When a federal minister brags about being a killer of child care, we know the country is down to scraping the sludge off the bottom of the political barrel," said Nancy Riche, vice-president of the Canadian Labour Congress.[28]

Then there are new problems for supervisors with information technology,[30] computers,[31] work redesign,[32] low morale as a result of downsizing,[33] lack of loyalty by employees as a result of their experiences during the recession,[34] etc.

The Problem-Solving Steps

NEW PROBLEM-SOLVING MODEL

The truth of the matter is that today all of us, East and West, are moving toward a new type of civilization, whether we realize it or not.

– Mikhail Gorbachev[35]

1. SORT OUT THE SYMPTOMS FROM THE REAL PROBLEM

For instance, if you notice that absenteeism is a "problem" in the new department that you have just been assigned to, sort out *why* the absenteeism is occurring. The unhealthy repercussions that you have to manage -- other employees' anger and resentment in asking them to take on more work, etc. -- are not pleasant, but these effects indicates a symptomatic situation for you. To clear up these symptoms, you must get to the root of the real problem.

2. IDENTIFY WHAT THE REAL PROBLEM IS

Begin by looking at the discrepancy between what you *want* and what *is*. Identify what it is you want and what it is you now have. It is very important, especially when the issue is important, that supervisors put pen to paper or flip chart (or fingers to computer!) in this part of the analysis because when it is "up" and "on the table," so to speak, the discussion will be much more concrete, and

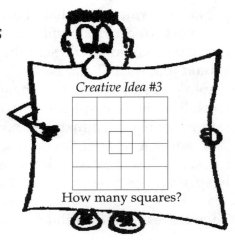

Creative Idea #3

How many squares?

not just theoretical.

As seen in chapter 3, in the organizing process, the supervisor can now ask *the key organizing questions* in identifying the problem.

The answers to these questions will get the supervisor past any superficial thinking on his/her part or on the part of the group. The question: "WHO is causing this discrepancy?" is a very important one. It relates to the 90 per cent Factor thesis in chapter 1, namely, that roughly 90 per cent of all problems are *relationship matters*, not technical ones. The "who" could be a group or a single person. The point is: a relationship dynamic is probably (at a 90% confidence level) out of whack and the supervisor will need to address this human relations need and problem. At this point, the solution may be straightforward: a simple talk with the individual(s), or training, or possibly disciplinary action.

> **WHAT**
> is the actual discrepancy?
> **WHO**
> is causing this discrepancy?
> **HOW**
> is the discrepancy affecting work?
> **WHERE**
> is the discrepancy most costly?
> **WHY**
> is the discrepancy happening?
> **WHEN**
> is the work going to get done?

3. CONFIRM AND DOCUMENT THE TRUE CAUSE OF THE DISCREPANCY

This is the final phase in the problem analysis/solving process. The supervisor, alone, or with a small group, has been able to distinguish between symptoms and the actual or real problem, and, in phase 2, has been able to ascertain the likely cause(s) of the problem. Now, the final verification step in the process will prove to the supervisor whether his/her analysis is correct. If it is, then the discrepancy should clear up when the supervisor applies the decision-making steps to solve the problem!

The Ideas Committee of the Valhalla Inn Markham convenes once a month to brainstorm new 'Made in Valhalla' services for immediate implementation. By creating a forum for submitting new, creative ideas, team members are contributing significantly toward meeting the hotel's objective of increasing business.

THE STEPS IN DECISION MAKING

The process of decision making has been called an "elusive concept."[36] We know that life doesn't always present us with clear-cut alternatives; we have our own biases; and circumstances impact on us to cloud even the best of

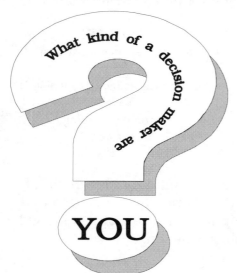

decision makers sometimes. But that doesn't mean we simply roll over and play dead and let others decide. The adage is correct, "Not to decide is to decide." We are decision makers just by *being*. Charismatic individuals exude something that catches our imagination and we automatically make a decision. It's all very spontaneous and we usually don't even realize we have made a decision.

In business a supervisor just can't make decisions "by the seat of the pants" all the time. Sometimes a supervisor goes with the best hunch or intuition when looking at alternatives, but, in important matters, and with serious problems to resolve, a more systematic process is crucial as well. The supervisor needs to know and follow the decision-making steps to weed out bias and error, and to make the best judgment. The best advice, of course, if a supervisor is not prepared and feels pressured into making a decision, is to wait until there is more clarity on the matter.[37] That's just good counsel, period! An experienced supervisor knows that that "waiting period" will not last forever. "Most good supervisors know that there are two cardinal sins in decision making: procrastination and vacillation."[38]

Supervisors and managers get paid to make good decisions. All decision making involves risk. Some supervisors are better at working in an uncertain or ambiguous working environment. Ambiguity seems to be commonplace today, and while it can lead to tremendous anxiety, it can also promote superior decision making.

Individuals or companies make decisions when a new situation has arisen, an on-going problem has to be resolved, or because the status quo is not good enough. With the Coca-Cola fiasco in the 1980s, Coke felt that the status quo for them meant certain losses. They decided to change their formula to counter this situation. Coke -- already the largest selling beverage company at the time -- weighed the actual losses against the *risk* of alienating its customers with the new coke. That decision proved to be a disaster.

LET'S REFRAME, FOLKS!

The skill of *reframing* is having "the power of perspective."[39] It's being able to see things from different viewpoints; we don't have to be unidimensional in the way we think and see the world. Two people can look outside on a dull February day; both see snow, but one "sees" the idea of a new invention -- what has become the Noma power shovel, for example!

The second person "reframed" the snow situation, and instead of just taking it "as is," reframed it, got another perspective, let the creative juices flow, and bingo! That's why the old expression, "Necessity is the mother of invention," is so true. Many of us need to reframe our lives and our work, especially in difficult times. A two-year recession, with 2,600 people a day being laid off in the U.S. alone, is a difficult time![40]

Since the only "constant" today is change, and change means learning, we are continually confronted with new learning situations. These situations force us to decide: for life or against life! Will we grow or will we stagnate? Will we accept life's challenges or will be become bitter and uninterested in life?

To meet life's challenges, personally and in our work, we need to reframe our life situations or to "put things into different contexts to give them different meanings; what we make important at that moment."[41] It is re-perceiving the experience or situation we are in so that it is positive for us, not negative. This can be done by reframing the *context*[42] (taking an adverse situation we are involved in and re-perceiving how it would look positive in another context). The expression, "if life gives you lemons, then make lemonade" is a good example of this context reframing. We can also reframe the *content* of a situation (taking an adverse situation we are involved in and re-perceiving what it means). For instance, the situation of a talkative employee could be content-reframed by seeing this employee as intelligent and having something to contribute.

Some supervisors may feel that reframing is selling themselves a "bill of goods." Not so. Why? Because the proof is in the pudding, so to speak. We get in life exactly what we measure out (in our thoughts, words, actions, perceptions). If we see the world as ugly, it is; if we see it as beautiful, it is. It's the evidence in the folk wisdom that says: before the age of 20 we have the face God gives us; from 20 to 40 we have the face we want to show the world; and after 40 we have the face we deserve! Life catches up with us.

Successful supervisors reframe so that experiences work *for* them, not against them.

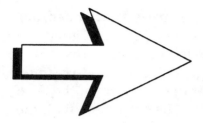

When the supervisor has identified the real problem in the situation, a new process begins in order to find a responsible solution. That is the decision making process. Like problem analysis/problem-solving, it too has definite steps.

1. DETERMINE THE KIND OF DECISION THAT IS NEEDED

Once the supervisor knows what the real problem is, the first step in the decision-making process is to answer the following question: "With *this* problem, what kind of result do I want in solving it?" That question asks the reason *why*, or the *objective* in solving the problem. The objective will guide the supervisor in the *kind* of decision that will be made. For instance, in the decision by senior officials on which plants in the U.S. and Canada will stay open, Robert Stempel, former chairman of General Motors Corp., said, "Innovative labour agreements and work arrangements are going to be part of our decision making."[43] This *kind* of decision making under these *kinds* of conditions is a serious moment in the management - union relationship. As well, in the area of information technology (IT), line managers -- and supervisors are line managers -- "are in the best position to lead in the use of technology to achieve business objectives."[44] Great West Life Assurance Co. of Winnipeg, Manitoba, for instance, several years ago distributed this kind of responsibility for applications development, and holds line managers accountable.

The kind of decision, or the decision's objective, could be: to increase sales, develop new markets, encourage positive morale, etc. A conflict could arise over the kind of decision that's needed in a situation like the following: As the new supervisor, you have determined that the excessive absenteeism is caused by older employees who have family responsibilities. You know that your company promotes a "family feeling": this is one of its corporate culture values. The objective or kind of decision that you envision, as a result of the problem, is possibly to introduce more flexible working hours. However, your boss has wanted to replace these "older" workers and sees this as an opportunity to suggest a disciplinary measure. At this point, of course, feelings, values, office politics, etc., come into play.

2. LOOK AT ALTERNATIVES TO SOLVE THE PROBLEM

Once the objective for the eventual decision is secure, the supervisor has the opportunity to allow the creative juices to flow by using the *brainstorming technique*, for instance. In brainstorming, ideas are simply tossed on to the table; they are not judged or evaluated; and the rule is, "the more, the better!" This is when it counts to have a positive corporate culture because employees will feel freer to "let loose" with ideas. Creativity does not occur in fearful environments. It was brainstorming that saved the GM plant in Arlington, Texas, when General Motors made their decision to close certain plants in North America. The Oshawa, Ontario, plant was spared, but not the one at St. Catharines, Ontario. At the Arlington plant, union *and* management both recognized "business realities," put heads together, brainstormed ideas and were successful. The president of the UAW Local 276 recognized the impact of brainstorming and the positive union-management relationship developed when he said, "It's No. 1 in making the decision."[45] And it was the brainstorming technique that got Olivetti Canada Ltd. its new advertising campaign, "The Renaissance of the computer" that increased requests for proposals on their information systems by more than 200% in the fall of 1991. Olivetti Canada's 33-year-old president, Mark De Simone, said, "We had an excellent September, October and December. Those three months were the best in our history in terms of revenue."[46]

Creativity does not occur in fearful environments.

3. EVALUATE THE ALTERNATIVES

When the brainstorming activity has exhausted itself, and there are enough ideas on the table, a technique called *force field analysis* can be used. This technique weighs the ideas as "forces for" and "forces against" reaching the

**ULCERLESS
DECISION-MAKING RULES![48]**
- Rule #1: Don't Sweat the Small Stuff!
- Rule #2: Don't Reinvent the Wheel!
- Rule #3: Don't Play Hero!
- Rule #4: Don't Panic!
- Rule #5: Don't Control Everything!
- Rule #6: Don't Fear Being Wrong!
- Rule #7: Don't Sit on Your Duff!
- Rule #8: Once You Decide, Do It!

objective. Not all of the forces are of equal weight or value. Once the forces are recorded (on a flip chart, for instance) as "for" or "against," a simple weighting scheme like "hot - cold" (e.g., is the idea "hot," a good one, or "cold," no good) and "rank ordering" can be used.

While there are very sophisticated statistical and mathematical tools in decision making,[47] a supervisor most probably would either not have reason to use them, or, if necessary, would be trained in their use. That would be particularly true in a sophisticated manufacturing environment.

Guidelines that a supervisor would rely on, at least initially, would affect his/her sense of confidence about a decision, the "feel" of it, how it fits into the organizational context, its timing, its importance, its probable impact on the company and/or individual(s) involved, its cost, and its implementation time. Finally, the supervisor actually makes the decision.

THE PROBLEM-SOLVING/DECISION-MAKING MODEL: A SUMMARY

DETERMINING THE PROBLEM
1. Sort out your symptoms from the real problem
2. Identify what your real problem is (asking the key organizing questions: what? who? how? where? why? when?)
3. Confirm and document the true cause of the problem

DECIDING TO RESOLVE THE PROBLEM
1. Determine the kind of decision you need (your objective)
2. Examine your alternatives to solving the problem
3. Evaluate your alternatives
4. Make your decision

IMPORTANT KEYS: RISK TAKING, GROUPTHINK, OFFICE POLITICS

For the supervisor, decision making is often accomplished in a context of risk taking, groupthink, and office politics.

RISK TAKING

Making a decision usually means that things will not stay the same; something will change. The most immediate risk is the "new." Often the supervisor will have to "satisfice": settle for objectives that are at least acceptable and relatively hassle-free, that don't impose an inordinate amount of hardship or danger.

Besides the quantitative measures of estimating used in business to gauge the probabilities of risk in a decision, *attitude* is also a major component in deciding how much risk to take. A tragic example of inappropriate risk taking around the safety issue is the "macho" and sexist attitude of some airline pilots.[50] The pilots' machismo attitude, for example, "discourages pilots from showing weakness" and this exposes them to taking foolish risks. In the federal inquiry into an Air Ontario jet crash, for instance, Randy Pitcher, in charge of making sure standards were maintained, said that airlines "must convince pilots there is nothing sissy-like about deciding not to fly because they are ill or having emotional problems." It is estimated that the NASA tragedy with Challenger occurred because attitudes blocked seeing the risks correctly.[51] The Canada Post strike in September 1991 is another example of a "macho standoff"[52] that put economic, as well as public relations, realities at severe risk: "Like two stubborn goats butting heads, Canada Post and its union prefer suffering pain to reaching a compromise."[52]

BIG BLUE TAKES THE POLITICS OUT OF THE OFFICE!

IBM Canada Ltd. is decentralizing the entire organization. In trying to solve its problems and make decisions, it has adopted a system of electronic meetings which apparently has taken "the posturing and politics out of meetings," because ideas can flow more freely. At a decision support centre at Queen's University School of Business, employees are in different physical spaces; all can "talk" at once for the system guarantees anonymity. The success of this electronic process does depend, however, on "a skilful facilitator to navigate the group through the session and help keep participants focused on critical issues."[49]

In the brokerage business, "bought deals" -- where brokerage firms put up their own money to buy an entire issue of shares from a company and then resell them as quickly as possible to their biggest clients -- are a good example of weighing the risks. The dealers often make a substantial financial loan in the hundreds of millions of dollars and must therefore know the risk factor involved.[53] As well, information technology (IT) has become so crucial in management's decisions *vis-à-vis* risk that a new, and challenging,[54] participant -- that of the Chief Information Office (CIO) -- is making its presence felt in the boardroom. American Airlines is a case in point: when it lost $50-million in revenue because of a glitch "in a new system for tracking seat utilization,"[55] the importance of a CIO role became part of their corporate agenda.

Our Vision

We will be Canada's leading network of business development professionals dedicated to client success through continuously improving organization effectiveness and individual performance.

We will achieve this by:
• Building trust partnerships
• Honouring our commitments
• Consistently exceeding expectations

[Gilmore & Associates is a Canadian owned and operated consulting and training design organization and designer of the total quality management **Compete To Win System**]

Much of the fear in the marketplace and in the free trade economic reality is the amount of risk business people feel exposed to. While many would want to "hunker down," so to speak, get protection from government and trade laws, others feel that, based on research and the Japanese experience, making better quality products and providing impeccable service will reduce that risk so that firms will be competitive and the #1 priority -- the customer -- will be better served.[56] In the business world that is being "globally restructured," other companies are "teaming up," developing partnerships, or merging. Again, all of this activity aims at reducing risk and maximizing profit opportunities.[57]

Even though research shows that organizations do not reward individuals or supervisors/managers for risk-taking behaviour,[58] managers and supervisors can still foster an ethical and positive corporate culture. Michael Barach, son of the founder of U.S. Shoe, said the real gift his father gave to the company was *not* in correctly segmenting the market but in creating "a beautiful corporate culture"[59] which rewarded risk taking, supported rather than punished those who had a bad year or two, and which allowed ideas to percolate up. Supervisors can also do a personal self-examination of their own blockages to risk taking and eliminate them. And they can get help: in an age of teamwork, it's all right for supervisors to enlist the pertinent help of subordinates in a decision, as Bankten Management Services Ltd., of Markham, Ontario, has done. Only in business six years, it has increased its revenues 50 per cent every year, and is now a $23-million company employing 23 people.[60]

GROUPTHINK

Another factor that the supervisor has to be aware of is pressure from the group to make a decision in a certain way. This pressure results in what is called *groupthink*.[61]

Reflective Exercise

Think of a decision you made that you felt pressured into?	
What were its consequences? Good? Bad?	
What kind of group pressure was it?	
What did you learn from this experience?	

Poor outcomes result if the supervisor, contrary to his/her own better judgment, allows others to dictate what they feel is the "right" decision to be made. Companies and individuals, during the recession of the early 1990s, realized that they had made financial decisions -- to buy a bigger home or to expand operations, for instance -- based upon what others were doing. Two years into the recession, many had gone bankrupt!

There are many examples of groupthink decisions: the lack of preparedness on the part of the U.S. Navy just prior to Pearl Harbor, the John F. Kennedy Bay of Pigs disaster, numerous decisions around the Vietnam War, the Gulf War, especially on Saddam Hussein's part. Iraq was in total "groupthink Catch-22 mode": for the generals to challenge Hussein meant death, to lose because Hussein's pressure forced them into a losing decision also meant death!

How does a supervisor recognize the pressures from groupthink and learn to avoid these pressures. Some pressures/cautions are listed below:[62]

Pressures for groupthink	Precautions
The group thinks it is above reproach, "can do no wrong." The group thinks everyone is in agreement on the topic. The group thinks its focus is ethical. The group thinks everyone communicates well. The group thinks it's okay and others are wrong.	As a supervisor, foster critical discussion. Challenge the status quo by remaining objective and on the topic. Use an ethical checklist. Videotape discussions for post-feedback critiques. Teach the group about projection and scapegoating.

OFFICE POLITICS

Organizational politics have been likened to a "double-edged sword."[63] In other words, the supervisor must realize that office politics has its "upside"[64] and its "downside."[65] Psychologist Christine Hansen writes, "Remember: all institutions are political environments. Your participation is not optional. Either you learn to manage change -- or you are managed. It's up to you."[66]

Effective politics is the art of persuasiveness. One of the most incredible acts of nonverbal persuasiveness happened with the birth of a baby on board a British Airways jumbo jet as it flew from New Delhi, through Soviet airspace, and into London's Heathrow airport![67] Four doctors on board assisted in the delivery in an economy section of the Boeing 747 that was curtained off. An even more persuasive move occurred on another jumbo jet, this time one flying from France to the Caribbean. The jet "was forced to turn back" after three hours in flight! Talk about power, and from a baby!

Older children know this art of persuasiveness -- and often several unusual techniques -- in "managing" their parents! Think back to your own childhood: didn't you go to one parent for one permission, and to the other for something else? Children don't confuse these "success lines" of persuasion.

Psychologist Christine Hansen writes, "Remember: all institutions are political environments. Your participation is not optional. Either you learn to manage change -- or you are managed. It's up to you."

What supervisors experience in the office is often an "updated" version of these earlier childhood versions "of getting what I want," that is, office politics. Some children have learned effective ways, or learned to make their ways effective; others have not, and suffer the consequences. There are ex-employees walking the street because they refused to "kiss butt"! Upon closer examination of these reasons, one often finds out that they just didn't have the skills to manage their relationships at work so as not to feel used, to feel they were degrading themselves. A positive ethical sense of persuasion will obviously take into account values such as respect[68] and dignity for others, fair play, and keeping the "big picture" in mind. Ethical persuasiveness will avoid manipulation. "Any act by a person in power that pressures another person to behave in ways that violate that person's sense of personal worth is a form of manipulation. At best, it's insensitive; at worst, it's a form of violence."[69]

A positive ethical sense of persuasion will obviously take into account values such as respect and dignity for others, fair play, and keeping the "big picture" in mind.

EMPLOYEE PARTICIPATION AND DECISION MAKING

A final consideration for the supervisor in problem solving and decision making is the issue of employee involvement and participation. Some feel that teamwork and employee responsibility is key; others do not. For instance, Ford keeps in touch with its employees through the use of TV[70] while Alias Research, of Toronto, which designed software graphics for *Terminator 2*, want "new staff and tighter controls"[71] as well as more participative decision making as a way to turn the company around.[72] Elliott Jaques, the French management expert -- whom one well-known management guru has called "neo - feudal"[73] because of his management philosophy -- believes that hierarchy is the way to manage because team-oriented organizations will have a problem of accountability. But Olivetti Canada Ltd. feels the more horizontal, rather than hierarchical, level is the recipe for its success in the future. President Mark De Simone told the Empire Club of Canada, "The most effective employees are the individual thinkers. These individuals expect the responsibility and the proper tools to support their decision-making. ... The successful firm will be transformed from a top-down hierarchical structure to one that is much more horizontal."[74]

Empowerment is a word that is not only familiar at the Valhalla Inn Markham, but is practiced by all levels of staff. "Providing our employees do not give the place away," says Graham Willsher, the hotel's general manager, "each and every line/staff member has the opportunity of rectifying any concern or problem a guest may have immediately, without the necessity of consulting a supervisor."

What is important for the supervisor to know in employee participation and decision making are the following realities:

(1) Employee involvement is critical when new changes are to be introduced. Of course, employees have to be mature or competent in the task(s) involved. Ignorance cannot be glossed over for a "politically correct" decision in favour of participation.

(2) Employees also feel more satisfied and produce more when they have a say in the matter.[75]

(3) When employees participate, the supervisor is sharing power. Too great a fear of losing control will not work. But if employees and supervisor are able to talk with one another, a true sense of empowerment can occur.

(4) Like a wise parent, only the supervisor can make some decisions.

(5) Total quality supervision involves participation which brings about a significantly better quality product.

(6) The kind of employee participation and involvement should match or fit the supervisor's style. The resulting behaviour does not mean that this relationship is a necessarily healthy one. For instance, an autocratic-style supervisor, with agreeably submissive subordinates who are quite content to let others take responsibility, is a rather dysfunctional arrangement.

(7) Employee participation, therefore, is neither good nor bad; it all depends on the situation and the context.

SUMMARY

Problems are part of life. They come in all shapes and sizes. *The problem is not the problem; it's what we do with the problem that counts.*

Problems are linked to decision making because decisions are made as a result of having problems. Identifying the correct problem is essential to making the correct decision.

The problem-solving steps include sorting out the symptoms from the real problem, identifying what is the real problem, and confirming and documenting the true cause of the discrepancy.

Reframing a situation is seeing it differently and can be done by *context* and by *content*.

The decision-making steps are: determining the kind of decision needed, examining the alternatives, evaluating the alternatives, choosing one to implement, and follow-up to see how good the decision was.

Important contextual elements include risk taking, the phenomenon and pressure of groupthink, and the reality of office politics.

Total quality management (TQM) supports pushing decision making down as far as reasonably possible. Participation is invaluable when changes are introduced.

TERMS/CONCEPTS

problem solving	brainstorming	office politics
decision making	force field analysis	ethical decision making
insight	risk taking	employee participation
reframing	groupthink	

DISCUSSION QUESTIONS

1. What is the relationship between problem solving and decision making?

2. Suppose you lost your wallet today. Using material from the text on problem solving and decision making, describe what you would do.

3. Describe a problem situation you have had which you felt you were highly creative in solving.

4. What is reframing? Give two examples each of *context* and *content* reframing.

5. What is the relationship of risk taking to decision making?

6. How could you see *groupthink* affecting a supervisor's ability to make an effective decision? Give examples.

7. Are office politics important? Explain.

8. How are employee participation and decision making related?

ASSIGNMENT

Instructions: Get into groups of 5-7 students each. Assume that you are all supervisors. The following fax has just come in from head office. You are to act on it <u>immediately</u>.

TO:	Field supervisors
FROM:	Sr. Vice-president, Human Resources
RE:	Immediate **30%** layoff action
DATE:	Now!

As you have been well aware for some time, our company has been losing money at a drastic rate. You were also aware that layoffs would be imminent.

This memo confirms the board's decision this morning to lay off **30% of all field service employees** <u>immediately</u>.

We regret having to do this, but economic times leave us no alternative if we are to stay in business. Please fax me your choices within one-half hour.

Below is a list of the ten employees working for you. You have only the information given below for each employee. <u>Your problem</u>: Which *seven* employees will you decide to keep? Make a personal decision for all empoyees first. Then, as a group, rank order the employees and give specific reasons. Be prepared to let the class know the three who will be laid off.

EMPLOYEES	Your rank	Group rank	REASONS
1. Male with AIDS; above average			
2. 50-year old; union steward			
3. 7-month employee; excellent			
4. Recently married; 5-year employee			
5. 10-year employee; above average			
6. Woman, 4 months pregnant			
7. Recent college graduate			
8. Engineer; critical to operations			
9. 15-year employee; large family			
10. Your spouse; average employee			

CHAPTER FIVE

MANAGING TIME AND CONDUCTING MEETINGS

Time is the scarcest resource, and unless it is managed, nothing else can be managed.

-- Peter Drucker[1]

LEARNING OBJECTIVES

At the end of this chapter, students will be able to:

- Explain that time management is self-management
- Cite organizational supervisory time concerns
- Identify major illusions about managing time
- Analyze the different time types
- Distinguish different approaches to spending time
- List common time wasters and time savers
- Explain the "TAO" of meetings

Opening scenario

O nce upon a time ..." When we hear those words the *child* in us immediately takes notice. Childhood memories and childhood stories come to mind and a feeling of expansiveness inside takes over. It's time to daydream, to let go. The Hebrew scriptures announce, "In the beginning ..." And we wonder. "Time ... is not so clear-cut when we come to mental and atomic events or to the early seconds of the universe, in which no independent clocks existed."[2]

For most of us, the mechanics of our consciousness get in the way of the more subtle movements of nature, and thus we are blocked, *in time*, from seeing more deeply into reality, which is *out of time*, so to speak.[3] Physicist Fritjof Capra says that in "eastern philosophy, unlike that of the Greeks ... space and time are constructs of the mind."[4] Stephen Hawking, the internationally acclaimed British physicist, says it's difficult to tell if we're going backwards or forwards in time because of the *rules* of the universe![5] Albert Einstein relativized Newton's concept of absolute time when he showed that time is a measure of each person's perception. Thus, time has a "mechanical," or sequential component (Newton) -- like 8:30, 8:31, etc. -- and a relative component (Einstein), relative to the observer.[6] Our conscious self, according to physicist F. David Peat, is not bound by any particular "order" in nature and is very sensitive to the movements of time. The bias, of course, in our daily living and in our society is for a "mechanical, sequential order of time that is essentially the same as Newton's" and our attachment to this interpretation of time blocks our efforts at creativity.

Fictionists and visionaries have often imagined what would happen if time were reversed. They speculate that clocks would run backwards, broken cups would suddenly reassemble, and people would "die, grow young," and then be "born"! Can some strange event cause our world to behave in this way? In fact, only one physical law would have to be reversed in order for this to happen. However, the celebrated British physicist Stephen Hawking demonstrates that if this pivotal law were to reverse, our psychological perception of time must also reverse. The universe would run backwards, but we would remember the future and ponder what the past has in store for us! In other words, our world would seem no different to us. We would remember the future births of our friends and hope their demises didn't occur too soon in the past! Even more bizarre, Dr. Hawking speaks of the concept of imaginary time which can proceed in any direction at all![7]

SOME OF THE STAGGERING IMPLICATIONS OF THE NEW UNDERSTANDING OF TIME

- We are not limited to what we think we are;
- The French philosopher René Descartes' "I think; therefore, I am" is incomplete. I am more than the sum of my thinking. I am also feeling, intuition, love, etc.
- Problem solving is possible because we can let go of thinking that puts reality into "little boxes";
- To say we have no time is to say we are dead!
- If true transformation of ourselves exposes us to "other orders" of time -- such as the more intuitive grasps of reality -- then we are bigger than we think we are;
- If the human journey, as physicists maintain, eventually takes us beyond a "rigid, mechanical, and limited"[8] way of seeing life to a more cosmic sense of unity with all of creation, then our world is not hopeless; and the move toward globalization is perhaps the initializing of this creative pulse;
- In spite of our resistance to seeing beyond ourselves and attempting to get "the big picture," life is relentless in compelling us to appreciate the diversity in nature, in the world, and in the universe;
- We really don't have a choice in becoming aware. The question is: will we co-operate with life willingly, or, as Carl Jung says, "as pigs to the slaughter"?
- We are not the centre of the universe, as much as we want to believe this illusion. We need an emotional, intellectual, and spiritual "Copernican revolution" -- or conversion -- to be healed as people and as a world;
- If business is to move into the 21st. century with a modicum of integrity, pride, and professionalism, it will need to transform its workplaces into *worthplaces*. A meditation on time is a good place to start.

We all take time for granted. We all say, "We'll just have to get more time!" Rather silly, isn't it, to say that? As a supervisor, if you find yourself saying, "But there's just not enough hours in the day!" something's not right. Each of us is given 24 hours each day. It's up to us to make use of these hours. Some people have something to show for their time; others do not. There are the winners and losers in life.

The purpose of this chapter is to examine time, what it is, how it affects us, how the supervisor can best make use of time, and, on a practical basis, how meetings are more effective when time is managed well.

TIME MANAGEMENT IS SELF-MANAGEMENT

Who we are and what time is are intertwined. Just as we cannot escape from ourselves, so we cannot escape time. We are; time is!

How is it that we never seem to have the time to do it *right*, but we always seem to find the time to do it *over?*[9]

A person is how a person lives in time! There's an old saying, "If you tell me how you spend your time, I can describe who you are!" In other words, *how* we spend the time each day is saying very clearly what our priorities are, and our priorities are indicators to values, and our values are the personal anchors that shape and focus our lives. Sometimes we don't know what our values are, but if we look at how we spend our time, we will find the clues to our values, and to who we are.

Some people make time, some pass time, some kill time, and others just waste time.

Time is all we have; no time, then death!

Our destiny is woven into the way we spend time. Discussing time can be a scary matter for some people. For instance, how would you answer the following questions in the reflective exercise below?

Reflective Exercise		
	yes	no
1. Are you unhappy with your life?		
2. Would you want to be doing something different?		
3. Do you know what you want from life?		
4. Does time "fly by" for you?		
5. Do you put off for tomorrow what should be done now?		

If you answered "yes" to all five questions, you need to start thinking seriously about where you're going in life. You may the kind of person who lets life *happen* to you, rather than *making* life happen.

The philosophy of time management as self-management holds that there are some key questions in life: where have I come from? where am I now? where am I going? The answer to the first question gives us a history; the answer to the second gives us a present; and the answer to the third gives us a future.

Thus, time management, in its basic consideration, is a reflection on the meaning to our lives. Does life make sense? Do I have a purpose to my life? Do I know where I am going in life?

A typical American's 41.8 hours of leisure per week break down as follows: 16.3 hours socializing with friends or family, 12.1 hours watching television, and the remaining 13.4 hours on all other leisure activities.[10]

Although these same "life questions" may not appear to be the immediate concern of the supervisor, the same principle of self-management is at work in *how* a supervisor manages his/her work time? Good supervisory self-management will lead to effectiveness on the job: a sense of purpose and direction. If my personal life has dignity and meaning, then my work life can also have purpose and direction.[11]

We live time. Time does not "fly." We use that expression probably because we are embarrassed by what we have to show for our efforts or because we didn't get done what we had planned. It's how we spend our time that counts, and in business today, as never before, time has to be spent ethically.[12]

Time and the supervisor's key work function of *planning* go together. A supervisor with poor time management is a supervisor with faulty planning habits. An effective supervisor plans his/her time to get the results intended.[13] The supervisor needs to keep in mind "Pareto's law of maldistribution," or simply, Pareto's law, coined after the Italian philosopher and engineer, Vilfredo Pareto, which states that 20 per cent of employees cause 80 per cent of the problems, an insight which helps to pinpoint problems more accurately.[14] Another way of stating this law is to say that "80 percent of our results come from 20 percent of what we do."[15]

Unlike many businesses, the hotel industry operates on a 24-hour basis. "Long hours are not a requirement of a manager's job," says the Valhalla Inn Markham general manager, "yet a 10-to-12 hour working day will still only cover 40 to 60 per cent of any department head's operating responsibility. Effective delegation and communication in the hotel business has to remain, therefore, the manager's greatest asset to ensure 'round the clock' effectiveness."

A TIME MANAGEMENT REFLECTION[16]

Instructions: In small groups, brainstorm ideas on the following questions. Be prepared to present your thoughts. Your instructor will help you round out your lists.

• Identify ways that a supervisor can CONSERVE time?

• Identify ways that a supervisor can CONTROL time?

• Identify ways that a supervisor can MAKE time?

Becoming a supervisor, therefore, in an important sense, is a calling to self-management and, therefore, time management. The more effective you are as a person, the more effective you will be in supervising and in time management. Olympic sports athletes, for instance, do what they do because they *do it*; and to do it, they need to plan and be organized, and that means managing their time. Isn't it true, "If you want something done, ask an organized busy person?" How many of us need help, but put it off because we say, "Oh, he/she will never get it done!"

Effective personal and therefore supervisory time management begins with being the best person we can be, maximizing our strengths, eliminating our weaknesses, and learning to know the difference!

THE SUPERVISOR AND TIME MANAGEMENT

Supervisors will not be effective without proper time-management skills. The major one, of course, is to have a personally balanced life: emotionally, physically, intellectually, and spiritually.

In addition to being personally organized and goal-centred, supervisors also need to be organized around their work requirements. Anticipating these activities can be very helpful in creating a productive day. Some organizational considerations that supervisors have to budget time for are listed on the next page:[17]

- time for doing things
- time for meetings
- time for relationships
- time for discussions
- time for office work
- time for giving instructions
- time for training and development

In an 8-hour or 480-minute day, it is estimated that a supervisor allocates his/her time as follows:[18]

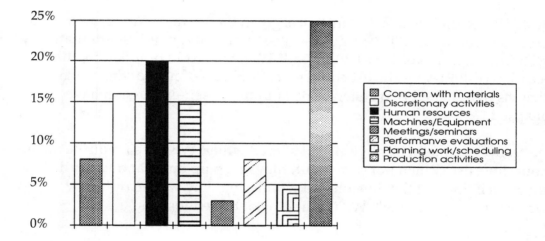

As you can see, a supervisor's time is cut out for him/her in rather practical, and consistent, ways. How does a supervisor, therefore, determine which activities deserve priority? While the emphasis on priorities would change from one organization to another, depending on the corporate culture, there are some priority guidelines most supervisors can follow. If you answer "yes" to the following questions, then the activity is "top" priority and needs immediate attention; if you answer half of the questions with a "yes," then the activity could wait a little while. This all depends, of course, on the context. Obviously, if you answer "no" to all the questions, the activity is not of immediate concern.

---

10 PRIORITY QUESTIONS

- Is it urgent?
- Is there minimum time?
- Is your boss expecting it now?
- Is there a crisis?
- Is it important to do?

- Is there a problem not doing it?
- Is it expected of you now?
- Is there a deadline?
- Is it the right thing to do?
- Is it important to you?

KEY ILLUSIONS ABOUT MANAGING TIME

We all live with illusions. For instance, given the Vietnam War era, the baby-boom generation, the "if-you-go-to-college-you-will-get-a-job-automatically" belief, the recession of 1981-83, the Gulf War, the world of inflation, the recession of 1991-92 -- the list could go on and on -- "most of the romantic illusions that fuelled two generations of limitless self-expression have collapsed."[19]

The reality of time in our lives is not spared either. We have favourite illusions about time also. When not sorted out, they creep up on us and we find ourselves living out the illusion and wondering why we are unhappy, or that "we just don't have time!" What are some of these illusions?

OUR FAVOURITE ILLUSIONS ABOUT TIME

---

1. *The illusion that the busier or harder we work the more effective we are.* Some people are very busy and manage to get much accomplished; others *look* busy, but it is all frenetic energy. The sixties's adage, "Just don't do something; stand there!" has a lot going for it for the frenetic types. The Ancient Greeks had the character Sisyphus: he worked hard all day rolling this huge boulder up the mountain, and when he got to the top, it rolled down the other side! And he then began to roll it back up, only for it to happen again! The "Sisyphus supervisor" needs to stop, slow down, get recollected, prioritize, and systematically begin working. The trick is to work smarter, not harder, and not always in "crisis management" mode.[20]

2. *The illusion that we are indispensable.* That's the sin of pride. The Ancient Greeks referred to this as *hubris* -- an inflated sense of ourselves. The Greeks told the story of Icarus who was given a pair of golden, but wax wings, by his father. He was warned not to go too close to the sun -- otherwise! Well, you guessed it! He plunged into the sea! The "Icarus supervisor" is flying around all over the place, but then overloads, and collapses. A collapsed supervisor -- however good his/her intent -- is useless.

3. *The illusion that it will "somehow" get done.* This is just wishful thinking. Jason in Greek mythology believed in this "until" illusion: until I get such-and-such done, then I can't do such-and-such! Some "Jason supervisors" never get what they need done because they are always trying to do "catch- up" and spend most of their time *preparing* to do things rather than *actually* doing their work.

4. *The illusion that there is just not enough time.* We know that this illusion is precisely that: all we have is time. In Greek mythology, Damocles was the person in the bed with the sword dangling over his head by a thread. He was in total fear and did nothing but lie there! The "Damocles supervisor" stays stuck, says "I can't," or "they won't" and then complains that there is not enough time to get things done. This supervisor must learn to believe in him/herself and realize that "can't" often means "won't"!

5. *The illusion that only others can make the decision.* This is the "passing the buck" approach to time management. The famous Garden of Eden or paradise story in Genesis has this. Adam said, "I didn't; she did!" Eve said, "I didn't; the serpent did!" So the serpent was blamed! The "Garden of Eden" supervisor is just being irresponsible, believing that others, high up in the organization, are more important, and hence, must make better decisions. This supervisor needs to learn how to live with the consequences of his/her own decisions, be delegated to, and held accountable.

THE DIFFERENT TIME TYPES

Just as there are different kinds, or types, of people, so people also relate to time differently.[21]

Time Type Questionnaire							
Instructions: Check off the one word in each row of four words that you prefer. When you have finished, add up each column (A, B, C, D) of checks. Place your total in boxes below.							
reality		imagination		system		tradition	
fact		theory		plan		memory	
engineer		architect		lawyer		historian	
proof		hypothesis		justice		mercy	
construct		design		rule		circumstance	
(A)		(B)		(C)		(D)	

(A)	(B)	(C)	(D)
_____	_____	_____	_____
present-oriented	future-oriented	linear-oriented	past-oriented

Although this Time Type Questionnaire is not a scientific test, it should get you thinking about your preference and sensitivity around time. For instance, if you had more checks in the "A" column, you are a "present-oriented" time type. What matters is here-and-now. In an organization, this is the supervisor who is "results-oriented" in approach. These kinds of supervisors have to learn not to have "tunnel vision" and begin to see the "big picture."

If you had more checks in the "B" column, you are a "future-oriented" time type. What matters are the possibilities. This type of supervisor can be effective in long-range planning for his/her department, anticipating problems, and working through complexities. They have to watch the "putting-off-till-tomorrow" syndrome.

If you had more checks in the "C" column, you are a "linear-oriented" time type: comfortable with past, present, and future realities. Because these time types take a more objective and analytical approach to work, they can appear cold and aloof at times. They have to learn that people count just as much as systems and ideas.

Finally, if you had more checks in the "D" column, you are a "past-oriented" time type. This type of supervisor is quite dependable, conservative in outlook and very respectful of what the company is and stands for. They need to be more open to new ideas and change, and, while tradition is important -- "this is the way we've always done it!" -- capitalizing on new opportunities will be what is important in the 1990s.

HOW WE SPEND TIME

What we say "after we say hello" refers to how we structure our time, and that, in turn, depends on whether we are whole in our personality or fragmented, and end up playing games to fill up the time-void, rather than be straight, open, and honest with people around us. Eric Berne, author of *Games People Play*, states that time and strokes go together. A stroke is a unit of recognition, "an act implying recognition of another's presence."[23] After we say hello to someone, that sometimes awkward moment right after confronts us with how we will spend our time with the person.

Strokes tend to be quite physical when we are infants and children. If babies are not stroked, their spinal cords literally shrivel up, which explains why Berne was so adamant in having people to "think sphincter."[24] As we get older, much of the physical stroking is replaced by symbolic or psychological stroking. Recognition then takes the place of physical stroking. Thus, Bell Canada advertises: "Reach out and touch someone!" If we don't get enough positive stroking -- that is, have enough time with positive experiences, feelings, thoughts -- we unconsciously look for negative stroking, especially as small children, because no stroking means death, and survival is the issue. Later survival needs are replaced by our needs to develop our potential and find meaning in our life circumstances.

Strokes are psychological food![25]

Since we cannot tolerate living in a vacuum, we will search for *some* way to structure our time to get the physical or recognition strokes we want. Whoever controls the supply of strokes is in a powerful position because none of us wants to be discounted, ignored, or dismissed as human beings. The pain of isolation and suffering is intolerable for us, and we do unbelievable things to avoid that fate, even committing suicide! When West Point cadet James J. Pelosi was alleged to have cheated in 1973 on an exam, he was given the *silencing* treatment. This lasted for one and one-half years, until he graduated. Outcome? "When you're right you have to prove yourself. I told myself I didn't care."[26] He shut down! Did he really have a choice? It was the genius of psychiatrist Wilhelm Reich and philosopher Hebert Marcuse to suggest that whoever controls the strokes controls the social order.

A sad contemporary political example of this control is North Korea's vision and implementation of "paradise," which in reality is a hell.

> *Controller of Strokes*[27]
> "North Korea's stark, mind-numbing uniformity, something even more chilling than the country's winter." Its current leader and absolute controller of strokes has set himself up to be treated "like a god." Everyone is told and indoctrinated into which strokes are important and which are not -- under pain of death: "... each of North Korea's nine provinces contains special execution centres where people who slander the Great Leader or his family are beaten to death with iron bars"!

THE STROKE ECONOMY

Strokes, and time, obviously mean much to people everywhere. It is no different in the office. Employees go to work each day, and if the magical SQ (Stroke Quotient)[28] level of at least 87 per cent of positive strokes is not secured during the work day, then complaints, dysfunctional spin-offs, etc., are likely to begin to occur! A person at a 60 per cent level of strokes, or lower, is desperate; and between 60-87 per cent, the person has to be careful and disciplined in rejecting negative and accepting positive strokes; over 87 per cent, the person has enough strokes in the bank "to assume a connoisseur's attitude." The supervisor, therefore, has an important role to play in managing what can be called the stroke economy[29] and being as straight and authentic as possible.

This supervisory modelling behaviour is critical in developing a healthy work environment so that employees can make time for work and for living rather than being dysfunctional and playing games. *"In general, a person who feels basically not OK will find it very difficult to stroke others."*[30]

BASIC QUESTIONS A SUPERVISOR NEEDS TO ASK:

What do I do to feel good about myself?
How am I in receiving compliments (positive [+] strokes)?
Am I good in complimenting (stroking) employees?
Are people in my department 87% "stroke secure"?

OUR DIFFERENT TIME FRAMES

1. **Personal time.** This can happen physically, when a person literally leaves the room, or psychologically, when a person's mind wanders, as in daydreaming, for instance. If a supervisor is very critical and condescending, employees will often withdraw and stay out of the way. The problem here is that these employees are spending energy on a dysfunctional behaviour rather than spending time accomplishing organizational tasks.

2. **Social time.** This is often the stereotypical and predictable social exchanges that go on in the office, for instance, the greetings in the hallways, the coffee-making routines, and include rituals. Rituals and social graces are very important to the Japanese and their workplace has capitalized on this time structure need.[31] Of course, imposing ritual and tightly controlling social time for employees can backfire, as it did with Seagull Pewter and Silversmiths Ltd., of Pugwash, Nova Scotia. The company and philosophy "is rooted in the Flower Child era" and it is "Seagull management's belief that distributing giftware and making money is almost incidental to its real purpose of making the world a better place."[32] Thus, Seagull's conflict is that its employees, while valuing a corporate social conscience in a company, find that the company is

taking it too far and demanding too much "personal development rituals" and seminars. The feeling with employees is that management is compulsive about its social philosophy.

3. **Small-talk time.** This is a way of spending time in getting acquainted, in using small talk,[33] or chit-chat, for instance, in conversations. It is less formal and stereotyped than social or ritual and is an important skill for supervisors to have. Often employees don't want to talk about anything personal or important, but they do appreciate their supervisor "just shooting the breeze." Small talk or "pastiming" can often be an opening for the employee to feel confidence in confiding a troubling family situation. At this point, the supervisor can act as coach or encourager, and perhaps point out the right person for counselling[34] or other form of employee assistance. Of course, too much pastiming is counterproductive; work needs to be done.

4. **Task time.** Activities make life convenient;[35] people like activities and they need to do "things" as well to feel productive. A supervisor's work day, as we have seen, is composed of many activities, such as tasks, meetings, discussions, etc. Sometimes a supervisor can "do things for doing's sake" and this is similar to "being busy for the sake of *busy-ness* (and not business)." This is the Sisyphus supervisor who just never seems to have time to do what needs to be done because he/she is always busy! Generally, though, activities help structure time for most people and, if they are not overdone, and a person takes time "to do nothing" once in a while, then they pose no problem.

5. **Waste time.** This exercise of one's time is counterproductive and often involves lack of purpose, direction, and dysfunctional behaviours in the workplace. How many times have we all gone to meetings, and come away after saying to ourselves, "That was just a waste of time!" The "waste" occurred because the group was off topic or playing head-games and office politics. This kind of a meeting, which happens all too frequently, is not a positive experience. A dysfunctional department is filled with *denial*. Structuring time with head-games just perpetuates denial of real issues, feelings, thoughts, etc.. Eventually people get sick of denial -- literally! Morale goes down, absenteeism and lateness go up. A wise supervisor budgets time well to avoid these potential problems.

Dysfunctional organizational relationships are the net result of an addicted supervisor interacting with codependent subordinates. *Addiction is a mind-altering substance, mood, feeling, thought, place, situation that has negative and often life-threatening consequences if played out fully.* Addict-supervisors are supervisors who play games. They are addicted to substances (alcohol, drugs, even work!), or moods (negative), or feelings (anger, frustration, etc.), or thoughts ("reduce costs at any costs"!). Since to confront an addictive personality is to usually incur his/her wrath, employees learn to "tiptoe" -- or be codependent -- around the addict-supervisor. Employees pretend; the supervisor plays games and "rants and raves." It's an extremely sick arrangement, and sadly, fairly common in today's organizations precisely this kind of dysfunctional or game-playing reality is so prevalent in our society: "... it is in the interest of the society to promote those things that 'take the edge off,' get busy with our 'fixes,' and keep us slightly 'numbed out' and zombielike. Consequently, the society itself not only encourages addictions, it functions as an addict."[36]

THE OPEN AND FUNCTIONAL SUPERVISOR

Openness consists of genuine caring[37] and is the ability to be appropriately present to the moment and the situation at hand with one's thoughts and feelings. It is very different from revelation, which is to expose one's inner feelings and thoughts -- skeletons in the closet, so to speak. Revelation needs to be done in the privacy of a trusted relationship; openness is a supervisory skill in using time well in expressing one's thoughts and feelings for the task at hand. That is, an open supervisor is able to share his/her thoughts and feelings appropriately, without panic, in a coherent manner, and in a way that allows the supervisor to remain true to core values and to the moment at hand. Developing a healthy corporate culture is a major way to increase openness.

The great fear for many people is that to be honestly open is to get exploited, taken advantage of. While that fear is realistic, the only real hope we have for human healing is in openness: interpersonally, in the family, in the office, nationally, and internationally.

THE PRACTICAL *DO'S* AND *DON'TS* OF MANAGING TIME

There are many ways in which people waste time, but there are also ways that people can make time work for them. *Exercise:* Look at the *time wasters* and *time savers* (page 112) and check off the ones that currently relate to you personally. Just be honest with yourself. When you have completed the list, add up your checks for both categories. Ask yourself, "Are you living quality time?"

THE "TAO" OF MEETINGS

The word **tao** [pronounced 'dowoh'] means "the Way."[38] It is a very intuitive word pointing to an even more intuitive reality -- absolute knowledge, awareness, or knowing. Being in the "tao" means being on the "way" -- having your act together, so to speak, being in touch, but in a genuinely profound way.

The TAO of meetings is a metaphor/acronym to help supervisors approach meetings more effectively. "T" is to developing a *topic* for the meeting: what it's all about; "A" is the *agenda*; and "O" are the *objectives*, the steps that will guide the supervisor to accomplishing the purpose of the meeting. There are some key tips provided to make meetings run more smoothly.

By extension, supervisors know whether a meeting is "on" or not, or whether it goes well. The TAO of meetings refers to the purpose, the process, and the fruit of meetings. Meetings can be time wasters, but they can also be productive.

In the final section of this chapter, the fundamentals of productive meetings will be presented, including their importance, the pitfalls, the key success points on a meeting checklist, and the outline of the TAO of meetings.

SELECTED TIME WASTERS	SELECTED TIME SAVERS
being unsure of what I want to do in life	knowing what you want to do in life
getting distracted all the time	living a balanced life
not managing interruptions	being a positive thinking person
not putting priorities on what I do	choosing to be proactive *vs.* reactive
not having a "to do" list	anticipating crises
giving in easily to temptation	knowing how to get positive strokes
sleeping in too much	having a personal philosophy of life
not interested in managing my time	being able to ask for help
afraid of tackling more difficult tasks	having a "to do" list
stalling and procrastinating	making priorities and adhering to them
never getting organized	knowing when to work, when to play
not having a settled lifestyle	doing first things first
lack of deadlines	eating well and regularly
not asking for help	getting adequate rest
inability to say "no"	choosing to be in the 20%: Pareto's rule
no daily plan	being able to sort for important things
no weekly plan	setting deadlines and sticking to them
no monthly plan	using technology (e.g., computers) wisely and efficiently
no 5-year plan	planning ahead
no life plan	learning time management, if necessary
fatigue	having something to read for line-ups
too much TV	doing difficult things when you're "up"
being too organized	having a daily, weekly, monthly planner
only mentally keeping track of things	eager to leave a mark in life
feeling you have to do everything "perfectly"	choosing "winners" as friends
	being efficient *and* effective
	getting feedback when necessary
	delegating when appropriate
	doing it right the first time (TQM)
	wanting to grow personally and professionally

"If you can motivate the team to be open in admitting a mistake or a problem and then have a culture where people are always willing to help solve that problem once it's identified, you just don't ever have these gigantic crippling problems. ... Everybody on the Compaq team makes these mistakes but we're in an environment where mistakes are not punished."[39] -- Rod Canion, founder and former president, Compaq Computers

"Time management is based on the assumption that time is an inelastic, finite resource."[40]

THE IMPORTANCE OF MEETINGS

As much as supervisors might say to themselves, "Meetings! Meetings! Meetings!" In our modern organizations and business life, there is no getting around "having to go to a meeting."

When much of life is going "high-tech," and the faceless relationship is upon us, it is still important to meet face-to-face. There is something very different about seeing another "in the flesh," so to speak. According to Peter F. Drucker, too many meetings are often a common symptom for poor organization.[41] In 1984 it was estimated that in the United States alone, there were more than 20 million daily meetings held! The costs: *$250 billion (!) a year!* 75% of the costs were for travel![42] In spite of all this, meeting face-to-face is still essential[43] and performs an indispensable function.[44]

Supervisors will meet for different purposes: problem solving and decision making, solving conflicts, planning and scheduling, restructuring and reorganization, team building, negotiations, performance reviews, general organizational meetings, etc. The list could go on. On an operational basis, supervisors will generally meet with one or two people or a small group to work out some glitch in scheduling or solve a problem, for instance, on the line or in data processing.

Meetings involve people; two or more people make a group. Thus, group dynamics and group processes begin as soon as people *meet*. It is important for the supervisor to keep in mind that *all* effective groups (and that includes what goes on in meetings *with groups*) go through four typical stages.[45]

In other words, (1) two or more individuals -- a group -- get together for some purpose: task accomplishment, fun. Even if the group has come about by accident, and if the individuals stay together for any period of time, a group will *form* where they will introduce themselves to one another, etc. After a settling-in period, (2) different opinions or feelings or thoughts may be tabled. This time of differences can bring up a lot of conflict, but if

- *FORMING*
- *STORMING*
- *NORMING*
- *PERFORMING*

The irony in these comments on the stages of groups in meetings is that for a group to do what it is supposed to do in a meeting, by definition it *must* go through the different stages successfully to have an effective group meeting. When groups short-circuit their developmental stages, decisions are made which are later often not fulfilled, information is held back which could have been helpful, and a general sense of sabotage and cynicism takes over. Meetings get short-circuited because the supervisor uses fear and power, rules and procedures, instead of common sense and shared values. In emergency meetings, not all of these stages can be honoured. But realistically, how many meetings in a supervisor's career are emergency ones?

the group is mature enough -- willing and able to deal with feelings while affirming (positive strokes!) one another -- they will eventually get through this. Many groups, and many meetings, get stuck in this stage. People get upset; nothing is resolved; angry words are exchanged; and people leave feeling bitter and resentful. If the group does get through this second phase, (3) it enters a third phase where common norms and standards and values are discussed and agreed upon. At this stage, the start of working as a team begins and group members feel more positive toward one another. They can even start liking one another because they now have a purpose for being together. As we have seen in chapter 4, *groupthink* can eventually set in and the group thinks that it is *it*! They know the answer! A dangerous point in group dynamics. On a national scale, it can lead to totalitarianism! Finally, (4) when the group has its major conflicts resolved and members feel a sense of purpose and mission, the group begins to perform its assigned task. Groups that arrive at this stage are maturing groups, open to change, but capable of doing what needs to be done as a group.

Effective supervisors know how to run effective meetings. Being an effective member of a group is a responsible role, and, as we shall see in chapter 9, means *both* supervisor *and* group members (employees) are skilled in *task* and *relationship* skills.

KEY PITFALLS

Besides the pitfall of not knowing anything about group dynamics and group stages, supervisors have to guard against other pitfalls.

The **size** of a group for a meeting is important for the supervisor to consider. If the supervisor wants direct face-to-face communication between each member, a group of five is ideal. If there are more than five members, special care must be taken to ensure direct communication occurs within the meeting format and that power struggles minimized.[46]

The **setup** for meetings must be attended to carefully as well. Important tips:

MEETINGS: IMPORTANT TIPS	
1. Figure out if there will be any costs to the meeting.	11. Be prepared with what you want to say.
2. Know why you are having the meeting. What's your purpose?	12. Hold only necessary meetings.
3. Have an agenda ready!	13. Stick to your time frames.
4. Plan your time and stick with it.	14. Don't let others manipulate or take over the meeting.
5. Train regular members in group dynamics and group stages.	15. Keep minutes for further review.
6. With new members, have a name plate on the table or "hello" card. If it is a name plate on the table, make it a "tent" shape and *print* the new person's *first* name on *both* sides of the tent card. If you use a "hello" card that sticks on, *print* the person's *first* name and have him/her place the card on the *right* side of a blouse or jacket. The reason for this is that people look to this right side first. (Most people will place their name tag on the left.)	16. Let people know when the final 10 minutes begins. This gives reassurance and security to those who may not want to be there, or who have other things to attend to and wonder whether or not the meeting will end as scheduled.
7. Make sure the room is set up the way you want it. If you are unsure how to set up a room well, follow this rule: make it so people can face and talk with one another.	17. In any small group discussions in a larger meeting, let the groups do their discussing; stay out of it; and let them present their findings.
8. Have the necessary materials ready.	18. In a plenary format -- when the larger group is attentive to you, or to another person speaking -- allow only *one* person to speak at a time. It's very frustrating to hear others chattering away while someone is trying to speak.
9. If using overheads, make sure they're clean, clear, crisp!	19. Nurture positive feeling within the group by projecting "up" feelings in your face, bodily posture, tone of voice, and the words you use.
10. If using a flip chart, print large, use key words, and use a dark pen!	20. Get a summary of the meeting to group members within a short period after.

THE TAO ITSELF

Perhaps the main reason why meetings break down is because they are not "on the **TAO**": Topic, Agenda, Objectives.[47] If supervisors can "follow the TAO" they will have more productive meetings. Supervisors would actually draft up this TAO before their meetings, submit it for minor modifications and approval by the group, and then they are ready to have their meeting.

TOPIC	AGENDA	OBJECTIVES
The *topic* is the focus of the meeting. It is the issue, the concern, the problem that needs to be discussed or resolved, or the matter that has to be resolved. Too many times employees go to a meeting and, if you ask them, "What was the meeting about?" they often can't say. This inability to express themselves results from supervisors not stating or forming a *topic*. An example of a good topic could be: "How will our department choose the best quality control software program available on the market today?" This topic is clear, open to discussion (because of the "how") and practical.	The *agenda* is the content or key points of the discussion that will occur in the meeting. The agenda works to solve the question in the topic; it is the plan of attack, the sequence of tasks to be followed to answer the topic question. Before the meeting, the supervisor would have had certain employees do research tasks to be prepared for this meeting. The agenda for this particular meeting on purchasing a quality control software package might include: (1) summary report on what is available on the market; (2) evaluation of the different products in terms of cost, complexity, and other criteria deemed appropriate; (3) the time for the learning curve involved; (4) the benefits; and (5) the implementation time. Each of these points would be alotted a certain amount of time, and the supervisor would perhaps allow a ten minute wrap-up so the group could make the decision.	*Objectives* are the steps the group takes for their one-hour decision-making meeting to complete their topic. If the topic positions the issue to be discussed, and the agenda is the format for the discussion, the objectives are the direction of the discussion. In our example, the objectives might be: the software program must be (1) cost-effective, (2) from a reputable company, (3) with good field studies, and (4) excellent support service.

Meetings can be boring; meetings can be "a pain"; meetings can just be a waste of time.

BUT meetings can also be productive and worthwhile, IF:

Meetings are planned and thought through

TAO

Group dynamics and stages are acknowledged

A structure such as TAO is used and followed

Supervisors won't get away without meetings, but they can make them work *for* them, not *against* them. This way, supervisors win, and so do employees.

SUMMARY

Managing time is akin to managing oneself. Good time management, therefore, is good self-management. If you tell me how you spend your time, you are telling me much about *who* you are.

Time has a fascination for people, especially for scientists and mystics, because time raises the big question of what reality is all about. Musings on time take us into the deeper recesses of the creative imagination on our human journey.

The key for supervisors is in transforming their workplaces into *worthplaces*.

Time can be conserved, controlled, or made. A supervisor has to budget time for tasks, meetings, discussions, administration, assignments, coaching. Key illusions about time are: that the harder we work, the more effective we are; that we are indispensable; that the work will "somehow" get done; that there is not enough time; and that only others can make decisions.

Just as people are different, so is their sense of time. There are present-oriented, future-oriented, linear-oriented, and past-oriented time types.

There are different approaches supervisors can take to spending their time: personal time, social time, small-talk time, task time and waste time.

Openness is a here-and-now skill expressing one's thoughts and feelings. It contributes immensely to a functional corporate culture.

There are some very practical do's and don'ts to managing time.

The TAO of meetings is a metaphor/acronym to help supervisors approach meetings more effectively: Topic, Agenda, Outline.

TERMS/CONCEPTS

time
self-management
time illusions
time types
approaches to time
personal time
social time
small talk time
task time

waste time
openness
dysfunctional
relationships
do's and don'ts of
time management
TAO of meetings
group stages

forming
storming
norming
performing
meeting pitfalls
topic (T)
agenda (A)
objectives (O)

DISCUSSION QUESTIONS

1. What does time mean to you?

2. Are you a good time manager? Explain your answer.

3. Why are good time management/self-management skills important for the supervisor?

4. Identify a situation from your experience where "Pareto's law" could be applied. Describe the situation and what you would do about it as a supervisor.

5. How can supervisors conserve, control, and make time?

6. List some organizational considerations that a supervisor has to budget time for.

7. Explain the five key illusions about managing time.

8. Which time type are you most like? Describe that type in detail, using your own personal work experiences.

9. What are *strokes*, and why are they important? How are they related to time?

10. What are the approaches to structure our time? Give examples.

11. List some time wasters and time savers.

12. What is the TAO of meetings?

ASSIGNMENT

Instructions: Study the "DO" and "DON'T" lists of ideas below on time management. Rank order the items in each list for yourself personally as to what is important (#1 = most important) for you to **do (DO list)** and what is important for you to **avoid (DON'T list)**. Complete the sentence in the shaded box below (right) for the #1 ranked item from each list.

Time Management*

DO		*DON'T*	
Establish an action list for the following day relating to meetings/phone calls/correspondence/project output, etc.		Shuffle paper from one pile to another. Handle and deal with each piece of paper only once.	
Purchase and devise a suitable time management system enabling you to organize project work/appointments/follow-up action/reference data, etc.		Put aside the important work projects. Handle immediately to reduce 80 per cent of stress.	
Establish "door-closed" periods where uninterrupted progress can be accomplished on projects requiring your attention.		Allow colleagues to interrupt meetings you are having with other personnel.	
Prioritize work to be accomplished in "degrees of urgency" (A,B,C) and always handle the most urgent first.		Write out memos or letters to be typed. Dictate wherever possible.	
Periodically, list on one page every single project or unfinished item requiring your attention and place in front of you constantly, deleting each item as it is handled.		"Work" all day. Take a break and relax. Productivity will increase.	
Delegate work, but not the responsibility, to others who are equipped to handle the assignment.			
Start work within one minute of reaching your office or work station, rather than talking to colleagues, fetching coffee, etc.		**[DO]** As a result of my #1 ranked choice, I will ...	
Make good decisions promptly to effectively handle workload.			
Allocate one leisure day per month, by yourself or with a colleague, to brainstorm and plan.		**[DON'T]** As a result of my #1 ranked choice, I will ...	
Always set deadlines (date and time) on projects requiring answers or action, both for yourself and for your subordinates.			

*Submitted by Mr. Graham Willsher, General Manager, Valhalla Inn Markham

PART TWO:

PERSONAL, INTERPERSONAL, AND GROUP DYNAMICS

Executive Summary

To be successful, supervisors must learn how to develop and manage business interpersonal relationships. Failure to do so will be a key stumbling block to being successful.

Understanding human behaviour has to begin with self-understanding. Unless a supervisor has insight into his/her own personality make-up, he or she is supervising by "hit-and-miss." There are interesting frameworks for human behaviour (ch. 6) that describe how personalities are formed and what makes for a healthy personality. Healthy supervisors foster healthy employees. A supervisor also needs to develop positive human relations (ch. 7), which includes awareness that meanings are in people, not just in words! Effective listening and speaking skills are the key skills for productive human relations. The core of listening is empathy; the key to communication is speaking for self. Supervisors also need to create a working environment that will motivate employees to do what needs to be done (ch. 8). Empowerment refers to genuinely bestowing power on to employees and trusting them to follow through. In today's work world, leadership often means choosing an appropriate style that will work in a situation (ch. 9). It also means providing vision and direction for employees to do what the supervisor wants them to do so that they want to do it. Finally, as in any relationship, conflicts are bound to occur (ch. 10). Effective supervisors know how to manage conflicts and to negotiate solutions for win-win results.

CHAPTER SIX

UNDERSTANDING INDIVIDUAL BEHAVIOUR

If you dig very deeply into any problem, you will get *people*.

-- J. Watson Wilson[1]

LEARNING OBJECTIVES

At the end of this chapter, students will be able to:

- Understand the importance of the examined life
- Outline the reality of the self-concept
- Identify key guidelines to understanding human nature
- Explain how individual behaviour is multidimensional
- Discuss the realities of *shadow*
and *projection* as ethical imperatives

Opening scenario

We are capable of the heights and we are capable of the depths! Effective supervision includes insight into human nature and into human motivation. Our world is shifting politically, economically, sociologically, spiritually and psychologically. The vision we once had of ourselves in the 1980s as yuppies, consumers, greedy, and me-oriented, because of its spirit of disillusionment is giving way to another vision: one built on outreach, conservation, and inner values. There is "an increased emphasis on that warm, fuzzy feeling that comes from social duty ..."[2] Former Global TV news anchorman Peter Trueman echoes this since he says that "the sweet smell of success" was all right for a while, but, when he took early retirement and moved to an island near Kingston, Ontario, with his wife, he has found he prefers "the aroma of our own bread baking.[3] It would be marvellous to think that this regeneration of attitudes has come about willingly, after much soul-searching, but it's probably more truthful to say that self-examination has been thrust upon us.

Vaclav Havel, former president of Czechoslovakia, has argued, "The point is that we should fundamentally change how we behave."[4] The change in attitude that he called for was to go beyond *only* trusting in technology and reason, abandoning the "arrogant belief that the world is merely a puzzle to be solved" and realizing that life itself imposes a soul, a spirituality into things. "Soul, individual spirituality, first-hand personal insight into things, the courage to be himself and go the way his conscience points, humility in the face of the mysterious order of Being, confidence in its natural direction and, above all, trust in his own subjectivity as his principal link with the subjectivity of the world -- these, in my view, are the qualities that politicians of the future should cultivate." He argues persuasively that "communism was not defeated by military force, but by life, by the human spirit, by conscience, by the resistance of Being and man to manipulation." For Havel, self-examination must include the life of the spirit, the soul-force. A revolution of the mind is needed: "At this crucial point in world history, we must rely on the eternal moral commandments -- the simple laws of morality and humanity, as Marx called them." In other words, people must reclaim basic intuitions about their behaviour.

THE IMPORTANCE OF THE EXAMINED LIFE

Maturity will develop either consciously, with the examined life, or unconsciously, without it. The major difference is that the examined life (or conscious reflection) has choices. When people are free, they can make choices. When they make choices, they are moral. When they are moral, they are human. Therefore, the examined life builds the humanity of each and every one of us.

Socrates said that self-knowledge was the basis of living and that the unexamined life was not worth living.

We mentioned in chapter 2 the challenge that the contemporary supervisor has with the tension of individualism *vs.* authenticity in supervising today's employees. While the culture breeds a cult of addictive consumerism so that one is measured by what one has or looks like, there is a parallel struggle going on as well: the search for meaning and personal authenticity. Speedy Muffler says it well, in a business context, by proclaiming that "at Speedy, you're a somebody!" In other words, you, the customer, matter.

The search for a meaningful life is the need we all have to know deep down inside that we matter, that we are significant. Not to feel significant is perhaps life's greatest pain. But significance comes as a result of self-examination and self-understanding because one then realizes that the examined life has depth and quality; it holds the depths but also the heights; and the person who lives the examined life experiences a joy and a deep conviction about living that is profound.

The examined life leads one on to the main focus of living, to the journey to individuation, or wholeness, or becoming the individual that nature, life, wants us to be. "Deep inside each organism is something that knows what that

> The Valhalla Companies' mission statement includes a commitment to providing the warmth of personalized service. At the Valhalla Inn Markham, all departments are in the process of preparing their own individual mission statements devised by all team members, thereby committing to "localized" standards of performance, which are nonetheless fully aligned to corporate principles.

organism's true nature and life goal is."[5] The journey to wholeness is a life task, with many dangerous, but also exhilarating encounters.

THE HUMAN JOURNEY

DESTINY
(What Life Wants of Us)

QUEST
(What We Want of Life)

STORY
(Interface of Destiny and Quest)

Life calls us to complete the task of *individuation* (Destiny); we also have to claim our gifts, talents, hopes, and dreams (Quest); and the resulting interface and interplay between Destiny (what Life wants) and Quest (what we want) fashions our life Story, and makes our human journey a unique journey, *this* journey, and no one else's.

"The great Law of the Universe ... is just this -- that what you think in your mind you will produce in your experience. As within, so without. You cannot think one thing and produce another." -- Emmett Fox[6]

This chapter is perhaps the most important of all for the supervisor. Unless a supervisor has self-knowledge and self-awareness to an adequate degree, he/she runs the risk of being a total failure. How can I manage others if I can't manage myself? How can I know what "makes others tick" if I don't know myself? The purpose of this chapter is to examine some personal frameworks that will assist the supervisor to have that self-knowledge in order to manage well.

THE GREATNESS OF LIFE

Our bodies[7]

1. The heart pumps 10 pints of blood every minute through 60,000 miles of arteries, veins, and capillaries.
2. We breathe 500 million times during an average lifetime.
3. Each person has 20 square feet of flexible, waterproof covering called the skin.
4. We have roughly 9,000 taste buds.
5. Every three years, 5 million hairs change.
6. We have 4 million receptors in the skin to help us feel, distinguish hot from cold, pain from pleasure.
7. We eat roughly 50 tons of food and drink 11,000 gallons of liquid in an average lifetime.
8. City residents will walk about 7,000 miles, country folk, almost 29,000.

Our world's sun[8]

1. The sun is a medium-sized star that is a million times the volume of the earth and always in a state of nuclear activity.
2. At its core, the sun's temperature is 25 million degrees Fahrenheit.
3. This sun-star uses more energy *in one second* than has been used by people since the dawn of civilization.
4. All the earth's reserves of oil, coal, and wood could fuel the sun's energy output to the earth for only a few days.
5. If you were 50 miles from a pinhead of matter from the sun's core, you would be burned to death since it is so hot.
6. In essence, the sun is like a huge hydrogen bomb, burning slowly.

THE REALITY OF THE SELF-CONCEPT

Speedy Muffler hits the nub of human nature and individual behaviour in its "At Speedy, you're a Somebody!" The basic need each of us has, of course, is the survival need. A baby's whole orientation is towards survival; everything the baby does is done for survival reasons.

Reflective Exercise

Take a few minutes and list some qualities about yourself that you like.

_____

_____

_____

_____

Now take a few more minutes and list some
things about yourself that you would like to change.

_____

_____

_____

_____

What you have described are features of your self-concept, or who you are --
at least, as you see it. An obvious application that the supervisor can make
here is the relationship of the self-concept to feedback, especially negative
feedback. We are all sensitive about negative feedback, or criticism, precisely
because it threatens our self-concept, or the "relatively stable set of
perceptions"[9] that we hold about ourselves. If these perceptions, or images of
how we see ourselves, break down, we fall apart. We are "together," so to
speak, because of these underlying images, perceptions, or self-concept, that
we are. The sum of these stable perceptions and images gives us our self-
esteem. We like, or dislike, ourselves -- our self-esteem -- in direct proportion
to the quality of our self-concept.

*A child's self-concept:
influence from the
parents' unlived life*

It's the *unlived
psychological life of the
parents* that creates
the greatest stumbling
block and psychic
poison for the child. In
other words, the
unlived life of the
parents is absorbed by
the child as a *lie*; lies
are the basis and core
of *neuroses*; and a
neurotic life condemns
one to pain and
joylessness.

This self-concept finds its roots in family life. In that sense
it is a "family affair."[10] A baby "becomes him/herself," in
many respects, according to *how* the parents view that
child. The parents at first reflect back to the child that he/
she is good, or, bad, loved, or not loved. It is not the words
that are spoken, but who the parents are that make the
most impact on the child. "Children are so deeply
involved in the psychological attitude of their parents that
it is no wonder that most of the nervous disturbances in
childhood can be traced back to a disturbed psychic
atmosphere in the home."[11] When children are neurotic, it
is really the parents who may be the principal cause,
because they *are* the fertile ground and psychic
environment for the child's mind. The strongest psychic
effect comes not from what parents are or are not doing,
but what they *should be doing*! It's the *unlived psychological*

life of the parents that creates the greatest stumbling block and psychic poison for the child. The unlived life of the parents is absorbed by the child as a *lie*; lies are the basis and core of *neuroses*; and a neurotic life condemns one to pain and joylessness.

As we grow and develop, this self-concept -- which gives us a percentage of positive and negative self-esteem images, or how we feel about ourselves -- is influenced, not only by environmental factors, opportunities, but especially by *significant others*. These significant others can be teachers, movie stars, heroes and heroines from contemporary events, etc. How many of us have said, "Had it not been for so-and-so, I don't know where I'd be today!" Someone of significance made an impact on us and that helped us to change. The real challenge of a marriage is that each person says, in so many words, that he or she will be in the other's life so that he/she can reach his/her potential. This is a very mature commitment, obviously. What often interferes with following through fully is that each person may try to get the other to bolster his/her self-esteem rather than affirm the other as he/she is. Each person is too needy to be able to stand back and witness the other person unfolding.

Gurdeep Singh is an excellent example of vibrant customer service. No fear here!

He is an attendant at the quaint Imperial Esso station in historic Unionville, Ontario. He greets customers with a great smile, genuinely asks how their day is, and when the car is gassed up, asks what else he can do for you. Excellent service. Excellent employee!

It is logical, therefore, for the supervisor to conclude that there will be employees who have "unfinished emotional self-concept business" that will at times interfere with work. If Bill, an employee, grew up in a home where his stroke quotient settled into a 70 - 30 per cent breakdown -- that is, 70 per cent positive strokes, but 30 per cent negative strokes, to make his 100 per cent -- then Bill will have that quotient as part of his self-concept and will be structuring it into his work world. He will be psychologically "at home," in a negative way, when he gets his 30 per cent negative strokes at work and his 70 per cent positive ones. Negatives could be: being yelled at by co-workers, coming in late often and getting reprimands.

Change is another way that the supervisor meets an employee's self-concept. Too much change creates what Alvin Toffler called "future shock"[12] and too much future shock creates dysfunction in individuals. They just don't behave maturely. This is a major concern during recessionary times. "It is no longer a matter of firms of different sizes. We are playing in different leagues."[13] There are many layoffs, and sometimes, back at work, managers and supervisors tend to use fear to maximize productivity. Does fear work? Not really. Fear may motivate in the short term, but it's a disaster in the long term![14] For instance, in this day of the *service organization*, companies risk a lot by using fear tactics. Fearful employees on the front line can leave a very negative impression with customers and these incidents can influence the bottom line quite directly by way of lost sales. Bill Easdale, the most senior Canadian at Toyota Motor Manufacturing Canada, Cambridge, Ontario, says that "fear of unemployment obsesses people, they dread what will come next. This causes them to make mistakes, causes injuries, inhibits productivity."[15]

KEY GUIDELINES TO UNDERSTANDING HUMAN BEHAVIOUR

We have seen that life is intolerable without a self-examination every once in a while. This examined life allows each of us to refocus and realign those pieces of our self-concept -- the *who* of who we are -- that need updating or disposing of. That can be a threatening process if it is imposed on us by future shock or events beyond our control, but it is a necessary task to live a whole life.

LIFE

▶ Choosing to be uncommon, to seize opportunities and to build a life that is vibrant and self-motivated.

▶ Choosing to risk, to build, and to dream; choosing to succeed or fail on one's own efforts.

▶ Choosing to stand tall as a human being, relying on one's integrity and sense of what is just, right, and good.[16]

There are two key guidelines that will help the supervisor make this self-examination more meaningful and practical.

1. All behaviour aims to unify and keep intact an individual's self-concept. *Everything we do, we do for a reason: known or not, wise or stupid, good or bad, mature or selfish.*

2. *Our ethics is our behavioural response to situations.* Values tell us what is good; ethics tell us what is right. An unethical action is built on a faulty valuing process or a violation of a value. Everything we do projects our ethical stance and hints at our core values. What is expressed *outside* is simply the result of what is conceived *inside*.

These two guidelines will help the supervisor realize that human nature -- and individual behaviour -- is goal-oriented and either ethical or unethical. The maturing supervisor or employee is congruent on both these matters: goals and ethics. Because of organizational restructuring there are often fewer employees and the need for on-going education in the area of the work/self-concept is paramount if companies plan to have loyal employees for the future. "There should never come a point in an employee's life when work and education are divorced."[17] Bank of Montreal chairman Matthew Barrett says, "We now have one and a half million unemployed. That's a human tragedy of enormous proportions. And it's unjust. A blameless minority are paying the cost of a restructuring that will benefit all Canadians. We cannot treat the unemployed as the canon fodder in our economic battles. That would be callous -- and also wasteful, since every unemployed Canadian is an unrealized asset."[18]

INDIVIDUAL BEHAVIOUR: PURPOSEFUL

There have been many efforts by philosophers and theologians throughout the ages, and social and behavioural scientists in our day, to explain what human nature is all about and what makes up the individual personality. All of these efforts point to one thing: human behaviour is goal-oriented, or purposeful.

Understanding individual behaviour on the part of the supervisor entails knowing key components of what it means to be human. This knowledge allows the supervisor to appreciate the human dimension much more empathically in employees.

We have often heard it said about people, "He is not himself today," or "She doesn't seem to be herself lately." The same can be said of employees as well. Each employee has different "parts' to him/herself. Each employee is a combination of different impulses: the impulse to know his/her direction and goals in life (*values*), the impulse to sort out and think through problems (*thoughts* or *ideas*), and the impulse that triggers emotions (*feelings*).

THE PART OF EMPLOYEES THAT FEELS

An employee's feelings signal a wealth of information, experiences, and associated memories. Common experience often says that a child is "a bundle of feelings." We also know that once a child begins primary school, much of his/her way of feeling is already encoded and later, as an adult, life will blossom or suffer depending on whether these childhood feelings have matured as well.

Supervisors will often experience the feeling side of employees by noticing their happiness in coming to work, their projection of self-and-other-worth and their pleasant dispositions. These employees have a positive sense and feeling about themselves and people around them. This state is nurtured by supervisors who build and promote healthy work climates and cultures.

Some employees, however, can have a feeling part that may have been damaged or stunted in its development. There may be residual negative feelings left over from childhood -- some conscious to them, many perhaps, totally out of reach. When the "right" moment of insecurity occurs in their later life situations, these "unfinished," that is, undeveloped feelings, may be

triggered. A negative feeling state emerges, one which triggers what could be called *TURTLE behaviour* in some employees (those who are fearful, who withdraw from conflict, who give in all the time, the *flight* posture), and *SKUNK behaviour* in other employees (those who judge and blame others for their mistakes, who criticize, who are angry a lot of the time, the *fight* posture).

Sadly, union - management relations often resemble this flight-fight, skunk-turtle, turtle-turtle, and skunk-skunk behaviour. Of course, nobody wins. Negative feelings in each group, management and union, take over. During the postal strike of September 1991, Diane Francis, editor of *The Financial Post*, was so disgusted with union chief, Claude Parrot's behaviour, that she wrote, "Parrot-the-carrot has his head in the sand," and, "It's about time the unions in this country were put in their place."[19]

Like a dysfunctional family, the postal workers' union and Canada Post seem rooted in inter-generational negative feelings.[20]

It should be mentioned that just because an employee is not fighting or being belligerent does not in itself indicate that the person is feeling all right. A supervisor may have some employees who are "quiet," but who also "mask" their feelings in moodiness, sullenness, sadness, agitation, and, in general, with a negative attitude. Just because they are quiet does not mean to say they are feeling good about themselves. There are numerous newspaper accounts of "quiet" people who have done some very destructive things to themselves and to others. While having a positive feeling self is an individual employee's responsibility, there are obviously employees who have not learned, or matured, into managing their lives in ways that maximize their potential.

THE PART OF EMPLOYEES THAT VALUES

Experts say that how we pick up information, or the imprinting that goes to developing our individual personalities, begins before we are born, while we are in utero.[21] More and more pregnant women speak, sing, and send positive messages to their unborn child in hope that the child will have a propitious start in life. This is an important consideration because it not only helps us to understand how our feelings about ourselves begin while we are just being formed, but also to understand what we need to do to take care of ourselves, or to cherish our valuing self. *As we have been valued, so we learn to value ourselves. As we have been treated (parented and taught), so we treat ourselves and others, unless we examine ourselves and make new choices.* Of course, later, as a child grows, other authority figures from school, society, and religious institutions come to play their parts as imprinters as well. We can assume that when supervisors naturally behave in a caring way, they have personally experienced positive parenting and valuing in earlier years.

Treating a child in a nurturing way while in utero, and in growing up, allows the child, and later the adult, to begin valuing him/herself in a nurturing, life-giving manner. There will be more positive strokes than negative ones, for him/herself and for others as well. The reverse is also true: if a child has been mistreated, or has received many more negative strokes than positive ones, the child will learn to "de-value" him/ herself, and others too. Supervisors need to be careful here if they catch themselves acting negatively with employees: are they just re-enacting what they have experienced from their own parents and authority figures? Most probably. The ground rule here is the Golden Rule: "Do unto others ..."

While supervisors may hold intellectually to the Golden Rule, unless they have examined and changed some of their immaturities, their words will simply be that -- words -- and their actions will betray them.

THE PART OF EMPLOYEES THAT **THINKS**

Behaviour is also understandable if supervisors realize
that in addition to a valuing self and a feeling self, there
is also a thinking self at work in employees. Some
employees complain by saying, "My supervisor treats
me as though I'm an idiot, that I have no brains at all!"
In this situation the supervisor is definitely not valuing
the employee's ability and capacity to think or to
problem solve. Giving employees a vote of confidence
in their competency allows them not to be afraid of
problems but to meet them "head on," so to speak, and solve them.

THE *SHADOW* KNOWS: A JUNGIAN ETHICAL IMPERATIVE

RECOGNITION OF THE SHADOW, OR
HOW TO AVOID **PINOCCHIO MANAGEMENT!**

Carl Jung, M.D., lived from 1875 to 1961. He was a youthful member in
Freud's psychoanalytic circle of friends, becoming president of the
International Psychoanalytic Association. But a split came around 1909 when
Jung felt that Freud was putting his Oedipus theory of the sexual libido above
important psychological truths. Freud asked Jung to promise him that he
would never abandon his sexual theory, and saying, "You see, we must make
a dogma of it, an unshakeable bulwark."[22]

Jung felt at this point that Freud was no longer concerned with scientific
judgment and truth, but only with his own personal power drive. A
contemporary biographer says that "Freud wanted disciples who would
accept his doctrine without reservation."[23] Jung, of course, would not. On
another occasion, on their seven-week trip to the United States in 1909, they
were analyzing each other's dreams. In helping interpret one of Freud's
dreams, Jung felt he needed more personal information from Freud. When he
asked for it, Freud looked at him very suspiciously, and then said, "But I

cannot risk my authority!"[22] Jung tucked that comment in the back of his mind, but he knew their relationship was finished at that point because "Freud was placing personal authority above truth." Eventually the break came when Jung published his own research and psychological conclusions, stating that **the overall purpose and thrust of life, and hence of human behaviour, is towards *individuation*: the psychic, in-born drive to become oneself and whole as an individual human being.**

For Jung, individuation, or becoming a whole human being, included integration of both conscious and unconscious contents and, especially, after 35 years of age, keeping one's ear to an inner spiritual pulse within the human psyche which guides each of us unerringly toward wholeness, if we co-operate, or toward potential destructiveness, if we refuse. Jung concluded from his medical psychoanalytic experiences with patients that all of them were healed when they regained a "religious outlook" on their life once more: "This of course has nothing whatever to do with a particular creed or membership of a church."[24] Freud rejected this hypothesis and stuck to his theory that the sex drive was the prime motivator of human behaviour, even going as far as to say that it must be the main cornerstone of his psychological discoveries.

THE REALITY OF PROJECTION

Jung believed that the first step on the road to individuation was a *moral* step: the psychological encounter with one's *shadow*. Our shadow side contains those elements that we have repressed over the years, or shoved into what the American poet Robert Bly calls the "bag."[25] We all have a "bag"; other people usually notice it; we don't because we only see it in *projection*, that is, "out there," in someone else.[26] As a society we are now, slowly and painfully with the recession of the early 1990s, coming face-to-face with the shadow or dark side of our 1980s prosperity: the greed, the lying, the selfishness and unethical behaviour that is costing us so much now,[27] or what this author calls *Pinocchio Management*. In the fabled tale, Pinocchio's nose got longer and longer every time he told a lie.

Pinocchio Management

We know we are projecting when the person, place, or thing "out there" *gets to us*, that is *affects* us emotionally to a considerable extent, whether that emotional affect is positive or negative. If a supervisor *really* gets worked up about an employee, perhaps gets into a rage over some incident, for instance, it is safe to assume that this supervisor is projecting a piece of his/her shadow on to that employee, in other words, seeing in the employee a negative quality that the supervisor *also* has, but fails to recognize, and, if confronted with that information and feedback, would probably get even more enraged! That doesn't mean that the employee does not, from a more objective viewpoint, also have that negative quality; but it is the fact that the supervisor is *so affected by it* that is cause for saying projection of a shadow content is occurring.

> A simple way to know if one is projecting a shadow content, either a positive or negative content, is to make the distinction between REACTING and RESPONDING. Having a reaction to someone or something is probably projection; having a response is authentic and real, and therefore clear.

War is the ultimate, and negative, projection of each faction's shadow side. Both parties in the conflict keep saying that the *other* is the problem! "The shadow ... is the archetypal urge for a scapegoat, for someone to blame and attack in order to vindicate oneself and be justified."[28]

The comic strip Pogo many years ago stated the matter well: "I have met the enemy and it is I!" Often a negative shadow projection is active in the conflict between union and management: each side claims that it is right; the other is wrong, or needs to change. Alex Tilley, the marketing whiz now part-owner of Tilley Endurables Inc., was fighting to save his business after he went into partnership with a shadow side of himself, a savvy number-cruncher named Dennis Hails. Their relationship began in "seemingly mutual convenience," but then deteriorated into major negative shadow projections: "animosity," "harassment," "sabotage," "malice," and ultimately, "weapons offences"![29]

There is nothing, for instance, as silly, and as sad, as seeing someone yelling at another about being rude! This is the case of the "protest" giving away the guilty clue![30]

Alcohol *does* open the door to one's shadow side. Those parts of ourselves that we keep in the background most the time will enter the light of day.

Christmas office parties[31] are another occasion for the repressed shadow of some supervisors and employees to show itself, especially when alcohol is used as a "shadow lubricant." Alcohol *does* open the door to one's shadow side. Those parts of ourselves that we keep in the background most the time will enter the light of day.[32] Sometimes these shadow contents emerge much to the supervisor's embarrassment or surprise. It's the proverbial *next day* that some people dread because alcohol let their shadow side loose and they may not remember what they did or said. They may even discover that they now face possible legal penalties or personal relationship problems.

The positive shadow

On the other hand, there are repressed, or unconscious contents, in each of us that are of a positive nature; they, too, are part of our shadow. A positive shadow content in an employee could be that part of the employee which could do a good job, but the employee's conscious self-esteem level doesn't believe that. This situation is a good opportunity for the supervisor to draw out this positive potential, or shadow, side of the employee. All effective training and development, therefore, from a Jungian viewpoint, is the maximization of the positive shadow potential side of an employee to accomplish organizational goals.

Another good example of a positive shadow projection is the experience of falling in love. How many of us have said "under the spell of love" (a positive shadow projection because it affects us so intensely) that the beloved is *so wonderful, so beautiful, so this or that*? We have all done that. But, after the honeymoon is over -- well, that's a different matter! "I loved you in the moonlight, and now I find I have to love you over the dishes."[33]

At that point, if the marriage or relationship is to last, each person must re-collect those positive projections and begin to see them in his or herself, and see that if they continue to project them only, first, the individual will become psychologically bankrupt, and secondly, the other person will have an impossible ideal and image to live up to. The weight of those projections will crush the relationship eventually. This same positive dynamic of projection is also at work when one joins a company and the new employee says, "It is *so great* to work here!" Eventually that projection will have to find its place. The employee will be forced to face reality. When the projection does find its place, so to speak, the employee will realize that the greatness belongs to him or her, and what makes this a *great* organization is that employees believe *they* are great, and act accordingly.

It can be just as difficult for an employee, for instance, to believe in his/her creative potential (positive shadow side) as it is to face a part of the personality (e.g., rudeness, a negative shadow side) that the employee was unaware of, but which co-workers experience. Performance appraisals, therefore, are opportunities for feedback to an employee about positive **and**, sometimes, negative shadow contents.

> "Nobody can make you feel inferior without your consent." -- Eleanor Roosevelt[34]

But since growth demands this on-going integration of shadow with the conscious view we hold of ourselves -- so that our personalities become more expansive and whole -- more and more companies realize that true managerial/supervisory excellence includes this on-going development of employees.

The reason Jung reminded us that the encounter with one's shadow side is a moral challenge is that none of us likes to see sides of ourselves that don't fit in with our ego, or conscious ideal of ourselves. Suppose, for instance, a supervisor keeps saying, "My door is always open," but employees are afraid to approach this supervisor, it's probably fair to say that what employees are reacting to is the supervisor's shadow: that part that does not want to meet with employees, which may believe that employees have nothing important to say or contribute. Employees would "pick up" this shadow side through uncomfortable or negative nonverbal communication on the part of the supervisor.

> "He that has eyes to see and ears to hear may convince himself that no mortal can keep a secret. If his lips are silent, he chatters with his finger tips; betrayal oozes out of him at every pore." -- Sigmund Freud[35]

The Valhalla Inn Markham is an excellent example of the positive belief in employees: The culture of Valhalla Markham's management style does not allow for merely meeting the specifications of a job description. "At every step of the way," indicates the human resource manager, "we attempt to stretch ourselves to surpass the objectives which we have devised for the hotel."

This supervisory self-fulfilling prophecy also works in triggering the positive shadow side of employees: if the supervisor believes that employees are good, creative, capable, competent, etc., most likely they will be like that. Economist Tom McCormack, of Strategic Projections, argues that Canadians should give thanks for the many blessings they have -- with the second highest standard of living in the world -- instead of continuing an ugly mood of depression and complaining, and even "cynicism."[36] He says, "If we choose to see ourselves as losers, we'll behave as losers. And sooner or later others will see us as losers, too."[37] Queen's University professor David Dennis even goes so far as to say Canada will cease to exist in 20 years because of its inability to compete globally.[38]

HOW TO RECOGNIZE A SHADOW PROJECTION

"What I see in other people is more-or-less correct if it only *informs* but it is definitely a projection if it strongly *affects* me emotionally."[39] If a supervisor, for instance, finds that he/she is *overly attached* to some person, place, or thing, this is called "shadow-hugging" and if the supervisor is *overly hateful, angry, frustrated* with a person, place or thing, this is called "shadow-boxing." It is easy to see that both shadow-hugging and shadow-boxing occur in many organizations: employees too dependent (shadow-hugging) on their supervisor, or employees always in conflict (shadow-boxing) with their supervisor.

RESOLUTION OF SHADOW AND PROJECTION

The following realizations are critical in resolving the shadow/projection reality:

- Shadow *and* projection go hand-in-hand.
- We become aware of our shadow self by recognizing it in projection, that is, in the other, and by having the courage to re-collect it as a part of ourselves.
- We are projecting if another person, place, or thing unduly affects us

emotionally. That happens when we just can't seem to "shake it" off, so to speak. A projection is definitely occurring if we feel consumed by the person, place, or thing, either positively, or negatively.

- Recognizing the shadow projection means realizing that what we are seeing "out there" in another person, for instance, is really a part of ourselves. It may, in fact, be a part of that other person, but it is also in us. This is more difficult to do when the projection is negative, that is, if we angrily, for instance, see the other as rude. We have to stop pointing the finger and realize that three are pointed back at us! Rudeness is part of us as well!

- The re-collection of our shadow projections is a life-long task, and an ethical imperative because (1) each of us is responsible for our own behaviour, and (2) to require others to carry our psychological task of living is to live out of their "psychological pocket," to be codependent, to not be ourselves, and, if carried far enough, to experience ourselves as empty and lacking meaning.

- In addition to taking responsibility for our shadow projections, we must learn to reverse the projections, that is, stop seeing the problem "out there" and recognize it as "within" us.

Coming to grips with one's shadow side is a great moral challenge for all of us, supervisors included. So much of the world is suffering, is in deep pain and agony because world leaders, politicians, and individuals cannot stop the negative projecting of their shadow selves. The Persian Gulf War was a major experience for all of us in seeing negative projection of shadow contents with each side claiming that the other was evil. It is irrelevant who is evil when it is estimated that perhaps over 150,000 people died in a matter of weeks![41] The experience is so unacceptable that the armed forces have to use "doublespeak," so that "collateral damage" really means *civilian deaths*, a "party" is really a *battle*, a "bag of tools" is really *weapons*, and to "deliver a package" is really to *drop bombs*![42]

Prejudice, and judging and blaming others, therefore, are really self-judgment and self-blame. "It is a curious psychological fact that the man who seems to be 'egotistic' is not suffering from too much ego, but from too little."[40]

Shadow and *projection* are such gripping realities that supervisors *have* to understand them as clearly as possible. That begins with self-understanding: how my own projections, especially the negative shadow ones, are destructive in relationships. By projecting I am fooling myself because I believe that it is always *the other* person who is at fault. Projection is "the pot calling the kettle black."[43] In organizations it is called "passing the buck," and there can be some terrible consequences.

SUMMARY

The unexamined life is not worth living because we are then at outside mercy of the forces. The examined life has faced the valleys as well as the mountain tops.

The examined life is worth living because it gives us choices, which gives us morality, which in turn allow us to be human.

Our self-concept develops from infancy and finds its roots in family life. A healthy family promotes a healthy sense of self-worth in its members.

Supervisors need to nurture a positive sense of dignity and self-worth in their employees by building a positive working environment.

All behaviour is purposeful. Ethics show up in our behaviour as an expression of our inner sense of values.

Individual behaviour is multi-dimensional. We are feeling, valuing, and thinking individuals.

The shadow is our alter ego, that side of ourselves that we have repressed, ignored, or left undeveloped. It is capable of reaching the heights -- the positive shadow but also capable of plunging the depths -- the negative shadow.

Developing as a full human being with a maturing self-concept means integrating more and more of one's shadow, both its positive and negative aspects.

The shadow, or instinctual side, of each of us is not experienced directly but indirectly, in projection, that is, in seeing the trait or quality (that belongs to us) in the other person or thing.

Projection and being unaware, go hand-in-hand. Becoming an aware individual minimizes projections so that reality is experienced as clearly as possible.

Supervisors need to be aware of their shadow sides and the mechanism of projection because these realities are active in the workplace, both on the part of supervisors themselves and on the part of employees as well.

When supervisors can appreciate the authenticity of growing as individuals, they can more readily acknowledge that need in employees. When that happens, a healthy corporate culture is established.

TERMS/CONCEPTS

spirit of acquisition
spirit of disillusionment
examined life
search for meaning
greatness of life
self-concept
unlived psychological life
significant others

shadow
Pinocchio Management
individuation
projection
reacting *vs.* responding
shadow integration
shadow *information*
shadow *affect*

DISCUSSION QUESTIONS

1. Describe in your own words the connection between "the *having* of things" and *"being* empty inside."

2. Why is the examined life important?

3. Discuss the influence of family life on the development of the self-concept.

4. What is the relationship between self-concept and supervising?

5. We have different "parts" to ourselves. Why is the reality of this information important for day-to-day supervisory practices?

6. Give a personal example to illustrate the *valuing, thinking,* and *feeling* parts of your life.

7. What is the psychological shadow? Why is it important in understanding individual behaviour?

8. Describe projection and its relation to the concept and reality of the shadow.

9. How does one come to recognize shadow projections?

10. How does one work on resolving shadow and projection issues?

ASSIGNMENT

Instructions: In the left column think of a person whom you greatly admire. List the qualities you admire in this person. In the right column, think of a person whom you dislike intensely. List the qualities or traits that you dislike so much. Both these persons can be public figures and/or personal acquaintances. Don't censor the qualities in either list too much; just write them down.

THE PERSON I GREATLY ADMIRE IS ...	THE PERSON I INTENSELY DISLIKE IS ...

The *shadow* contains those qualities and traits, both positive and negative, that already exist in us, but of which we are unaware and which we end up *projecting* on to others, truly believing that these self-qualities in fact only belong to the other person. Our positive and negative self-description (above), while not obvious to us, is obvious to our family, friends, and co-workers, and is the more true the more the other emotionally affects us **intensely**. That is, the more we strongly like or dislike some quality or trait in the other, the more sure we can be that it already exists in us. It may or may not be a reality in the other person.

CHAPTER SEVEN

COMMUNICATIONS:
DEVELOPING EFFECTIVE HUMAN RELATIONS

Reviewing has one advantage over suicide: in suicide you take it out of yourself; in reviewing you take it out of other people.

-- George Bernard Shaw[1]

LEARNING OBJECTIVES

At the end of this chapter, students will be able to:

* Recognize the need for effective human relations
* Understand the *70 - 30% Dilemma: People Have Meanings!*
* Identify the important skill of speaking for self
* Know the difference between understanding and agreement
* Discern the key components of the communication process
* Describe the key to the art of listening
* Explain how to define issues

Opening scenario

A contemporary and very tragic case of inadequate and missed communication was the crash of the two 747s in Tenerife, Canary Islands, in 1979.[2] Jacob Veldhuyzen van Zanten, the 50-year-old pilot of the KLM 747, was also chief of pilot training for KLM. This was a very prestigious job. Already a potential communications problem was brewing: who would challenge or say anything to such a senior and well-respected person, even when danger was apparent? Charisma and position have their appeal, but also their deadly undertow! Other constraints impacted on the communication process: the KLM crew was almost at its limits for flying time before being required to take a rest. They hurried to get back to Amsterdam in time. Getting in late could possibly result in a heavy fine or prison term because of the strict Dutch disciplinary measures! *But then the fog rolled in.* The Pan Am and KLM jumbos had to reposition themselves. By then the fog was too thick to see anything. Eager to take off, the KLM 747 roared down the runway slamming right into the Pan Am 747 at 130 miles a hour! The KLM pilot had throttled before getting clearance, but anticipating it; the Pan Am pilot missed the side exit to park because of the fog; and communications got garbled between cockpits and tower. Result: 583 dead!

The greatest communications tragedy of all was the bombing of Hiroshima on August 6, 1945. The Potsdam Declaration was a document that asked the Japanese to surrender on July 26, 1945. It was signed by the United States, Great Britain, and to the surprise of many Japanese, China. The Japanese felt good about the document because it stated that Japan would not be wiped out if they co-operated. The Emperor told Foreign Minister Togo that all was acceptable. At that point the full cabinet met with the Allies to discuss the declaration and Japan's response. When Prime Minister Suzuki met with the press the next day it was decided that he should treat the matter in a light-hearted way. Suzuki said the Japanese cabinet was following a policy of *mokusatsu*, a word that could be translated as either *to ignore* or *to withhold comment*. Sadly, the Domei News Agency chose the wrong meaning, giving the impression to the Americans that the Japanese were ignoring the threat and couldn't care less. On August 6, 1945, the atomic bomb was dropped![3]

THE NEED FOR EFFECTIVE HUMAN RELATIONS

There are three main reasons for the supervisor to develop effective human relations skills: (1) the need we have for one another, just as human beings; (2) the need to create justice in the *worthplace*;[4] and (3) the costs of unsatisfactory human relations.

OUR NEED FOR ONE ANOTHER

A true reflection on life shows that *we are crafted in relationship*, that is, we find ourselves, our meaning and identity, in relationships. Chapter 6 on understanding individual human behaviour highlighted the importance of the developing positive self-concept in a child for mature adult functioning. We can say here that this self-concept develops within relationships. As a child I am what you believe me to be, but then gradually I learn to believe in me, in my own talents and potential. But that counsel also comes from effective parents and teachers primarily. As we grow we gradually internalize this vocation for self-autonomy. As an adult I should be able to be in a relationship as an interdependent individual, sometimes dependent, sometimes independent, but mainly mutually interdependent.

An American Indian legend tells about a brave who found an eagle's egg and put it into the nest of a prairie chicken. The eaglet hatched with the brood of chicks and grew up with them.

All his life the changeling eagle, thinking he was a prairie chicken, did what the prairie chickens did. He scratched in the dirt for seeds and insects to eat. He clucked and cackled. And he flew for a brief thrashing of wings and flurry of feathers no more than a few feet off the ground. After all, that's how prairie chickens were supposed to fly.

Years passed and the changeling eagle grew very old. One day, he saw a magnificent bird far above him in the cloudless sky. Hanging with graceful majesty on the powerful wind currents, it soared with scarcely a beat of its strong golden wings. "What a beautiful bird!" said the changeling eagle to his neighbour. "What is it?" he asked. "That's an eagle, the chief of the birds," the neighbours clucked. "But don't give it a second thought. You could never be like them.

So the changeling eagle never gave it another thought. And it died thinking it was a prairie chicken.[5]

"If I am because I am I
And you are because you are you,
then I am and you are.
But if I am I because you are you,
and you are you because I am I,
then I am not and you are not."

-- Rabbi Mendel[7]

Adults with a fractured self-concept are either overly dependent or independent in relationships. That is what is known as codependency in relationships: not being myself, but being what the other wants me to be. Terry Kellogg, the family systems/codependency expert from Lifeworks Communications, says that "much of our adulthood is a re-enactment or a reaction to unresolved childhood experiences."[6] Even if Kellogg's comment is only partly true, it is still essential for supervisors to develop as a positive self-concept as possible so that they can supervise well. We see through our own self-concept filter, and if it is dirty or shattered, we may be of little help to others.

Each of us in life is seeking some sort of contact: with ourselves and with one another. We cannot survive without contact. Something or someone has to remind and tell us that we're alive. It takes a very special person to be *totally* isolated as a hermit. In the western world, at least, most of us will have contact with someone in one way or another. We know that contact is important because so many people suffer from loneliness; loneliness is the absence of contact. More precisely, loneliness is the absence of meaningful contact. Some have many people around them, but they are still lonely. One has only to go to the contemporary place of worship, i.e., the shopping mall, to realize that many people can be there, but if there is no significant contact, they are still lonely.

The Valhalla Inn Markham has recognized that in an industry where a diverse mix of ethnic races joins forces to present a warmth of personalized services, communication becomes paramount to its success. To this end, the hotel established a 200-foot *Communications Corridor* displaying visual forms of information relevant to business and social endeavours of common interest to all employees. Its golden rule -- no memos!

It is the same in our interpersonal communications. Whenever we speak, we strive for contact, for meaningful contact. We seek to be understood, in other words. One way or another we will make contact -- unless we become that totally isolated hermit mentioned above. No two people can come together without some sort of contact being established! Contact is the interpersonal goal. We can illustrate that by the following diagram:

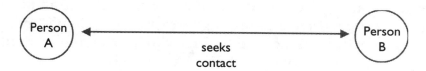

Contact will occur one way or another, positively or negatively. Isn't it better to aim for a positive experience of contact? To do this we will need to use as many effective communication skills as are necessary. We want this contact because it brings us recognition for who we are, and we hope for understanding. It only makes sense that if to use effective communication skills facilitates this process, we had better make use of them. Sadly enough, some people seem content to live with negative contact. These kinds of relationships tend to be interpersonally abusive and destructive. The choice is really ours.

Below is a model showing that, despite our natural seeking and yearning for contact, often it doesn't occur as easily as we would like.

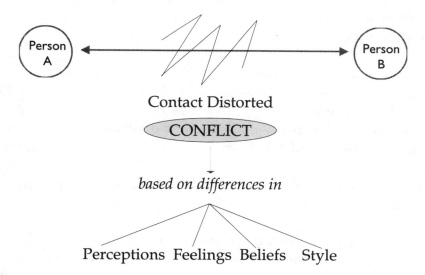

As can be seen, conflict often arises *on very natural grounds* precisely because there are differences in people's perceptions of what is or is not; people's feelings, whether values or one's emotional set; people's beliefs, the mindset

We all need strokes: solid, positive, life-giving strokes. If we don't receive positive strokes, then we will look for negative strokes (often unconsciously), because no strokes means death, and survival is the issue.

through which we all filter our information; and people's style. Each of us, through experience, training, and preference, act, see, and react to life differently. Because these potential conflictual differences are bound to occur, communication skills become critically important.

The *quality* of our relationships[8] is one of the factors determining whether or not we are healthy or sick. Sick relationships create illnesses; healthy relationships create health. We need effective human relations for many reasons, among which are our physical needs, our ego needs, social needs, and practical needs. Medical research shows a wide range of medical problems occurring as a result of lack of close relationships:[9]

a. When people are socially isolated they are two to three times more likely to die prematurely than are those with strong social ties. It doesn't seem to matter what kind of relationship the person has, as long as the person has *a* relationship. Relationship ties increase longevity, in other words;[10] a relationship heals.[11]

b. Before the age of seventy, divorced men die from heart disease, cancer, and strokes at double the rate of married men. Hypertension claims three times as many of these same men. Five times as many divorced men commit suicide; seven times as many of these same divorced men die from cirrhosis of the liver; and ten times as many die from tuberculosis.[12]

c. Cancer, of all types, is as much as five times higher among divorced men and women than among their single counterparts.

d. A Swedish study found that poor communication can contribute to coronary disease. This study involved thirty-two pairs of identical twins. One of the siblings had heart disease. While there was not much difference in obesity, smoking habits, or cholesterol levels of either party, what researchers did find was that there were significant differences with poor childhood and interpersonal relationships, that is, the ability to resolve conflicts and the degree of emotional support given by others.[13]

e. Researchers have also found that death increases when a close relative dies. In a Welsh village, when citizens lost a close relative, within the year deaths were five times greater among those who had suffered from this relative's death. In other words, we need our relationships.[14]

JUSTICE IN THE WORTHPLACE[15]

Common sense and experience tells you that if you treat employees unfairly you will end up the loser in the long run. Some supervisors never understand that and go on about their business as if people didn't matter and were there for their every whim and fancy. These kind of non-caring and unethical supervisors are losing out not only in terms of productivity but also in terms of organizational effectiveness and profit.

Employees evaluate the sense of justice in terms of *equity* or the *fairness* they perceive in situations, structures, and relationships. Widespread knowledge and practice of psychology and the social sciences in this century have made our psychological worker aware of realities such as self-esteem and values in the workplace. Today's employee wants a *worthplace*.

Injustice occurs because employees *perceive* inequities. Employees don't like to be treated unfairly; never have and never will. The history of humankind is filled with stories about injustices and the wars and conflicts people got themselves into to fix up their actual or perceived grievances.

In today's society there are many new factors that contribute to actual or perceived injustices in the work environment.[16] We have mentioned one of the factors already: future shock, the impact of the amount and speed of change that is happening in our world. Even anticipating what the Canada Pension Plan will be like is placed in the future shock category.[17] There are

Justice in the workplace, or, as a matter of fact, justice *anywhere*, does not have to be justified. It is justified solely on the basis of its being integral to humanness. Lack of justice therefore is lack of humanness. As such, this lack, if extensive enough, can promote very evil consequences.

A *worthplace* is a working environment where a conscious effort is made to articulate and put into practice values that promote human dignity, freedom, and affirmation. Perhaps the demands of this vision explain in large part why there is such a lack of justice in many workplaces.[23] As with any relationship, it takes time, patience, effort, and commitment to realize a just working environment.

"radical reorganizational changes, layoffs and plant closings."[18] There is a new world order.[19] Insecurity is a prevalent feeling for many in the early 1990s as employees try to grapple with these elements of future shock and the globalization of the work environment.[20]

Another factor that can contribute to perceived or actual injustice in the workplace is the new kinds of jobs and skills required by business today. For instance, Roy Woodbridge, president of CATA -- the Canadian Advanced Technology Association -- says, "People with software skills have a very strategic role to play in the transformation of the Canadian economy yet the human resource dimensions of this shift to the information age have never been adequately assessed. ... As a result, the country as a whole is beginning to pay for that neglect."[21] As well, some employees will be deemed redundant, or their skills obsolete, and they will feel that it is unfair to be "dehired" when someone, even legitimately more skilled, but with less experience than they, replaces them. To balance this possible perception of injustice, David Olive says, "Canadian workers must be given the tools to enhance their own productivity."[22]

A supervisor who is commited to developing effective human relations will realize that many employees go to a *workplace* each and every day, but how many can say they go to a *worthplace*, a place that (1) is worth going to, (2) values each and every employee, and (3) places the highest values on the acknowledgment, the affirmation, and the promotion of human dignity as the *core* of the work environment?

Supervisors who create *worthplaces* know the tremendous importance of feelings of justice that must exist in the work environment, and they seek to promote those feelings of justice through concrete acts of fairness in working relationships. They do this because *to promote justice is the right thing to do*, but they also know that, on a practical basis, an unjust workplace is certainly not a healthy working environment or *worthplace* because it fosters absenteeism, abnormally high turnover, high grievance rates, lack of commitment, physical and psychological withdrawal, and numerous arbitrations.

Worthplace supervisors encourage communication among themselves and their employees and they especially try to communicate accurate perceptions of work justice and attend to any actual perceptions of injustice because they know that however "perceived" -- rather than actual -- the injustice may be, it is very real to the employee and often due to inaccurate and insufficient information; and a worthplace supervisor knows he/she can do something about inaccurate or insufficient information. Employees want to be informed: "employees generally have three communication needs. They want to know where the organization is heading and how it will get there and -- most important -- what all that means to them."[24] The Canadian Manufacturers' Association has found that "the top six supervisory roles, in order of importance, are motivating employees, controlling and improving productivity, handling performance issues, improving productivity, coaching and counselling employees, and helping employees cope with change."[25]

> "At the Valhalla Inn Markham," says general manager, Graham Willsher, "we are always trying to improve our human relations skills. This means that you, the customer, profit because our staff will genuinely listen and speak with you about your concerns. We haven't forgotten why we are in business: to serve you! That is the main focus, and one we will work at unceasingly."

Justice builds on an accurate sense of information, that good and fair things will happen, and that bad and unfair practices will stop. Parents know about this "sense of fairness" that children have by instinct. Children can live with fairness, but not injustice. Injustice breeds contempt, rebellion, and self-and-other hatred.

In today's work environment it is ethically imperative for supervisors to put justice at the top of their priority list. So much time and energy is squandered, so much profit is lost[26] and heartache and sorrow are suffered, both on the job and in home situations, that to do anything less than create justice in the workplace would be abhorrent at best, and evil at worst.

THE COST OF UNSATISFACTORY HUMAN RELATIONS

Perhaps *the* major business example of costs, both human and financial, in our society from unsatisfactory human relations occurs when a strike happens. In 1992 North America had its first NHL strike! When the NHL Players Association at the time turned down the NHL's offer, president John Zeigler said, " We are at an impasse and [the players] have taken their offer off the table. ... It's a sad day, my friends, a sad day."[27] NHLPA labour lawyer John Quinn said this rejection throws the whole structure of the NHL into chaos and, "If I were the owners, I would not sleep very well tonight." Tough words, tough feelings, tough losses! The costs? The CBC alone faced a potential loss "as high as $60 million, which would represent over half the $108 million cutback in 1990 that closed or gutted 11 TV stations."[28] Finally, a good dose of what Henri Bergson, the French philosopher, called "common sense"[29] appeared and the strike was settled. "What we got was common sense on both sides [owners and players], and now the deal's done."[30]

In British Columbia's 1992 bitter pulp labour dispute, Eric Mitterndorfer, president of Pulp and Paper Industrial Relations, pointed out that the direct costs of the strike were about $2 million a day in lost pay for workers and more than $16 million a day in lost pulp and paper production. In 1992 alone B.C. market pulp firms lost $250 million and newsprint makers an additional $152-million![31] On a national basis, besides the frustration and costs, estimated to be around $300 million, of the October 26, 1992 referendum on the Charlottetown Accord, it is estimated that "the doubts about whether Canada can stay united ... costs Canadians at least $15 billion a year."[32] Human relations costs money!

"When the human heart stays home, so does dedication, loyalty, and working to the maximum potential."[33]

A survey by Public Agenda in the U.S. found that only one in four employees is working up to speed and 75 per cent said they could dramatically increase their performance! The international temporary personnel service, Accountemps of Canada Inc., in one survey found that employees, *at all levels*, really only worked one-third of each working day! Both surveys showed that employees don't mind working, but they want challenge and caring! "Management's heartlessness prevents most of them from contributing their best efforts."[33]

Fountain Tire Ltd., an Alberta tire retailer, presents a different story though -- this time a positive human relations one.[34] Besides winning the Canada Award for Business Excellence in marketing (CABE), Fountain builds relationships by fostering trust. Jim Pangle, manager of the commercial truck centre in Edmonton, says that head office managers "treat everybody like another human being and equal to themselves."

Finally, former chairman of the Bank of Montreal William Mulholland, in a speech at Queen's University, referred to a study by the Business Roundtable and Ethics Resources Centre in Washington, D.C., which tracked companies over a 30-year period.[35] The criteria for these companies: (1) at least 30 years in business, (2) a codified set of ethics, and (3) an excellent record in practicing what they preached. The results?

- A 10.2% growth in profit since 1953 (1.5 times higher than the GNP for that period);
- Net income 24.5% greater (GNP net was only 11.7 times greater); and
- Shareholders, originally with $30,000, now pocketing $1,878,221 since 1973 (the Dow Jones Industrial average being worth $276,000).

THE 70 - 30% DILEMMA: PEOPLE HAVE MEANINGS

We're not what we seem to be. You must have had the experience of meeting someone for the first time, not liking the person, but after a few more encounters, seeing a different side to them, a side that was very attractive to you. What's the old saying, "You can't judge a book by its cover"? That's especially true when it comes to people.

We all try to be congruent with ourselves. Each of us wants his/her behaviour to reflect inner choices. This is the psychological way to say what the moral philosophers have been pointing out to us: we are by nature moral. We communicate just by being alive. Another way to say that is to say that *we cannot NOT communicate!* A majority of the things that will trouble a supervisor will have to do with relationships with employees.

The 70 - 30% Dilemma is the following:

If we assume for a moment that we present ourselves -- 100 per cent of who we are -- in any relationship, we know also that there seems to be a mix of *what* we communicate with *how* we communicate. John Welch, chairman of General Electric, and once known as "Neutron Jack" -- because he was known to destroy people but leave the office buildings intact! -- has had a major conversion to this *how* of relating and communicating. In the company's 1991 annual report, he writes, "We cannot afford management styles that suppress and intimidate."[36] Companies had better learn this crucial distinction and practice it, because customer service and loyalty and effective human relations are the next corporate battleground for profitability.[37] Martin Peskin, senior vice-president of Cara Operations Ltd., and in charge of its Harvey's hamburger chain, reiterates this same message in saying that attitudes have changed in the 1990s: "Value is what is important. I think we're out of the greedy 1980s, that mindless race for money. I think the recession was the catalyst for a new emphasis on value. People know what they want, and they will pay for it."[38]

We cannot NOT communicate!

What is more formally known as verbal (the what, the words, the content) communication and *how* is more formally known as nonverbal (meaning, context, medium) communication. The "communication barometer" illustrates this (p. 159):

Our total message is 100%, but what comes through consistently is a mix of 30% (my words) and 70% (the meanings we attach, consciously or not, by the way we pronounce them, or make sounds). While it is not fair to be suspicious of people when they talk, or to start "reading people," it is legitimate to be aware of the communication mix. Real listening[39] occurs on the 70% level. This kind of listening demands time, patience, and involvement.

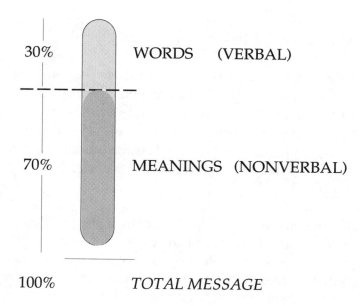

30%	WORDS (VERBAL)
70%	MEANINGS (NONVERBAL)
100%	*TOTAL MESSAGE*

Three elements are communicated nonverbally, or in the 70 per cent zone:

- Our *interest* in the other person or topic;
- Our *top dog* or *underdog* attitude in the situation which sends a message about who is in charge: you or I? and
- Our *like* or *dislike* of the person or topic.

These three elements point out to another person quite a lot about our communication and how we do it -- in short, who we are. This occurs irrespective of the words we are using. It is the 70% Factor, rather than the 30% Factor -- in what is called the 70 - 30% Dilemma -- that is the more important part of our communication and also the area for the most trouble.

The 70 - 30% Dilemma tells us that we must examine the *way* we talk, our *intentions* in the words we use, the gestures we make, the facial expressions and bodily movements we use. When we find through feedback that we were not understood or were ignored or were argued with, it is important to sort out where the crux of the matter is: in our *way* of communicating (the 70 per cent), or in the topic itself (the 30 per cent). It could be that what we have to say is of no interest. But that is life! We're not always scintillating!

THE IMPORTANT SKILL OF SPEAKING FOR SELF

All the communication skills are important. But if we were to isolate one skill in particular, that would have to be the skill called "speaking for self." When I speak for self, I am taking responsibility for what I am saying, whether that be a feeling or a thought. If more people would use this skill, there would be less defensiveness in our (business) interpersonal communications.[40] Speaking for self means that I ground what I am saying in my experience, not yours, nor theirs (i.e., other people's).

This means that the use of the pronoun "I" becomes very critical, and it also means that there is less ineffective use of the pronouns "you," "it," "we," and "they." Speaking for self says, "*I* am feeling this way; *I* did such and such; *my* experience is ..." When I speak for self, the other party may disagree with me (which is perfectly legitimate), but at least there is emotional room for this other party to consider disagreeing with the content. Too often we get caught disagreeing about the *way* something was said, or *how* it was said. Speaking for self minimizes this risk to a great extent. An example may be helpful in illustrating the difference between self- and other-responsibility in communicating:

> One morning your supervisor comes rushing into the office and can't wait to tell you about her weekend at the convention in Las Vegas! She begins, "We get to the airport late Friday afternoon, and you know what it's like when it's the last minute, and you're racing to beat the clock, and the taxi gets caught in traffic; so you say, 'Can't you get me there any faster than this?' You feel very frustrated in these circumstances. Anyways, at least you have time to read ..."

And she goes on with her story. This kind of monologue happens all the time, in homes and in offices. Do you notice that there is something very important that is missing. Your boss hasn't really told you *her* experience. She's been busy putting *you* into the scene, and you, the listener, never do get her direct thoughts or feelings. There is quite a difference when someone says, "You're really scared when you're in a situation like that," in describing an event, and the more appropriate and effective way of speaking for self, "*I* really get scared when *I'm* in a situation like that!" "Speaking for self" makes the speaker take responsibility for his/her own experience.

A neutral example has been used to demonstrate this skill. However, when the content of a message that is being spoken is highly charged emotionally, it becomes absolutely necessary to use this skill of *speaking for self*. Sometimes a supervisor will have to counsel an employee. Especially if the matter is delicate or threatening, the supervisor can speak for self and position the issue from his/her point of view rather than using the "you" pronoun and have the employee feel blamed.[41] The pronoun "you" does get the other person anxious, and he/she then feels that self-defence is the only posture at this point. This is ironic because the one reason that people want to communicate is to make valuable contact, let defenses down, and be more themselves! No one can blame another person for speaking for self about his/her own experiences. Another person may disagree, however. If a person does blame the other, that says more about the immaturity of the speaker than it does about the listener.

THE DIFFERENCE BETWEEN UNDERSTANDING AND AGREEMENT

Each of us wants to be understood. Many mix up the goal of communication and think that it is agreement; it is not. The goal of communication is understanding, and if agreement should occur, then that is a gift.

If the contact is effective, we experience understanding; if it is not, we experience misunderstanding. The reason that you or I begin a conversation in an interpersonal situation is not only to make the necessary interpersonal contact that is vital to us in life, but also because we hope that the communication of our message will not only be accepted, but, to the best possible extent, understood. In other words, you know what I mean by the words I use. That is a tall order, and while we often fall short of understanding someone, it is our personal and ethical responsibility to make the best effort possible. That's why effective listening skills are so important as well in our interpersonal communications. When I feel understood, I know that you know what I mean; and I also know that I am accepted.

Many mix up the goal of communication and think that it is agreement; it is not. The goal of communication is understanding, and if agreement should occur, then that is a gift.

Therefore, understanding and acceptance go hand in hand. You may totally disagree with me but that does not nullify the understanding and acceptance that I have received and experienced from you. None of this, of course, can be done without a willingness and a decision on the listener's part to "be there" for that other person, because when someone feels understood, and therefore accepted as a human being, that person has received a great gift indeed.

It is also in the gift of understanding and acceptance from the other that I am able to accept myself, and in accepting myself, I am also able to make a decision to change because I perceive a freedom and an interpersonal environment where risk and innovation are possible. Many people don't change from self-defeating attitudes or behaviours precisely because they don't feel understood, and therefore accepted. They make the fallacious, but psychologically pertinent, decision for themselves that it is better to be in a prison of one's own making than to risk potential rejection by another. If we could only realize that we're all striving for the same thing: contact, understanding, and acceptance!

THE KEY COMPONENTS OF THE COMMUNICATION PROCESS

A relationship has an opportunity to *develop* when two essential factors interact: *self-disclosure* and *acceptance of feedback*, or *speaking* and *listening*.

A relationship has an opportunity to *grow* when there is an appropriate balance of self-disclosure, or speaking, and of receiving feedback, or listening.

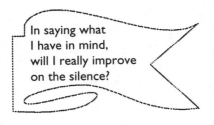
In saying what I have in mind, will I really improve on the silence?

In the same way that "all work and no play makes Jack a dull boy," so "all talk and no listening" makes a relationship lopsided, and "all listening and no talking" makes a relationship unbalanced -- *if this is the habitual pattern*.

TO CREATE JOB FIT, A SUPERVISOR NEEDS TO

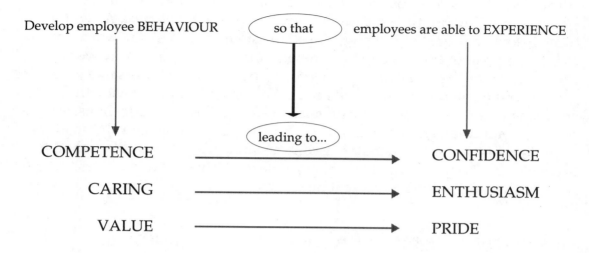

Develop employee BEHAVIOUR

so that

employees are able to EXPERIENCE

leading to...

COMPETENCE → CONFIDENCE

CARING → ENTHUSIASM

VALUE → PRIDE

THE BASIC COMMUNICATION PROCESS

Communication occurs between a *sender* and a *receiver*. One person sends a message; the other receives it. *Feedback* occurs when the message is acknowledged and, if desired, more information is exchanged. The diagram below illustrates this process:

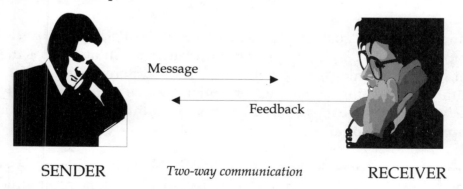

Message

Feedback

SENDER   *Two-way communication*   RECEIVER

Typically people communicate *something*, with a mixture of *verbal* communication, that is, words (what is called the *social dimension* of the communication, accounting for up the 30 per cent of the content) and *nonverbal* communication, that is, meanings (what is called the *psychological dimension* of the communication, accounting for at least 70 per cent of the content). Thus, the communication process *always involves the 70 - 30% Dilemma*. As will be seen below on the art of listening, effective listening "hears" the words, but "listens empathetically" for the meaning of the words. That is why we say *meanings are in people, not in words!* Different people can use the same word, or words, but mean different, or even opposite, things. People provide the meaning of words by their tone of voice, their emphasis, their feelings, etc. If a supervisor asks an employee is she has finished the project, and she answers, "Yes," in a pleasant voice, that gives one meaning. Another employee might give his "Yes" with a sarcastic or angry tone to it. They both said "Yes," but they both communicated different messages.

SOME COMMON BARRIERS TO EFFECTIVE COMMUNICATION

Conflict occurs when there are differences. As we shall see in chapter 10, conflict is the result of different goals that people have. A diagram can illustrate the conflict barrier as follows:

What kind of different goals might cause this conflict? Perhaps the *perceptions* of the supervisor and employee are very different concerning what is the real problem. There is nothing wrong with this, but the difference does offer an opportunity for listening so that the perceptions can be aligned as closely as possible. We all perceive life differently; effective communication skills allow us to appreciate each other's difference.

A second potential barrier is the supervisor's *dislike* of the employee. As we saw above in the 70 - 30% Dilemma discussion, dislike will be communicated nonverbally often by the speaker. If it is conveyed deliberately, then the supervisor is asking for trouble. His or her job is not to start fights and conflicts, but to get work done. If a supervisor does indeed dislike an employee, listening to the employee will be next to impossible *unless* the supervisor identifies something about the employee that is good and connects on that level.

A third potential barrier can be a supervisor's *feelings*.[42] Feelings are like spaghetti: they can be very difficult to manage at times. This is a situation in which the personal maturity of the supervisor is critical: the feelings are all right; it's what the supervisor does with them that counts. In chapter 5 we studied the reality of the shadow and projection: self-reflection will help the supervisor sort out if the feelings are his/ hers and need to be dealt with on that level, or if they need to be part of the communication. If they are, then the *speaking for self* skill above is *absolutely necessary!* It's important for the

> **Supervisors' common communication barriers:**
>
> - Different perceptions of goals
> - Particular dislike of an employee
> - Supervisor's own feelings
> - Lack of good listening skills
> - Pressure of *political correctness*

supervisor to communicate: "*I feel angry* [for instance] about what you're doing," not, "*You* make me angry!" The employee will hear the use of the pronoun "you" as a judge-and-blame statement and all it will do is get defences up. Meanwhile, the purpose of the communication in the first place was for openness and dialogue![43]

A fourth potential barrier may be the *lack of good listening skills* on the part of the supervisor. In this case, the supervisor should get help, either through on-the-job training and development courses or training at a local community college. Supervisors spend about 40 per cent of their working day listening to employees and colleagues[44] "even though we spend 70 per cent of our waking hours in verbal communication"! If a supervisor's salary is $40,000/annum, this means that $16,000 of salary is for effective listening skills on the job! Multiplying that 40 per cent factor by supervisors' salaries in Canada would produce a tidy sum! The important question is, of course: is the money justified? A fifth, and final potential barrier - especially prevalent today - is the crusade for political correctness in the words we use. The world-renowned literary critic Northrop Frye of the University of Toronto, says that society can kill freedom by killing the capacity to speak freely. Indeed, "the kernel of

Will we lose the connection between our language and physical and historical reality through politically correct thought? If so, we will be in danger of not remembering how to express ourselves or to understand and shape future events as they impact on us. "What is really oppressive to women and men in our language is its very debasement. In 'flattening' our language, we are flattening our own selves. Rather than beating it down further, we should instead be trying to understand how we got into this terrible mess."[46]

everything reactionary and tyrannical in society is the impoverishment of the means of verbal communication."[45]

While it is important for supervisors, like anyone, to avoid sexist and racist language, sometimes the *fear* of making a mistake when communicating is more of a barrier than it need be. Employees and supervisors who use their negative shadow side to get power and control by judging and blaming others with their "wrong" use of words can be quite destructive. In this instance, "political communication" becomes a game of the hunter and hunted. Then it loses its effectiveness because no one gets really concerned about the issues or the inappropriate words that need to be changed.

Doublespeak in organizations compounds this problem of the meaning of words and creates a further barrier. When a National Airlines 727 airplane crashed on May 9, 1978, killing three of the fifty passengers on board, the airline netted $1.7 million as an after-tax insurance benefit for its stockholders; not wanting to talk about the crash in the annual report and wanting a way to explain the $1.7 million, National added a footnote explaining that the money came from "the involuntary conversion of a 727"![47] The Nazis used the term "Final Solution" to mask the murder and killing they were doing! An anaesthetist at St. Mary's Hospital in Minneapolis in 1982 gave a fatal dose of nitrous oxide, killing a mother and her unborn child. What did the hospital call this mistake? In doublespeak it was a "therapeutic misadventure"![48] In the corporate boardrooms, communication via doublespeak proliferates. Laidlaw, the garbage and school bus conglomerate, wrote that its August 31, 1991, year-end was "extremely challenging"![49] What did that mean? It was their way of explaining how the recession and recycling produced a loss for them of $344 million (U.S.)! In fighting software piracy, is filing criminal charges against those caught a new method? Not really. It's "an enhancement" to the way business is done now![50]

When Air Canada uses phrases like "industry restructuring" and "made-in-Canada solutions," what precisely do they mean? They "seem to be Air Canada code words for ridding themselves of Canadian Airlines International Ltd. of Calgary as a competitor ..."[51] Companies don't *fire* or *lay off* employees today; that's too harsh a word. What happens instead? There is "repositioning, involuntary force reduction, rightsizing, downsizing, reshaping, redeploying, reducing duplication, focused reduction, de-selection, involuntary methodologies, employment security policy"![52] The list could go on.

Where does that leave supervisors and employees? Often they are left with the feeling that nothing counts any more. It's all gobbledegook! And trust in words and belief in authentic communication becomes tenuous.

THE POLITICALLY CORRECT COMMUNICATOR[53]
Something To Think About ... Seriously!

For the last twenty years business has been evolving more positively along the continuum of effective human relations.

After the American Revolution and later, in the nineteenth century, business was primarily occupied with being business, i.e., the nuts and bolts of "good" financial and manufacturing practices. "Good," of course, wasn't inclusive of treating workers fairly and humanely. Hence, the beginnings of unions and the personnel movement, now called human resources management. Theoretically speaking, if management had "played fair," and treated workers as valuable, self-determining individuals, unions would be unnecessary. That didn't happen, and we don't live in an ideal world.

So business has had to change. Even now, the $1.2 million federal government study by Harvard economics professor Michael Porter concludes that Canadian companies, managers and workers, have to change attitudes if they want to remain competitive in the future.[54]

Business has indeed been changing, perhaps not as dramatically and aggressively as it should, but we are much more aware of human issues today than twenty years ago. Discussions and legislation on human rights, employment equity, sexual harassment, the ethics of advertising, environmental ethics, and the irreversible self-actualization mindset of today's employees more than proves this.

But now we seem to be caught in a new dilemma. Just when we have become conscious enough of some of our most pressing human and ethical business issues, and after companies have spent millions of dollars over the last twenty years in training and development activities so that more managers and employees are able to speak more compassionately, effectively, and decisively, the "thought police" have moved in. The "thought police" are those who fail to distinguish offensive speech (such as the racist remark or ethnic joke) from the appropriate expression of dissenting speech. Will we lose what we have gained? Even the Canada Council *seems*[55] to have its thought police to enforce its "cultural appropriation" and "authenticity of voice" rules: writers, artists from one culture not being allowed to write or paint, for instance, about another culture; an Italian, for instance, not being allowed to write about the Chinese since he or she is not Chinese, etc.[56] The politically correct thing to say is also strongly affecting the advertising industry in what it can and cannot say. Advertising fails if there is no emotion in it, according to John Bliney, creative director for Mediacom Inc., who says there's "a pervasive attitude of political 'correctness' ... sapping the creativity of Canadian advertising." According to Bliney, "We're getting into a 'Big Brother' type of society, where we're very limited in what we are allowed to say."[57]

In a 1991 *Toronto Star* editorial cartoon[58] there were pictures of five people. The first person says, "Anti-semite!" The second says, "Sexist!" The third person cries, "Racist!" The fourth person cries, "Homo-phobic!" And in a box to the right is the fifth person who observes, "I imagine a time when religion, gender, race and sexual preference would have nothing to do with my freedom not to like someone ..." Like others in society, business people are caught in this dilemma: having learned many of the skills to speak openly, humanly, and clearly, they are now in danger of being labelled *because* they spoke! Carl Jung said one time that he would always hold the right to disagree with someone, but, by the same token, would fight to the death to uphold the other person's right to speak as well.

> The main confusion today is that communication is equated with agreement. This is the #1 mistake and assumption of ineffective communicators. Anything that devalues relationship, that skews or tramples on dignity and respect, is a major ethical problem. It is simply and unequivocally just not right.

The purpose of effective communication is understanding, and, if agreement occurs, then this is gravy! This is especially true in conflict situations. Otherwise, we just erect walls and pull out the artillery. In this kind of a set-up, the party that has the thickest wall and the better guns supposedly wins. In human relations, this kind of competition is self-defeating and usually unethical because it makes a travesty of relationships. It takes a mature individual to (1) maintain relationships, (2) affirm each party's dignity and respect, (3) strive for understanding, (4) speak well, and (5) uphold the inalienable right of both parties to disagree.

The "politically correct thought police" violate this basic ethical principle. Ethically they are "fascists of the intellect and of the spirit." Christina Sommers, associate professor of philosophy at Clark University in Worcester, Mass., in challenging the extremes of politically correct feminists, says, "These people are influential monsters of correctness, putting slogans into student minds rather than clear thinking."[59] A rather nasty comment, in graffiti form in London, England, speaks volumes about this politically negative attitude, this time on the subject of equality of the sexes: "Women who seek equality with men lack ambition."[60] Pointing fingers, judging, and blaming are unethical and destructive gestures. Hopefully business people will not be seduced into this politically correct thinking vice. Business has worked too long now to develop some of the required relationship skills. In many companies and departments, meetings are more effective because managers and employees communicate well. To have these gains snuffed out because of the *fear* and threat of any thought police would be a travesty, interpersonally and ethically.

THE KEY TO THE ART OF EFFECTIVE LISTENING

We can't speak of effective communication skills without also mentioning the art of listening. If there is one cry that we hear from children, spouses, students, and employees it is that "no one listens to me." There must be some truth to the statement because it is said and heard so often. If effective listening has occurred, a person will feel understood and accepted. It may be hard work and take some time, but it *can* happen.

We can make the distinction between hearing and listening. We hear many things at the same time -- the trees, the wind, the airplane, the birds, etc. Hearing is the passive experience of taking in information: information comes to us. But listening must be active; there is a presence and an alertness (in mind, body, spirit) that we need to have *vis-à-vis* the other.

If I listen to you, I feel with you; I *empathize*. *That's the key: empathy.*

Listening is hard work. It means a decision to commit oneself to be with the other person in his/her need to be understood. In listening, there is an intensity which demands discipline and attention in the here and now. If I listen to you, I feel with you; I *empathize*. *That's the key: empathy*. And empathy is shown by the absence of a judge-and-blame attitude or words, and by a willingness to "walk a mile in the other person's shoes" and genuinely relate to their experience.

Effective listening is a major way to show care and compassion for someone. Since meanings are in people, and not really in words, when we listen to another, we are saying that we care enough about that person, as a person, to go beyond the words to the core -- or meaning -- of what the person is saying. We do not let the other's words sidetrack us, or get emotionally involved with their literalness. We reach beyond the words to the meanings, and in so doing begin to accept them as a human being. This *empathic contact* is life-giving to us and we are renewed.

If supervisors could learn this empathy skill of listening to the employee's *meaning behind the words*, there would be a lot more effective communication on the job. Not to feel listened to - when the matter is important to you -- is to feel dismissed. Like children, employees pick up this non-acceptance by feeling that they are "bad," that there is something wrong with them. If employees still harbour a childhood way of handling this sense of dismissal, rather than a more mature adult response, they will either take a *turtle* approach, and go away, feeling personally wounded, from the supervisor, or take a *skunk* approach -- and start acting out their sense of rejection. *Turtles* implode their frustration; *skunks* explode it. Both are unhealthy. One acts in; the other acts out. A supervisor with good listening skills will seek to avoid those two extremes in his/her employees and offer, through empathetic listening, an *understanding* of the employee's need, concern, or problem.

Diagrammed below is an uncomplicated model of the listening process: If supervisors can learn to go beyond the words and begin to listen to an

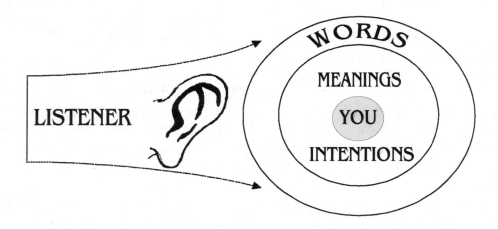

employee's meanings and intentions, little by little the real issue will become visible. The beauty of this approach is that the supervisor will have helped to unlock the door employee's real needs and be accepted and understood by him/her. This listening technique builds self-and-other esteem, affirms the dignity of both parties, and keeps open the channels of communication and productivity.

DEFINING ISSUES

When people communicate, they communicate some *thing*. That "thing" is called an issue. If the moment is one for chit-chat communication, then it doesn't make too much difference what one talks about as long as the interpersonal time is quality time. But if there is something important to talk about, then it is important to know the kind of issue it is.

Solve the riddle!					
63	61	94	18	52	46
6	4	7	9	5	?

Illustrated on page 172 is a model to look at *issues*. There are four quadrants (I, II, III, IV) for issues, and if we place the normal statistical bell-curve on the model, it becomes more clear that we start at a low end and move to a high end. The more we move from one quadrant to the next, the more critical become our skills in communication and listening. Not only that, if we should begin a conversation at quadrant #III (which is often the case in a performance review session), we have to recognize that (1) the issue is much more personal than a topic issue (e.g., the weather), (2) the interpersonal tension is usually at a higher level because feedback to one person is occurring, (3) communication and listening skills become critical, precisely because (4) there is fairly high interpersonal activity at this stage.

Usually *topic* issues deal with more impersonal matters, such as the weather, chit-chat matters, and social talk. *Me* issues move up the scale a notch. Now I am telling you something about myself, an issue probably more threatening, especially if the issue about myself is something I feel frightened about, scared of, or embarrassed over. Third, *you* issues get to be even more risky and potentially fraught with tension. Any time a supervisor has to give a performance evaluation session to a low performing employee, he/she is walking into potentially defensive territory, especially if the employee feels he/she has been doing a good job. The supervisor will be giving feedback to "you," the employee. Communication skills are vital at this point. Finally, there are *us* issues, matters that are of mutual concern. For instance, when there is a conflict or disagreement between a supervisor and employee, both may try to prove their point, or argue for their case over the other's. True communication will occur when both parties seek understanding in the matter. This means truly listening to the other party. Depending on the intensity and emotion involved in the *us* issue, both parties will need to be keenly aware of their skills and limitations.

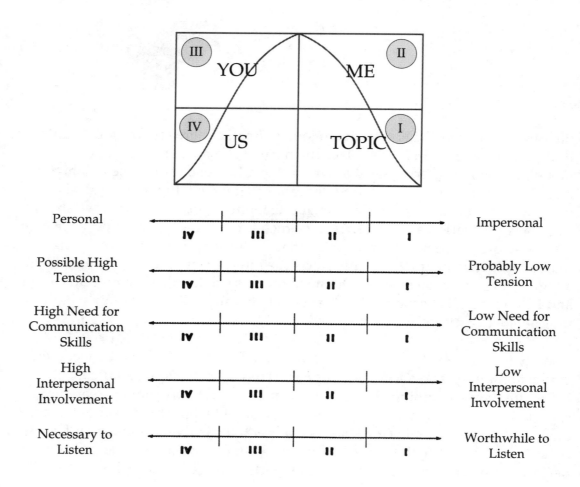

This is illustrated even more clearly by the following examples between a supervisor and an employee:

ISSUE	STATEMENT
#I: TOPIC	"Did you enjoy the Grey Cup today? I thought it was terrific!"
#II: ME	"Jim, I'm not feeling too good about what happened during the meeting we just had." (Notice the speaking-for-self skill)
#III: YOU	"Jim, I need to talk to you about something which really bothered me that you did during our meeting."
#IV: US	"Jim, we need to talk about our avoiding each other. I'm not happy with what's gone on. I've heard you say something similar as well."

As you can see, the level, intensity, and degree of involvement for each of the issues is quite different. It is much "safer" to talk about the Grey Cup, or the World Series, in a discussion between husband and wife than it is to talk about something as personal and potentially emotionally laden as their sexual life. Both kinds of issues have their place within the relationship, but both demand perhaps different levels of skills to be effective. One can, by choice, raise the seriousness, if you will, of a topic issue to that of an "us" issue, in which case, the same logic and wisdom apply.

Finally, in deciding to talk about an important issue, it is a good idea to ask the following organizing questions:

- *WHAT* KIND OF ISSUE IS IT?
- *WHOSE* ISSUE IS IT?
- *WHEN* WILL WE TALK ABOUT IT?
- *WHERE* WILL WE TALK ABOUT IT?
- *HOW* WILL WE KNOW WHEN TO CLOSE?

All of the above questions are important in order to place the issue within a positive context and give the discussion the best chance of success between the two people.

SUMMARY

We are searchers for meaning. We seek to understand and to be understood.

What we seek for is contact. For most of us, this occurs within an interpersonal relationship. The choice is not whether we will make contact. Rather, it is *how* and the kind of contact we will make.

Effective contact is challenged by potential conflict, which is based on differences between people's perceptions, feelings, beliefs (or assumptions), and personal styles.

"Speaking for self" is a skill to facilitate positive interpersonal contact. When I speak for self I take responsibility for my experience. Effective interpersonal contact allows our communication to be understood. In this way, we also feel accepted.

Listening allows us to hear the *meaning* of the speaker's words. Understanding, acceptance, and meaning reinforce one another. Listening is the key.

People communicate around issues, which can be (1) TOPIC issues, (2) ME issues, (3) YOU issues, and (4) US issues. All issues are discussed in a setting. The more important the issue is, the more care should be taken with the setting.

TERMS/CONCEPTS

worthplace
contact
70 - 30% Dilemma
content
context
speaking for self
understanding
agreement

communication process
social dimension
psychological dimension
political correctness
doublespeak
turtle approach
skunk approach
issues

DISCUSSION QUESTIONS

1. Why is there a need for effective human relations?

2. Choose two personal examples in which ineffective human relations caused you problems. What were they? How did they affect you?

3. "We see through our own self-concept filter, and if it is dirty or shattered, we may be of little help to others." Discuss.

4. Why is justice in the worthplace such an important ethical issue?

5. "People have meanings." Show how this communication principle illustrates the 70 - 30% Dilemma?

6. What are the realities that are communicated nonverbally? Give examples from your own personal experience.

7. Describe the "speaking for self" skill.

8. What is the difference between understanding and agreement? Illustrate this difference with an example from your work experience.

9. What are some common barriers to effective communication?

10. Discuss doublespeak and political correctness.

11. What is the key to effective listening, and why?

12. Define *issues* and give personal work examples.

ASSIGNMENT

Instructions: Answer the "Test on Listening Habits" for yourself. Add up your totals to find out what kind of listener you might be.

Test on Listening Skills	Circle the number below to indicate the **extent** of how well you listen				
	Very little	Little	Some	Great	Very great
1. I listen empathetically to people.	1	2	3	4	5
2. I am able to stop mind-wandering when listening.	1	2	3	4	5
3. I concentrate on what the other person is saying.	1	2	3	4	5
4. I listen even when I don't agree with the other person.	1	2	3	4	5
5. I ask the the other person to repeat if I don't understand.	1	2	3	4	5
6. I listen even when I am tired to someone who needs me.	1	2	3	4	5
7. I look at the other person when I am listening.	1	2	3	4	5
8. I find something to like when the other person is boring.	1	2	3	4	5
9. I know my "hot buttons" in my communications.	1	2	3	4	5
10. I listen for feelings as well as content.	1	2	3	4	5

Scoring: Although this is not a scientific test, it can be helpful for you to take stock, so to speak, of your skill in listening. Below is the scoring key.

40 — 50	--	*Excellent* listening
30 — 40	--	*Superior* listening
20 — 30	--	*Average* listening
10 — 20	--	*Poor* listening
0 — 10	--	*Inadequate* listening

CHAPTER EIGHT

MOTIVATING AND EMPOWERING FOR PRODUCTIVITY

People will swim through shit if you put a few bob in it.

-- Peter Sellers[1]

LEARNING OBJECTIVES

At the end of this chapter, students will be able to:

- Define and describe motivation
- Describe the basic motivational process
- Identify what employees want from their jobs
- Describe the elements of performance
- List selected theories of motivation
- Distinguish ways to nurture a motivational environment

Opening scenario

*T*here is a practical and attitudinal change taking place in our workplaces today, a new shift in consciousness from competitiveness to co-operation. Jean Monty, Bell Canada chairman, says, "We cannot meet the challenge of competitiveness without a locomotive, and that locomotive is big business. ... It is no longer a matter of firms of different sizes. We are playing in different leagues."[2] Old league rules of protecting one's turf at any expense[3] is giving way to mergers, partnerships, alliances, and co-operative affiliations are becoming more common. The playing field has changed![4] And so IBM and Apple Computer team up.[5] Then Apple Computer Inc. enters into a partnership with Sharp Corp. to produce the next-generation personal information devices.[6] IBM and France's Groupe Bull also team up;[7] Aikenhead forms a strategic marketing and merchandising alliance with Montreal-based retailer Groupe Val Royal Inc.;[8] SHL Systemhouse Inc. and BCE Inc. (which has Bell Canada as its utility arm) are seeking partnership approval;[9] Northern Telecom and Motorola combine to zero in on the cellular market;[10] Unisys and Motorola form a technology partnership;[11] two very different advertising companies, McKim Advertising Ltd. and Baker Lovick/BBDO -- McKim being creatively safe and Baker being creatively assertive -- merge to create Canada's biggest ad agency;[12] AB Volvo and Procordia AB merge in a deal which "comes at a time when the European car, food, and drug industries are consolidating";[13] and Four Seasons Hotels Inc. enters a joint venture with EIE International Corp., the Tokyo-based parent of the Regent Hotels International Ltd. group.[14]

Even management and unions are getting together. "There's a new mood at many workplaces."[15] Unlike the U.S., Canada, with its higher unionization rates and different values, is seeing management *and* unions establishing co-operation and achieving innovations "through more joint efforts."[16] What does co-operation look like? At Hamilton Wire Products Ltd., management showed its books to the union as a way of being honest with them. Allan Harrison, company vice-president, said showing the books helped the union see what was real. According to Harrison, "We figure, 'Let's get the employees in on it.' We're trying to get co-operation up to a new level. ... It helps employee morale and motivation."[15]

WHAT IS MOTIVATION?

In this chapter we will be studying a basic question: why do people do the things they do? *There is always a reason!* There is always what is known as a *motivator*. The purpose of this chapter is to understand these "reasons," mainly through the eyes of Abraham Maslow's *needs hierarchy*, but also, through quick reference to B.F. Skinner's idea of *rewards*, Frederick Herzberg's idea of *higher level needs*, David McClelland's idea of *acquired needs*, and Victor Vroom's idea of *expectations*. Each of these psychologists studied why we do what we do and has proposed an answer.

Perhaps it was fear of going out of business; perhaps it was good will on people's part; or perhaps it was just accumulated experience that said goals would be attained if companies developed a *spirit of co-operation!* During General Motors' restructuring process, discussions were held over whether its Oshawa, Ontario, plant would survive. The history of worker relations ("including absenteeism and stability"[17]) was to count as one of the three criteria in GM's decision-making process. This explained why GM's assembly plant in Kansas City, Kan., in spite of lacking a strong supplier based around it, but with good transportation links, was a strong contender at the time: the workforce had a good reputation. "Management and labour have a co-operative relationship. Their top people meet regularly and workers talk openly about shared goals of raising quality and productivity and reducing costs. Grievances are few and there is an overtime agreement."[17] In the w ords of L.D. Edwards, a 28-year veteran of GM and president of United Auto Workers' Local 31, labour relations were "as good as any in the corporation." As to whether this spirit is felt deeply within by other businesses and/or unions remains a matter for debate. The alternative in recessionary times is rather stark! The point is: the people factor has to become just as important as the financial factor.[18]

Martin O'Neil, president of the Bata Shoe Organization, planned a renewed motivational environment through what he called "a cultural revolution" with no layoffs (which he considered bad management), just-in-time inventory controls, and production circles. For him, Bata's new mission statement would

The Valhalla Inn Markham, during tough economic times, has increased its expenditure on motivational and technical training for all employees with strong emphasis on personal development. It is the belief of the hotel that no employee will fully benefit from managerial or supervisory skill training unless the individual is focused on, and acts upon, personal goals.

read: "We will be No. 1 in the marketplace. We will be faster than the competition."[19] At Air Canada, even though 1991 had been its most difficult year ever, Michelle Monette been given the green light to implement the Idea Action motivational program. The airline was hoping to gain nearly $25 million with this approach! Why did the program work, according to Monette? *Because of a principle of empowerment:* employees were able to claim ownership of a chunk of the company; they had vested interests in the company. Idea Action was a 13-week idea generator: Air Canada's 20,000 employees were broken into teams, given 4,000 projects on which to save money, and then turned loose for ideas on how to do precisely that. Monette claimed, "It's changing the way we do business, forever!" An additional bonus was the communication employees had with one another. Monette said, "People have never talked to each other so much. It opened management's ideas to the skills and ideas of front-line employees."[20]

A survey of executives and personnel directors at 100 of the largest 1,000 U.S. companies showed that workers rarely quit because of money, but because they didn't get opportunities or recognition.[21] In another survey involving eight Canadian companies in four Canadian cities and 81 companies in 65 U.S. cities, results showed similar patterns: workers were frustrated because they

---

WHY DO WE DO THE THINGS WE DO?

WHY?

THERE IS ALWAYS A REASON!

"felt their efforts and contributions were not recognized." The irony of the situation was that these same workers felt proud of their companies and were committed to them! Angela Murray-Franklin, organizer of the survey for Towers Perrin in Calgary, said, "Employees want to make a contribution to their companies' bottom lines, but they feel they aren't used to their full extent. In particular, they feel powerless to affect the results of their work group, let alone their company. They want direction and measurable goals."[22]

Reflective Exercise

Think back to a job in which you felt underutilized. What was that job? What were the *feelings* and *thoughts* you had as a result of this underutilization?

FEELINGS	THOUGHTS

Why do employees do what they do? The answer lies in what motivation is all about. A simple and straightforward definition of motivation is the following:

MOTIVATION IS THE WILL TO ACHIEVE[23]

Employees are willing to achieve because they have *needs* (Abraham Maslow), or because they get *rewarded* (B.F. Skinner), or because they seek *satisfaction* (Frederick Herzberg), or because the achievement fulfils a *learned need* (McClelland), or because of what they *expect* (Vroom) for doing something. We will highlight Maslow's approach in detail, but also provide thumbnail sketches of the other approaches.

Irrespective of the approach one settles on to define and describe motivation, there is one common theme: human beings *do everything for a reason,* conscious to them or not. Even the psychopathic killer in that sense has a "reason," bizarre and skewed from reality though it may be. Human beings don't do things willy-nilly. The diagram below illustrates this process.

Why we do the things we do!

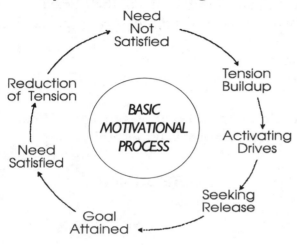

To the person doing something, something *must* be done. This "pull" to do something builds up tension within the person; the person seeks a tension outlet; when the tension is released, the person feels relieved. The cycle is complete.

Motivation, therefore, becomes the regulatory process within each of us for need-satisfying and goal-seeking behaviour.[24] In a work situation, it refers to "the arousal, direction, and persistence of behaviour,"[25] or "the forces within an individual that account for the level, direction, and persistence of effort expended at work."[26]

Thus, motivation as the *will to achieve* means that employees will do something because they *want* to (arousal); they know *what* and *how* something needs to be done (direction); and they *complete* what they started (persistence).

DOING IT THE RIGHT WAY!

Isadore Sharp, chairman of Four Seasons Hotels, says that quality service for the customer is the key today. "Employees cannot be customer-driven and rules-driven at the same time." Mr. Sharp asks the question, "How do we at Four Seasons motivate our employees? We do not. We hire people who are already motivated. Then we treat them the way we treat our customers. We do our best to give them what they want. And what employees want from management is respect, appreciation and integrity." The key point for Mr. Sharp is this: TREAT YOUR EMPLOYEES THE WAY YOU NEED TO TREAT YOUR CUSTOMERS![27]

THE BASIC MOTIVATIONAL PROCESS

When children are four or five years of age they become insistent in asking *one* question: the *WHY* question. The constant questioning for an answer to their *whys* can be rather annoying to parents at times, but the drive to ask the question *why* is quite typical of the human condition.

Victor Frankl, Jewish medical doctor who was in Auschwitz for three and one-half years, concluded that if people have a *why* (that is, a reason) for what they are going through, they can get through any *how*.[28] In other words, if I know *why* something is happening, I can then manage the situation more effectively.

FOR INSTANCE:

- One writer wonders what could be the reason for people to chase the almighty dollar "70, 80 and 90 hours of each and every week of their lives in the high-pressure seclusion of their high-rise offices." He asks, "Is money really the only measure of success?"[29]

- Judy Mann is one of Hong Kong's classic success stories. Cheetah Management Co. Ltd. is her own international clothing company. But has success brought her happiness? She says, "I would like to do something more meaningful. I can't wait until I don't have to make money. ... If you have no time to enjoy your money, then you are miserable."[30]

> How's this for recognition!
>
> A woman named Sarah Clifton, who worked for W.L. Gore & Associates, had to go on a business trip. Not knowing what title to give herself, she asked Bill Gore himself. The result? They agreed she would call herself *Supreme Commander*.[31]

Supervisors are also people who constantly ask *why*. If they can understand *why* an employee does a certain thing, or behaves in a peculiar fashion, they feel more secure in supervising the employee as well as *including* the employee's motives, as best they can, in setting organizational goals.

"In my opinion, there is a misconception that a manager can motivate his or her workforce," says Valhalla Inn Markham general manager Graham Willsher. "I strongly believe that this is not possible. What *is* possible, and I feel proud of our management team having achieved this during our first two years of operation, is *creating the environment* which allows employees to motivate themselves."

Everything we do, consciously or not, we do for a reason. We don't always know *why* we do something or behave in a certain way, but we wouldn't do something or act in a certain way unless it fulfilled a *need* for us.

Motivating employees, or rather providing a motivational environment for employees, means that supervisors must (1) understand some key approaches that psychologists have researched to answer the question *why* employees do what they do, as well as (2) identifying and being sensitive to the needs of employees. These two factors will greatly help supervisors *get employees to do what they want them to do so that the employees will want to do it!*

The key responsibility here is to listen to the employee who always says, in one way or another, *"Take me into consideration and understand what motivates me! Don't discount or ignore me! I count! I'm a somebody!"*

So there is an answer to *why*. The answer is found in the *needs* we have, needs that seek an outlet. Otherwise we wouldn't do what we're doing.

THE LITTLE RED HEN[32]

Once upon a time there was a little red hen who scratched about the barnyard until she uncovered some grains of wheat. She turned to other workers on the farm and said, "If we plant this wheat, we'll have bread to eat. Who will help me plant it?"

"We never did that before," said the horse, who was the supervisor.

"I'm too busy," said the duck.

"I'd need complete training," said the pig.

"It's not in my job description," said the goose.

"Well, I'll do it myself," said the little red hen. And she did. The wheat grew tall and ripened into grain. "Who will help me reap the wheat?" asked the little red hen.

"Let's check the regulations first," said the horse.

"I'm on my lunch break," said the duck.

"Out of my classification," said the pig.

"Then I will," said the little red hen, and she did.

At last it came time to bake the bread.

"Who will help me bake the bread?" asked the little red hen.

"That would be overtime for me," said the

horse.

"I've got to run some errands," said the duck.

"I've never learned how," said the pig.

"If I'm to be the only helper, that's unfair," said the goose.

"Then I will," said the little red hen.

She baked five loaves and was ready to turn them in to the farmer when the other workers stepped up. They wanted to be sure the farmer knew it was a group project.

"It needs to be cleared by someone else," said the horse.

"I'm calling the shop steward," said the duck.

"I demand equal rights," yelled the goose.

"We'd better file a copy," said the pig.

But the little red hen turned in the loaves by herself. When it came time for the farmer to reward the effort, he gave one loaf to each worker.

"But I earned all the bread myself!" said the little red hen.

"I know," said the farmer, "but it takes too much paperwork to justify giving you all the bread. It's much easier to distribute it equally, and that way the others won't complain.

So the little red hen shared the bread, but her co-workers and the farmer wondered why she never baked any more.

WHAT EMPLOYEES WANT FROM THEIR JOBS

In a classic survey by L. Lindahl on "What Makes a Good Job?"[33] workers in different organizations were asked to rank order ten factors that researchers had placed before them. Then their immediate supervisors were asked to rank order the items in terms of how they thought the employees would rank them.

Instructions: First rank order the items for employees and then for supervisors, with a "10" being *not important* and a "1" being *the most important*. Correct answers will be found at the end of the chapter.

WHAT MAKES FOR A GOOD JOB?		Supervisors	Subordinates
1.	Good working conditions.		
2.	Feeling "in" on things.		
3.	Tactful discipline.		
4.	Full appreciation for work done.		
5.	Management loyalty to workers.		
6.	Good wages.		
7.	Promotion and growth with company.		
8.	Sympathetic understanding of personal problems.		
9.	Job security.		
10.	Interesting work.		

A demotivating environment can develop quickly when supervisors and managers misjudge the real needs of employees. For instance, the once proud employees of Walt Disney Co. began calling their corporate headquarters in Burbank, California "Mauschwitz,"[34] and "Duckau,"[35] and their chairman, Michael Eisner, as one of the Italian Medicis, in spite of the fact that $3 of the $57 a share stock price in 1988 was believed to be because of his leadership.[36] Attitude surveys done by William M. Mercer Ltd. of Toronto consistently show that workers want to be informed about decisions affecting them. Sometimes employees believe that their managers hold back information to maintain power and control and that the top-down model of managing leaves little room for them to contribute. Employees did not make radical suggestions for managers to implement, but simply for them to take courses on people skills! And what do the employees themselves want? (1) To be valued as people as well as workers, and (2) for a management style that makes them part of the decision making, with greater responsibility.[37] Finally, in the WorkCanada survey of 2,400 workers, carried out by the Wyatt Co. consulting firm in the spring of 1991, results showed that Canadian workers were happy with their jobs, but not with their supervisors or management's decision-making efforts. According to these workers, people skills were sacrificed for strategic planning and business opportunities. What do these workers want? (1) To be asked what they think of key work-related issues, and (2) to be able to participate.[39]

The Key!

Worker Rick Pederson, of Northern Telecom's Morrisville, N.C. plant says, "People know their jobs inside out. ... They don't know how to deal with each other."[38]

It also helps to sprinkle the workplace with some kindness. Researcher Dr. Alice M. Isen, of the University of Maryland, Baltimore County, says that a little kindness can go a very long way to promote creativity, reason, and co-operation in other people. People who have been put into a good mood as a result of kindness have better memories and increased creativity. Isen says, "Some people think the way you motivate others is to criticize. They may try to work harder, but their performance won't be as good."[40]

ELEMENTS OF PERFORMANCE

Today, of course, *performance is the name of the game.* We hear expressions like, "Those who don't perform are gone!" "Perform or else!" "It's performance that counts!"

But what's a fair way to evaluate someone's performance? Some companies are tying performance to social responsibility and non-financial measures. For instance, at Colgate-Palmolive Co., a senior executive's bonus hinges "on hiring or promoting at least one additional woman or minority member."[41] At Xerox Corp., bonuses are measured by customer service surveys. In Pittsburgh, Pennsylvania, Aluminum Co. of America bases a chunk of the bonus on managers' safety records. While we have seen in chapter 2 that social responsibility expenditures reduce profits in the short and long term after a certain point, they do contribute to long-term profits up to a break-even point, but, as well, says Diane Posnak, the managing director of Pearl Meyer & Partners, New York compensation specialists, these non-financial measures are becoming more and more a part of compensation programs.

"Commit yourself to performing one ten-minute act of exceptional customer courtesy per day, and to inducing your colleagues to do the same. In a 100-person outfit, taking into account normal vacations, holidays, etc., that would mean 24,000 new courteous acts per year. Such is the stuff of revolutions." -- Tom Peters and Nancy Austin[42]

Sometimes performance is evaluated by the stock market -- "sort of a Nielson for the boardroom"[43] -- especially for top executives. Sometimes a chairman's departure will raise stock prices, sometimes lower it. For instance, because of his highest credibility rating in the pharmaceutical industry, if P. Roy Vagelos, chairman of Merck & Co., were to leave, that action would lower the $150 stock price by $5 or $10, according to Neil Sweig, an analyst with Prudential-Bache.

In what is known as the *corporate governance movement*, large institutional investors want more of a say in how and what senior executives are paid. The emphasis is on aligning executive pay with performance. In 1990, was Steve Ross, chairman of Time Warner Inc., worth $78 million (U.S.) and Roberto

Goizueta, chairman of Coca-Cola worth $80 million? At least one person, Coke's spokeswoman, Linda Peek, said that Goizueta was well worth what he got: "The success record of the company speaks for itself. More than $50 billion have been added to the wealth of Coca-Cola shareholders over the past 10 years, and $22 billion of that in just the last year."[44] But, in recessionary times, with the thousands of layoffs, when top American executives earn 109 times the pay of the average worker -- 17 times more than what top Japanese executives and 35 times what top British executives earn -- these "fat cats cause resentment."[45]

When researchers try to understand *why* employees do what they do, what motivates them, or what factors affect their performance, they settle on four main variables or factors that affect performance in work organizations.[46] They are listed below:

PERFORMANCE

is the result of one's *ability, effort, opportunity*

(where)

ABILITY

is a result of *technology, knowledge, skill, strengths,* and

EFFORT

is a result of *needs, goals, expectations, rewards,* and

OPPORTUNITY

is a result of one's *current situation* and *past performance!*

Thus, supervisors will get significant performance from their employees (1) if they have the *ability* to do what they're supposed to, that is, when there is adequate technology, they have the know-how, the skill and necessary strengths; (2) if they put in the necessary *effort*, that is, the amount of energy and willingness employees expend on a task to meet their needs, goals, expectations, and sense of adequate rewards; and (3) if there is the *opportunity*, that is, the organizational support to do what needs to be done. A final factor in this formula, of course, is the indispensable *feedback* to evaluate and improve performance, whether that evaluation is quantitative and/or observational. At Allegheny Ludlum Steel Corporation, chief executive Richard Simmons relies heavily on the quantitative measuring stick: "It's simple. If you can't measure it, you can't manage it."[47]

Not all companies and their managers and supervisors are as strict, but will also include the MBWA concept: *Managing By Walking Around*, where less managing is really producing more productivity.[48] Quad/Graphics computer company even translates MBWA as "management by walking away"! They feel that responsibility should not be too tightly defined. Instead, it should be *"assumed and shared"* so that work *never* becomes someone else's responsibility.[49] The Ottawa-based computer software company Cognos Inc., learned this the hard way. Sticking to a rigid, centrally controlled management style produced a very rough ride in 1989 and early 1990. Vice-president Robert Minns described chairman Michael Potter as "clinical, rational, and hardheaded." That approach to performance, even according to Potter now, was "at the expense of hands-on management in the trenches or holding customers' hands."[50]

> MBWA: "management by walking away"!

Thus, to create optimum performance means to create an empowered supervisory management/leadership environment, which is the result of developing five realities:[51]

- Cultivating accurate self-awareness and self-understanding;
- Understanding different organizational perspectives and viewpoints;
- Valuing differences and diversities;
- Developing honest and open communications; and
- Forming common purposes.

SELECTED THEORIES OF MOTIVATION

Different psychologists have sought to scientifically explain *why* people do what they do. While the theories may seem confusing at first, they do point to one thing: *people do what they do for a reason!* Performance just doesn't happen "out of the blue," so to speak. Some of the key people over the last number of years who seriously worked at answering the *why* question are listed below. Each researcher has given an approach to the solution. For you, the student of supervisory dynamics, it is important to know that different approaches do exist, and if you want to do further research, the main idea of each approach is given. We will concentrate mainly on the *need hierarchy* approach by Abraham Maslow.

THE MOTIVATIONAL NEED HIERARCHY

The late American psychologist Abraham Maslow developed what came to be known as the *need hierarchy*. Maslow postulated that you and I do what we do because of **needs**. He was trying to respond to the question that people have always asked themselves: *Why do we do what we do?* Maslow's answer was the following: people do what they do because they have needs that seek fulfilment. When people have adequately satisfied one need level they spontaneously move to another, and so forth. People without needs are dead people! We all have needs and it is important that we adequately satisfy the one or ones seeking our attention.

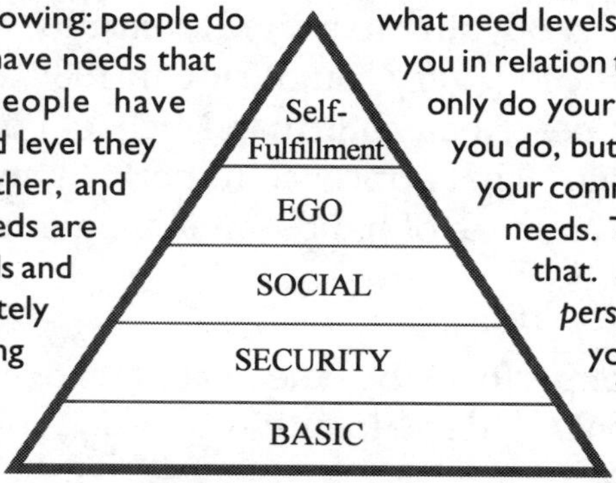

We could further describe the needs as *primary level needs* (Basic, Security, Belonging, or Social) and *motivational level needs* (Ego, Self-Actualization). In other words, unless we have the primary needs more or less adequately fulfilled, it is very difficult, if not impossible, to perform well on the motivational need levels. It

is difficult, for instance, to fulfill our need for recognition (Ego need) when we don't have anything to eat (a Basic need)!

The *Need Sensitivity Inventory* (pp. 191-92) is a simple learning tool to get you to think about what need levels you perceive are influencing you in relation to your role as a student. Not only do your needs influence you in what you do, but also in what you say; that is, your communication is *flavoured* by your needs. There is nothing wrong with that. A need level *positions your perspective* in communicating and you will talk around this need. The content of your convesations will refer to this need level, either consciously or unconsciously. If marks are the most important thing to you (a Security need), you will talk to your classmates and friends about how well you are doing, or the fear (or reality) of not doing well on an exam or test. An adequately satisfied need no longer demands attention. We

The pyramid levels from top to bottom:
- Self-Fulfillment
- EGO
- SOCIAL
- SECURITY
- BASIC

move on to other need levels. Should a situation arise where previously satisfied need levels are activated, then we will move to those levels again.

The **Basic** need level refers to your need for physically safe conditions, air, food, water, etc. The **Security** need is your need to protect the basics; it is an insurance need level, so to speak. On the job it refers to salary, pensions, benefits; in school it can refer to grades, expectations, knowing where you stand in a subject, etc. The **Social** need level is your need for relationships. The **Ego** need level is your need for recognition, positive feedback, valuing as a person. This occurs in school when professors affirm you, when you receive special recognition for outstanding work, etc. And the **Self-Actualization** need level is your need to be creative, to "do your own thing," so to speak, to be trusted because you will follow through. A high score here would indicate that you see yourself as a self-starter with a need for accomplishment and that you are making a unique and positive contribution. This need level, of course, demands *willingness* and *internal discipline* on your part to make your mark in life. To fulfil yourself in life is the most important task of all. All the more reason to get started now!

NEEDS SENSITIVITY INVENTORY

Adapted from: Michael E. Rock, Ed.D., John Miteff, M. Comm., 1982
(1992 revision, especially for Community Colleges)

Listed below are 20 statements. Read each statement and evaluate it for yourself by circling a number to the right of the statement. As you do this learning exercise, think of your day-to-day college/class situations and the degree to which the statement reflects present reality for you. The response categories are: 1 = to a **very little** extent; 2 = to a **little** extent; 3 = to **some** extent; 4 = to a **great** extent; and 5 = to a **very great** extent.

To what extent do the following statements reflect my present reality?	very little	little	some	great	very great
1. Assurance of regular classes.	1	2	3	4	5
2. Constructive feedback and recognition.	1	2	3	4	5
3. Good working relationships in class.	1	2	3	4	5
4. Clear-cut expectations from professors.	1	2	3	4	5
5. More challenging opportunities.	1	2	3	4	5
6. Only good grades.	1	2	3	4	5
7. More meaningful assignments.	1	2	3	4	5
8. Friendly relationships in class.	1	2	3	4	5
9. Individual recognition for my work.	1	2	3	4	5
10. Improved physical conditions in class.	1	2	3	4	5
11. Positive feedback from my professors.	1	2	3	4	5
12. Clean washrooms in the college.	1	2	3	4	5

13.	Harmonious relationships in class.	1 2 3 4 5
14.	Knowing where I stand with my marks.	1 2 3 4 5
15.	A sense of accomplishment in class.	1 2 3 4 5
16.	To see myself as a *self-starter*.	1 2 3 4 5
17.	Reassurance around tests or exams.	1 2 3 4 5
18.	To work well with members in class.	1 2 3 4 5
19.	To be valued by my professors.	1 2 3 4 5
20.	I *urgently* need a break.	1 2 3 4 5

Scoring: Transfer the number you circled on the *Needs Sensitivity Inventory* to the appropriate space below. Add up the numbers in each group. Then transfer the small BOXED TOTAL score to the *Needs Sensitivity Inventory Profile* (below). Follow instructions on the *Profile* sheet.

NUMBER.	SCORE	NUMBER.	SCORE	NUMBER.	SCORE
1	. . . .	3	. . . .	5	. . . .
10	. . . .	8	. . . .	7	. . . .
12	. . . .	13	. . . .	15	. . . .
20	. . . .	18	. . . .	16	. . . .
BASIC need		**SOCIAL** need		**SELF-ACTUAL-IZATION** need	

NUMBER.	SCORE	NUMBER.	SCORE
4	. . . .	2	. . . .
6	. . . .	9	. . . .
14	. . . .	11	. . . .
17	. . . .	19	. . . .
SECURITY need		**EGO** need	

Transfer your boxed numbers above to the appropriate levels below. Place a dot (•) in that space. Join all five dots with lines to give yourself your visual profile. High score indicates need is active.

	BASIC	SECURITY	BELONGING	EGO	SELF-ACTUALIZATION
20					
18					
16					
14					
12					
10					
8					
6					
4					
2					
0					

The concept of a *need hierarchy* was first advanced by W.C. Langer,[52] but it was made popular by Abraham Maslow in the 1940s,[53] even though two management authors have written, "Research has not been kind to Maslow's need hierarchy theory"[54] because studies have shown no *consistent* support for his *five* need categories but only for perhaps "two or three levels,"[55] or that workers progress up the needs hierarchical ladder systematically as Maslow claimed.[56] Instead, workers are usually only able to relate to the *distinguishing idea* of lower-order and upper-order needs.[57] Thus, there is still a controversy among psychologists over whether there is actually a hierarchy of needs.[58]

Maslow also claimed that once one need level was satisfied adequately, a person moved to the next. But, with self-actualization, it has been found that satisfaction at this level only motivates the worker for more self-actualizing activities! The implication, of course, for the supervisor is that *self-starters become more self-starting in an open and motivational environment!* Rigid, authoritarian -- what psychologist Douglas McGregor calls Theory X, or autocratic supervisors[59] -- falsely believe the opposite about workers: that if you give workers freedom, they will abuse it. True, some will. Supervisors who believe in their employees -- what McGregor calls Theory Y supervisors - will thrive in that atmosphere. It is important to know the difference between the two types of workers. The conclusion to this short discussion of Maslow is that the supervisor needs to recognize the *different or multiple needs*[60] of workers that may be operating simultaneously.[61]

People do what they do for a reason!

In spite of the controversy and research on Maslow's need hierarchy model -- which he modified as he got older into two need levels: (1) physiological/ safety and (2) self-esteem/self-actualization[62] -- most supervisory and management texts make mention of his theory because it is *intuitively* pleasing at least and has been accepted by many managers.[63] More important, however, is the fact that research does support the movement from lower-level to higher-level needs as being important to individuals.[64] We are not made for surival alone but for accomplishing greatness. Effective supervisors know how to create a motivational environment which draws out this greatness.

BRIEF NOTES ON OTHER KEY RESEARCHERS WHO GIVE ANSWERS TO *WHY* WE DO THE THINGS WE DO

B.F. SKINNER[65] said that we do things for *rewards* and *to avoid punishment*. His could be called "the carrot and stick approach": the carrot leading us when we're hungry and the stick prodding us when we're lazy.[66] Skinner built on E.L. Thorndike's 1911 "law of effect"[67] (satisfied activities will likely re-occur; uncomfortable ones will not) and J.B. Watson's 1919 theory of "behaviourism" (that thoughts and beliefs are inconsequential in understanding *why* we do what we do; rather, behaviour is best understood by observing its consequences).[68]

> **Note:** *punishment* only works in the short run, and even then is open for abuse by supervisors and probably doesn't accomplish the real objectives at all because of its side effects: sabotage, getting even, etc. Ugly examples of the use of punishment involved the giant retailer W.T. Grant that went bankrupt in 1975 with its "negative incentives" program. It was a practice (1) to cut the tie of any sales managers who did not meet quota, (2) to get a pie in the face for "bad" performance, (3) to be forced to run around the store backwards, and (4) have peanuts pushed up their noses![69]

"Yes, companies should install the latest computer, the most advanced software. But put the fanciest boxes on the desks of workers who lack commitment, and there will be few gains" -- Gedas Sakus, president, Northern Telecom Canada[71]

FREDERICK HERZBERG[70] said we do things based on whether we are *dissatisfied* or *satisfied*. However, removal of what he called our "dissatisfiers" does not necessarily lead us to be motivated. It may simply mean that we are just now *not* dissatisfied! Only "satisfiers" (such as achievement, recognition, responsibility, etc.) motivate us. Herzberg applied his theories to work environments to develop job enrichment.

DAVID McCLELLAND[72] said that we do things because of our *learned* needs for *achievement*, *affiliation* (or friendship), and *power* (or our ability to have an impact on and influence others). Research has shown that individuals who have strong needs for power tend to be supervisors who are excellent performers; even their co-workers will rank them high on leadership skills.[73]

VICTOR VROOM[74] said that we do things because of our *expectations* that something good will happen if we do such and such a thing. Behaviourism claims to set up a work situation *so that* a supervisor gets what is intended; expectancy theory claims that if workers *believe* they will fulfil a need based upon what a supervisor expects, then the supervisor gets what is intended. Behaviourism *says* that it will happen; expectancy theory *believes* that it will happen.

NURTURING A MOTIVATIONAL ENVIRONMENT

There are a number of practical things a supervisor can do to nurture a motivational environment. The situational context, of course, has to be kept in mind.

Money is one such practical matter. Although recessionary times challenge the supervisor to monitor closely financial rewards, the fact remains that money does peak employees' interest! What does research and experience say to the supervisor concerning money?

Research gives mixed reviews.[76] The real answer to the question, "Does money motivate?" is this: *It all depends.* Money means so many things to so many people, for instance. For one employee, money will motivate because it reflects an ego need, that of importance. Perhaps it's not so much the quantity of money, but the *fact* that money has been given as a recognition reward. For another employee, money may not mean as much; what really matters is job security. When most employees are concerned with having enough cash flow during a recession, the money aspect seems to take a back seat to just having a job. Union - management talks reflect this impact. While Bob White, head of the Canadian Auto Workers, says that "workers don't need unions to lead them backwards"[77] and must hold the line against management, a

"Today, when I look for managers for clients and my own staff, I look for high-impact players, change agents, drivers and winners, people who are extremely flexible, bright, tactical and strategic, who can handle a lot of information, make decisions quickly, motivate others, chase a moving target and shake things up." -- Jeffrey Christian, CEO, Christian & Timbers, Cleveland-based executive search firm[75]

"distinctly Canadian" settlement on overtime had 77 per cent of GM workers at the Oshawa, Ontario, auto plant, on a second vote, deciding to be more flexible to try to save their jobs.[78] George Peapples, GM Canada president, told the Winnipeg Chamber of Commerce, "The bottom line is that like automotive workers across all of North America, Oshawa workers will have to become more competitive if they are to retain their jobs."[70] Perhaps a more worthwhile area that supervisors can reflect on is *how* monetary rewards are given out. The supervisor needs to ask: (a) Does the money for this employee reflect actual performance? (b) Is the money rewarding what needs to be done? (c) Does the employee need higher pay? If the answers to these questions are "yes," then money can motivate.

Flexibility is another option the supervisor may need to develop to nurture a motivational environment. Having flexibility in working hours is becoming more and more a critical issue because of single parent families[80] -- usually the woman with children[81] -- and the commuting problems in big cities, and just the idea of having options can be motivating to some degree. "Some corporate employees have started to spend two or three days a week working at home, to avoid the traffic snarls and to see more of their children. Human resource experts say this trend is being fuelled by a shift in values, from the office workaholism of the 1980s to a greater emphasis on family ties in the 1990s."[82]

Reducing office space can be a major cost-reducer. Instead of continually using the layoff option as a way to reduce costs, telecommuting is become popular as a viable alternative. It is estimated that 23 per cent,[83] or anywhere from 400,000 to 3.4 million Canadians, work from their homes. This number has

A greater emphasis on family ties

SUCCESSFUL SUPERVISORS	
• Treat employees with dignity and respect • Give appropriate recognition • Develop their employees' potential • Trust their employees by delegating • Give appropriate and timely feedback • Use a collaborative supervisory style • Provide training and development • Speak to and listen to employees	• Encourage employees to try new approaches • Give clear expectations for work and rewards • Eliminate unnecessary need for threats • Nurture an ethical working environment • Demonstrate confidence and pride in their employees

grown 60 per cent over a two-year period (1990 - 91). The corporation is picking up on this as well. "Telecommuting holds the answers to a wide variety of corporate conundrums, not the least of which is the prime downtown office space, which, on some parts of the planet -- Tokyo for example -- rents for more than $200 a square foot."[84]

Accommodating home and work[85] is an option that is becoming more prevalent and is working well despite the sense of isolation[86] that some employees experience. While new technologies -- such as computers, faxes, and modems -- can often reduce the need for staff, "home offices are also being established by corporate employees who have hung on to their jobs. Instead of burning the midnight oil at the office, they're investing in home computers and working evenings at the dining-room table."[87] Selected examples of companies experimenting or utilizing the home-work connection are the federal Department of Consumer and Corporate Affairs in Ottawa, a small pilot group with IBM Canada Ltd. in Ottawa, and Royal Insurance Co. of Canada, which has most of its claims adjusters in 20 Canadian cities working from their homes.

Job enrichment takes a job, and as originator Frederick Herzberg has shown, increases the motivational elements in it. If an employee is working at a boring job, the supervisor could include more opportunities for the employee to assume more responsibility by delegating more responsibility, for instance, or by involving the employee in more planning and decision-making activities and by giving task-specific recognition and positive feedback. However, not everyone is happy with a job enrichment possibility. Some may feel that this is just a euphemistic way for management to make employees work harder and take on more stress. For example, with Northern Telecom's adoption of CIM (computer integrated manufacturing) for most of its North American plants and its aim to be #1 before the year 2000, "competing globally rather than locally,"[88] the emphasis now is worker team involvement. Donald Noble, executive vice-president, said NT is "increasing the decision-making authority of employees" and giving them "greater freedom to act and to innovate." This self-directed team approach, said David

It means rethinking the corporate culture, going from managing by authoritarianism to managing by empowering.

McCormick, manager of quality engineering at Northern Telecom's Calgary switching plant, has meant shaving "$2.10 off the average hourly cost of labour and material." What are the "challenges" though with this? It means rethinking the corporate culture, going from managing by authoritarianism to managing by empowering. "The battle is between thinking and control," according to Ms. Anna Versteeg and her very successful plant in Morrisville, N.C. But questions still remain for workers: what about the additional stress? Are workers working themselves out of jobs? Are they stressing themselves even more now?

Job enlargement, on the other hand, is another motivational possibility and means taking a job and adding a greater variety of tasks to it, redesigning the *range* and skill levels of a job, which gives employees a number of tasks to do rather than the same ones all the time. "Job enlargement ... decreases the probability of worker alienation or boredom by increasing the variety of skills each worker has to master. In its simplest form, managers increase skill variety in workers' jobs by giving workers more tasks."[89] Rover Group PLC, of London, England, is a case in point. They feel if they can't beat the Japanese they're going to join them -- in style and techniques -- just to stay competitive and in business! "In Rover's case, that means overhauling work patterns that have been in place for decades and persuading the unions to accept radical changes, including ... requiring ... workers have skills to do multiple jobs."[90] Acceptance of this approach, in Rover's case, was eased because the unions could read and understand a balance sheet!

Money

Flexibility

Home and Work

Job enrichment

Job enlargement

Job rotation

Training and Development

Job rotation is a form of job enlargement and, initially, while it does give variation to a worker's job, its motivational impact is limited. Workers could be rotated from one similar task to another every few hours to avoid the problem of boredom. Automakers and assemblyline plants, such as Motorola and Philipps, would use this technique. Resistance from unions has gradually waned since they see it is in their own best interests to accept this approach because the company can be more competitive.[91] On a managerial level, job rotation is used, for instance, at Bell Canada. Bell Canada's job rotation "program includes rotating line managers into the personnel department and personnel officers into line management positions."[92] The federal government, with its Senior Executive Management Development Program, rotates its new managers through some of the 64 departments.[93] Large organizations will also rotate their promising managers through human resource departments, and not just as observers.[94]

Training and development is an invaluable way to motivate employees. In the fast-work environments today, in our global economic competitive world, to neglect training employees is business suicide.[95] Gordon Simpson, president of Simpson Management Systems Inc., says, "The challenge has been identified. It is time to address it head on. ... The choice is to compete, to outperform other nations, to deliver superior products and services at the right price or to become an economic backwater."[96] Superior performance has certainly worked at Wal-Mart Stores Inc., the U.S.'s largest retail chain, which hopes to start up in Canada in the near future. When Sam Walton, the founder, died on April 5, 1992, he was a multi-billionaire. "But I always had confidence that as long as we did our work well and were good to our customers, there would be no limit to us."[97] Customer service was the cornerstone to his success: "Customer service became part of a Wal-Mart employee's job description."[98] Employees were known as "associates." Sam Walton's innovative philosophy and his cheerleading skills that convinced his employees to be efficient and service the customer "enabled Wal-Mart, which began with a single store in Rogers, Ark., in 1962, to ring up $43.9 billion (U.S.) in 1991 sales and dethrone Chicago-based Sears Roebuck and Co. as the largest retailer." Canadian business struggles with investing in its employees,[99] even though in 1980 it was estimated that $100 million was spent on training.[100] One company that does

> "I always had confidence that as long as we did our work well and were good to our customers, there would be no limit to us."
> -- Sam Walton, founder, Wal-Mart Stores Inc.

value, promote, and train employees is IBM Canada Ltd.[101] It invests *13* days a year in employee training, about $75,000 per employee![102] IBM is now starting to export 70,000 (!) days of teaching experience in training to its external customers, with most of the skills being "'soft' skills such as how to sponsor promotional conferences, how to co-ordinate mass mailings, or how to place effective 'cold calls' to prospective clients."[103] It considers education a profit centre! The Royal Bank's Miro Skrivanic, manager of technology training, says corporations are going with IBM because they know exactly what they're going to get.

Personally speaking:	*Speaking as a supervisor:*
☞ Develop a personal philosophy of life for yourself. Know who you are and have an ethical balance sheet.	☞ Create a motivational environment so employees will want to do what you want them to do.
☞ Know what it is that motivates you and the goals you wish to attain.	☞ Realize that employees have differences.
☞ Learn to make choices rather than simply reacting all the time.	☞ Productive employees will be satisfied employees.
☞ Develop an action plan for yourself with realistic time frames.	☞ Make sure employees have a vested interest in what they are doing.
☞ Do what you love to do.	☞ Be responsive to employees, not only in what they do, but also in how they do it.
☞ Be kind to yourself.	☞ Provide feedback, feedback, feedback.
☞ Be kind to others.	☞ Sincerely believe that employees are the best resource you have.

Answers to "What Makes For A Good Job?" (p. 185)
SUPERVISORS' ANSWERS: 1=9; 2=2; 3-10; 4=1; 5=8; 6=5; 7=7; 8=3; 9=4; 10=6
SUBORDINATES' ANSWERS: 1=4; 2=10; 3=7; 4=8; 5=6; 6=1; 7=3; 8=9; 9=2; 10=5

> ### THE PRESSURE IS ON FOR PERFORMANCE
> Linamar Machine Ltd., of Guelph, Ontario, knows this only too well. Having just won a $40-million contract on a Rockwell deal -- the only Canadian company among 20 bidders -- it sticks to its knitting: "A record of product excellence, technical ability and, of course, price."[104] At Aikenhead's Home Improvement Warehouse, a division of Molson Cos. Ltd. of Montreal, in its first store in Scarborough, Ontario, Robert Wittman, vice-president of merchandising and marketing, said, "We're looking to change the rules." Richard McDonald, a former electrician who now manages the store's electrical department, knows what changing the rules looks like: if a customer asks for help and personnel just point a finger in a direction, this is a no-no. Customers will be walked to the part of the store where their product is and have all their questions answered. If that doesn't happen, says McDonald, "Someone will probably stop you and have a word about the culture."[105]

SUMMARY

People always do what they do for a reason. This reason is known as a *motivator.*

Generally speaking, employees want to make a contribution to the company but often find lack of recognition a stumbling block to creativity and productivity.

Motivation can be defined as *the will to achieve* and is a regulatory process within each of us for need-satisfying and goal-seeking behaviour.
The basic motivational process has the following components: an *unsatisfied need* leading to the buildup of *tension* which triggers *drives* which seek *release.* When the *goal* has been *attained*, the *need satisfied*, there is then a *reduction of tension* temporarily, or until the next time.

Employees rank *appreciation for work done* as the highest on their list for what they want from their jobs.

Productivity is measured by one's performance which is the result of one's ability, effort, and opportunity.

A key person who attempted to answer the question of why we do the things we do is Abraham Maslow with his hierarchy of needs.

Other key people who have tried to answer the why question include B.F. Skinner (rewards and punishments), Frederick Herzberg (satisfaction *vs.* dissatisfaction), David McCLelland (achievement, friendship, power), and Victor Vroom (expectations).

Redesigning jobs can often motivate employees. Key considerations for the supervisor are: money, flexibility, accommodating work and home, job enrichment, job enlargement, job rotation, and training and development.

TERMS/CONCEPTS

motivation

hierarchy of needs

motivational process

empowerment

performance

corporate governance

MBWA

punishment

money

flexibility

home and work

job enrichment

job enlargement

job rotation

training and development

DISCUSSION QUESTIONS

1. What does it mean when it is said that people always do something for a reason?

2. Think of a personal need you have. Using the basic motivational process model (p. 182), diagram and explain how your need could be satisfied.

3. Describe what performance is all about.

4. Your friend has been promoted to supervisor. He/she comes to you and says, "I don't know much about supervising, but the money's good, so I took it." What would you tell your friend?

5. Identify three theories of motivation and their basic philosophy.

6. *"Punishment* only works in the short run." Discuss.

7. What are some practical things a supervisor can do to nurture a motivational environment?

8. In you own words, what impact will the *home - work* motivational option have for the future of the Canadian work environment?

9. What is the difference between job enrichment, job enlargement, and job rotation?

10. "A supervisor cannot motivate, only provide a motivational environment." Discuss.

ASSIGNMENT

Instructions: (1) In the box below describe the "best" job that you have had to date. Identify the industry, the time frame, the context, and the content of the job.

| |
| |
| |
| |
| |
| |
| |
| |
| |
| |

(2) Form small groups. Discuss your "best" job with group participants, and then isolate those factors that made it a "best" job. For example, a factor could be "money" or "responsibility," etc. When you have finished be prepared to present your group's findings to the class.

FACTORS INVOLVED IN A "BEST" JOB	
1.	6.
2.	7.
3.	8.
4.	9.
5.	10.

CHAPTER NINE

LEADING AND CHAMPIONING TEAMWORK

The Bitterness of poor quality remains long after the sweetness of Low Price is Forgotten.

-- Wall sign, Print Three shop[1]

LEARNING OBJECTIVES

At the end of this chapter, students will be able to:

- Describe the difference between leading and managing
- Identify managerial elements of success and failure
- Discuss how assumptions influence leadership
- Describe the Leadership Climate Model
- List the key elements of power
- Describe elements of effective teamwork
- Explain transformational leadership

Opening scenario

One of the most significant examples of the critical importance of teamwork involves the decision whether to keep open GM's Oshawa, Ontario, auto plant or close it down. Gary McCullough, car plant manager, said GM in Detroit was looking for what they called *responsiveness* -- "a team of workers and managers that is willing to become steadily more productive while meeting daily schedules."[2] One thing was for sure: "Real change is needed and it's needed quickly," said GM Canada president George Peapples to the Winnipeg Chamber of Commerce. "It's not a situation where we're asking for concessions. What we're asking for is an attempt to design a new working relationship."

Teamwork at the Schneider Corp. plant in Kitchener, Ontario, did bring a real turnaround in 1991 with an operating profit of 4% in 1991 compared to the 2.5% in 1990![3] At the Crayola crayon plant in Lindsay, Ontario, they adopted "high-velocity manufacturing" for their winning formula which allowed for a quick response to customer orders and a 22% increase in profits in 1991. Customer service (in addition to new products and some price cuts) had done it again![4]

Leadership, then, posits a constructive vision of who and what we can be. Effective leaders, in business as elsewhere, mobilize the focus for vision for those around them, stimulatee the imagination in others, and in that way promote the human. Effective leaders also know how to wait. Timing is everything. Albert Einstein once said that he knew why there were so many people who loved chopping wood; in this activity they could immediately see the results![5]

Abitibi-Price Inc.'s "last stand"[6] has CEO Ron Obedlander harnessing "a new spirit of teamwork to turn its paper mills into money mills." His method? The religion of management and people. "He wants to persuade 24,000 Abitibi employees to believe in themselves, in their work, in their company."[7] To implement his vision he has created a new position: senior vice-president of organizational leadership and innovation with Jean-Claude Casavant at the helm. Casavant says, "Our future depends on our attitude and our ability to do things better."[8]

THE DIFFERENCE BETWEEN LEADING AND MANAGING

Leaders and managers are different.[9] The qualities for each can exist in one person, but they are two different, and necessary, groups of elements for any business. As the first level of management, supervisors need to realize that in addition to being "operational," if they want to be leaders as well they also need to be "visionary."

Through the use of what is called employee "empowerment"[10] or "ownership" by employees of what they do, Amdahl Canada, the computer company, is making a difference. Ronald Smith, the president, said, "The difference now ... is that it became their own idea." At Levi Strauss & Co. (Canada) Inc., workers are willingly taking pay cuts in return for greater responsibility; and Alan Torrie, president of MDS Laboratories Canada, painted a similar picture when he said, "In the midst of change we can't offer security, but we can assure people we will give them choices. ... The best you can offer these days is no surprises, fair treatment and respect. ... We try to provide enough information to allow them self-determination."

One writer's image of the *manager* is the following: "Managers are positive, action-oriented people. An employer's job is to give them a positive, supportive environment that can help them do their best in bad times as well as in good."[12] Problems that bother many managers include not being challenged sufficiently, inadequate autonomy, lack of constructive feedback, rewards and compensation that don't fit, insufficient information about company decisions, and little involvement in strategic planning, instead, in these recessionary times, they were burdened mainly with "putting out fires."

"Nowadays when the idea of a community of mankind is triumphing, creating a world without frontiers or walls, I appeal to you knock down the last wall - the wall of indifference." -- former Soviet foreign minister, Edward Shevardnadze[11]

Warren Bennis says *leaders*, on the other hand, share some common characteristics: a guiding vision, passion, integrity, trust, curiosity, and daring.[13] He makes an interesting distinction between leaders and managers when he says, "I tend to think of the differences between leaders and managers as the differences between those who master the context and those who surrender to it."[14] In other words, the leader looks at the forest, the manager looks at the trees! Both are needed, and some companies need the emphasis differently, depending on their circumstances and situation. The positive side of the supervisor-manager, in this understanding, is the ability to do the "nuts and bolts" of the job, with the down side being, of course, getting too caught up in the details, developing "tunnel vision," and missing the forest for the trees.

The supervisor-leader, on the other hand, has the ability to grasp "the big picture," to look down the road, to exploit crisis and complex situations, with the down side being, of course, becoming too uninvolved in the day-to-day operations, bypassing the important facts and details, and missing the trees for the forest! "Those without vision and perspective are equally lacking in an essential leadership trait as those who can't get things done. Being unable to see the forest for the trees and being unable to trim the trees for the forest are equally damaging limitations."[15]

Reflective Exercise

Which image most appeals to you?

- BASE of the mountain? ⟶ ▢

- SUMMIT of the mountain? ⟶ ▢

If you chose *base*, your preference may be toward *managing*; if you chose *summit*, your preference may be more toward *leading*. The point to remember is that "balanced and integrated" organizations are the ideal because "they value management, leadership, and the variations in between."[16] In the balanced and integrated organization, differences are recognized, valued, cherished, and worked with. The hands-on supervisor-manager learns to work with the more intuitive supervisor-manager. Neither one has the truth, but *gauges whether, in this particular situation or environment*, one approach may be more appropriate or effective than the other.[17]

MANAGERIAL ELEMENTS OF SUCCESS AND FAILURE

The Centre for Creative Leadership in Greensboro, North Carolina, has identified key clues for managerial success or failure.[19] In studying differences between 20 successful and 21 derailed managers, in spite of the fact that both groups had made sacrifices along the way, had good career pedigrees and excellent technical skills, successful managers had superb interpersonal skills, were good negotiators, comported themselves gracefully and with poise under stress, had a good sense of humour, took responsibility for mistakes, and were conceptually strong in focusing on problems to solve them, whereas the derailed executives' biggest flaw was their *insensitivity to people*. The lack of good people skills was the downfall of 75 per cent of the derailed managers! The "fatal flaws" in the managers' leadership profile that the study uncovered included: "aloofness, arrogance, betrayal of trust, abrasiveness, rebelliousness and overmanaging. The ability to understand other people's perspectives marked the difference between those who fulfilled their early potential and those who didn't."[20]

> "In the new world order, the most important key to our success - as a nation -- lies in the skills, knowledge and talents of people -- our work force. Indeed, in the information age, brainpower will be the premium commodity."[18]

In another study, with 44 service sector managers, "effective" managers communicated well and spent their time on human resource management: motivating, training, and managing conflict whereas what were called "successful" managers spent most of their time politicking and interacting with others.[21]

To state it once again: business and society need individuals who can manage and lead, individuals who can take care of the nuts-and-bolts of business and individuals who can envision a future not in existence. But success and effectiveness still rely on the key skill identified in chapters 1 and 7: the human dimension or people skills or sensitivity to relationships. CEO Lawrence A. Weinbach, of Chicago-based Arthur Andersen & Co., an executive development company, says, "Pure technical knowledge is only going to get you to a point. Beyond that, interpersonal skills become critical."[22]

"No matter how charismatic, visionary, brilliant, daring, competent or creative they are, leaders are human; they all have flaws. If not recognized and corrected, some of these flaws may precipitate dramatic downfalls. Ambitious people who don't deal with interpersonal blind spots may crash and burn on their way to the executive suite -- or after they arrive."[23]

While managers are "operational," tending to the day-to-day activities and functions of the organization, leaders are "visionary," carving out a niche, envisioning a strategic alliance or partnership, and generally going where the organization has not gone before. The deal that Quebec-based Bombardier made in buying de Havilland is a good example of visionary "niche-making": the acquisition has now made it possible to have a "totally integrated industry."[24] Married couple Kishore Sakhrani and Elizabeth Thomson, with their company ICS International, also found a niche by initially helping companies gain tax benefits by incorporating overseas, but are now expanding into trade services to represent overseas companies doing business in Asia by arranging their trade finance packages.[25] Finally, Dr. Ronald Colapinto found a business niche, because of a provincial billing quirk, in opening up his "personal" clinic *vs.* the hospital setting he had worked in for years. He said, "In the hospital I was doing what everyone else was. The patient was just an arm and a leg you had to work on, it wasn't personal at all. Here you have to speak to the patients, often meet them several times, both them and their families. My work here is much more like what a family doctor does and I enjoy that very much. And I think there should be more of it in hospitals but they are too big, too impersonal."[26]

Thomas Watson, Jr., founder of IBM, said that "the real difference between success and failure in a corporation can very often be traced to the question of how well the organization brings out the great energies and talents of its people."[27] A leader is also a protector of values for the organization and "fails when it concentrates on sheer survival. Institutional survival ... is a matter of maintaining values and a distinctive identity."[28] Lest we forget, we are reminded, "So it is at once attention to ideas and attention to detail."[29] The vision and and the practical must go hand-in-hand. Vision without substance is simply fantasy, and structure without vision is blind. Effective organizations and supervisors know the difference.

VALUES[30]

A Personal Vision for a Preferred Future
by
Stephen E. Quinlan, president
Seneca College, Toronto, Ontario

In the decade of the nineties, Seneca College will commit itself to a philosophy and method of operation which fosters and promotes access, excellence, and personal achievement by adherence to the following principles:

☐ Quality teaching and active learning will be the heart and soul of Seneca College. The collective efforts of all employees will be concentrated to ensure that student success becomes our most important objective;

☐ In recognition of the vital role that employees play in ensuring successful student outcomes, principles of employee empowerment, decentralization, and local autonomy will govern our organizational structures;

☐ The goals of the College shall at all times unselfishly include opportunities for the unskilled, underemployed, and those who have been or are facing layoff to upgrade and retrain in a discipline where opportunity and job potential is apparent;

☐ By example, by practice and through curriculum, the College will commit itself to promoting racial tolerance, employment and educational equity, and harmony between and amongst stakeholder groups, while at all times respecting individual dignity, worth, and well-being;

☐ Subjects and courses that are considered vital to the future well-being of our nation and contribute to the growth and development of our community will be offered on at least one College campus, provided that they can be offered in a cost efficient/cost effective manner;

☐ The College will act in a fiscally responsible and prudent manner, and at all times stand accountable to its community for its actions;

☐ In respect of future generations, the College will assume a leadership role in efforts to protect and restore the environment of all living things;

☐ In recognition of the need for strong bonds to employers, active advisory committees and meaningful partnerships will be established for all programs.

HOW ASSUMPTIONS INFLUENCE LEADERSHIP STYLE

Theory X and Theory Y are two frameworks of human behaviour that researcher Douglas McGregor identified to highlight how our underlying assumptions about human nature influence our approach to leadership.[31]

The type of elevator-style music piped through to the public facilities of the Valhalla Inn Markham was an annoyance to one of the restaurant servers. The general manager invited the employee to visit the supplier's audio library and select the music style most suitable for the hotel. "I was convinced that the staff member knew more about the average guest's taste than I did," said the hotel's general manager. "She appeared delighted to be the catalyst in making an important decision for the hotel."

Theory X assumptions look at more of the negative side of the human experience in relation to work and say that the average worker is lazy, dislikes work, avoids responsibility, and has to be pushed. Theory Y assumptions look at the brighter side of the human experience in relation to work and say the average worker is eager to work, has self-control, is willing to learn, seeks responsibility, and in contemporary work organizations has been underutilized.[32]

A further extrapolation of McGregor's Theory Y is Louis A. Allen's Theory M.[33] The key word in this theory is *some*, that is, *some* employees are lazy, *some* are self-centred, and *some* are irresponsible and need to be pushed. On the other hand, *some* employees are eager, *some* want to take on more responsibility, and *some* employees are ambitious and want to be leaders; "the majority fall somewhere in between."

Assumptions such as those outlined in Theories X, Y, and M influence a supervisor's leadership style. A Theory X supervisor will be more autocratic and, in the worst of situations, be abusive and a bully with employees. Morale will be low; absenteeism will be high. Toronto's department of public works suggests this pattern, with an absenteeism rate of 30.4 per cent in 1991 for its 761 unionized employees.[34]

It's important that supervisors reflect on their own assumptions so that they get the results they want from their workers. A Theory X style is not wrong all the time, only when it promotes abusive and dysfunctional consequences or when employees are capable of doing their work and need little tracking. In a situation where employees need guidance, however, when there's a lot of uncertainty, where competency is low, an autocratic or directive style is appropriate, and employees will flower under this style because they will feel secure, protected, and directed. On the other hand, a Theory Y style can become dysfunctional and inappropriate when employees are floundering and the supervisor provides little input and resources, but leaves employees on their own. It is appropriate, though, when employees are competent in their work, and harmonious in their team relationships. A Theory M supervisor will weigh the leadership climate factors -- and use a more directive style of supervision if employees need direction, and give infrequent supervisory input if employees are competent and know what they doing.

DIFFERENT APPROACHES TO LEADERSHIP

For many years it was assumed that leaders were of a certain ilk, had certain traits or characteristics. For instance, what was called *The Great Man* or trait theory[37] described what some believed about leaders: leaders were honest, intelligent, social, achievers, initiators and task-oriented. People who had these "traits" were prime candidates to be leaders! The late Sam Walton, who built the Wal-Mart empire, would be considered a good example of this trait approach.[38] Tom Monaghan, founder of the Domino pizza empire, is another example.[39] In a research study conducted by Judith B. Rosener, Ph.D., at the University of California, Irvine, she discovered that women have "dramatically different leadership traits from those of men"[40] and suggests that this woman's approach may be the leadership style of the future. What exactly is happening? She says that the male model of hierarchy and control is not necessarily better or worse than the female model, but it is certainly getting to look old-fashioned, antiquated and often unmanageable. "Female executives, the study concludes, tend to lead in non-traditional ways: by sharing information and power. They inspire good work by interacting with others, by encouraging employee participation, and by showing how employees' personal goals can be reached as they meet organizational goals."

"It's no longer enough to be hewers of wood and drawers of water ... We rely too much on selling logs and not enough on cutting them to meet the demanding specifications of foreign markets." - Frank McKenna, Liberal Premier, New Brunswick[35]

— — — — — —

"From now on we must demand an answer to a very fundamental question: Is this economic proposal or that social program, or this business initiative or that labour demand more or less likely to improve our competitive position in the world. If the answer is that it's likely to worsen it, we should not do it. Period." - - Matthew Barrett, Bank of Montreal Chairman[36]

Over the last forty years, study and research has been on-going in relation to leadership. Of special note are the Michigan studies,[41] which described an *employee-centred* and a *production-centred* supervisor, and the Ohio State University studies, which described supervisor/leader behaviour as high in *consideration* (or the relationship dimension) and high in *initiating structure* (or the task dimension). A spin-off of this research has been the very popular and successful *situational leadership* model by Paul Hersey and Kenneth Blanchard.[42] For them, a supervisor's leadership style is influenced by the leader (who she is, what his personal strengths are, what her capabilities are as a person, etc.), the situation itself (its context) and the people (employee(s), group) the supervisor will lead. This model is intuitively and practically invaluable for any supervisor -- or teacher or parent!

The Rock-Miteff *Leadership Climate Model*[43] and discussion (next page) is a composite of the leadership research and experience, and portrays a simple scale that supervisors can follow in managing an employee or group.

SUPERVISOR - EMPLOYEE INTERFACE:[44]
Managing those you supervise

Common sense and research both show that we usually need to provide different strokes for different folks, that is, that every relationship is different, and each person in our charge has different needs and abilities and degrees of willingness. Employees know what should be done in a situation, but the truth of the matter is that they sometimes do not accept the situation for what it is. No change happens without an act of acceptance.

Two key ingredients in a situation are understanding and acceptance. The Rock-Miteff Leadership Climate Model does not minimize the superior's commitment to being part of a process of managing subordinates. As a matter of fact, it highlights the responsibility of the supervisor even more and gives the path and rationale to manage each individual or group based on the *climate* the supervisor is able to ascertain. The supervisor's job is to decide to be part of the process. The decision itself goes a long way towards helping supervisors accept the differences in the relationships they have to manage.

BUILDING THE MODEL: THE *WHAT*

The primary work responsibility of any subordinate is the work that needs to be done. Work accomplishes *strategic goals* that a supervisor has developed and answers the question: *what* is it that we have to do? But in relation to that work, there are specific *climate* elements that influence its accomplishment. For instance, doing something "well" will often mean different things in different situations and with different employees. This situational variety requires that supervisors supervise in specific ways.

BUILDING THE MODEL: THE *HOW*

Thus, a second key ingredient is the *climate* a supervisor must foster if work is to be done effectively. A healthy work environment accomplishes *climate goals* that a supervisor has developed and answers the question: *how* will employees do what they need to do? Supervisors not only manage some*thing* but also some*one*. What should that look like? Does a supervisor relate to every employee the same way in their work? Or must the supervisor pay attention to other factors as well? The main priority is to establish at least quality relationships, irrespective of the amount of supervisory leadership needed.

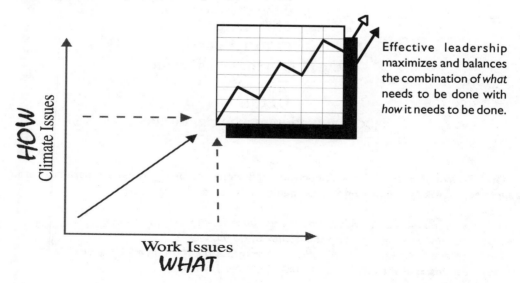

Effective leadership maximizes and balances the combination of *what* needs to be done with *how* it needs to be done.

ADDITIONAL CONSIDERATIONS

Effective leadership, therefore, depends on *how* a supervisor manages *what* needs to be done. An additional consideration that is very important is the *competency* of the employee or group the supervisor is managing. Competency refers to an employee's *ability* to do the work, *knowledge* of the work, *background and experience* to do the work, and *responsiveness* to doing the work. Effective supervisors also know that each employee has different levels of competency. Knowing the situational climate can often help the supervisor avoid anger because an employee will or will not do a particular thing. Many of us get angry when someone under our care does not follow through, especially if this not following through is a repetitive pattern. Supervisors may understand why a subordinate is not following through, but unless they are also willing to *accept* the situation as it is to begin with, they will only end up blaming the employee. A more mature posture is to (1) know what's going on (*understanding*), (2) accept that it is happening (*acceptance*), and (3) decide on ways to manage the employee to do the job more effectively (*decision*).

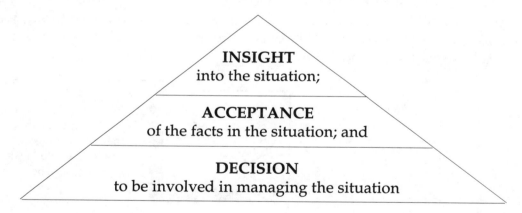

INSIGHT
into the situation;

ACCEPTANCE
of the facts in the situation; and

DECISION
to be involved in managing the situation

When a supervisor asks, "How *competent* is *this* employee or group on *this* particular *task?*" the supervisor is asking and making a quick mental diagnosis of the following:

• What is *this* employee's (group's) **knowledge base** for *this* particular work?
• Does *this* employee (group) have the **ability** to do *this* work?
• Does *this* employee (group) have sufficient **background experience** for *this* work? and
• How **responsive** is the employee (group) to doing *this* work?

All four questions need to be asked to make an informed diagnosis because the answers to these four questions will give the supervisor a fix on the competency level of the person (or group) doing *a particular* work assignment. Of course, the more experience a supervisor has in asking these questions in a situation, the more accurate the diagnosis should become.

To be effective, therefore, means that a supervisor not only wants to get the job done, but is also concerned with how the job gets done. There is a difference between success and effectiveness: success is attaining your goal; effectiveness is how you attain your goal. If you start out from point A and want to get to point B, and you actually do arrive at point B, then you are successful. How effective you are is another matter. If you created interpersonal havoc on the way to attaining your goal, you were successful, but you were definitely not effective! Many organizations mistake this important distinction. In their efforts to meet the "bottom line" (i.e., to be successful), they sometimes do it in a very self-defeating and destructive way for themselves and their employees. The results of being successful can often, ironically, create employee morale problems, tardiness, absenteeism, lying, theft, alcoholism, and a workplace that is not too pleasant to work in. This is the foolishness of supervisors who think that all that matters is success. Not only does the work environment suffer, but often many home situations as well. This poses a real ethical concern then for the supervisor: success *vs.* effectiveness. A supervisor can be successful but not effective; but to be effective, a supervisor will necessarily be successful! Problems at work are often ventilated in a negative way in the home. Spouse, children (and dog) suffer. It doesn't have to be that way. Managers, teachers, and parents can learn how to "grow up" and become effective. If one is effective, one is also successful. But success does not necessarily mean that one is effective. This is a major point. Effectiveness, in the final analysis, is the

At a meeting of restaurant staff at the Valhalla Inn Markham, the hotel's general manager requested the attendees to detail any challenges which had not been addressed to date. One employee suggested that the restaurant shouldn't open so early on the weekends. Amused laughter followed from her co-workers. When asked why she was making the recommendation, the employee indicated that results had shown that few, if any, guests eat breakfast at such an early hour. The result of one person's clear-thinking view? The restaurant opened a half hour later each weekend, saving the hotel thousands of dollars a year in labour costs.

net result of how insightfully the supervisor can answer the question, "How do I assess *this* situation in such a way that I can weave together the proper emphasis on *what* needs to be done with *how* it is to be done?"

Effective supervisors experience more and more satisfaction in the quality of their work. To be effective demands hard work and a commitment to follow through. For supervisors to expect each time that because they *say* that something must be done, it *will* necessarily be done, is naive. Life does not work that way. To be human is to err. Supervisors must learn to cope with employees who do make mistakes, who are often not responsive to doing work, but must be supervised so that they become more competent employees.

SITUATIONAL CLIMATE

Once we have the constituent elements in a leadership situation, a supervisor must choose a style of intervention that will best get the results wanted. Listed on the next page is the Rock-Miteff Leadership Diagnostic Chart model that provides a visual aid in understanding the different styles. It is called *climate* because a supervisor's leadership posture in any situation sets a tone, a psychological breathing environment. If the climate is polluted, employees won't be able to breathe; if there is clean air, the possibility for effective work is greatly enhanced. Supervisors may have all the techniques, and know all the theory, but if they cannot set a positive, growth-filled climate, then it is not of much use.

As the *competency barometer* goes up for the individual or group, the level of supervision goes down, until finally, when employees (or groups) are sufficiently competent and can do the job on their own, there is minimum supervision, precisely because they can take care of themselves without outside help. Seasoned employees don't require the same monitoring that new employees require. However well-intentioned supervisors might be in getting involved in the details of the work, seasoned employees will find this an interference. By the same token, if supervisors misjudge the situation and assume that an employee is highly competent in a certain line of work, and the employee isn't, this will create anxiety and concern because the employee will experience no direction.

SITUATIONAL STYLES:
An Explanation

Simply put, if an employee is low in competency on a task, the safest bet is for the supervisor to **DIRECT** the employee. This doesn't mean that the leader-supervisor has to act like a tyrant. Direction can be given firmly and precisely without tearing a strip off the employee. **Style #1 -- DIRECT**: placing a high emphasis on the job being done and a low emphasis on relationship contact, not because a supervisor doesn't care about the employee, but rather, that the work takes priority at this point in time.

When the employee begins to acquire facility with the task, to keep on directing will simply be more of a hindrance. Therefore, a supervisor's best bet now is to use **Style #2 - INVOLVE**: listen to suggestions, make recommend-

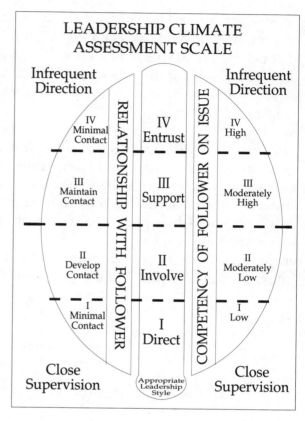

LEADERSHIP CLIMATE ASSESSMENT SCALE

ations, and begin to initiate a more open concern for the interpersonal relationship dimension. The supervisor still does not back off the task, but begins to develop the first overt steps to relationship contact. **Style #2 -- INVOLVE** -- places a high emphasis on the job being done but also the moderately low level beginnings of relationship contact. The assessment reads that employees are learning the job well, and beginning to work together - hence a moderately low to moderately high level of competency will occur at this level. The supervisor might also realize that some employees may never be able to move much higher on the competency scale than this and will need to accept them as they are. Even though competency on *this* work will not go higher, positive relationships are still ethically required.

In the next stage, the employee or group has matured and become competent in their work. The supervisor must now back off directing or being involved and simply use **Style #3 -- SUPPORT**: telling the individual or group that the supervisor is there for them, and that the quality of human relations is very important. The employees know that they are self-starters as far as their work is concerned, and this in itself is a very positive stroke. Thus, **Style #3 -- SUPPORT** -- recommends low emphasis on the work (because the employee or group knows how to do the job) but moderately high emphasis on relationship contact.

Finally, when the supervisor realizes that the employee knows the work quite well and is able to work on his/her own, then **Style #4 -- ENTRUST** -- is needed: simply delegate the work. If a group of employees is involved, the supervisor will assess, not only their competency level, but also *how* well they work together (their human relations dimension). Thus, with **Style #4** there is low emphasis on the work and low emphasis on relationships because the employees know how to do their work (the *what*), and they work well together (the *how*). Listed below is a diagram outlining the process:

			WHAT (the *work*)	HOW (work *relations*)
	HIGH	THEN	—	—
If competency for the work is ...	MODERATE	THEN	+	+
	LOW	THEN	+	—

— means *de-emphasize*
+ means *emphasize*

RESPONSIVENESS -- AN IMPORTANT KEY

Common sense tells us that this model is not only intuitively accurate, but also practically useful. However, its simplicity is also really only on paper. With live human beings in a work situation, supervisors must make the best *judgment calls* they can each and every time.

Working this model will often demand patience, commitment, and follow-through. Otherwise, we simply give up or lose interest ourselves because we're too tired, or under stress, or we simply don't like the person or group very well.

Perhaps the most trying component to deal with at times is the employee's lack of responsiveness in doing the work. When employees are unwilling to do the work -- even though they are work-competent -- the supervisor has to actually get *involved*. These are moments in supervisory dynamics when *maturity* -- what could be described practically as *the ability to accept what we **don't** like*[45] -- is most aptly tested and refined. If unresponsiveness occurs at any of the stages, the supervisor must first examine what is happening -- make a situational diagnostic -- and, if necessary, to take action. Unresponsiveness on the part of employees when they are *low or moderately low* on work-competency is managed by the supervisor focusing in more deliberately on **what** needs to be done, and de-emphasizing relationship contact. When employees are fairly competent in what they are doing, and there is an emerging responsiveness, the supervisor's best strategy is to focus in on the employee work relationships. If this intervention or team-building suggestions do not help, then the supervisor has no alternative but to de-emphasize relationships and re-emphasise the work that needs to be done.

LONGEVITY AS A RESULT OF TEAMWORK?[46]
In 1960, Japanese men had a life expectancy of 65 years. In 1970, they were tied with Canadian men at 69. But since then Japanese working men have been #1 in living longest -- at 75 years in 1986! Canada is still only 73 years, still ahead of the U.S., Britain, and France. How do the Japanese do it? "No one can be sure how Japan did it, but its fabled industrial job patterns seem to fit the social-envelope theories. Factory workers are organized in teams, they work together, each feels support from the others."

KNOW THE KEY ELEMENTS OF POWER

For some people, *power* is a dirty word. But it need not be. In a supervisory context, it is the ability to influence employees to meet personal and organizational objectives. In the discussion on office politics, we saw that a newborn baby wields incredible power -- enough to turn around a 747 jumbo jet, and its passengers after take-off!

There are a number of ways to look at power and its application.[47] A supervisor, being in a leadership role, has two *sources* of power at his/her disposal, one organizational (position power), the other, individual (personal power):

Position power gives the supervisor (a) the power to *reward*, or use intrinsic and extrinsic rewards to control employees; (b) the power to *coerce*, or deny rewards and administer punishments to control people; and (c) *legitimate* power by formal management to position him/herself as authentically responsible for what goes on.

Personal power allows the supervisor (a) to employ *expert* power by way of any special knowledge or skill or experience as a means to control employee's behaviour because they have need of that knowledge, skill, or experience; and (b) to capitalize on *referent* power, or the need employees have to identify with a supervisory personality they admire and respect.

AN ETHICAL DILEMMA

Some supervisors may try to meet organizational objectives with only position power. In other words, lacking personal power (no expert power because they might be the boss' adult-child (i.e., a dysfunctional relationship), and possess no referent power because employees don't identify and respect the supervisor), some supervisors wield power and try to be influential by using their position power status only: (a) "You'll have that promotion, if you join me for dinner after work!" (reward power to justify compliance in a sexual harassment situation); (b) "You'll do this, or else!" (coercive power); and (c) "I'm the boss and that's why!" (legitimate power).

Clearly, these are unethical situations in which position power is used to manipulate, intimidate, and subordinate! Supervisors have to examine if they are falling into these ethical traps. Since the only power an organization gives a supervisor is legitimate power, that is, the *right* to supervise in *this* situation, with *these* employees, with *these* constraints and objectives, the supervisor needs to quickly understand how important the informal organization is for increasing an ethical and respected power base in the organization. Again, much of the real power supervisors have has its source in "the eye of the beholder," that is, supervisors may have legitimate or formal position power, but if they are perceived by employees as incompetent (no expert power), as puppets of management (no true reward power), and as "dimwits" (no referent power), then the task of supervising will be stressful and the benefit of being effectively supervised will be lost.

THE RELATIONSHIP POWER LINE

The following model of the Power Line describes a view of power within relationships:

It has been demonstrated by stress medical doctor Hans Seyle that when people respond to danger, as with animals, their bodies go into a fight - flight mode: ready to flee if the danger is too great, ready to fight if warranted. Seyle also pointed out that sickness occurs when this fight - flight dynamic is always at high tension, that is, a person is always in flight mode, or always in fight mode. It's the balance that counts.

In interpersonal relationships it is the same thing. When stress or anxiety or insecurity develeops in a relationship, individuals have three options: (1) *solve* the relationship problem, (2) take *flight* from the relationship, and (3) *fight* the relationship.

Mode #1 -- Solve the relationship problem: With this approach, a supervisor would be using ***POWER FOR* ...** task accomplishment, sorting out issues, addressing concerns, anticipating problems, etc. Included in this approach are often the necessary skills of speaking and listening.

Mode #2 -- Take flight from the relationship: With this approach, a supervisor would be using ***POWER OVER ... SELF***, that is, taking that very same power and energy that could solve the problem and internalizing the problem such that he/she withdraws, avoids, keeps distance, feels depressed, and blames him/herself for the problem, saying, "I always screw up!" Obviously, this is not an effective approach in using power. "Flight supervisors" use a **TURTLE** style of supervision.

Money talks and, therefore, money and power go hand in hand. Often it is not a money problem per se, but rather, a power problem!

Mode #3 -- Fight the relationship: With this approach, a supervisor would be using *POWER OVER ... OTHERS*, that is, taking the very same power and energy that could solve the problem but externalizing the problem by judging and blaming others, accusing them and projecting anger and frustration only at them, denying any responsibility, and in effect saying, "It's always YOU who screw up!" Obviously, this is not an effective approach in using power. "Fight supervisors" use a **SKUNK** style of supervision.

KEY ELEMENTS OF EFFECTIVE TEAMWORK[48]

Teams consist of two or more employees "who interact and co-ordinate their work to accomplish a specific objective."[49] The Japanese turnaround at Ontario's Mitsubishi Midland plant provides a good example of supervisors utilizing effective teams in a Canadian environment.[50] Organizations such as Chrysler Corp., Digital Equipment Corp., Microsoft Corp., and MICA Management Resources Inc. say teamwork will be the work style of the future.

"In the end, it's the people that make the difference. In a pitch like this, when all the agencies are good, what is going to take it over the top is the passion and the enthusiasm of the people." -- Ian Seville, vice-president, Cossette-Communication Ltd.

The work world is too complicated for any one single individual to master.[51] "Perhaps the most important function of work groups is that they provide a means for accomplishing complex jobs beyond the capacity of any single individual."[52] This is the synergy principle in business: the whole is greater than the individual parts by themselves. When McDonald's was looking to spiff up its image, it dropped its old agency of 12 years, Vickers & Benson Advertising Ltd., and gave the $10 million account to Cossette-Communication Ltd. because it was impressed by "the credentials of its agency and staff -- the 'synergy and chemistry. We were looking for a fit,' Mr. [Gary] Reinblatt [McDonald's senior vice-president and national director of marketing] says."[53] Cossette's vice-president, Ian Seville, said, "In the end, it's the people that make the difference. ... In a pitch like this, when all the agencies are good, what is going to take it over the top is the passion and the enthusiasm of the people."

"The simple fact is that times -- and people -- have changed."[54] Pillsbury Canada Ltd. has capitalized on this new mood. Realizing that employees are their greatest asset, they have also seen that treating employees well benefits the corporation. Donald Maldeis, a union man and mixer at Pillsbury's Midland, Ontario, plant, is also a convert. He readily admits that employee relations have improved dramatically through the use of the company "people focus" and teams. At Campbell Soup Company Ltd., the team concept has caught on as well. According to Peter Barkla, vice-president of human resources, supervisors are more like coaches or leaders.

Research shows that team effectiveness consists of productive output and personal satisfaction.[55] Team cohesiveness consists of team interaction, shared goals, and shared values. Team members need to get to know one another; they need a common objective, and they need to be able to identify with and share similar values and attitudes. A work team, as a whole, develops excellent cohesiveness also if it is in competition with another group, if it experiences success, and if outside evaluation gives it favourable ratings.[56] This schema of team elements is quite understandable if one studies a sports team.

Organizational benefits of teams include the unleashing of enormous energy in employees, the fulfilling of employees' needs for belonging, the expansion of job knowledge and skills, and the increased flexibility to the organization.[57] Teams also have costs: supervisors will have to relinquish some of their power. Insecure or status-conscious supervisors will feel threatened by the team concept, or the self-managing team. J.E. (Ted) Newall, the former chairman and chief executive officer of Du Pont Canada, Inc., who assumed the new duties of president and chief executive officer of Calgary-based Nova Corp. in September 1991, made a difference when he taught managers to create a climate where the talents, energies, and imagination of employees were unleashed and self-management became the norm for everyone. For him, business excellence and people excellence went hand-in-hand and could not exist without each other.[58]

Create a climate where the talents, energies, and imagination of employees are unleashed and self-management becomes the norm for everyone.

TRANSFORMATIONAL LEADERSHIP

Transformational leaders are able to inspire employees with a vision they look forward to embracing, provide a corporate value system that employees willingly adhere to, and establish mutual trust with employees.[59] Transformational leaders create vision, mobilize commitment, and institutionalize change.[60] The traditional transactional supervisor/manager is distinguished from the emerging transformational supervisor by the following characteristics: they are self-confident in their abilities and judgments; they have a vision about where they want to take their company; they are passionate about their vision; they behave in unconventional ways; and they are catalysts for changing the status quo.[61] Anthony Eames, president of Coca-Cola Canada Ltd., is another example of the transformational leader.[62] No one can remain indifferent to transformational leaders: they arouse emotions! They transform employees' expectations so that employees do more that they thought possible.

SUMMARY

Leading is different from managing. Managers are "operational" and manage the day-to-day details. Leaders are "visionary" and attempt to grasp "the big picture."

Insensitivity to people is the major stumbling block for supervisory success.

Theory X and Theory Y assumptions about people influence supervisory styles.

The Rock-Miteff *Leadership Climate Model* approach to leadership discusses the *work* to be done, the kind of *human relations contact* appropriate with employees, and the *competency* and *responsiveness* of employees to get work done. An appropriate mixture and balance of these variables leads to effectiveness.

Power can be both positional (reward and legitimate) and personal (expert and referent).

The Relationship Power Line helps us examine our power. Do we use *power for* solving problems, to put ourselves down, hide and escape (**Turtle** approach), or to put others down, attack and belittle (**Skunk** approach)?

Teamwork is the contemporary work style. Organizations promote teams to unleash the enormous energy that employees have.

Transformational leaders inspire employees with a vision. They also provide a corporate value system, and mobilize commitment and excellence.

TERMS/CONCEPTS

leaders
managers
managerial success
managerial failure
insensitivity to people
Theory X
Theory Y
Theory M
trait theory
employee-centred supervisor
production-centred supervisor
Leadership Climate Model

competency
effectiveness
situational climate
situational styles
responsiveness
maturity
position power
personal power
Relationship Power Line
Power for/Power over
teamwork
transformational leadership

DISCUSSION QUESTIONS

1. "Leadership is influence." Discuss this statement in the context of the supervisor's responsibilities.

2. What are the key elements of managerial success and failure?

3. Why is establishing a system of core values at the heart of managing an effective organization?

4. How do assumptions about people influence one's leadership style?

5. Explain the situational approach to leadership. Use a personal example to highlight its key features.

6. Why is it important for supervisors to nurture the situational climate in their organizations?

7. Describe the importance of responsiveness as a key in assessingl the leadership climate.

8. What are the key elements of power? Explain how they interface with the Relationship Power Line.

9. Describe elements of effective teamwork.

10. Discuss transformational leadership. Use a personal example to highlight its key elements.

ASSIGNMENT

Instructions: Think of the one "best" manager that you have ever had and the one "best" leader you have ever had. These people may have been parents, teachers, or actual managers or supervisors. List their characteristics in the appropriate column below.

"BEST" MANAGER	"BEST" LEADER

Overall, which type of individual would you prefer to work for: a manager or a leader? Why?

CHAPTER TEN

HANDLING CONFLICT AND NEGOTIATIONS

The secret of walking on water is knowing where the stones are.

-- Herb Cohen, negotiator[1]

LEARNING OBJECTIVES

At the end of this chapter, students will be able to:

- Describe the nature of conflict
- Know why conflict arises
- Examine functional *vs.* dysfunctional conflicts
- Identify conflict resolution styles
- Identify ways to cope with criticism
- List the basic skills of negotiation
- Develop a win - win approach to negotiating

Opening scenario

*N*egotiations can be big and small. Negotiating the sticker price on a new shirt is different from negotiating on the billions owed, for example, by the Reichmann empire![2] The very private Paul Reichmann -- "The Philosopher King" and "Canada's Most Powerful Businessman,"[3] - had a record $20-billion debt task,[4] and owed *91 creditors*![5] Only when the the bankers felt they had all the facts and figures would the "real negotiations"[6] begin!

The TradeSource Inc.[7] group of businesses provides an excellent example of business negotiations. With its hundreds of companies and individual professionals, members are able to "trade" services and products with one another through the computerized TradeSource Inc. system, but without using cash! Members are responsible for taxes and charge regular prices, but in "trade dollars" (TDs). This computerized negotiation service is perfect for those who have something to offer but may not have the cash for a trip, for instance, to Hawaii. If the trip is regularly $7,000, and the member has that amount in TDs, it's a simple matter of computerizing the transaction/negotiation through TradeSource Inc., and *voilà*! The member and spouse are now in Hawaii! What was negotiated or traded? Perhaps the member had a chiropractic or limousine service, or was a retailer. When enough TDs were earned through trading their own service or product, all they had to do was phone TradeSource Inc. For the chiropractor, $7,000 worth of service to other TradeSource Inc. members cost him/her time; for the limousine service, $7,000 worth of service to members cost perhaps $700 out-of-pocket expenses (gas, maintenance, etc.); for the retailer, the $7,000 product might have cost $1,800 out-of-pocket expenses. For the chiropractor, the $7,000 Hawaii trip results from enough time; for the limousine operator, the $7,000 trip cost $700 in real dollars; and for the retailer, the $7,000 trip cost $1,800 in real dollars. Hundreds of companies and professionals are willing to negotiate and trade in such a fashion. After all, in the given example, the retailer still saves $5,200 on the trip!

Life is a negotiating process: I do something for you, you do something for me; "I scratch your back, you scratch mine"! In an organization supervisors and employees must constantly balance their own needs and those of the organization.[8]

THE NATURE OF CONFLICT

Conflict is the result of two interacting parties having different goals that cannot be achieved at the same time. If you want to go to Montreal for the weekend, and your friend wants to stay home, the difference raises a conflict.

Reflective exercise

Think back to a time when you had a conflict with someone. Describe that conflict below in terms of the different goals each of you had.

_____

_____

_____

_____

For some people, conflict is "bad." Perhaps that reflects their family upbringing. Perhaps it reflects the fact that conflicts at home were not resolved very fairly or effectively.[9] But conflict is inevitable and can be a healthy sign for a relationship or organization. Just as two individuals can have conflict, so there can be conflict between groups in an organization. Robert Townsend, who made Avis Rent A Car a success, said good managers don't eliminate conflict but deal with it openly. But his ground rule was the following:

> *Keep all conflict eyeball to eyeball.*[10]

Competition by itself is not necessarily harmful. It can be the stimulus for further discovery and development. The old axiom, "Necessity is the mother of invention," can be quite helpful here. Many thrive on competition. In the auto industry, "less well known is that adversity, competition and prodding by governments on the environmental front have led to renewed inventiveness."[11] Necessity forced Novatel Communications Ltd., of Calgary, to consider selling to Northern Telecom Ltd. NT would get the company for just under $30 million and its back orders for $100 million! Why? "Novatel has been a financial drain on Alberta and its sale would give the government some cash."[12] The problem with competition arises when it generates destructive patterns.[13] That is why, for instance, there are rules, procedures, and roles in every organization. These realities cut down on the amount of conflict because they allow employees, and outsiders as well, to know what some of the expectations are. Of course, they don't guarantee that everyone will follow the rules!

Productivity and profits are lower for groups that compete with each other. Some supervisors may feel that groups will be more motivated if they compete against each other. "Unfortunately, as seductive as this theory may seem, competition between groups frequently increases conflict between groups without increasing productivity."[18] Ironically, groups that co-operate generally have a higher-quality product.[19]

Conflict can be (1) *intra-personal*, that is, within an individual him/herself, and not related to others directly. If it becomes severe enough, counselling or therapy, or perhaps medical intervention, is needed;[14] (2) *inter-personal*, that is, between two individuals; (3) *inter-group*,[15] that is, between two different groups in an organization, for example, production and finance, union and management,[16] often showing up in tersely worded memos, unanswered phone calls, misinformation and disagreements over minor details. "If left unchecked, it can lead to missed deadlines, aborted projects and disgruntled customers. 'It' is that eternal source of workplace tension commonly known as interdepartmental conflict: plain old bad blood between work groups"[17]; (4) *inter-organization*, that is, when two organizations go at it "tooth and nail," so to speak. Again, a classic example was the fight between Penzoil and Texaco during which Texaco had to pay Penzoil a court-ordered $3-billion (U.S.)![20] In 1984, when Texaco acquired Getty Oil Co., Penzoil sued, claiming interference by Texaco because it had prior claim on the acquisition. A jury originally awarded them $10.53 billion (U.S.), but that was appealed and reduced to $3 billion (U.S.). "The wire transfers to Texas Commerce Bank NA of Houston [for Penzoil Co. from Texaco Inc., in White Plains, N.Y.] began at 10:03 a.m. Ten minutes and four transactions later, the transfer was complete"; and (5) *international*, that is, when two countries don't see "eye to eye." The Gulf War between the Allied Coalition and Iraq was a classic example of international conflict.[21]

Traditionally it was assumed that Adam Smith's "invisible hand"[22] would guide market forces so that the common good would win.[23] But is that necessarily true? For one university professor, the answer is yes: "The presence of women in the workplace didn't come about as a result of preferred hiring programs. It is largely the result of economic pressure levied by the 'invisible hand' of Adam Smith."[24] Adam Zimmerman, chairman of Noranda Forest Inc., makes an urgent call "for a major leadership effort ... to improve the inherent strengths of market forces" to build Canada's future.[25]

For others, a more guarded or *centrist approach* is important, for they insist that governments over the last 10 years have been naive in relation to this invisible hand allocating resources fairly and efficiently in society: "A more constructive direction for Canada would be a centrist approach which recognizes that if market forces -- competition, incentives, openness - are crucial to economic growth, then government is crucial to making the market work smoothly and efficiently."[26] A. Paul Gill, an organizer with the Canadian Farmworkers Union, says it even more strongly: "Our standard of living is not the result of market forces; it is the result of decades of struggle by unionists, some of whom suffered, even died at the hands of police during events such as the On To Ottawa Trek in the 1930s."[27]

One thing is certain: the idea of conflict has changed over the years. The traditional view was that it was dysfunctional because it blocked employees, for instance, from producing in an organization. A good example of this kind of dysfunctional conflict was the Canadian engineering firm that discovered it was costing them "$12,000 a year per employee in time and  materials, and $30,000 if project days are taken into account."[28] Traditionally a s well, performance appraisals of supervisors who had "conflict" in their departments tended to be more negative.

But while there are numerous examples to support this, a negative view of conflict need not prevail.[29] A more accepting view of the role of conflict in our lives is taking hold: conflict is seen as natural and inevitable. For instance, researchers have discovered that while all marriage relationships have conflict, happy couples are those who can fight well![30] Effective organizations use conflict to their benefit as a stimulus to growth and a catalyst for change,[31] and believes that to suppress it would possibly cause even further damage.[32]

WHY CONFLICT ARISES

While it is true that conflict arises because of different goals[33] needing attention at the same time by two parties, in organizations these "differences" show up in a variety of ways. For instance,[34] supervisors will experience conflict in the organization because (1) **resources** -- such as money, information, supplies -- **are scarce**. This "scarcity reason" is causing what could be called *New Deal thinking*: "The overall trend is doing more with less," says Jo Ann Compton, a partner in charge of Executive Search with Coopers & Lybrand Consulting Group. "It's getting more difficult to make money and corporations are cutting back. They're trying to get individuals to work harder, to wear more hats, to be more productive. And they're giving those individuals less than before."[35]

> Most conflicts tend to lie somewhere between being healthy and competitive and being totally negative and disruptive.

A second reason for conflict is (2) **task**, or jurisdictional, **ambiguity**: uncertainty over what and how something needs to be done. This seemed to be quite apparent in the conflict of Thomas Johnson, the U.S. banker who temporally replaced Paul Reichmann as president of Olympia & York Developments Ltd. The definition of his role and responsibilities had come under discussion.[36] Then he left amid much speculation. Did he not feel he was getting paid enough? Was the conflict over financial strategies for O&Y too much? One bank executive said, "Paul Reichmann doesn't want to take his medicine."[37]

Sometimes (3) a **communication breakdown** can create conflict. We saw in chapters 6 and 7 that we all see the world through our own perceptual filter.

Supervisors communicate from their perceptual base as well. If a supervisor thinks one way, and the employee thinks a radically different way about the same situation, these perceptual differences will be communicated. The trick, as we've seen, is not forcing one's view or perception on to the other, but communicating so that understanding may occur. Agreement is not the goal of communication; understanding is, and, if agreement does occur, that's a nifty by-product. Supervisors, especially in large Canadian cities with ethnic populations, will have many opportunities to manage potential communication conflicts with their multicultural workforces.[38] John Welch, chairman of General Electric Co., who had "earned the nickname Neutron Jack on his reputation for eliminating people while leaving buildings standing" said his new *work out* program would reduce conflict and promote more productivity "by encouraging communication outside traditional channels and having factory employees participate in workplace decisions."[39]

A fourth cause of conflict is often (4) **personality clashes**. Some people just "rub others the wrong way." Two interesting, and very different, personalities are those of the father-son team that runs the Quebecor Inc. printing empire, one of Canada's 50 biggest public companies. The father, Pierre Péladeau, is beginning to pass on the reins to his son Pierre-Karl. The father is outspoken, racist, and sexist in some of his comments, and unpredictable. The son, by contrast, who is age 30, is smooth, likeable, competent, down-to-earth, and a quick learner. Pierre-Karl says that while his father is flamboyant, he is not as much so as Robert Campeau or Robert Maxwell. "Sometimes he will say things that people won't like, but he is quite frank. I don't have a problem living with that, but at the same time I'm different from him."[40]

(5) **Status** can also be a cause of conflict, as was the case between Paul Reichmann and Thomas Johnson (above), and is particularly evident (as will be seen in chapter 15) when women seek equality, not only in society, but also in business. When the federal government said it would not obey any commission that was forcing it to give retroactive pay-equity adjustments to its lowest-paid employees, Liberal MP Marlene Catterall said the Canadian government was cheating women out of $1 billion, "paying its

> "If a man takes off his sunglasses I can hear him better." -- Hugh Prather[41]

"Whenever a manager or supervisor tells me that a staff member is *opinionated* or *vocal*, I usually sense that a high level of conflict is about to take place," says assistant general manager for the Valhalla Inn Markham Michelle Chisholm. "My experience tells me that in this type of situation, the manager or supervisor is the one who probably lacks effective communication skills, and the staff member is the one who likely has something valid to contribute, yet is frustrated by the lack of response."

debt to Wall Street but wiping out its debt to women."[42] The focus of *status* is built right into the title: National Action Committee on the Status of Women. Judy Rebick, its president, said, "The government is basically saying that it won't pay the cost of equality." Supervisors need to realize that the juxtaposition of power and status differences is also at the root of conflicts concerning workplace sexual harassment.[43]

Call it the *challenge of consumer conflict*, it should be pointed out that sometimes a supervisor will need to *promote* "situational conflict," in the best sense of the term, because of changes and challenges from the external environment. The current recession, of course, is creating this kind of conflict for business and is forcing many businesses to restructure, downsize, and reorganize. When a supervisor/manager says, "The competition is gaining on us. We need to do something about that," that is provoking conflict because the supervisor is inviting employees to change. If the world were perfect, supervisors could set up these "learning/change" situations; employees could adjust; and a new state of affairs would accrue. But the world isn't ideal. Sometimes change and conflict are forced on to us. Many of Burger King Canada Inc.'s franchisees felt the hand of "force," from its "big cheese."[44] "He's scaring the hell out of some franchisees," says Ron Groswell, a Burger King Canada franchisee in Sudbury, Ontario. "I have never seen a guy who can put his fist on the table and make things happen the way Alain Germain [the president] has done." Many of the franchisees have had their contracts terminated "amid a raging fight with head office."

Today's business constant is change and those companies that can adjust and meet new challenges will survive. "Change appears to be the norm rather than the exception today as companies seek ways to increase efficiency without escalating expenses."[45] The demise of the Beaver Canoe chain of clothing stores may have occurred because they did not change, or introduce conflict early enough, to anticipate market trends, according to Coopers & Lybrand analyst Howard Petrock. "You may be hot today, but that doesn't mean much for next year."[46] For six or seven years, Beaver Canoe had good times, but, said Petrock, it didn't change that much and when teenage shoppers are as fickle as they are, if a company doesn't adjust fast, it goes out of business. A retailer selling young, casual, trendy clothing is in a fast-moving environment. Change and conflict go hand-in-hand. To want the status quo is to go out of business. With a teen market now worth an estimated $6 billion and expected to grow to $10 billion by year 2000, Levi Strauss & Co. (Canada) Inc. is a company that meets conflict and challenge head-on by "sticking to the knitting" in its ads, providing "a sense of security in the teens' hectic lives" through "psychological and physical comfort,"[47] and with Nike Inc., by catering "to teens' seemingly contradictory need for both conformity and individuality."[48] To keep trendy, Glenn Wakefield, national advertising manager for Nike Canada Ltd., for instance, said he's marketing new shoes -- style and colour -- every *three* months now instead of the usual six months!

FUNCTIONAL *VS.* DYSFUNCTIONAL RESPONSES TO CONFLICT

The core of a dysfunctional system, be it family or organizational, is the reality of *denial*. In a dysfunctional family or organization, members *deny* that a problem exists and feel that if they just get the structure right, then all will be well. "Addictive organizations believe if they can get the form right, they do not have to deal with the underlying disease process."[49] Since conflict can be so painful and threatening at times, it presents a unique opportunity for supervisors to choose to be effective. Harmful conflicts are *dysfunctional* and beneficial ones are *functional*.[50]

> "Our marriage used to suffer from arguments that were too short. Now we argue long enough to find out what the argument is about." -- Hugh Prather[51]

A chart is provided on page 240 to quickly recognize clues in identifying functional *vs.* dysfunctional conflict.

HOW TO RECOGNIZE CLUES IN A FUNCTIONAL *VS.* A DYSFUNCTIONAL CONFLICT	
FUNCTIONAL CONFLICT	**DYSFUNCTIONAL CONFLICT**
Both-and thinking	*Either-or* thinking
Co-operation	Antagonism
Understanding	Power playing
Focusing on issue	Drifting *(kitchen sink fighter)*
Doing one's "homework"	Ad hoc arguing *(foresight* vs. *shortsightedness)*
Getting positive results *(increased interpersonal involvement; growth in relationship; safe outlet for feelings of frustration and aggression; establish a personal identity); put into perspective "goal aspirations"*[52]	Getting negative results *(resentment: one "winning", the other "losing"; future threat to relationship; personally destructive)*
Increased level of interaction	Decreased level of interaction[53]

CONFLICT RESOLUTION STYLES

Conflict can be resolved in more than one manner. Many supervisors may rely only on one style; it may or may not be effective. Self-reflection will show that most of us have a bias. Let's examine once again and fill in more of the **Relationship Power Line** from chapter 9 (p. 241).

One way to anticipate your bias might be to ask yourself the following question: "As a child, in the game of hide-and-seek, what did you do most: *hide* or *seek*? While there is nothing wrong with "hiding" as part of a game, if this *hiding instinct* is really part of a supervisor's conflict resolution style, then, in relation to the Power Line, this supervisor would tend to blame self,

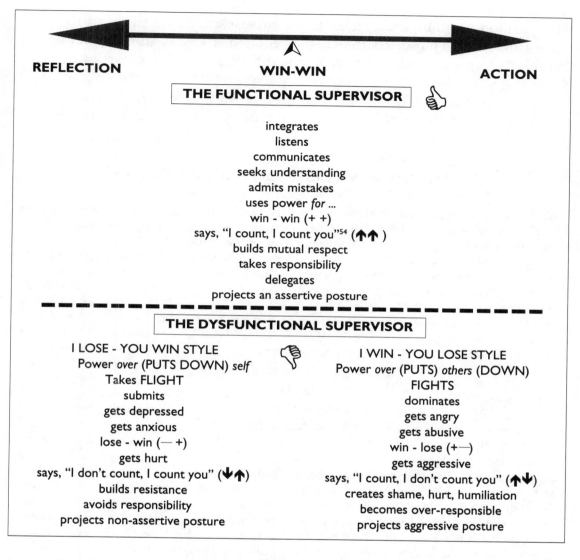

<--- REFLECTION   ↑ WIN-WIN   ACTION --->

THE FUNCTIONAL SUPERVISOR 👍

integrates
listens
communicates
seeks understanding
admits mistakes
uses power *for* ...
win - win (+ +)
says, "I count, I count you"[54] (↑↑)
builds mutual respect
takes responsibility
delegates
projects an assertive posture

THE DYSFUNCTIONAL SUPERVISOR 👎

I LOSE - YOU WIN STYLE	I WIN - YOU LOSE STYLE
Power *over* (PUTS DOWN) *self*	Power *over* (PUTS) *others* (DOWN)
Takes FLIGHT	FIGHTS
submits	dominates
gets depressed	gets angry
gets anxious	gets abusive
lose - win (— +)	win - lose (+—)
gets hurt	gets aggressive
says, "I don't count, I count you" (↓↑)	says, "I count, I don't count you" (↑↓)
builds resistance	creates shame, hurt, humiliation
avoids responsibility	becomes over-responsible
projects non-assertive posture	projects aggressive posture

internalize the conflict, and back away. The *seeking instinct* can be exploited by organizations with their sales people, but if a supervisor, for instance, has this as a dysfunctional style, it can come across as "judge-and-blame," as putting others down, and as using power to attain the goal, instead of a win-win collaborative process. When Warren Moysey was fired from the helm of Central Guaranty Trust Co. over conflicts and disagreements between himself and the board of directors, he said, "I was forced out ..."[55]

The question could be asked, then, of the supervisor: (1) when a conflict occurs, do you get tense, internalize the problem, and stay stuck? or (2) when a conflict occurs, do you get upset, blame the other party *"for starting it,"* and then force your objective irrespective of the other party? or, when a conflict arises with another party, do you instinctively want to resolve it, listen to conflicting viewpoints until the matter is resolved (a win - win posture)?

Conflict Occurs Over Definition of Relationship Rules[56]

All messages exchanged in a relationship become part of a larger system of rules concerning who has the right to say what to whom and under what circumstances. Because every act of communication between relational partners either establishes, maintains, or negates a relationship rule, interpersonal conflict erupts over seemingly innocuous issues. Imagine, for instance, that a wife says to her husband, "Take out the garbage," and the husband angrily replies, "You take it out for once, and stop trying to control my life." Many people would say this couple was arguing over the garbage. It is possible, however, to contend that the husband and wife were arguing about a relationship rule: Does the wife have the right to order her husband to do a particular household task? In this example, the wife's command, "Take out the garbage," would have established her right to tell her husband what to do, to direct his behaviour. By angrily refusing, the husband attempts to negate that relationship rule and to clarify his position: If his wife attempts to *order* him to behave, he will angrily refuse.

Every message has two components: content and relationship. The content level is obvious -- it represents the informational segment of the message. But every message also says something about the relationship between sender and receiver, and conflict usually erupts over this relationship level. Consider the following example: You and your roommate have agreed that you are both responsible for tidying up and taking care of your own clothes and dishes. One day you are late for school and leave your dirty dishes in the sink, planning to wash them as soon as you return. When you get home from school, your roommate says, "You slob, you left all the dishes in the sink. Get in there and clean them before my friends arrive." Your immediate response to this situation is, "I'll wash them tonight. I don't have time now." You say this even though, on a rational, logical level you know and agree that your dishes are your responsibility. In this situation it is not the content of the message that bothers you but rather the relationship aspect. You are saying, in effect, "You cannot order me around. We do not have a relationship where you can tell me what to do." Relational partners often think they are arguing over the content of messages, when, in fact, they are arguing over the relationship rules being established.

> *All messages exchanged in a relationship become part of a larger system of rules concerning who has the right to say what to whom and under what circumstances.*

Supervisory Conflict Situations:
A Self-Test

Instructions: Look at the five evaluation criteria in the box below. For each column choice (A,B,C,D,E) per statement, place a number (1,2,3,4,5) from the evaluation criteria guide below in each column to the right of each of the 20 statements that follow that best reflects what you would typically *feel* in a similar situation. REMEMBER: THIS IS A SELF-TEST ON HOW YOU WOULD INITIALLY *FEEL* IN THE SITUATION DESCRIBED. The Self-Test does not ask you to mark down what you would do. *Just be honest with yourself.* At the end of the exercise you will be able to obtain your score, with an explanation.

Your evaluation criteria guide

1 = **definitely not like me**, not what I would typically *feel* like doing
2 = **somewhat like me**, what I would typically *feel* like doing
3 = **occasionally like me**, what I would typically *feel* like doing
4 = **generally like me**, what I would typically *feel* like doing
5 = **most like me**, what I would typically *feel* like doing

Your column choices

A. Back away from the employee or situation. Your feeling is: "I don't need this. Just leave me alone."

B. Try to 'deal' with the employee. Your feeling is: "I win some; he/she wins some. We don't get exactly what we each want, but better something than nothing."

C. Cushion the employee's feelings to make sure he/she does not get more upset. Your feeling is: "I want peace at all costs. I don't need any hassles."

D. Use pressure on the person or situation to do what you want. Your feeling is: "I'm in charge. Just do what you're told."

E. Work out the problem with the employee. Your feeling is: "I know we've got a problem, but I'm going to stick with it until we get it resolved."

SITUATIONS	A	B	C	D	E
1. Word somehow leaked out that you were going to lay off 12 of the 26 employees. A really angry union steward comes to your office demanding a full explanation.					
2. You're a new supervisor in the sales department. Jim, who has the best sales record, is also the one who leaves early on Friday and comes in late on Monday morning. He					

SITUATIONS	A	B	C	D	E
jokingly told you he doesn't want you "messing up" his routine.					
3. Harriet, a long-time employee, typically makes popcorn in the microwave for lunch almost every day. The office smells like a movie theatre. You don't like that.					
4. After a big fight with Bill, the computer technician, you realize you need his help again.					
5. Two customers have complained about Geoff. You like him; he's great with people. But he gives off body odour.					
6. Your boss has told you that there will be no increases this year. Instead, you have to ask employees to take a pay cut.					
7. You notice that two employees are arguing quite loudly in front of some customers.					
8. Jenny, a very strong and opinionated person, is back smoking quietly in her office. The rules say, "No smoking!" She has ignored you for the most part because you're young.					
9. Richard "squealed" to you about Muriel's use of the photocopier for her own personal use.					
10. Jennifer just told you that Jo, your buddy, made a pass at her.					
11. You pick up the phone and overhear two employees discussing you in a very unfavourable light.					
12. According to you, one of the secretaries spends too much personal time on the phone.					
13. John really irritates you when he speaks because of his high-pitched voice. You think he's whining all the time.					
14. Gino said he would have the project completed today for your important meeting. He didn't get it done because he was away sick. He didn't tell you that until he got back today.					
15. You and your secretary had a bitter argument just before you both left work yesterday. It is now 7:55 AM. The secretary begins at 8:00 AM, but is usually in at 7:40 AM to get things ready.					
16. Margot has asked you to join three others for a drink after work. Andrew is part of that group. He's a loud mouth and you don't like being around him.					
17. Sandra is very angry with you because you forgot to mark in all her overtime this month and she didn't get					

	A	B	C	D	E
paid what she was expecting. She's threatening to talk to your boss.					
18. For the past week, Julian has not gone out of his way to speak to you. Some days he has not even said hello. He has quite a temper.					
19. You suspect Arnold has a drinking problem.					
20. David is going to receive an "unsatisfactory" performance review from you this morning. He thinks he's done a good job.					

Explanation:

The Self-Test was designed as a quick way to get you to put your *feelings* on paper about conflict situations. To have a feeling does not mean that you have to act on it. You might *feel* like **forcing** your choice in the conflict situation, for instance, but, given more conscious thought, you might act differently. At least know or acknowledge that this is probably how you would feel, and if to act on your feeling would bring dysfunctional consequences, that you would hopefully make a more adult decision to act more maturely.

There are five typical styles of conflict resolution.[57] All the choices or styles have their costs (–) and benefits (+). Like many things in life, what to do often depends on the situation. These are listed in the chart below.

A = AVOID
+ = when your objective is not all that important and you don't care about the quality of the relationship.
– = when you're just scared and not willing to face up to your responsibilities.

B = COMPROMISE
+ = when resources are scarce and you realize that neither of you realistically will get what you want.
– = when you don't want to be more assertive and work at a better solution.

C = PLACATE
+ = when the objective is not important, but your relationship is.
– = when you "stuff your feelings" in order to be "nice."

D = FORCE
+ = when your objective is critical and relationship matters have to take second place.
– = when you're being a bully.

E = RESOLVE
+ = when it is important that both parties "win."
– = when it takes too much time in an emergency situation.

Now graph your score by placing a dot in the appropriate box for each style and joining all the dots. Check out with your friends or family their perception on your *highest* score and your *lowest* score. Friends and family can often give us excellent corrective feedback. If your highest score is RESOLVE and your lowest score is AVOID, you are saying that in conflict situations, you typically *feel* like solving the conflict (RESOLVE) and you definitely *do not feel* like walking away from the conflict (AVOID).

MY PREFERRED CONFLICT RESOLUTION STYLE(S)				
100 95 90 85 80				
75 70 65 60 55				
50 45 40 35 30				
25 20 15 10 5 0				
A = AVOID	B = COMPROMISE	C= PLACATE	D = FORCE	E = RESOLVE

Questions you need to ask yourself

1. Do you act in relation to how you feel with your highest scored choice?
2. Would your best friend agree with your self-assessment?
3. Are you surprised that you might feel a certain way, yet act differently?
4. How open to change are you?
5. In conflict situations, are you more a TURTLE, a SKUNK, or PROBLEM SOLVER?
6. Do you let your feelings block you from making effective choices?
7. Is your highest scored choice or style effective for you?
8. As a supervisor, would you be effective managing conflicts?

COPING WITH CRITICISM

No one like to be criticized. The English writer Samuel Johnson, said that "criticism is a study by which men grow important and formidable at very small expense."[58] Each of us has a self-concept and a self-image that can be quite fragile at times, so fragile that it can even contribute to disease in us. Dr. O. Carl Simonton, the oncologist who treats cancer with the aid of visualization therapy, draws a profile of a cancer-prone person, who is self-pitying and has a very poor self-image.[59] The world's most often cited psychologist, Dr. Hans J. Eysenck, Ph.D., D.Sc., says, "Dramatic results from studies completed in Europe over the past several years point to a very strong connection between certain personalities and specific illnesses."[60]

One of the threats to our self-image is criticism. Criticism says that we're not perfect, or, at least, others think or feel that we're not.

We like to see ourselves in the best possible light, and we hope that others see us that way as well. Some may be so thick-skinned that they say they don't care what others think or say about them.[61] But, for many, how others think and feel about us is very important. Shannon Smith, president of Premiere Image Inc., and Lynne Mackay, president of Image Consulting, image consultancy firms, know this: "Corporate responsibility often goes to those who offer the best package - mere business ability and intelligence is, sadly, often just not enough."[62] One writer says that "the C-Factor" -- comfort and conformity to the corporate culture -- *is* more important than ability,[63] and another writer says that our corporate image even affects the bottom line.[64] Teenagers are quite sensitive about how they look and what others think of them,[65] so much so that the fad for teenage cosmetic surgery is worrying experts.[66]

Criticism can create and does sustain conflicts. Phillip Anthony Clarke, 20, received 10 years for killing Desmond Cole, 23, after they got into a "macho" argument about music preferences. They hurled insults at each other; the dispute escalated; and Clarke, "to save face," said the judge, got a gun and shot Cole in the chest![67]

To work for a supervisor who "always criticizes" is not much fun at best, and probably quite abusive at worst. Critical or controlling supervisors will create havoc in the workplace. Employees will resent them, sabotage materials, absent themselves, and develop other dysfunctional behaviours. A corporate culture will be developed whereby employees will always feel that they are being judged and blamed. They might not have concrete facts to explain their feeling, but to them, the feeling is real. Research has also shown that a supervisory culture, or organizational unconscious,[68] that is poisoned in this way is very expensive to the company.[69] The formula is:

> ## *When criticism goes up, profits go down!*

Criticism can be the major piece in a dysfunctional culture or supervisory experience. Because we are all tender and sensitive around our self-concept -- precisely because it is who we are -- criticism tends to elicit aggression and counterattack. War is the ultimate negative conclusion of attack and counterattack. Mikhail Gorbachev, former president of the Soviet Union, said "that today all of us, East and West, are moving toward a new type of civilization, whether we realize it or not."[70]

Will conflicts ever go away? Will attack and counterattack ever stop? Not likely, given the present state of development in human nature. But there is still hope: "The most exciting breakthroughs of the twenty-first century will occur not because of technology but because of an expanding concept of what it means to be human,"[71] and because we do have certain skills available that will minimize the impact of conflicts and criticisms so that a more healthy win-win possibility emerges. But it will not emerge without involving protecting the self-concept.[72]

Benjamin Franklin once said, "Love your enemies, for they will tell you your faults."[72] When people feel criticized, the critic is often perceived as "the enemy." Rather than going into one's shell, and becoming a TURTLE, or going on the attack, and becoming a SKUNK, there are other options.

The two skills, and their component parts, for coping with criticism are as follows:[73]

SKILLS FOR COPING WITH CRITICISM	
Seeking out more information, by	**Agreeing with the critic, by**
• Asking for more information; • Guessing about specifics; • Paraphrasing the critic's comments; • Finding out how your behaviour is bothering the critic.	• Agreeing with the truth; and • Agreeing with the critic's perception of the conflict.

Let's examine each of these skills in more detail.

(1) Seeking more information allows you room to have concrete data and begin to calm down. Sometimes there **is** (a) information that can be quite helpful, and before "jumping the gun," so to speak, you inform yourself. From ch. 6 we learned that if the other person or party *informs* us, then most probably we are not projecting something on to that person. However, if we feel turmoil and *affect* inside from a critic's remark, we know automatically that there is some truth to his/her statement, even if it was said badly, incorrectly, or inappropriately. In other words, the critic's remark found a "hook" in us and a tender part of us felt exposed. We try to cover this psychic nakedness often by going into our shell and being a TURTLE ("you can't hurt me now!") or by getting defensive and attacking the other person (the SKUNK -- "I'll get even, you S.O.B.!"). If the critic can't recall exactly what is bothering him/her, then try (b) guessing: "Is it this? that? because I ...?" The criticism may have come in a moment of anger and the critic also is too afraid to explain more. If guessing doesn't resolve the conflict, continue and (c) paraphrase, or summarize the meaning, intention, as you perceive it, that the critic had in the criticism.

"Delighting customers all of the time is not always possible," according to Graham Willsher, Valhalla Inn Markham's general manager. "Conflicts between hotel guests and staff occur as they do in any business. I have found that by saying (and believing) that I am fully responsible for my staff's actions and comments we tend to weather the storm and pacify the most irate of guests. Passing the buck or condemning individual staff members only angers the guest even more."

A projection is an unconscious psychological activity. That's why we don't know we're projecting! But we can detect the experience by this major clue: if another person criticizes us, and we are informed by this new information, and don't have a major affect, or reaction, then we're probably not projecting. If we do have a major affect, and "go nuts," so to speak, whatever it is we accuse the other party of -- even if the other party began the criticism first -- we also have a part of that nastiness, or greed, or stupidity, etc., in us. The criticism has acted as a "trigger" for us to ventilate a shadow piece of ourselves. It is an ethical obligation to pull that projection back, stop the judging and blaming -- especially when we feel justified and want to get even! -- and use the coping with criticism skills to defuse and manage the situation and relationship. In the privacy of our own thoughts later, or in the presence of a trusted friend or spouse, we can reexamine, re-evaluate, and redirect our projection so that it doesn't "pop out" and create problems for us in the future. In this way we "own" more of humanity, be it base or profound, for in this ownership lies our human destiny and the integrity of our human journey.

Finally, you may clear the matter up by (d) asking the critic how your behaviour is bothering him or her. You may not be able to do anything about that (for instance, being hard of hearing), but, at least you'll know why the person was criticizing you. Maybe your acceptance of the critic's pain will dissolve the conflict.

(2) Assume you've gone through skill #1 -- seeking out more information, but you haven't progressed all that well. Skill #2 -- agreeing with the critic -- can be extremely helpful. Sometimes people will shake their heads in disbelief when this idea of agreeing with the "enemy" is brought up. "After all," they might say, "haven't I suffered enough?" It's not a question of being a masochist here; it's a question of maintaining relationship -- if that is important to you. As a supervisor, interacting with employees on a daily basis, the quality of your relationships will be critical to your success, financially, from a health point of view, and from the point of view of your general well-being. As pointed out above, if you do experience yourself having an *affect*, i.e., getting ticked off, hurt, angry, etc., recognize at least that you too have some part to play in the criticism; you're not totally "clean," psychologically; you are projecting some of the problem too.

Thus, (a) take the grain of truth there is in the criticism and use it for your own growth. That's the only way we can truly grow. It's painful at times, as we all know, but the rewards are in an enhanced view of ourselves, life, and the world around us. If none of that works for you, then you can at least (b) agree with your critic's right to have their perception, however silly or vindictive or juvenile you think it is. In a society which honours and values freedom of speech -- in spite of the pressure to be politically correct -- how we handle criticism can be a rather poignant and personal moment of greatness: supporting the right to the critic's perception and opinion as your concrete commitment to a vital anchor in the democratic process that holds our society together. That's idealistic, but it is the basis of a truly free society, and when the human development index compiled by the UN Development Program that measures life expectancy, literacy, and standard of living for 160 nations is acknowledged, Canada is still the best place in the world to live![74]

The fear is that if we continue to draw the battle lines in our society and country, we will spend our time fighting and not making Canada competitive. "Our failure to develop new ways to produce wealth is increasingly eroding our ability to sustain the social and political institutions that have made Canada a tolerant, fair, and decent society."[75]

BASIC NEGOTIATION SKILLS

Negotiating is distinguished from general conflict resolution by three features: it is (1) deliberately set up,[76] (2) in a reciprocal, two-party fashion, in order (3) to make a decision.[77] It is "particularly appropriate in situations where some individual or group will clearly lose out in a change and has considerable power to resist."[78] It is also one of the decisional roles that a manager/ supervisor has to practice, whether in union contracts, budget proposals, allocation of resources, hiring of new personnel, work assignments, compensation, purchases, or for department interests.[79] It has also been described as "a process in which two or more parties, having both common and conflicting interests, state and discuss proposals concerning specific terms of a possible agreement."[80] An excellent example of a structured negotiation -- instead of competitive bidding -- is the case between a manufacturer and a government department when it is purchasing a product, especially if the manufacturer is the only supplier. In this situation, the terms of the contract are set after both parties negotiate the deal.[81]

The restructuring of the Reichmanns' $14 billion Olympia & York Developments Ltd. debt was a classic example of the need for negotiations. If a key description of stress is lack of information, then the O&Y situation highlighted this perfectly. Indeed, anxious and stressed lenders were *clamouring* for more information, more disclosure, and an end to the Reichmanns' secrecy culture and strategy. "Additional disclosure is part of the negotiation process," said an O&Y insider.[82]

In the negotiation process, there is a "bargaining zone" with bargaining ranges: the initial offer point, the target point, and the resistance point.[83] The give-and-take happens within these points. An initial offer is placed on the table; both parties have a goal, or target, or objective in mind that they want to reach; and each party has a point beyond which they will not go unless they end up giving in completely, in which case they walk away feeling defeated. It was John F. Kennedy who stated, "Let us never negotiate out of fear; but let us never fear to negotiate."[84]

Negotiating skills are important for the supervisor in the on-going balancing acts that are part of today's organizations. Bell Canada, for instance, in 1987, tried to get the CRTC (Canadian Radio-television & Telecommunications Commission) "to 'rebalance' rates -- ... lower business rates while raising local ones. The CRTC said no."[85] In the case of Burger King Canada Ltd., distribution contracts were renegotiated "to make everyone in the system more accountable to head office."[86]

CLOCKS ARE OUT, BRAINS ARE IN![87]
A Negotiated Settlement

Algoma Steel Corp. Ltd.'s new collective agreement is turning upside down the traditional image of the brainless worker who does what he is told, gets paid, and then goes home. In a new and "interesting adventure," says Leo Gerard, outgoing Canadian director of the United Steelworkers of America, Algoma's new survival plan, based on West German and Scandinavian models of co-determination in drafting its unique collective agreement, and decided on after a negotiated process, will see supervisors in redefined roles as "coaches" and "co-ordinators," meeting, on a day-to-day basis, with work groups of employees, both groups "jointly responsible for completion of tasks, planning, scheduling, budgeting and administration." Not so kind are the words of *The Globe and Mail's* business writer, Terence Corcoran, who said the union had to do something to put a "positive spin" and dress up these union concessions, and said, "... spare us the social-democracy co-determination propaganda."[88]

Negotiating can be approached in the following two basic ways:

The *fixed pie* approach,[89] whereby each party wants the biggest slice and makes negotiating efforts for that purpose. Union - management relations and starting salary issues will often have that dynamic. This approach and method assumes that what each party has between them is limited, and "may the best person win!" The problem with this negotiating approach is that is sets up a "we *vs.* them" mentality, the "good guys *vs.* the bad guys" syndrome; and, since we have seen, each of us wants to see ourselves -- our self-image -- in the best possible light, so this approach fundamentally comes down to "We're the good buys; they're the enemy!" Neither party will win; neither party will lose. When the relationship between the parties is an on-going one - family, friends, co-workers, union, management -- the damage from such an adversarial dynamic can become quite extensive. As pointed out, Canada Post and the postal workers union have had this traditional antagonism for many years.

The *expanding pot* approach,[90] whereby both parties realize that there is enough for all, and that attitudes, information, and effective behaviour will allow both to win.[91] Although it is difficult, a supervisor can *reframe* a *fixed pie* approach into an *expanding pot* approach in negotiating, but this effort requires the following tactics:[92]

- *develop superordinate goals* Common
(goals bigger than both parties, but that each wants)

- *tackle the issues, not the people*
(focus on problems, issues; be objective; do not personalize)

- *focus on mutual interests, not on positions*
(establish what is common to both parties)

- *expand the pot*
(invent options through creative thinking)

- *determine what is objectively **fair***
(develop and agree on criteria of fairness)

Thus, negotiation is a process employed to influence the *outcome* of a situation. When it is done well, both parties can win. Ineffective or twisted negotiations in organizations leave hard feelings, lost profits, and dysfunctional work relationships.

DEVELOPING A WIN - WIN APPROACH IN NEGOTIATING

Above all else, supervisors want to leave work at the end of the day and feel good about what happened during the day. Employees are no different. Often good feelings are a result of common sense. Such was the case eventually with the NHL strike in the spring of 1992. According to New York Ranger forward Mike Gartner, a member of the union's (NHLPA) negotiating committee, there was a turnaround from "a lose, lose, lose situation where the players were losing, the owners were losing and the games were losing, to a win, win, win situation," which turn of events Toronto Maple Leaf general manager Cliff Fletcher called "common sense."[93]

> Keep your affairs in suspense.
> Make people depend on you.
> Avoid victories over your superiors.
> Control your imagination.
> Know how to take and give hints.
> Know how to be all things to all men.
> Without lying, do not tell the whole truth.
> Be a man without illusions.
> Behave as if you were being watched.
>
> -- Baltasar Gracian, Spanish Philosopher,
> Seventeenth Century[94]

The dysfunctional win - lose and lose - lose approaches to negotiating, as well as to supervising, use the following six steps:

- unreasonable starting positions
- limited authority to make compromises
- emotional tactics and immature behaviour
- macho attitudes not to back down
- minute changes in positions
- disrespect for time frames

The net result of these approaches, of course, is that bad feeling wins the contest. This was the case with negotiations on the beer disputes between Canada and the U.S. which became so quarrelsome, competitive and problematic that they prompted one trade official to say, "The negotiators are going to need a few beers themselves by the time this is all over."[95]

A more healthy win-win approach to negotiating and supervising, on the other hand, helps both parties -- employees and supervisors -- meet their needs. "Successful collaborative negotiation lies in finding out what the other side really wants and showing them a way to get it, while you get what you want."[96]

Key things to do in win - win negotiations:[97]

- Do your homework and be prepared
- Build trust and relationship with the other party
- Gain the commitment and support of the other party
- Learn to manage disagreements by seeking understanding
- Be smart enough to bring in a trained third party if necessary

WHEN TO COMPETE, WHEN TO CO-OPERATE

Ideally organizations and supervisors would all work from a win - win, collaborative, and co-operative model in their day-to-day activities. But that's not reality.

Co-operation means that members in an organization are "all singing out of the same hymnal," so to speak. Each person knows what the "score" is, each is prepared and trained, and a great "symphony" called the organization emerges.[98] "Management's job is to provide an environment in which people can do their work."[99]

Competition means that member goals are "negatively linked,"[100] thus creating a situation where one party wins, the other loses. Losing typically creates problems of self-esteem, whether that be for an individual, group, province, or country. Nobody likes to see him/herself as a "loser." To save face, people get defensive, blame others, become disruptive, get depressed, sabotage work efforts, etc. "Winners" (at the expense of others), on the other hand, may develop a cockiness, an arrogance that is misplaced, an abrasiveness that is difficult to deal with, and an attitude of invincibility and lack of vulnerability that can be very problematic. "Winners" often like to run their opponent's faces in the mud. Again, the net result is dysfunctional relationships where *addict* (the one with power) and *codependant* (the one who tiptoes around the addict) play out the travesty of their lives. How many organizations or departments are there where addict-supervisors have created a whole department basically of codependants, employees who are afraid to speak up, to get involved, to challenge, and to be creative.

BUT IS COMPETITION ALWAYS BAD?

The answer, of course, is no! Sports can be a good example of the positive value in competition. In sports, contestants are measuring themselves against a standard of excellence. "The key rule for using competition is to avoid it when individuals or groups are interdependent and must co-operate to reach the organization's goals."[101] There can also be very damaging consequences when sports uses an athlete, when her value is only *what* she can do and not also *who* she is, as in the case of Elizabeth Manley, Canada's Calgary Olympic silver winner, who fell into black despair, severe depression, and mental illness when she was 17 years old in 1983. "Although excellence is measured by results, a young person's sense of self-worth can become twisted."[102] A supervisor can use competition positively by answering "yes" to the following questions:[101]

- Is it going to hurt the team/department?
- Is it fair for all involved?
- Is there a limited time period?
- Will it be rewarding for those involved?

If a supervisor can answer "yes" to all four questions: (1) that the competition, for instance, is between two different organizations, (2) that both parties have an equal chance to win, (3) that when the competition is over, it will not be held against the loser, and (4) that a winner is not going to be penalized or isolated from the group, team, or department -- then, and only then, should competition be a possibility.

We would be remiss at this point in our competitiveness to remain a country not to remind the supervisor of the incredibly important times we live in as Canadians. We are so lucky and yet many of us forget that. We need to remind ourselves what Jean Monty, Bell Canada chairman, has said: "Let there be no misunderstanding: there can be no economic strength if we are constantly quarrelling among ourselves over political power. History will not deal kindly with us if we do not grab hold of the constitutional challenge and forge a new national alliance."[103]

Constitutional Affairs minister Joe Clark is an excellent example of one Canadian, through credibility and trust, in a very significant and sensitive role, amidst the angry constitutional debates, who tried "to broker a new deal for Canada" through a win - win solution. He readily admitted his greatest frustration was "that our system operates as though what is at issue is a traditional negotiation among governments." Indeed, the very existence of Canada as a nation seemed to be at stake and that Canada would hold together because the relationship was fundamentally more important and valuable than taking positions. In a speech in February 1992, in Saskatchewan, he said:

> We can be the first generation of Canadians to pass on to the next less than was passed on to us. There is nothing automatic about this country. Canada was not here at the beginning of the last century. There is no logic that says it must be here at the beginning of the next.
>
> We have to work to keep it. We always have. Keeping it large without destroying its diversity has always been our challenge. And it's been our achievement up until today. Our challenge is to sustain that achievement.[104]

SUMMARY

Conflict is the result of two interacting parties having different goals that cannot be achieved at the same time.

Competetion by itself is not necessarily harmful.

Conflict can be intra-personal, inter-personal, inter-group, and inter-organization.

Conflict arises because of a scarcity of resources, task or jurisdictional ambiguity, communication breakdown, personality clashes, and status. *Situational conflict* can bring out the best or worst in people and organizations.

Functional conflicts contain both-and rather than either-or thinking, co-operation *vs.* antagonism, understanding *vs.* power playing, and increased levels of positive interaction *vs.* decreased levels of negative interaction.

Supervisors (in a positive vein) can adopt a reflective, a win - win, action-oriented approach to solving conflicts, or supervisors (in a negative vein) can adopt a TURTLE, a lose - lose, and a SKUNK approach to solving conflicts.

Conflict resolution styles include the following: AVOID, COMPROMISE, PLACATE, FORCE, and RESOLVE. Each style has its costs (−) and benefits (+).

Criticism threatens our self-image because it says we're not perfect. Seeking out more information and agreeing with the critic are the two main skills for coping with criticism.

Negotiation includes the following factors: it is deliberately set up, in a reciprocal, two-party fashion, in order to make a decision.

The negotiation process has three bargaining zones: the initial offer point, the target point, and the resistance point. Win - win negotiations build trust, gain commitment, and support and seek understanding.

TERMS/CONCEPTS

nature of conflict
types of conflict
causes of conflict
situational conflict
denial
functional conflict
dysfunctional conflict
Relationship Power Line
relationship rules
content level

relationship level
conflict styles
criticism
negotiation
fixed pie approach
expanding pot approach
supraordinate goal
win - lose approach
lose - win approach
win - win approach

DISCUSSION QUESTIONS

1. Define conflict and illustrate it from a personal work example.

2. What does it mean by saying, "Keep all conflict eyeball to eyeball"?

3. Describe the different types of conflict.

4. Why does conflict arise? Support your answer with actual work examples.

5. What is the differences between dysfunctional and. functional conflicts?

6. Why are conflicts experienced as negative so much of the time?

7. Using a personal example, describe what relationship rules mean.

8. Discuss the conflict resolution styles.

9. What is criticism? Identify and explain the skills for coping with criticism.

10. How is negotiation different from conflict? Identify and explain the two basic ways to approach conflict.

11. How can supervisors develop a win - win approach to negotiating?

ASSIGNMENT

Instructions: Listed below are the five conflict resolution styles used in this chapter. Describe a situation for each when you used the style in a positive way and when you used the style in a negative or dysfunctional way.

	POSITIVE EXPERIENCE	NEGATIVE EXPERIENCE
AVOIDING		
COMPROMISING		
PLACATING		
FORCING		
RESOLVING		

My most effective situation _____

_____

My least effective situation _____

_____

PART THREE:

HUMAN RESOURCE DEVELOPMENT DYNAMICS

Executive Summary

Globalization, complexity of legislation, and diversity in the workplace in Canada make it imperative that today's supervisor manage the human resource function as expertly and humanely as possible.

Perhaps the most important activity that a supervisor can perform is the selection, orientation and development of employees (ch. 11). This is the "entry point," so to speak, for all the other activities the supervisor will do. To maintain an effective workforce, the supervisor will then need to provide feedback and evaluation of job performance (ch. 12). Sometimes that feedback will also be in the form of disciplinary measures. To neglect the union dimension and the labour - management dynamic is to commit an act of folly (ch. 13). Experience, as well as legislation, compel the supervisor in a unionized environment to become proficient and knowledgeable as quickly as possible. Health and safety, as well as work-related stress issues (ch. 13), demand increasing amounts of a su-

pervisor's time, not only because of the enormous financial costs incurred by business with these issues, but also because they are ethical imperatives. Changes in society and new legislation for the workplace demand that the supervisor also pay sigificant attention to the emerging social dynamics of the workplace (ch. 15): employment equity, pay equity, racism, discrimination, etc. The workplace needs to reflect its society. Increasingly this means in some cities in Canada a workforce that may be as much as 46 per cent multicultural! Finally, supervisors also have to manage those employees who have problems (ch. 16). Living in an addicted society only encourages these problems, but it is still a reality for the supervisor to address.

CHAPTER ELEVEN

SELECTING, ORIENTING, AND DEVELOPING EMPLOYEES

These people [her Jewish parents in Auschwitz], who had lost everything and practically everyone, never lost hope ... From their shared history I have learned the importance of tolerance, of open-mindedness, of optimism, of civility, of commitment, of integrity, and of justice. And from their shared history I have learned to fear only indifference and irrelevance. ... Ambition for me is a competition with time, not people.

-- Rosalie Abella,
100th woman on federal bench[1]

LEARNING OBJECTIVES

At the end of this chapter, students will be able to:

* Demonstrate the role of human resources management
* Distinguish among job analysis, description, specification
* Identify the necessary steps in the selection process
* Describe the critical role of orientation
* Understand the importance of training and development

Opening scenario

*H*iring the right people for the right job at the right time is both an art and a science. As a science there are key markers that companies follow, such as proven methods of interviewing and testing procedures, as well as required legislative procedures, such as targets and goals for employment equity, and policy requirements for a collective agreement. As an art, the supervisor, for instance, has to keep in mind the company's corporate culture and the "fit" for the potential employee. For instance, Donald MacDonald, former Liberal finance minister, now says, "Some of the people there now are good technicians but are lacking in the breadth of vision or imagination that my colleagues had."[2] The "hiring and promotion bottom line," however is still: "May the best qualified *human being* get the job."[3]

The summer of 1992 found the Canadian economy with 462,000 less people working than the summer of 1990! This loss "... can easily outstrip the so-called efficiency gains."[4] Margaret Regan, a human resources expert at Towers Perrin, calls the layoffs a "knee-jerk reaction" and says, "The Japanese think we're out of our minds."[5] Sociologist Michael Unseem, of the Wharton School of Business, says "... companies with a history of repeated bloodletting have trouble attracting new talent when they need it."[5]

This is the new selecting, orienting, and developing environment for supervisors today. Times have changed. Two views: One view says that workers are more than ever demoralized[6] which will mean an increased pressure on workers to work harder and perhaps not complain about a demotion because of the job-loss threat. The other view says that this "economic - end-of-the-world mentality" neglects the good things that have occurred, the most obvious one being Canada's being relatively low inflation. As Canadians we may be missing the forest for the trees!

Today's supervisor perhaps lives in "the best of times" and "the worst of times." The best wisdom for the supervisor may be the following bit of folklore:

When you can't change the direction of the wind - adjust your sails.[7]

A main responsibility of the supervisor is to select, orient, and develop employees. The purpose of this chapter is to highlight the key elements in this process by situating them within a discussion of the emergence of human resources management within this century.

THE ROLE OF HUMAN RESOURCES MANAGEMENT

The field of personnel, or what is now called *human resources management* (HRM), has finally come of age. In the last twenty years alone (1971 - 91), the number of human resource managers has increased from 4,055 to 28,659![8] Human Resources (or HR) is finally losing its "Goody-Two-Shoes image."[9] The HR professional is becoming more and more a part of the strategic direction of the company or organization. Human resources is too complicated and potentially explosive an area to neglect. Dale Kerry, vice-president for human resources at Jannock Ltd., says the HR person's strategic role is now in "optimizing the company's investment in its people."[9] This is particularly true in areas such as layoffs, the launching of a new product, team-building and efforts at retraining. Royal Bank chairman Allan Taylor, says, "Canadian companies have a miserable record of investing in their people. Eighty-five percent spend nothing on training."[10]

The role of the human resources department is to promote the efficient utilization of human resources, to assure an on-going succession of well-trained employees, to maintain morale and productivity, and to promote and actualize a quality of work life that brings out the best in employees. These aims are directed at ensuring organizational excellence and effectiveness.[12]

HRM-Europe?

HRM-Europe seems to be at a crossroads, according to IMD, the Swiss management school and the EAPM, the European Association of Personnel Management. There are tensions over turf, power and influence -- potential *shadow* temptations, as we have seen (ch. 6) for many people. Unlike North America, where HRM is seen more strategically as an integral part of doing business, HRM-Europe is struggling to be relevant and credible. Will it pass the grade? If it meets the joint research committee's conclusions about the three external influences impacting now and for the future on HRM-Europe: "demands for quality, customer service and technological innovation."[11]

A simple' but interesting way to look at the importance of effectively managing human resources can be seen in the diagram below.

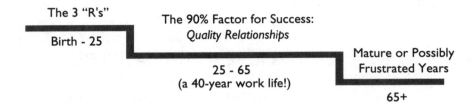

The 3 "R's"

Birth - 25

The 90% Factor for Success:
Quality Relationships

25 - 65
(a 40-year work life!)

Mature or Possibly
Frustrated Years

65+

While society prepares us for what it thinks we need to be successful during our first 25 years of life, we soon realize that we have a work life of 40 years![13] And 90 per cent of the success in these 40 years will be based on how well we manage our relationships.

JAPAN: MANDATORY RETIREMENT? OR ECONOMIC PANIC?	
Japan Inc. is in the process of self-examination. It is estimated that by the year 2002, about 40% of the population will be over 50 years of age. That number will increase to 50% by the year 2025. Political science professor Michael Donnelly said that because of these raw facts the "energy, verve, and vitality"[14] of the country itself could quickly disappear over these next 20 years. The BIG QUESTION is the following: "How will Japan Inc. keep its business operating?"	In addition, there are the following added problems: (1) an expected shortage of workers, (2) a growth in population in the 25 - 34 and under 5 age brackets *only*, (3) a male-dominated culture and managerial workforce, (4) a 40% labour force of women in lower-paid jobs, and (5) expectations that traditional roles of child-care and elder-care be provided by women. "Already, many senior managers are staying on into their seventies."

The important question that needs to be asked at this point is the following: what has all this discussion on the role of human resources management got to do with the supervisor? The answer is clear: "all managers are human resource managers."[15]

Today employees are considered the organization's most important resource.

The Royal Bank of Canada puts it this way:

> "No one, it seems, has bothered to point out that treating workers as feeling human beings rather than as factors of production is simply a matter of doing the right thing. ... Organizations ... are moving away from the tough-guy primitivism which for too long has been held up among North American management as an admirable quality. They are moving towards a more civilized society -- one in which the 'basics' of work and love need no longer tear people apart emotionally."[16]

It was not always so. Employees were virtually slaves in earlier centuries, to be used and disposed of by businesses for their ends. "Owners and managers were virtually dictators."[17] It was little wonder that employee resentment and hostility grew; so did unions. The age-old supervisory problem of employee absenteeism was directly linked to how workers were treated. Today absenteeism accounts for more lost days than strikes! The costs are staggering: ranging from an estimated $1.5 to $15 billion per year![18]

Reflective exercise

Think back to a work situation when you chose to be absent because of bad working conditions. List some of the factors involved.

_____

_____

_____

_____

_____

_____

Which factor was most critical? _____

Thus, human resources management is not only a separate staff function[19] within a large organization, but it is also a central responsibility of every supervisor in order to maintain an effective workforce. In some situations it could mean the difference of the firm staying in business or not.

JOB ANALYSIS, JOB DESCRIPTION, JOB SPECIFICATION

Before a supervisor can select, orient, and develop employees, some key activities must first take place. If the organization is large, the following activities have been performed by the human resource management department, but also in co-operation with supervisors and managers throughout the organization. In a small organization, it is the supervisor's responsibility to make sure job analyses, job specifications, and job descriptions are completed. These activities depend on the *kind* of organization it is, its organizational structure, mission, and strategic plans. As we have seen, human resource managers are becoming integral to strategic planning in the organization: "Now the person in charge of human resources," says Dale Kerry, vice-president for human resources at Jannock Ltd., "is a full-fledged member of the management team with the strategic role of optimizing the company's investment in its people."[20]

JOB ANALYSIS

The first activity in determining the job needs in a particular work area is done through what is called **job analysis** which is "the process of determining the nature or content of a job by collecting and organizing relevant information"[21] or "a systematic process of collecting data and making certain judgments about all of the important information related to the nature of a specific job."[22] In other words, job analysis gives the supervisor "all the basic features of a job"[23] and "reveals the actual tasks, activities, and skills related to jobs currently existing."[24]

In selecting its supervisory contingent, the Valhalla Inn Markham has been consistent in securing individuals who have displayed, through the selection process and past employment performance, the right "attitude." Less than 50% of its supervisory and management team had prior experience in the positions to which they would be appointed, possessing instead the necessary personal skills which would make the hotel successful. The results over a two-year period indicate that the Valhalla Inn Markham has one of the lowest turnover statistics in this employee category within the hotel industry.

Job analysis is important for many reasons. In a litigious society, not knowing what a job consists of, in order to defend supervisory actions in relation to it, is tantamount to political and economic suicide. A supervisor may say that an employee has a "bad attitude," but *what* behaviours indicate that and are they integral to the job? Job analysis is critical also for compensation and pay equity purposes (ch. 15). While all employees want to be treated equitably and fairly, they especially want to be *paid* equitably and fairly; and they want to know that the "system" is free of bias and discriminatory judgments, whether intended or not. For instance, in 1977, a human rights tribunal voted in favour of Ishar Singh, a security guard, in his request to wear a turban and a beard as a sign of his religious faith. It was found that Security and Investigation Services Ltd. did not *intend* to discriminate against him, but that their policy did *in fact* do so and hence they breached the human rights code.[25]

Mismanagement in compensation matters, or the perception of unfairness, can create an intolerable working environment, for both employees and supervisors. Finally, job analysis is the basis for all the human resource activities that the supervisor will be involved in, such as the recruiting, selecting, orienting, developing, appraising, and compensating of employees.

STEPS IN A JOB ANALYSIS

If a supervisor has to personally oversee setting up, monitoring, and completing a job analysis for his/her department, there are some sequential steps to follow. They are as follows:

1. Overall knowledge of the organization, its purpose, mission, culture, product or service, and place on the organizational chart.

2. The purpose of the job analysis must be determined. Gathering information and data relevant to this purpose becomes more focused then.

3. Jobs that need to be analyzed need to be identified. Information and charts from predecessors can be quite helpful here.

4. A data-gathering activity needs to be conceived to reflect steps #1 - 2. For instance, the supervisor might find it appropriate to design a data-gathering instrument, set up an interview or an observation process on the actual jobs being analyzed, isolate critical or important incidents integral to a job, or use a combination of all these approaches. What the supervisor will be investigating and gathering are the duties, responsibilities, skills, working conditions, and performance standards required for a particular job.

> 5. If necessary, the supervisor can also consult the Canadian Classification and Dictionary of Occupations (CCDO), which has classification structures to arrange jobs for the supervisor/manager into occupational categories and the kind of work performed. The CCDO is issued by the federal department of Employment and Immigration Canada.[26]

JOB DESCRIPTION

At this point, when adequate information is compiled, the supervisor is able to begin to design job descriptions, job specifications, and their attendant job standards.

"A **job** can be defined as one or more tasks that an individual performs in direct support of the organization's production purpose."[27] A job description, then, should tell someone *what* needs to be done in order to "get the job done." It would also spell out the working conditions, the responsibilities or duties involved in the job, the reporting relationships or lines of authority, the expected standards of performance, and the kinds of interpersonal relationships required. Good job descriptions will help the supervisor distinguish the many "relationships among jobs."[28]

JOB DESCRIPTION*

POSITION TITLE: RESTAURANT MANAGER
DEPARTMENT: RESTAURANT, LOUNGE, ROOM SERVICE AND MINI BAR
REPORTS TO: GENERAL MANAGER
SUPERVISES: ASSISTANT RESTAURANT MANAGERS
                 RESTAURANT SUPERVISORS
                 RESTAURANT AND ROOM SERVICE WAIT STAFF
                 BARTENDERS
                 MINI BAR ATTENDANTS

POSITION SUMMARY:

Responsible for the operation of the restaurant, lounge, room service and mini bar departments as it pertains to policies, procedures, standards and guest services. The Manager is also responsible for all controls, revenues, and assists with the marketing of the facilities.

(cont'd)

* Valhalla Inn Markham

DUTIES AND RESPONSIBILITIES:

(cont'd)

PRIMARY:

1) Provide food and beverage services to guests of the hotel through the restaurant, lounge, room service and mini bar departments.
2) Provide direction and support to the department management team ensuring that proper supervision is provided to all operating departments.
3) Supervise, direct and train the department staff to ensure maximum productivity and guest services while performing their duties.
4) Establish the highest standards for cleanliness, maintenance and safety throughout the operations. Resolve safety issues immediately.
5) Enforce approved control procedures and policies throughout the operations.
6) Plan and execute the appropriate daily menus for all operations within the department in conjunction with the Executive Chef, assistant managers and staff.

SECONDARY:

1) Participate in the costing of menus and ensure that all product is sold at an acceptable profit margin.
2) Plan and execute timely promotions for all operations within the department.
3) Assist the Food & Beverage Controller with inventory taking, evaluate the results and take appropriate action to rectify concerns.
4) Actively participate in the creation of new department menus.
5) Create and maintain a professional, progressive and co-operative environment.
6) With the Human Resources Manager, interview and select department staff.
7) Train new staff and provide ongoing technical and motivational training for all staff.
8) Create work schedules providing staff coverage that will ensure adequate guest service.
9) Ensure that the daily, weekly and bi-weekly payroll procedures are completed accurately.
10) Convene department, management and staff meetings on a regularly scheduled basis for the purpose of providing direction, receiving information and providing the necessary motivation to all department employees.
11) Co-ordinate, develop and maintain a Procedures Manual for the restaurant/lounge, room service and mini bar.
12) Be proactive in determining and meeting guest needs.
13) Act as the hotel's duty manager as per the schedule and/or as requested.
14) Attend and participate in department head, operations, and division meetings as required.
15) Ensure that all staff understand and follow the hotel's policies, procedures and regulations as outlined in the Employee Handbook; and, ensure that all staff are familiar with the hotel facilities and services.

JOB SPECIFICATION

Besides needing to know *what* the job is or entails, the supervisor will need to know *who* the potential employee is who will actually fill the position and what demands will be made on the employee, in essence, what *kind* of employee is needed to do the job. It is at this point that the supervisor tries to match the skills, abilities, and characteristics of an applicant to the specific job. Typically, a job specification *specifies* what experience and training are needed, the level of education, and the quality of skills and abilities needed. This "who-does-the-job" endeavour is the business of the job specification which offers qualifying guidelines to the supervisor on the type of employee needed. Job specifications, or the identification of the human qualities needed by the job applicant, are a critical component because they must be job-related, free of discriminatory requirements, and realistic.

JOB SPECIFICATION*

JOB REQUIREMENTS: FOR RESTAURANT MANAGER

EDUCATION: Certified post secondary education in the hospitality field is preferred.

EXPERIENCE: Minimum 2 years' experience as a restaurant manager or, where appropriate, 3 years as an assistant restaurant manager.

SKILLS REQUIRED TO DO THE JOB:

1) Above average level of accuracy and detail-oriented.
2) Above average verbal and written communication skills.
3) Above average ability to create and compile reports.
4) Able to provide leadership.
5) Full working knowledge of the following computer program: Remanco.
6) Advanced level of knowledge and understanding of food & beverage principles.

PHYSICAL DEMANDS:

1) Able to stand and walk for a minimum of 8 hours per day.

(cont'd)

---

* Valhalla Inn Markham

JOB STANDARDS: (cont'd)

1) Arrive at work in business attire, including name tag and proper shoes.
2) Maintain a friendly, professional and close working relationship with co-workers, management and other hotel employees through co-operative and effective communication.
3) Understand and follow the hotel rules and guidelines as outlined in the Employee Handbook.

Employee Handbook
TABLE OF CONTENTS

A Word From The General Manager
Mission Statement
Who Are We?
The Organization Chart
Telephone List
Your First Three Months
Career Development Plan
House Rules

      Security
      Authorized/Unauthorized Areas
      Lost & Found
      Visitors on Site
      Telephone Calls
      Requesting Time Off
      Calling in Sick
      Calling in Late
      Staff Entrance/Exit
      Smoking Policy
      Equipment and Tools

Uniforms, Grooming and Hygiene
Lockers
Breaks and Meals
What To Do If You Are Injured
What To Do In An Emergency
Employee Benefits and Payroll

      Rate of Pay
      What Happened to OHIP (Ontario Hospital Insurance Plan)
      Pay Day
      Overtime
      Statutory Holidays
      Sick Pay
      Bereavement
      Scheduling Policy
      Personal Change and Status Information

Employee Conduct
Disciplinary Guidelines
Causes for Termination
Terminated Employees
Staff Bulletin Boards
The Twilight Zone (staff communication corridor)
Statistics About the Company
Addresses of The Companies and Properties
A Closing Word

(con't)

4) Have complete knowledge of service procedures and departmental guidelines as outlined in the department Procedures Manual.
5) Know how to safely use the following equipment: Remanco hardware; photocopier; 2016 Meridian display telephone; confirmed hardware; beverage dispensers; calculator; fax machine.
6) Respond to all guest compliments and complaints and report the action and result to the General Manager where appropriate.
7) Practice progressive coaching techniques to change employee behaviour. When necessary, administer disciplinary action.
8) Be familiar with the Career Development Plan and know how it is administered.

DATE CREATED/REVISED: April 19, 1991

For instance, job "streaming" was alleged by Diane Gale, a former deli manager, to have taken place at a Miracle Food Mart grocery store. She claimed that the company "streamed female employees into the lowest-paying jobs as cashiers and clerks." She eventually quit in 1989 for another line of work. The lawyer for the provincial Human Rights Commission said Miracle Food Mart's job classifications showed men being placed in the highest-paid jobs; only four women were among the 179 grocery/produce managers. With no actual job descriptions, and an informal method of promoting employees, the bias swung strongly in favour of men. As of July 1992, the Commission had not ruled on the matter, but it was considered a precedent sex-discrimination case for the retail and grocery industry.[29]

VIRGIN AIR ATTENDANTS?

A blatant example, from Canada's point of view, of a discriminatory job specification is that involving China Air and its recruitment problem: it wants female virgins for flight attendants! Hao Yu-ping, the school director, says the new recruits must be virgins. The problem is that not many pass the so-called "chastity test." Hao thinks the sexual history [a job specification] of these potential flight attendants makes a difference. Her reason? "We can't have our girls fooling around with the passengers!" Are there any other job specifications for this "figure of awesome authority"? You bet! All applicants must "have odorless armpits, no pockmarks and a 'correct political attitude'," the latter point meaning, in Hao's job specification book, no boyfriends![30]

GLASS CEILING? OR STEEL CEILING?

In male-dominated Poland, now that communism is gone, so are the jobs. Even though women make up 48% of the workforce, 53% are unemployed. Why? The answer lies in discrimination. "Potentia employers now are free to advertise for male chief accountants or female secretaries, for a worker who is young, childless or pretty."[31] As a matter of fact, the Polish word "businessman" has no female equivalent! A poll taken by the largest newspaper showed that 75% of Polish men want women to take care of the house and children; 60% of women agreed with them!

In summary, when the supervisor has completed a job analysis (if necessary) and developed job descriptions and specifications, he/she is in a much more intelligent (as well as legal) position to appreciate the interplay among the various elements: the job itself, what is required to do the job, and the qualifications necessary to do the job well. Of course, these activities of job analysis, description, and specification will have to be updated over time. This will be more so as government regulation and societal expectations grow and change. "Human resources management will increasingly dwell on matching corporate needs with personal needs as the competition to hire skilled, educated and experienced workers intensifies."[32]

THE SELECTION PROCESS

With jobs classified (job analysis), with tasks specified (job description), and with potential candidate qualifications identified (job specification), the supervisor is now ready to recruit employees.

Recruitment means to attract, identify, screen, interview and hire the appropriate candidates for the job(s) needing to be filled. In large organizations, it is the co-responsibility of the human resources manager *and* the supervisor to work in tandem. This can be not only helpful, but also critical because the supervisor cannot be expected to know all the human resources implications, organizationally and legally. But they are important. In smaller organizations, with no human resources manager, the supervisor will recruit, interview, and hire by him/herself. In both situations, the supervisor will need to match the organization need with the right candidate. If supervisors can remember that this selection process may the most important function in the company, then the decision to recruit and hire carefully will take on the pre-eminence it should. Supervisors get the employees they deserve!

"More and more individuals will have to divide their time among working for pay, raising children, and caring for aged parents. ... The changing nature of family life presents a growing challenge to North American business to adapt to social realities. ... A new type of male worker has also arrived. ... He is likely to have a different set of values from men in the past, defining success in terms of all aspects of his life and looking upon his career as only part of the whole."[33]

Nᴇᴄᴇssᴀʀʏ sᴛᴇᴘs ɪɴ sᴇʟᴇᴄᴛɪɴɢ ᴇᴍᴘʟᴏʏᴇᴇs

❶ *recruiting* inside, outside
❷ *screening* job applications
❸ *interviewing* job applicants
❹ *assessing* job applicants
❺ *reference checking* job applicants
❻ *selecting* and *hiring* job applicants
❼ *placing* job applicants

RECRUITING INSIDE/OUTSIDE

To comply with employment equity requirements and to make sure that *all* employees in the organization know about a job opening, the supervisor will post the job. This job posting and internal method of recruiting can be done through memos, bulletin boards, and newsletters. "In a U.S. study, 76 per cent of the organizations reported that they fill a majority of their openings internally."[34] Another internal strategy supervisors might access is the HRIS (Human Resource Information System) that their company might have installed.

HUMAN RESOURCES: COMMENTARY BY SYD YOUNG

[Interview with Mr. Sid Young, a 24-year veteran of the Toronto Metropolitan Police Force, was the Human Resources Manager from 1985-88, responsible for putting in place the first employment equity program that the Force established. In 1988 he was seconded to the Ministry of the Attorney General as the Cross-cultural Police Co-ordinator. In essence he worked with police forces across the province of Ontario, assisting them to develop employment equity programs for their respective police forces. He was subsequently reassigned to the Court Services as manager in charge of all policing activities (such as training and education, the day-to-day operations) at Old City Hall in 1991 and is responsible for 120 employees. This is the first of a series for this and subsequent chapters.]

The issue of selection within the context of an equitable work environment is not a stand-alone piece because when an organization embarks on its recruitment and selection of employees, it first has to look at its proper human resources strategy: the analysis of the organization, where the organization is, the design of the program which meets the needs of the organization, the implementation of that particular program, and the monitoring of those programs once they are in place. Selection is a piece of that.

The organization has to look at how it sells itself. For example, if any organization, once it has completed its analysis, determines that it doesn't reflect the community that it serves -- this is particularly so within the public sector -- then the organization has to put in place unique marketing or recruitment strategies which are designed to attract qualified people who are not represented within the organization (e.g., visible minorities, aboriginals, physically disabled, and women). Recruitment strategy, therefore, has to be based on the needs of the organization. I call that marketing. Develop the program, go to those areas and people where the kinds of people you need are available, and sell the organization and job opportunities to those people. There are many ways to do that, but that is a concept that the organization has to be very much aware of.

Once that is completed, then the organization must look at the selection tools. How are positions made in terms of who gets hired? If, for instance, we sell the organization to women, native people, minorities, and the handicapped, and then these people apply for jobs, if we use biased or inappropriate selection tools, these people will possibly be screened out. So the kinds of tools and kinds of processes that the organization uses must be carefully examined to ensure that the organization does not have an adverse impact on people once they come to the door looking for jobs. This also extends itself to the kinds of people interviewing, the interviewer training that is provided so that they too understand the organizational goals and the people whom they are interviewing and that any test(s) is job-related.

To recruit outside the organization, a supervisor has many avenues to pursue. A supervisor can respond to mailed-in résumés. In these recessionary times, many supervisors are swamped with would-be applicants. Michael Stern, president of Michael Stern Associates Inc., a Toronto recruitment firm, speaks about the "30-second reading" that a résumé gets. According to Stern, "The average executive recruiter, or human resources manager, makes the first cut after spending only about 30 seconds on each résumé -- so it has to do its selling fast."[35]

Also, depending on need and circumstances, just placing a sign on a store window for walk-ins - such as at a donut shop or gas station -- may be all that is needed. An approach that is sometimes overlooked is employee referrals. Having a personal recommendation from a present employee can be a cost-effective as well as a positive recruiting technique. Of course, in larger companies, more sophisticated approaches will be needed, such as newspaper articles or ads as well as accessing the hundreds of Canada Employment

Centres (CEC) that the federal government has set up across Canada. These centres are the meeting-grounds, so to speak, both for employers and would-be employees. A computerized data bank of information gathered from these employers and would-be employees matches the needs; would-be employees get a chance to be interviewed, and employers are able to advertise nationally.[36]

THE COST OF HIRING[37]

$$C/H = \frac{SC + ST + MT + PC + T\&R + Misc.}{H}$$

where C/H is the Cost per Hire; SC is Source Cost (methods used to attract job applicants, e.g., advertising costs, agency fees); ST is Staff Time (hours staff put into the process costed against salary, benefits, etc.); MT is the Supervisor's Time (costed against salary, benefits, etc.); PC is the Processing Time (the effort and time it took to get the hire's record checked, any medical exams, etc.); T&R is the Travel and Relocation costs (if any); and Misc. are the Miscellaneous costs, the unplanned expenses the supervisor didn't expect; and all of these costs are divided by the number of new Hires (H).

Another possibility for the supervisor is the many community colleges and universities throughout Canada. Notices are often placed on bulletin boards in business departments with potential job openings. Supervisors can also hire outside placement agencies and "headhunters" to recruit for them, but a word of caution is in order here: know the agency, its philosophy, its track record, its credibility, and its service response. With headhunters, find out who they are, their ethics, and whether or not they can be trusted. The headhunter may be more interested in getting the 30 per cent commission than getting the best fit of new employee and company. Finally, a supervisor can also post in a union hall any notice of an opening, especially in those trades which demand this process as part of the collective agreement.

SCREENING JOB APPLICATIONS

Screening job applicants is an important activity because it helps the supervisor sort out the more appropriate candidates from those who are not.

Of course, employment equity considerations and legislation has to guide supervisors as well. However the potential job applicant heard about the job, the supervisor needs now to cull the résumés or application forms that were submitted. Most companies and organizations use application forms.[38] If the supervisor advertised effectively, the job applications should reflect this; if not, a supervisor could have hundreds of applications from people seeking work, even if the industry is not their preferred choice. An application form (standard type) enables clearer comparison of applicants.

In addition to this more frequently used biographical application form, sometimes supervisors will use WABs, or weighted application blanks as a predictor of work behaviour and performance. This application form is "weighted" in favour of certain desired options by the supervisor, and job applicants are then sorted according to the weighted criteria and the factors that reflect a particular criterion. For instance, past performance records, as well as research, might indicate that to the supervisor that excellent employees have consistently had three characteristics. These would be given higher weights in relation to other characteristics. Or, "two years of secondary school receives a certain score and four years another. Scores are determined by analyzing the relationship between the responses to items and measures of job performance such as absences, productivity, and turnover)."[39] Criteria, of course, have to be job-related and be predictive of future excellent employee performance. The job applicant(s) with the most weighted points would be screened and brought in for an interview. "Results of several past studies have in general supported the validity of application blanks. However, applicants may often exaggerate or give totally untruthful information in their application forms."[40]

> In general, studies have supported the validity of application formsl

INTERVIEWING JOB APPLICANTS

Interviews are used by most companies and organizations in selecting their personnel. However, there are problems as well with the use of the interview.

Is it that good a predictor of job effectiveness, for instance? "The accumulated evidence has documented the poor accuracy of traditional, unstructured interviews in predicting job performance."[41] Research indicates that if the same interviewer does the interview twice, there is good reliability with the process;[43] however, if different interviewers are involved, there is low reliability with the process. What does show promise is the use of a panel of interviewers[44] who combine their insights, remarks and judgments, and are able to give a more accurate assessment of a potential job applicant. What is called behaviour description interviewing, which uses specific job-related questions to guide the interview, shows much promise. Unlike the 14 per cent accuracy rating generally applicable to interviews, behaviour description interviewing techniques can reach a 50 per cent accuracy mark!

Validation studies on interviewing have been able to show that the best estimate of interview validity is still only 14 per cent! In other words, you only have a 14 per cent chance of getting the best potential candidate(s) for your company![42]

Yet the interview is still used. And realistically, it will continue to be used. "The interview has been raked over the coals by many knowledgeable people (especially research workers) and in turn praised to the heavens by others (usually personnel people)."[45]

INTERVIEW HURDLES FOR SUPERVISORS[46]

- the supervisor's *personal background* and frame of reference (i.e., how the supervisor sees the world, personal philosophy on life, stereotypes, prejudices). In today's legislated working environment, self-examination is particularly important with the new employment equity legislation that supervisors must cope with *in spite of how they feel*;
- the *psychological influences* that impact on the supervisor (e.g., how self-confident the supervisor feels);
- the impact of *body language*, both from the supervisor and job applicant, in the interview;
- the supervisor's own sense of importance in the interview (e.g., status, ability to be credible);
- the supervisor's environmental constraints in the interview (e.g., physical layout, privacy, comfort, distractions);
- the supervisor's communication skills (e.g., ability to be understood and to understand the meaning of what the job applicant conveys);
- ability to ask the appropriate *kinds of questions* (in terms of their ambiguity/abstractness/clarity, and whether open, closed, probing, loaded, confrontative); and
- NOT BEING PREPARED!

There seem to be four main reasons for the continuance of the interview:[47]

1. Supervisors will say that they can only get a "feel" for a candidate in the interviewing process, such as interpersonal skills, the potential "fit" required to work in a specific corporate culture, etc.
2. Supervisors find the interview easy to do, especially when there are only a few job applicants.
3. Supervisors, especially long-time supervisors, sincerely believe that they can make good "judgment calls" about potential job applicants in an interview.
4. These kinds of "street smarts," or intuitive judgment making, reinforce for the supervisor that "getting the right person essentially boils down to experience."
5. Supervisors believe also that the interview is a time and place to enhance the organization's image and to promote the company.

The supervisor needs to prepare for the interviewing process, which includes not only having adequate training for interviewing, but also planning the time and kind of interview to be held: for instance, whether it will be a structured or an unstructured interview, a stress interview (used particularly by the police and armed forces to identify which job candidates have "the right stuff" for the stress-related work they will be involved in), a problem-solving interview (which requires the interviewee to solve a series of problems presented that will be crucial for the job performance), or a mixed interview which would combine planned and unplanned questions).

At this point, the supervisor needs to develop an interview guide which would include such items as how the opening will be, the kinds of structured questions that will be asked, and how the interview will end. Questions that are sometimes on an interview guide would be: (1) Describe your last job; (2) Tell me (us) something about yourself. The data required needs to be job-related, clear of any human rights violations, and specifications (e.g., speech, personality), able to be behaviourally anchored. These activities would have been completed *before* using the data sheet and supervisors would need to be trained in spotting these behaviourally anchored specifications in potential job applicants.

The supervisor also has to keep in mind the necessary legislative guidelines from the Canadian Human Rights Commission on the kinds of questions that can be asked and those that need to be avoided or reworded in order to avoid a potentially discriminatory focus. The Canadian Human Rights Act, passed by Parliament on July 14, 1977, and effective in law in March 1978, states in its Guide[48] that

> *Every individual should have an equal opportunity with other individuals to make for himself or herself the life that he or she is able and wishes to have, consistent with his or her duties and obligations as a member of society.*

To accomplish this aim, the Act specifies ten grounds on which discrimination is forbidden, the assumption being that if these discriminatory practices were removed, *all Canadians* would have a better and more equal opportunity to make and live the life they want to have. Former Justice Minister Kim Campbell planned to amend the Act by adding the "sexual orientation" prohibition in areas of federal jurisdiction. Ontario, Quebec, Manitoba, and the Yukon already ban discrimination on the basis of sexual orientation.[49] Perhaps even the traditional concept of the family as two people of the opposite sex[50] will be changed for reasons of pension and job benefits, in spite of the federal government on June 16, 1992, defeating "amendments to the act governing public service pensions that could have seen pension and survivor benefits extended to gay and lesbian couples in the federal public service."[51]

The ten currently prohibited grounds of discrimination are: race, national or ethnic origin, colour, religion, age, sex, marital status, family status, pardoned conviction, and disability.

The Canadian Human Rights Commission has resources and guides on the kinds of questions allowed in an interview. In relation to age, the supervisor cannot ask, "How old are you?" but can ask, "Are you between the ages of 18 and 65?" Again, if supervisors are concerned about a past criminal record, they cannot ask, "Have you ever been in jail?" but can ask, "Have you ever been convicted of a crime for which you have not received a pardon?"

BEING GAY, BEING A 'FAMILY,' AND GETTING WORKPLACE BENEFITS

Government employee Brian Mossop had asked for time off to attend the funeral of his partner's father. He was denied the request. A human rights tribunal ruled in his favour, saying his collective agreement at work discriminated by excluding same-sex couples from its definition of family. The federal government appealed the decision and it was overturned in 1990 by the Federal Court of Appeal, which said same-sex couples are not families under the law. That decision was in turn appealed to the Supreme Court by the Human Rights Commission. The Court ironically rejected Mossop's "family status" *human rights* claim on February 25, 1993, but said a future claim might have a different outcome, if argued under the Charter of Rights and Freedoms, and if the Canadian Human Rights Act was amended to include sexual orientation as a prohibited ground of discrimination.[52] In August 1992, an Ontario Court of Appeal had ruled that the Canadian Human Rights Act does in fact discriminate on sexual orientation. The Canadian Human Rights Commission gave their blessing to this ruling, in effect making *sexual orientation* the eleventh prohibited ground of discrimination in Ontario.[53]

The Canadian Human Rights Act covers federal departments, agencies, crown corporations, and any businesses under federal jurisdiction, such as banks, airline companies, and railway companies. The provinces, in their provincial human rights laws, will cover areas not under federal jurisdiction, for instance, the age groups protected under human rights acts which vary considerably from one jurisdiction to another. Supervisors need to contact their provincial human rights commission office to be informed in this matter. There also may be what is called a reasonable exception: a bona fide occupational qualification (BFOQ) or bona fide occupational requirement (BFOR). To refuse to hire a blind person as a taxi driver would seem to be discrimination based on the Act, but this "reasonable" BFOQ exception is allowed because of the obvious potential harm were it not granted. Thus, a BFOQ is deemed absolutely necessary to do the job.

If there is a problem that cannot be resolved, provincial and federal human rights commissions are in place to deal with the matter. The "sophistication"[55] of the case will usually determine if

"For example, the Supreme Court of Canada has ruled that wearing a hard hat is a bona fide occupational requirement and that there is therefore no duty to accommodate persons of the Sikh religion who are required to wear a turban and no other head covering. While the Court repeated its finding in *O'Malley vs. Simpsons-Sears Ltd.* that it is not necessary to show an intention to discriminate in order for there to be a violation of human rights legislation, the hard hat rule was allowed because it was being applied to all employees and therefore the Federal Court of Appeal ruled it a bona fide occupational requirement."[54]

it is a provincial or federal matter. Obviously it makes eminent sense if the company or organization can handle the complaint at the local level.

ASSESSING JOB APPLICANTS

Sometimes supervisors will need to use tests in determining the appropriate qualifications of candidates. As in other selection matters, strict adherence to human rights legislation, as well as tests that are job-related, must be maintained. The supervisor may want to use tests that check an applicant's abilities, aptitudes, or skills.[56] Obviously, if the supervisor has no training or certification in administering these tests, then the appropriate professional must be brought in. Other tests that may be important are: language tests, personality tests, and interest inventories. It is important for the supervisor to keep in mind the reality of "adverse effect": even though there may be no preconceived intention to discriminate, the effect of a supervisory or hiring policy may in fact adversely affect a job applicant or employee. Such was the situation stated earlier of *Singh vs. Security and Investigated Services Ltd.*, Ontario Board of Inquiry, May 30, 1977. The company wanted clean-shaven and properly cut hair on all its employees. Singh, a Sikh, could not fulfil this requirement because of his religion. "The board of inquiry found that although the company did not intend to discriminate against Sikhs, it nevertheless discriminated against the applicant through the effect of its employment policies."[57]

The question of ethics, both inside and outside the organization, is also a noted topic these days.[58] Outside the organization, for instance, in the retail industry, because of shoplifting, more than $2 billion was stolen in 1991. "'That's more than the total profits of the retail industry,' Mel Fruitman, vice-president of the council, told reporters yesterday at a loss prevention conference. 'This money could have been used to buy new inventory, hire more staff," and help pull the country out of recession.'"[59]

The U.S. Chamber of Commerce estimates that workplace theft amounts to $7,125 stolen per minute.[60] Also, "35 percent of business failures in the United States are caused by fraud artists ... an estimated 25 percent of companies will be defrauded at some point, with small firms being particularly vulnerable ... perhaps 75 percent of business fraud goes undetected."[61] One business fraud that *was* detected involved an employee charged by a Workers Compensation Board "with two counts of fraud under $1,000, two counts of forgery and two counts of uttering a forged document."[62] The Police Investigation Support Squad was brought in to investigate. They discovered that the employee had manually altered two paycheques by increasing their amounts. The WCB's regular payroll verification process caught this problem; hence the employee was charged.

Inside the organization interest in **honesty tests** for job applicants is growing with the use of pencil-and-paper tests and polygraph or lie detector tests. Paper-and-pencil tests have been shown to reliably cut losses by as much as 50 per cent![63] The difficulty in trying to assess something like honesty is to determine what it means exactly. Some provinces allow these tests; Ontario does not.

REFERENCE CHECKING JOB APPLICANTS

Most organizations make background checks on potential employees. It is very foolish if a supervisor neglects this important step in the selection process. One in 200 American applicants was found to have fraudulent credentials![64] Some supervisors may have what is called the "name, rank, and serial number" approach to references, that is, only say or write as little as possible in case they are sued for slander or libel. Toronto employment lawyer Howard Levitt counters this reluctance and caution this way in regards to an employee who has been fired: "As a rule, a former employer cannot be sued for libel or slander by a terminated employee as a result of a reference, even if the information provided in the reference is damaging and inaccurate. Information provided in a reference is protected by the courts."[65]

SELECTING AND HIRING JOB APPLICANTS

When the selection and interviewing procedures have been completed, the

REFERENCE CHECK FORM*

	COMPANY	COMPANY	COMPANY
	CONTACT	CONTACT	CONTACT
	TITLE	TITLE	TITLE
	PHONE	PHONE	PHONE
What sort of employee was _____?			
Did he/she get along well with other staff members?			
Did he/she take direction well?			
Were there any problems regarding punctuality or attendance?			
Was he/she conscientious?			
Why did he/she leave?			
Is there anything specific that you feel I should know about this person?			
Were it your company policy, would you rehire _____?			
Confirmation of salary earned			
Should any employer be openly hostile or unresponsive, obtain a second opinion. For those unwilling to give references over the phone, have applicant call for permission or send form letter by fax.			

* VALHALLA COMPANIES LIMITED

supervisor must make a choice or choices. At this point, the supervisor can rely securely on the information and qualifications of the applicants.

PLACING JOB APPLICANTS

After the job applicant has been hired, the supervisor has one more task: to make sure that the new employee is placed in the new job. All the recruiting and selecting efforts have led to this one objective: to fill a vacancy.

THE CRITICAL ROLE OF ORIENTATION

Too often, when supervisors have spent so much time and effort to find and hire the "right" employee, they leave the employee on their own after they become part of the organization. Orientation is a critical first step in the socialization task for the new hire.[66] Orientation makes the new hires find their "turf," so to speak, "get the lay of the land" at the very outset and balance out any unreal expectations. The orientation is strongly influenced by the new hire's co-workers, supervisors, and informed sources of information along the way.[67] The main purpose is to develop and sustain organizational commitment in and from the new hire.[68]

> "Orientation ... may incorporate information about the firm's history, founders and their successors, present executives and their major areas of responsibility, and organizational chart. Orientation also usually includes explanations of the policies of the firm, the responsibility of each employee for carrying out these policies, and the rules that govern behavior within the firm. The latter usually cover days and hours of work; doors by which to enter and leave; space in which to store coats and other belongings during the workday; use of employee lounges, lunchrooms, and restrooms; medical services available; emergencies; and other important directives."[69]

HUMAN RESOURCES: COMMENTARY BY SYD YOUNG

Let's assume the right people, well qualified, are chosen for the job(s). The organization has expended a lot of cost to go out and recruit the very best people. It is important at this point that the organization have in place a proper orientation and training program so that when these people come on board, they

> too can succeed, that they don't come on board feeling that they're not wanted, but rather, that they belong to the organization. This is a process that requires commitment of senior managers; it requires policies on appropriate conduct. A proper orientation program doesn't happen by itself. It has to be managed and managed effectively. If management does all this, and if it is clear that the employee will not succeed, then management must take a position and realize that the employee will have to be dehired.

Most new hires are likely to quit in the first six months after being hired;[70] it's important to reduce this high turnover because it is expensive to start over again. A poor orientation program can be costly to a company; besides, employee productivity will not be as high or as satisfactory -- factors leading to greater dissatisfaction and turnover.[71] A social orientation program at Texas Instruments is credited with a 40 per cent drop in early career turnover.[72] Shown below is a model of an orientation plan. As can be seen, the new hire is looked after regarding many important items to the business.

Socialization is the continuing process of orienting the new employee so that he/she becomes a company or organizational person. It is the process which eventually allows the employee to call it "his/her company." Organizational theorist Dr. Edgar Schein describes this process as a three-fold one: entry phase (what we are calling orientation); socialization phase; and mutual acceptance phase.[73] The Procter & Gamble company is known for its "testing" of newcomers to help them fit in with their achievement-oriented culture.[74] In this kind of a socialization, a formal breaking of expectations occurs and the new employee learns to do it "the company way." At Hewlett-Packard Co., it is known as the H-P Way. Founder Bill Hewlett says the "Way" can only be captured by its "spirit": "There is a feeling that everyone is part of a team, and that team is H-P."[75]

ORIENTATION PLAN*

EMPLOYEE'S NAME _____

JOB TITLE _____ DEPARTMENT _____

DIVISION _____ HIRE DATE _____

EMPLOYEE #: _____ PAYROLL # _____

LOCKER #: _____ SUPERVISOR _____

(cont'd)

* Valhalla Inn Markham

CHECK ITEMS RECEIVED

Employee Card ❑   Combination Lock ❑   Uniform ❑   Employee Benefits Book ❑

Staff List & Titles ❑   Name Tag ❑   Job Description ❑

THE FOLLOWING ITEMS WILL BE ADDRESSED WITH YOU BY THE HUMAN RESOURCES MANAGER:

	DATE & INITIALS
1. Tour of the Hotel	
2. Goals & Mission Statement	
3. Orientation Video	
4. Introduction to Management Team	
5. Organization Chart & Reporting Structure	
6. Sign-up with company:	
Application/Resume	
Personal Action Form	
TDI	
Manufacturers' Life Application	
Payroll Information	
7. Career Development Plan	
8. Review of Company Benefits	
9. Payroll Information & Time Clock Usage	
10. Review of Company Policies, Procedures & Standards	

Safety, Accidents & FA		Lockers	
Fires & Evacuation		Smoking	
Probationary Period		Security	
Uniform/Dress Policy		Vacation	
Personal Phone Calls		Breaks/Meals	
Disciplinary Procedures		Dismissal	
Causes for Discipline		Overtime	
Awards & Privilegs			

THE FOLLOWING ITEMS WILL BE ADDRESSED WITH YOU BY YOUR DEPARTMENT HEAD:

1. Tour of the Work Area	
2. Full Explanation of Job Description, Responsibilities & Tasks	
3. Introduction & Training on Department Equipment	
4. Introduction to Supervisors & Department Staff Members	
5. Sanitation/Hygiene Standards	
6. Washroom Locations	

(cont'd)

DATE & INITIALS

7. Working hours
8. Department Policies, Procedures & Standards

Supply Requisitions		Hygiene	
Schedule Requests		Uniforms	
Vacation Requests		Sanitation	
Leaving Work Area			

I have received full orientation and acknowledge that all of the listed items have been discussed.

EMPLOYEE'S SIGNATURE _____

DATE _____

DEPARTMENT HEAD'S SIGNATURE _____

DATE _____

HUMAN RESOURCES MANAGER'S

SIGNATURE _____

DATE _____

THE IMPORTANCE OF TRAINING AND DEVELOPMENT

An on-going and critical task that the supervisor must manage is the training and development of employees. Karen Hanna, Director Human Resources at Levi Strauss Canada, emphasizes the matter succinctly by saying, "You have to invest in development."[76] This is especially true today with so much new information, technology, and know-how impacting on the workplace. Obsolescence is a real threat.[77] A perfect example of obsolescence interfering with productivity is Domtar Inc.'s new $1.2-*billion* paper mill complex in Windsor, Ontario, which could not operate efficiently, not only because of the downturn in the economy for paper products and the sophisticated technology contained in the football-sized complex, but also because union contracts "forced the hiring of workers from the St-François mill, many of whom were used to 1940s-vintage machines. The new mill's technology belonged more to the 21st century."[78]

HUMAN RESOURCES: COMMENTARY BY SYD YOUNG

"Danger of the Rear View Mirror Approach in Canada"

If the organization is not utilizing its employees to their fullest, it is selling itself short. This is particularly true of ourselves as Canadians. We are setting ourselves up to compete in particular with the United States and with Mexico. Canada has approximately 27 million people. If you take out the number of people who are (1) under 16 years of age, (2) over 65 years of age, (3) disabled, unable to work, etc., we have a very small group of people in this country who produce what we have. If we again take out of that working group people who do important work -- such as government workers, teachers, doctors, firefighters, nurses, etc. -- we find that this group does not produce anything that is saleable *per se*. We cannot trade those kinds of services with Mexico or with the United States. We, as a nation, must work harder and produce more. Large and small organizations have to select the very best and most productive people for their organizations, train these people to standards, provide a climate in the organization for these employees to produce to their best, and provide systems for on-going excellence. If that does not occur, we are heading for a debacle in this country: we will not be able to compete! We spend too little money in training and developing our employees as it is right now. *We don't look ahead very well.*

"*Training* is defined as any organizationally planned effort to change the behaviour or attitudes of employees so that they can perform to acceptable standards on the job."[79] Training that prepares employees for future positions in the organizations is known as *development*.[80] The difference between *training* and *development* is "more one of degree, level of abstraction, and methods."[81] Mike Kennedy, a management training consultant in Montreal, points out that "companies are opting for short programs to impart specialized skills" and that "problems from globalization and downsizing are increasing the responsibility of individual managers and forcing companies to deal with change."[82] Robert Stoeckler, a consultant with Right Associates in New Jersey, agrees: "The ultimate security for employees is understanding their own skills."[83]

John Denomy, manager of education quality at IBM Canada, says, "Canadian companies will have to improve the quality of their work forces ... There will be little room for unskilled employees, cumbersome layers of management, or the types of jobs in which employees passively perform assigned tasks without having to think for themselves."[84] And at Levi Strauss Canada, it is

As part of their employee development program, the Valhalla Companies have introduced an Action Planning Worksheet which is completed by all levels of management for their own position. An annual document, the APW defines the objectives and goals of the individual, the means to achieve the targets, the necessary tools required to meet the objectives, and the measuring stick for success.

the same commitment to development: "Each year it shuts down for a day to review corporate values and apprise employees of its multipoint mission statement. The firm also pays employees to attend regular classes in English as a second language."[85] At the new Chrysler plant, workers are taking great pains to "do it right as any workers in the greatly admired Japanese car factories" training being management-directed to accomplish this objective.[86]

Ironically, too, it is sometimes the training that employees have received that is one of the reasons some are questioning the many recessionary layoffs. Training has provided better critical thinking skills! Margaret Regan, a human resources expert at Towers Perrin, calls it a "knee-jerk reaction" and says, "The Japanese think we're out of our minds."[87] CEO Roland Boreham Jr. reiterates this sentiment by saying that "you have a lot of training, experience, and skills going out the door, as well as company loyalty." And Michael Unseem, a sociologist at the Wharton School of Business, concludes, "companies with a history of repeated bloodletting have trouble attracting new talent when they need it."

CORPORATE COMMITMENT: TRAINING AND DEVELOPMENT

How committed are Canadian and American business to training and development? In a detailed questionnaire on total quality management (TQM) that was sent out to businesses around the world, "North American companies took an average of 20 hours to fill in the questionnaire. The Japanese spent an average of 400 hours."[88] This doesn't sound like a lot of commitment compared to the Japanese. In the United States, it is estimated that about $60 billion is spent each year on training, with 8 million employees, involving 15 billion work hours![89] On the Canadian side, Matthew Barrett,

chairman of the Bank of Montreal, said, "Canadian business invested only $1.4-billion in in-house training last year."[90] John Cleghorn, president, Royal Bank of Canada, writes, "In the late 1980s, per capita spending by Canadian companies [on workforce training] was half the level in the United States and less than a quarter of what is spent in Germany. How can we hope to compete if we are not leading in the development of our work force?"[91]

Others will say that Canada does spend a lot, close

to $200 million a year which represents roughly $16/employee or 1% of corporate profits.[92] In the 1980s the Canada Employment and Immigration Commission was allocating $140 million to employers to train their employees and the federal government's Canadian Jobs Strategy program was allocating $1.65 billion.[93] At IBM Canada Ltd., training has become more important than ever. It is showing this commitment by increasing spending on training by 20%, or $50 million! What are the areas of concentration? "Such skills as decision-making, working in a team, showing leadership, communicating verbally and in writing, thinking laterally and how to use stress constructively."[94] And finally, "GM Canada is spending $24-million (Canadian) on training."[95]

However, training and development efforts are increasing because of the knowledge worker and the needs of the marketplace. What is sorely lacking in Canada is a concerted public commitment to research and development. Among the 24 nations in the Organization for Economic Co-operation and Development in the late 1980s, Canada ranked 14, just behind Turkey! This was because Canada was still only spending 1.2 per cent of its gross domestic product on research and development! Thomas Di Giacome, chairman, Manulife Financial, says, "Canada's industry currently spends just 0.5 per cent of GDP on training initiatives. This must change if we are to equip young Canadians with the tools they need ... to make this country a world-class competitor."[96]

MULTICULTURAL TRAINING FOR THE WORKPLACE

An important training area for the supervisor now and for the future will be the sensitization of employees to the diverse workplace. In a speech on Friday, April 11, 1986, the then Minister of State for Multiculturalism stated, "Our society has become *irreversibly* multicultural and multiracial."[97] And John Samuel, demographer at Carleton University in Ottawa, says, "We are a nation of minorities."[98] By the year 2001, Metro Toronto alone will have 45 per cent of its population as visible minorities. The workplace will reflect that reality as well. Will supervisors be ready? Will employees? In 1962, "only 3 per cent of Metro's population was composed of visible minorities. Today, it's one person in four. And more than 100 different languages and dialects are spoken in greater Metro." Lawyer Malcolm MacKillop says that as the workplace becomes increasingly diverse, employers will have to deal with racism more and more.[99] McKillop gives two situations: one involving a factory that provided microwave ovens in the lunchroom, some employees complaining to

"It is only when a man is truly able to confront another with openness, directness, and honesty; when he is able to trust and assume responsibility for another; when he meets another's Thou; only then does a man experience genuine humanity."[100] -- Stephen M. Panko, on Martin Buber

management about the smell of Indian food being heated, and the other a case of the kitchen employees complaining that staff members of another race smelled bad in the hot surroundings. Supervisors cannot leave these potentially explosive situations to chance.

Racism will be a possibility if the supervisor does not set a proactive training and development focus for employees. "Racism is endemic. It's in the air people breathe. It's part of daily life. It's inescapable and soul-destroying."[101] The Stephen Lewis 37-page report highlighted the need for education and training to combat racism.[102] "The reality, significance and promotion of multiculturalism rejects saying that because others are different, they, therefore, are unacceptable."[103]

Also, depending on the level of sophistication of a supervisor's responsibilities and the global competitive environment their company is working in, a supervisor may be involved in international business. To do this well will demand cross-cultural training to prepare employees to work and relate to people offshore, or to spend time offshore as part of the work demands. "Inadequate training has been well documented, ranging from the loss of business deals worth millions of dollars, the break-up of profitable joint-ventures, and the loss of valuable local employees, to high turnover rates and premature returns among maladjusted overseas employees."[104] It is estimated by Graeme McDonald, Asia Pacific Foundation president, that "by the end of this decade, more than 70 percent of all world trade will be with or among the economies along the western shore of the Pacific."[105] This reality will demand "people with Asian skills and networks, firms with Asian partners and alliances," in short, multiculturalism, to survive economically. Ironically, if ethics and the human factor do not convince supervisors and employees to honour differences and diversity, the reality of economic survival will! Effective cross-cultural training will also be important in Canada for the future. Records have shown that at the federal Indian Affairs Department; systemic discrimination has been on the rise "against natives, women and disabled."[106] As well, lack of cross-cultural training has contributed to tension between natives and non-natives. An interesting example of one person trying to heal some of this tension is that of Crown Attorney Rupert Ross, not your ordinary lawyer. He hails from a prominent lawyer's family, became a dropout to be on the road with a rock band during the 1960s, went back to law school years later, and now, at age 46, finds himself fully at home in a northern city. His job? Continuing to learn the wisdom of traditional native ethics and philosophies and applying this "training" in the courtroom to bring a more holistic sense to court proceedings. The North for him is a personal experience: "I got to see a whole bunch of wisdom in people who didn't have a formal education and a whole bunch of human generosity -- all the things I thought were important about life." His has written a book on his experiences called *Dancing with a Ghost: Exploring Indian Reality.*[107]

SUMMARY

The HR professional is becoming more and more a part of the senior strategic direction of the company or organization. Human resources is too complicated and potentially explosive an area to neglect.

All supervisors and managers are human resource managers.

Job analysis gives the supervisor all the basic features of a job and reveals the actual tasks, activities, and skills related to jobs currently existing.

A job description tells *what* needs to be done in order to "get the job done" and spells out the working conditions, responsibilities or duties, reporting relationships or lines of authority, expected standards of performance, and the kinds of interpersonal relationships required.

Typically, a job specification *specifies* what experience and training are needed, the level of education, and the quality of skills and abilities needed.

Recruitment means to attract, identify, screen, interview, and hire the appropriate candidates for the jobs needed to be filled.

Recruiting includes: posting inside, outside the organization, screening job applications, interviewing, assessing, reference checking, selecting and hiring, and placing job applicant.

Legislative guidelines implemented by the Canadian Human Rights Commission on the kinds of questions that can be asked and those that need to be avoided or reworded in order to avoid a potentially discriminatory focus are crucial.

The ten currently prohibited grounds of discrimination are: race, national or ethnic origin, colour, religion, age, sex, marital status, family status, pardoned conviction, and disability. An eleventh may be added: family (sex) orientation.

Orientation helps the new hires find their "turf," so to speak, to "get the lay of the land" at the very outset and balance out any unreal expectations.

Training is defined as any organizationally planned effort to change the behaviour or attitudes of employees so that they can perform to acceptable standards on the job. Training that prepares employees for future positions in the organizations is known as *development. Socialization* is the continuing process of orienting the new employee to become a company or organizational person.

Training in race relations and multiculturalism is crucial today.

TERMS/CONCEPTS

personnel
human resources management (HRM)
job analysis
job description
job specification
recruiting inside/outside
screening job applicants
interviewing job applicants
interview guide

Canadian Human Rights Commission (CHRC)
assessing job applicants
reference checking
orientation
training
socialization
development
multiculturalism

DISCUSSION QUESTIONS

1. What is the role of human resources management in business?

2. Employees are considered the organization's most important resource. Discuss and give examples from your own experience.

3. Describe the differences among job analysis, job description, and job specification.

4. What are the key steps in the selection process?

5. Why is selecting employees perhaps the most important task for supervisors?

6. Why is orientation important? Identify Schein's three-fold phases to job orientation.

7. Define and describe the difference between *training* and *development*.

8. What is the commitment level of Canadian companies to training and development within their organizations? Discuss.

9. What is the role of multicultural training in the workplace?

10. What is cross-cultural training? Why is this important to supervisors?

ASSIGNMENT

Job description

Using the model on pages 270 - 271 as your guide, design a job description for a job you have had. Use the following headings:

- Position title
- Department
- Reports to
- Supervises (if applicable)
- Position summary

- Duties and responsibilities

  - Primary

  - Secondary

Job specification

Using the model on pages 272 - 274 as your guide, design a job specification for a job you have had. Use the following headings:

- Job requirements

- Education

- Experience

- Skills required to do the job

- Physical demands

- Job standards

CHAPTER TWELVE

DISCIPLINING AND
EVALUATING JOB PERFORMANCE

As in everything else, I must start with myself. That is: in all circumstances try to be decent, just, tolerant, and understanding, and at the same time try to resist corruption and deception.

-- Vaclav Havel, playwright,
former President, Czechoslovakia[1]

LEARNING OBJECTIVES

At the end of this chapter, students will be able to:

- Identify the factors in employee performance
- Distinguish between *proactive* and *reactive* discipline
- Understand how to conduct a disciplinary interview
- Identify the key steps in a performance appraisal
- Discuss the addictive process and problem employees
- Describe the role of the supervisor as counsellor

Opening scenario

*T*oday the key to the future is performance and productivity. Employees know that; so does management. Some believe that quality is quite fine and employees need a chance to expand their potential; others believe that Canadian companies lag far behind in productivity. An optimistic view, or a pessimistic view? As with many things in life, the answer lies somewhere in between: it's some (and ironically, the sum Σ) of both points of view. *Some* companies fall below effective performance; others surpass the mark and are quite successful.

Peak performance is very much tied to our self-concept and self-esteem, how competent we feel and the impact or significance of what we do on those around us.[2] Canadian Dave Clark, former head of Campbell Soup Co. Ltd., Canada, said, "I wanted to prove myself under adversity," when explaining his resistance and performance to keep the Canadian subsidiary -- and holding its own -- from being absorbed by its U.S. parent. He follows what he calls his MAHS -- *Management Ah Hell Syndrome:* "Life may be a marathon, but it's actually run in a series of sprints. As soon as you meet one challenge, you have to say to yourself, 'Ah hell, here comes another one.'"[3]

At Mars Inc., the candy bar company, "The Five Principles of Mars"[4] -- Quality, Responsibility, Mutuality, Efficiency, and Freedom -- go a long way in setting performance standards and expectations. Employees are called "associates" and "everyone, from the president on down, is paid a 10 per cent bonus for arriving on time." The Crayola staff at the Binney & Smith (Canada) Lindsay, Ontario, plant have made a success story of their Canadian operation. They have opted for efficiency, quality, and a decentralized working environment.[5]

Canadian companies do want to do well and succeed. The early 1990s brought news of a lot of doom and gloom, but also the reality that "Canadians had already embraced competitiveness."[6]

Job performance - what we do and how we're rewarded at work for it -- is making, and will continue to make, Canada the great country it is.

The purpose of this chapter is to examine common understandings of perform-ance: discipline as modelling, both in its corrective and proactive sense, and performance appraisal, giving feedback to employees so that they know where they stand as well as identifying areas where improvement and development may be possible. Failure to do that, besides missing the mark on employee development, can also contribute to unpleasantness on the job and wrongful dismissal lawsuits.[7]

Reflective Exercise

Identify the key performance factors that allow (or could allow) you to do an excellent job in your work.

_____

_____

_____

_____

_____

_____

FACTORS IN EMPLOYEE PERFORMANCE

Work or *job performance*[8] is the sum (Σ) of *who* you are and your *abilities* measured against the *energy* you put into doing something, which, in turn, is measured against the amount of *backing* your company or organization gives you. The pre-eminent responsibility of all supervisors is to achieve excellent performance, or "the attainment of organizational goals by using resources in an efficient and effective manner."[9] We can represent this by the following equation:

WORK PERFORMANCE

(Σ one's *abilities*)(*energy* input)(company *backing*)

What is obvious here is that peak performance is the **product** of a *process*: *who* an individual employee is (with skills, talents, abilities, etc.), the amount of *effort* this employee puts into doing the job, and the organizational *backing* and support that the employee receives. As you will notice, the issue of "hard work"[10] is not factored into this equation. There is a reason for this: excellent organizations measure their success, not by "a hollow ritual" that reinforces "a corporate culture that equates achievement with kilowatt hours,"[11] but by actual results. Harold Geneen, once head of ITT, put the matter this way:

Do You Feel Overworked?

David Harrington, company official for the time management people Priority Management, said, "Productivity is not only a function of how long people work, but also how long they do not work."[16] In recent research his company completed on 1,000 middle managerial and professional people across Canada, only 2% felt they were leading balanced lives! Economic uncertainty and fear of job loss were concerns even overriding family priorities. According to Harrington, improved productivity will come to those companies who can close the gap between employees' personal goals and the demands of the workplace. Otherwise, worry, concern, and insecurity were undermining work performance. Smart companies know this reality of managing the home-work dynamic and tension. Alan Torrie, president of MDS Laboratories Canada, says, "We're talking balance between people and profit. Between thinking and feeling. Between the personal and professional."[17]

"Only performance is reality. Performance alone is the best measure of your confidence, competence, and courage. Only performance gives you the freedom to grow as yourself."[12] The Hewlett-Packard Co. believes that also when it says that a great company's performance "has a track record of meeting its objectives."[13] In a strong survival instinct move, the United Steelworkers union has transformed themselves into an organization that also aims for peak performance. A new policy document, adopting experimental new policies, states: "Unions should be prepared to make an active contribution to the performance of the firms that employ their members in the areas of productivity, product quality and effective organizational design."[14] Even the performance of boards of directors of companies is being challenged.[15]

What's changing, therefore, in the world of business is not only the concept of *performance* but also the *expectations* surrounding its reality. A much greater emphasis is being placed on excellent companies *modelling*, by way of a healthy corporate culture, what is expected to achieve results. It's not any more just, "I put in a good day," but rather, "I put in a good day, and I have met these stated objectives well." Binney & Smith (Canada), a subsidiary of Binney & Smith International (owned by Hallmark Cards Inc., of Kansas City, Mo.), and their Crayola factory in Lindsay, Ontario, are a perfect example of this shift from doing what employees felt was their job only, to modelling a structure and culture that integrates the work-team revolution for increased performance and profits. Employees are more satisfied; boring jobs and mindlessly toiling away have been replaced by involvement -- more work, to be sure, but a much stronger competitive position. The result? "So far in 1992, the average cost per crayon is down 9 per cent. Last year, inventories fell 75 per cent while profit was up almost 140 per cent."[18] How were supervisors prepared to accomplish this remarkable success story? "Supervisors ... received exhaustive education in interpersonal skills, problem-solving, conflict management, maintaining self-esteem and providing positive feedback to negative situations."

Sometimes, however, employees do not meet the objectives. That may be because an employee is in need of help (corrective discipline) or because the supervisor is not modelling (proactive discipline) appropriate expectations.

PERFORM OR ELSE!

An Interview with Mr. Knut Brundtland*
President, Canada Welcome Pack

In today's business environment, it's "compete or die" on several levels. It's compete or die on cost effectiveness, for instance, because North American industry have not invested sufficient money in upgrading their manufacturing facilities. Survival rests on the basis of an unprotected marketplace. As such our production scale is not really the right scale for world competition. We have been geared toward the Canadian market and we have been allowed to develop a cost structure behind tariff protectionist walls to serve this particular market. Canada is 27 million people. Now we have a direct access, if we include Mexico as well as the United States, to 350 million people! Our production infrastructure will have to be re-geared to the new market.

There is a lot of the pain right now. When we went into the free market with the United States, we said to ourselves, "It is a good thing. It allows production of scale; costs will be brought down, etc.," but we did not take into account that Canada represents just a 10% expansion for the U.S. market whereas with us we have to gear up a whole new manufacturing structure from Canadian factories. We have a 90% expansion challenge! In other words, we have to re-invent, but the Canadian economy is not really led by innovation. It is led by

* Saturday, June 19, 1992

being given innovations and product development particularly from the United States, but also from Germany. We are a country of "daughter companies," or subsidiaries. Michael Porter, from Harvard, pointed out that Canada is one of the biggest pulp and paper and lumber producers in the world. BUT: we don't even make a chain saw! They are imported from Sweden!

Human Resources and Survival Time!

We have been paying attention to the line that "human resources are our biggest resource," but it's a lot of lip-service. There are a few companies doing it, but, in the main, it is lip-service. I don't know how it's going to change, but I do believe that *in theory* managers believe that human resources are important and that corporate culture to support and feed the growth of the individual in the company is important. I am not so sure they have assigned sufficient funds to develop those resources and whether they have the techniques and capabilities and true dedication to making it happen. I put question marks on that.

Description of Performance

The demands today placed on the individual's ability could well outstrip the individual's actual capability. Therefore, to increase their capability you have the whole notion of training and development and the motivation to continuous training of people. But there's no time for that. When people are scared and frightened, and the pressure is on from the shareholders, and the chief executives from the mother country -- typically down in the States, or Germany, or Great Britain,

or Holland -- when people are frightened and pushed beyond their ability, they do things under rational circumstances that they would not do. There is a bigger need for training today because the time lines are collapsing in developing new products and processes and demands on individuals to be more effective must be evident fast! It's survival time!

There is also a lot of conflict today because of perceived ineptness, that people are not "up to snuff"; they don't know their stuff; they come to meetings but haven't done their homework; they can't answer questions. I have found many more conflicts from *lack of competence* as compared to divergent management styles. And this problem fosters problems on the relationship level. *The corporate culture has a tremendous responsibility to allow for competition while disallowing lack of corporate manners.*

Managerial incompetence generates such derision and resentment. There are techniques, such as a corporate culture inventory, attitude surveys, etc., that can ferret out these problems, but I don't know how many companies actually do that. Companies that do have a better climate, more personal growth and achievements, more proficiencies than the companies that do not, because they unearth and solve managerial problems. The mere fact of doing these surveys is a very powerful signal to the individuals within the organization that *this* company means business in putting wrong things right! This is *modelling* behaviour. Efficiency and competitiveness begin to happen when supervisors learn to address communication, cultural and ongoing training problems.

> Students need to be told that this *do or die work environment* is a reality now. But they also need to be prepared to negotiate when they go into a new situation as to how their continuous proficiencies should be ensured. I think it is important that they take personal responsibility for their own proficiencies, that they keep up in the literature, in the periodicals and that they exercise interest in their chosen profession to keep themselves current.

PROACTIVE AND REACTIVE DISCIPLINE

PROACTIVE DISCIPLINE

Excellent companies strive for excellent results. The key is in the modelling of behaviour that is exhibited and the expectations around performance. In the broad sense of the term, *discipline* is the shaping of behaviour to corporate culture and strategy expectations.[19] Discipline shows *what* (strategic goals) to do and *how* (culture goals) to do it. Discipline, therefore, in its most positive root form, is occurring all the time. Many people think discipline has to do with punishing someone and is *reacting* to something that was supposed to be done or not done. That's a very narrow interpretation.

The word *discipline* comes from the Latin *disciplina*, and the word *disciple* calls forth the word *mentor*. The mentor-disciple relationship has a long history. The ancient Greek philosophers were mentors; their followers were often disciples. The world's great religious leaders also had this relationship. Today's manager-mentor (and supervisor-mentor) fulfils that role as well.[20]

HUMAN RESOURCES: COMMENTARY BY SYD YOUNG

"Modelling job performance"

If we are going to ask employees to follow rules and standards, those rules and standards must be clear, articulated by the organization and employees trained to those standards. This all starts when we are hiring the right kinds of productive people. The organization is *modelling* from the very beginning. It is not something in the abstract, but part and parcel of the concept of hiring and developing of employees, training them to standards and feeling confident that they *can* follow standards. The supervisor, with an under-performing employee, needs to coach, support, document, use patience and identify the talent that is there. Remember: the organization has probably spent a good deal of money on this employee to date and to dismiss that person because of a poor job performance evaluation may be quite hasty. If the person is loyal to the organization, it's a matter of spending more time with the person and guiding him to acceptable performance standards. The old adage, "Success is a combination of preparation and opportunity" is quite apropos here. The organization has saved an employee. And by the same token, management must not be afraid to make a decision, after all these things are done, if the employee shows no sign, or is unwilling or able to meet the standards, to let the person go.

The key in the mentor-disciple relationship was always the following: the mentor *modelled* what was expected; the disciple learned how to do what was expected, and one day the disciple would in turn become the mentor. This is illustrated with the diagram below:

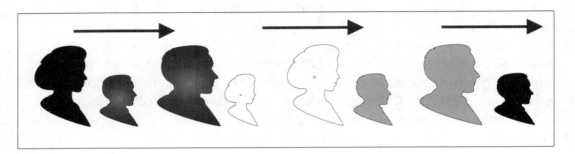

In its broadest sense, therefore, to discipline is to model expected behaviour. Ross Cooley, senior vice-president of North American sales for Compaq Computer Corp., illustrated the modelling process when he said, "The days of double-digit increases is a phenomenon that won't be repeated. We're not modelling our company to try and get back to that."[21] In the new ruling from the CRTC which allowed open competition in long distance telephone calls, Unitel Communication Inc., with its two bosses, William Stinson and E.S. (Ted) Rogers, would be going head-to-head with Bell Canada and BCE Inc. Unitel had to blend two different styles of bosses, who provided two different

Two models, two 'disciplines,' two different messages

"disciplinary" models to employees: Mr. Stinson was "the model of the bureaucratic organizational type," while Mr. Rogers was entrepreneurial, a risk taker with "a voracious appetite for debt" who "loves to speak his mind to the public." Two models, two "disciplines," two different messages. If disciplined well and proactively, employees find direction, structure, and well-being.[22] From an ethically responsible, environmental business point of view, the essence of discipline as modelling is seen in the "shift from the still-dominant notion of dominion over the earth to one of stewardship, an environmentally responsible model that will affect the nature of enterprise at every level."[23] As we will see also in chapter 15, the impact of Ontario's new Employment Equity Act will serve to "discipline" the workplace of the future. Tara Seon, manager, employment equity services, Consumers Gas, says that employment equity is "about focusing on qualified candidates, making sure we cast the net out wide enough, and if necessary, putting in place special measures to get us moving towards equity in employment. It's about looking at our organizations for perceived and real barriers that inhibit equity."[24] This "equity" framework is discipline in its positive sense of "shaping" employee behaviour to certain standards of performance.

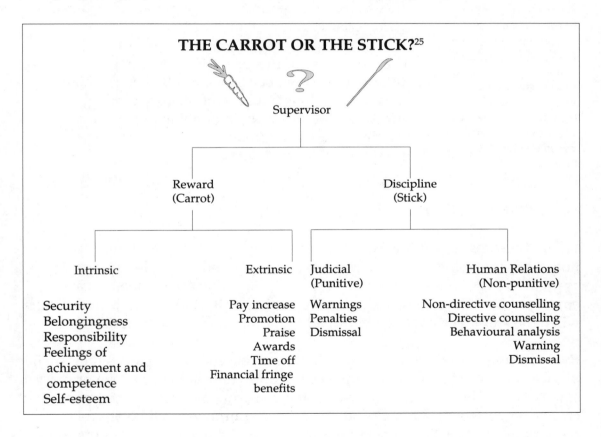

THE CARROT OR THE STICK?[25]

Supervisor

Reward (Carrot) — Discipline (Stick)

Intrinsic	Extrinsic	Judicial (Punitive)	Human Relations (Non-punitive)
Security	Pay increase	Warnings	Non-directive counselling
Belongingness	Promotion	Penalties	Directive counselling
Responsibility	Praise	Dismissal	Behavioural analysis
Feelings of	Awards		Warning
achievement and	Time off		Dismissal
competence	Financial fringe		
Self-esteem	benefits		

A healthy corporate culture "disciplines" by the very nature of its corporate mission, values, goals, and objectives. Employees "know" -- not only formally, but especially informally -- what is expected of them and the levels

"Confronting employees over sensitive issues such as performance standards remains our biggest challenge," says the Valhalla Inn Markham's general manager. "The key to overcoming the hurdle is to confront people and situations *immediately*. Confrontation is not a 'dirty deed' if handled in a positive understanding way. Employees appreciate immediate response to their performance; they don't appreciate being 'dumped on' weeks later when the situation can become emotionally divisive."

of excellence and appropriate behaviour that are expected from them. Researchers have shown that higher levels of performance are possible, in 90 per cent of cases, when goal setting is combined as a motivational experience with communication.[26] This is discipline in its most positive and proactive sense: vision, example, and cultural ethos providing leadership. A proactive "disciplinary" corporate ethos is self-discipline. It is a corporate environment where the very highest of ideals are sought after, technically, managerially, and personally.

Thus, the irony of this proactive understanding of discipline is that supervisors, just by being who they are, are modelling, and therefore, disciplining. Effective supervisors, by modelling positive and healthy behaviour, implicitly give direction and discipline their employees.

REACTIVE DISCIPLINE

When the word "discipline" is used, most people are likely to think about the notion of an employee doing something wrong. If modelling is a proactive approach to discipline, corrective or *reactive* discipline is a response to an employee for deliberately not doing something well, at all, or in the right way, when the employee has been informed of performance expectations.

Every business needs rules and regulations. In excellent companies they are in place as final reminders; in mediocre companies they are used as the primary supervisory "club"! A rules-only-oriented company models expectations for employees, but often from a position of threat. Employees will often follow these rules religiously, but never perform beyond the literal level of the rules, or worse, follow them stupidly! Work-to-rule union - management disputes more than prove this point. On page 309 is a sample Employee Conduct Guidelines model taken from the employee handbook.

EMPLOYEE CONDUCT GUIDELINES*

Your conduct not only reflects what and how you feel about yourself, but it also represents the company. We expect you to **always** be friendly, courteous and helpful to our guests and each other. Your smile goes a long way. Don't hesitate to share it ... it's contagious.

The following is a list of guidelines you should use when making decisions about yourself and your job. Professional conduct is important and your adherence to these items will ensure that we protect the image of ourselves as well as the hotel.

1. Smoking is not permitted in the hallways, public or food areas.
2. Chewing gum is not allowed in public areas.
3. Alcohol and drugs do not mix with work.
4. In case of misunderstanding or argument, call for a Supervisor right away.
5. Abusive language with customers or colleagues is absolutely unacceptable.
6. You should be prompt when reporting for work. You are expected to report to work in time to permit uniform change and other pre-work preparation prior to the start of your shift.

---

* Valhahha Inn Markham

As can be seen, these employee conduct guidelines are just common sense and most people would readily agree. Of course, depending on the industry, kind of work, or situation, other "rules" would be applicable. For instance, companies have rules around parking, tardiness, moonlighting, insubordination, poor customer service, sleeping on the job, leaving early, sexual harassment, office romances, etc.

There are times when employees will not, for different reasons, follow the rules or guidelines. At that point, the supervisor has to implement *reactive* or corrective discipline. The process is essentially the same in union and non-union working environments, except that in a unionized environment, the supervisor must follow the procedures laid down in the collective agreement and any penalties outlined in the contract. Supervisors must also know their *zone of reactive disciplining*, that is, to what extent consequences can be applied without more senior levels of management being involved. In difficult situations, and if the company has a human resources manager, it is always safer to discuss the matter before reacting, to make sure proper employment standards, legislation, and rules have been followed. Again, this is not only common sense, but in today's litigious working environment it is dangerous not to. Naturally, the supervisor should be secure in knowing that instructions were given clearly and concisely, and that the reactive discipline is the fair and logical step to take because the employee has not followed the rules. We saw the application of Douglas McGregor's "hot stove rule" in chapter 3: "any disciplinary action should be similar to what happens when a person touches a hot stove: with warning, immediate, consistent and impersonal. A supervisor should sit down, weigh and chart out the possible infractions and their consequences, and be prepared in case a reactive disciplinary action is needed.

Typically, in a reactive disciplinary situation, a supervisor will use the following procedures and *document everything*:

The progression from verbal warning to firing usually takes time, except for situations that call for immediate dismissal -- such as possession of weapons, theft, sexual misconduct, deliberate falsification of personnel records, etc.[27] Even here, with increasing government legislation, companies are finding that it is not as easy to invoke the *termination-at-will doctrine* from yesteryear.[28] Supervisors and managers will increasingly need to justify their firings. Listed below are examples of "Disciplinary Guidelines" and "Causes for Termination" from an Employee Handbook.

DISCIPLINARY GUIDELINES*

This company has a three-written-warning notice system. An accumulation of the three written warnings will result in immediate suspension/termination of your employment.

We realize, especially when you are new, that you will make mistakes. However, it is necessary for us with the size of our staff to have such a system.

(cont'd)

---

* Valhahha Inn Markham

The first occurrence of any infraction of any of our House Rules for the reasons listed below may simply result in a verbal warning; thereafter, any reoccurrence will be in writing.

Warning notices are issued for the following reasons:

1. Any violation of our house rules or your department policies and procedures.
2. Unnecessary abusive language or treatment or co-workers.
3. Any rudeness with customers.
4. Unacceptable dress code.
5. Lateness for work. Your first two may be verbal; an accumulation of three warning notices in a three-month period may result in termination.
6. Excessive time spent on breaks during shifts -- (including unwarranted time spend on personal calls).
7. Not maintaining our standards of cleanliness or hygiene.
8. Ineffective performance on job description.
9. Minor insubordination.
10. Refusing any justified request for service by guests.
11. Discussion of pay rates with other employees.

CAUSES FOR TERMINATION

Immediate termination could result from any one of the following:

1. An accumulation of three written warning notices.
2. Serious infraction of any House Rules.
3. Failing to report to work without notifying your supervisor or the manager on duty in your department.
4. Giving or receiving of any product(s) without accounting for it.
5. Theft from a hotel guest/customer, the house or fellow employee.
6. Adding gratuities to guest checks without their authorization.
7. Violence of any kind.
8. Use of intoxicating drugs or alcohol before or during a shift.
9. Possession of, or selling of drugs, to fellow employees or guests.
10. Visiting an unauthorized area without permission or management, at any time.
11. Negative discussion of tips/gratuities with customers.
12. Gambling with guests or fellow employees.
13. Sleeping on the job.
14. Breaking a security lock in order to use a fire exit.
15. Deliberate or careless damage to hotel property.
16. Inefficiency -- careless or inefficient performance of duties including failure to maintain proper standards of workmanship.
17. Insubordination -- including failure or refusal to perform the work assigned by your supervisor.
18. Working overtime without prior department head approval. Not reporting properly on Time Sheets when absent or late, or punching a timecard other than your own.

(cont'd)

19. Being present at guest functions or on the premises including guest rooms, restaurant or lounge without prior approval.
20. Dishonesty, theft or commission or any other crime, including falsifying employment application or other official hotel documents or records. Removal of company property without proper authority, including but not limited to pilfering and stealing, including "found" items from the premises.
21. Causing a serious guest complaint.

WHAT HAPPENS IF THERE IS A GRIEVANCE?

A grievance is a *formal* complaint between a supervisor and an employee. "Many grievances stem from perceived injustices or injured feelings rather than from contract violations on the part of supervisors."[29] Unionized employees in Canada are protected under their collective agreement and are entitled to an arbitration process. If a dispute "goes to arbitration," a binding arbitration agreement seeks to provide justice both for the supervisor and for the employee. This was what was hoped for, for instance, in the resolution of the Eric Lindros hockey affair. In June 1992 when three teams were deadlocked over when he would play for (Quebec Nordiques, Philadelphia Flyers, New York Rangers), for the first time in NHL history, said spokesman Gary Meagher, a trade dispute had gone to an outside arbitrator: "All three teams agreed to submit to binding, independent arbitration and waive all rights to appeal the decision through the courts."[30]

Often arbitration is the only way to interpret or to apply the collective agreement in a practical way on a particular matter. The complaint or grievance-arbitration process is a dynamic one, and if worked at well, can establish meaningful precedents for both parties. At Algoma Steel, the new collective agreement resembles the *co-determination model* (management - worker partnership) in West Germany and Scandinavia. While there is criticism of this approach here in Canada, Leo Gerard, outgoing Canadian director of the United Steelworkers of America union, said that management still has the authority to discipline workers, but under what is called the new *justice and humanity provisions*, "a worker cannot be suspended or fired until the entire grievance and appeal process has been exhausted."[31]

Depending on the complexity of the grievance, the complaint could be resolved with the supervisor, union steward, and employee. This is the beginning phase of the arbitration process. The matter could stop there or it could go to "final arbitration." A typical grievance procedure is charted below:

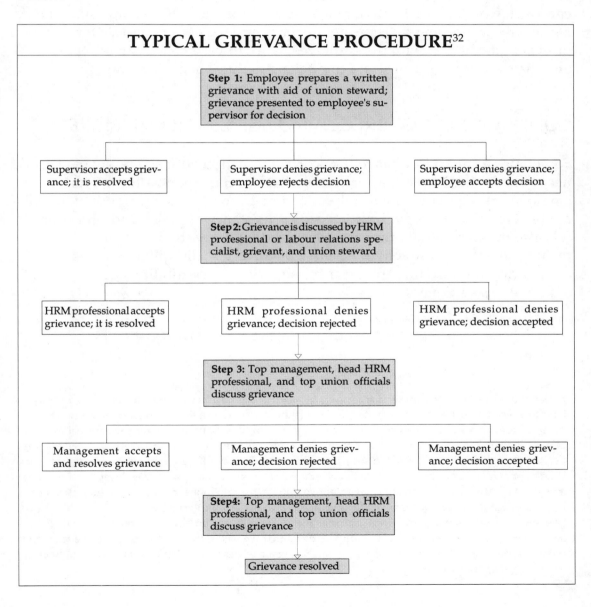

TYPICAL GRIEVANCE PROCEDURE[32]

Step 1: Employee prepares a written grievance with aid of union steward; grievance presented to employee's supervisor for decision

| Supervisor accepts grievance; it is resolved | Supervisor denies grievance; employee rejects decision | Supervisor denies grievance; employee accepts decision |

Step 2: Grievance is discussed by HRM professional or labour relations specialist, grievant, and union steward

| HRM professional accepts grievance; it is resolved | HRM professional denies grievance; decision rejected | HRM professional denies grievance; decision accepted |

Step 3: Top management, head HRM professional, and top union officials discuss grievance

| Management accepts and resolves grievance | Management denies grievance; decision rejected | Management denies grievance; decision accepted |

Step4: Top management, head HRM professional, and top union officials discuss grievance

Grievance resolved

It behooves the supervisor to develop a positive relationship with the union steward so that grievances can be resolved as early and as quickly as possible. It is a cost-effective way, and a way to keep stress to a minimum as well. An effective supervisor will be "keeping his/her ear to the ground," and be able to spot potential trouble areas. This is a time when effective human relations can work wonders! As in all disputes, supervisors need to remain calm when a grievance is presented, listen, get the facts and the correct motive for the grievance, be honest with the employee, work toward consensus, openness, and dialogue, and demonstrate competence, ethical behaviour, and fairness.

CONDUCTING A CORRECTIVE DISCIPLINARY INTERVIEW

Sometimes a supervisor has to take corrective action with an employee. This is necessary for the employee's sake as well as for the organization's. The employee needs to understand that a certain behaviour is not accepted or will not be tolerated; the organization needs consistency of policy and procedures. It is also important that other employees realize that action was taken regarding a certain infraction. Reactive or corrective discipline establishes boundaries; it is also important for the supervisor's credibility and for a sense of justice for employees.

HUMAN RESOURCES: COMMENTARY BY SYD YOUNG

"Fair, But Not Necessarily Equal"

Evaluation processes by themselves are generally subjective unless they are quantifiable. A good system has to be developed; managers and supervisors must be trained to use those tools, and at the same time, those systems have to be used fairly. It must also be an on-going process. Before the formal meeting several informal meetings should have taken place for the employee to know precisely where the performance evaluation is going. No surprises. There is a distinct difference in my view between equal treatment and fair treatment. For example, if you were to say to me, "Sid Young, I want you to run a mile or the 100-yard dash, and I'm going to put you up against Ben Johnson." You know as well as I that I will lose. But if you provide training for me, if you take my age into account in relation to his, if you give me the proper dieting, etc., if you factor all these things in, I might give Ben Johnson a good run for his money. But if you treat us equally, you are saying that we will both start together, do the race, and then you will look at the results and Ben Johnson is going to beat you. That is *equal treatment*, but it is not necessarily *fair treatment.*

Before a supervisor conducts a corrective disciplinary interview, he/she must emotionally create an atmosphere that will promote as much dialogue as possible. No one wants to hear bad news. As we have seen, we are all sensitive about our self-image and how others see us. Emotionally the supervisor must get a "fix" on his/her feelings, the facts involved, the possible interchange that will take place in the interview, and how the resolution of the situation will occur.

HANDLING THE CORRECTIVE DISCIPLINARY INTERVIEW

The interview is best handled if the supervisor is able to honestly and factually answer the following questions.

1. Why are we getting together?

This is the question that tries to describe the purpose and objectives for the corrective disciplinary interview. In a unionized workplace, the objective would be to have all parties satisfied that the issue was fair, equitable, addressed, and resolved within the context of guidelines of the collective agreement.

2. What is it that we have to talk about?

This is the question that is answered by both parties knowing what the agenda is, with the supervisor having documented the honest facts about the infraction.

3. What are the possible constraints impacting on the interview?

This is the question that the supervisor must often give much thought to *before* the interview. The supervisor must anticipate the mood of the employee, his/her possible defensiveness, the main objections that the employee may put forward to rationalize the infraction, and the strengths and weaknesses that the supervisor feels as well in doing this kind of an interview. Not every supervisor is comfortable conducting a corrective disciplinary interview. The supervisor must know his/her weak spots, acknowledge them, but not let them interfere.

4. What is the best way to begin?

This is the question that the supervisor must answer very directly for him/herself. The opening can set the tone, the climate, and demonstrate the perceived competence of the supervisor, and the willingness of both parties to be as open and forthright as possible.

(cont'd)

> ### 5. What are the best procedures for the meeting?
>
> This is the question that helps the supervisor set out an agenda for the meeting and how both parties will act. After the opening, the supervisor needs to state formally what the problem and infraction is, ask the employee to respond and clarify his/her position, assess the situation with this "updated" information, and then determine, if the employee is indeed responsible for the infraction, what the consequences are, and to communicate these consequences to the employee. The supervisor would also tell the employee how he/she could "redeem" him/herself for future records, and also what will happen should this infraction occur again.
>
> ### 6. How will the interview end?
>
> This is the question that the supervisor asks in order to visualize as positive a conclusion to the meeting as possible. It is an important question because sometimes the interview might turn into a debate without the supervisor wanting that. Visualizing an ending, after guilt has been fairly assessed, will make sure that the meeting stays centred on its purpose: to deal with an infraction by an employee. The employee needs to know that it is *future behaviour* that will count now. An infraction happened; it was dealt with; penalties were assigned; it is time to move on.
>
> ### 7. How will follow-up happen?
>
> This is the question that helps the supervisor document what happened in the interview, the new information, the consequences or penalties assigned, and how the interview went. The supervisor also needs to evaluate his/her performance skills in the interview: Was I fair? Did I address the problem? Did I avoid personalizing? Did I allow time for discussion? Did I take decisive action? Was I clear? If "1" is poor and "7" is excellent, how would I rate myself?

KEY STEPS IN A PERFORMANCE APPRAISAL

Providing feedback to employees is a key supervisory activity and responsibility. It lets employees know where they stand. In its most positive sense, it is an on-going developmental activity that the supervisor does, but it is also a training and development opportunity of the first order for the supervisor as well. Performance appraisal is a more or less formal time set aside for the supervisor and employee to talk about how adequately the employee met objectives, to identify developmental and training gaps, to determine how these gaps can be filled, and to set new objectives to close the gaps. Performance appraisal, therefore, is an educational learning tool and implies growth. It is "the process of collecting, analyzing, evaluating and communicating information relative to individuals' job behaviour and results."[33]

However, it is not always seen in organizations in such a positive light, if it is done at all. Organizations that take it seriously know their employees more honestly and are able to balance realistic assessments with salary increases, new promotional opportunities, and chances for personal development.

In doing performance appraisals, supervisors need to make sure that the "performance" they are appraising is job-related. This is a human rights requirement as well as a justice requirement.

In its efforts to monitor guest services throughout the Valhalla Inn Markham, the hotel has created a *Customer Service Team* whereby assistant managers and line staff are encouraged to participate in evaluating specific services offered by individual departments. Recommendations for improvement are brought forward by the team for consideration and implementation by the department concerned.

Supervisors also usually need appropriate training in doing performance appraisals,[34] especially on recognizing how to avoid many of the common performance rating errors, such as the *halo effect* (seeing a candidate only in the best possible light), or the *horn effect* (seeing a candidate only in a bad light), or the *central tendency* error (grouping most of the candidates in the middle where the employees are evaluated as "average" since the supervisor is reluctant to mark "high" or "low," if necessary), or the *recency effect* error (evaluating and being influenced by what happened most recently with that employee). All of us have biases. The trick is to know which ones "hook" us the most, and to avoid them. In today's work environment, with its emphasis on equity and non-discrimination, supervisors who still have "macho attitudes" should quickly "revise" they since these can get them into a lot of trouble. If the perception exists that an employee was evaluated solely on gender, or colour, or age, or personality, a very real problem can arise. It's illegal; it's unethical; and it is just not right. Personal prejudices, therefore, must be examined, acknowledged, and minimized. Liking or not liking an employee is not a basis for evaluation; job performance is.

There are different methods to do performance appraisals; each has its costs and benefits. Perhaps the most common and easy to use is the *graphic rating scale*, which has a number of specific items which the supervisor is able to

Personal prejudices, therefore, must be examined, acknowledged, and minimized. Liking or not liking an employee is not a basis for evaluation; job performance is.

check off using a scale. "It is estimated that over 95 percent of the major U.S. corporations use this method to appraise employee performance."[35] The main disadvantages are that it often personalizes the factors for the supervisor so that the supervisor bases the evaluation on personality rather than performance factors, and it assumes that if an employee is good on one factor, e.g., communication, that the employee may also be good on another, e.g., leadership. On page 319 is an example of a "Performance Evaluation Form" graphic rating scale.

Another technique that can be used is the *ranking order* technique, placing employees in a hierarchical ranking order from best to worst. This can be helpful if not all employees are excellent performers, but it creates resentment when most of a supervisor's employees are. Who wants to be #2 or #3 when #1, 2, and 3 are more or less arbitrary levels since everyone is more or less excellent? It's somewhat analogous to the Olympic skiers: the difference between first and second place is often quite minuscule. We expect these hierarchical rankings at the Olympics, but it is obvious that this kind of a ranking technique could be a disaster for the supervisor in the office. There is also the *MBO* technique that we looked at in chapter 3: agreed-upon objectives and their attainment are discussed and new objectives designed with the employee. But this is quite time-consuming. A supervisor can also use the *essay* technique and write out descriptions of an employee's behaviour, but that is really time-consuming. Most unions do not find this essay, or anecdotal method, acceptable for pay, promotion, or dismissal justifications.[36] Finally, there is what is called the BARS method: the

The key is for the organization and supervisor to determine what is excellent performance.

behaviourally anchored rating scale technique, "sometimes called behavioural expectation scales ... whose scale points are defined by statements of effective and ineffective behaviour."[37] (The assignment at the end of the chapter has an example and asks you to write your own.) The key is for the organization and supervisor to determine what is excellent performance, what is substandard performance, and then the varying degrees in between. Some authors consider it "very accurate";[38] others say that "research shows BARS do not outperform other simpler, less costly

PERFORMANCE EVALUATION FORM*

NAME OF EMPLOYEE _____

DEPARTMENT_____ JOB TITLE_____

DATE OF EVALUATION _____ EVALUATED BY_____

SKILLS PERFORMANCE

	1	2	3	4
GROOMING/UNIFORM	1	2	3	4
PUNCTUALITY/DEPENDABILITY	1	2	3	4
ACCEPTS RESPONSIBILITY	1	2	3	4
ABILITY TO WORK WITH MINIMUM SUPERVISION	1	2	3	4
QUALITY OF WORK	1	2	3	4
USAGE OF EQUIPMENT	1	2	3	4

ATTITUDE PERFORMANCE

		1	2	3	4
COMMUNICATION		1	2	3	4
LEADERSHIP		1	2	3	4
ASSERTIVENESS/SELF-MOTIVATION		1	2	3	4
ATTITUDE TOWARDS:	PERFORMING JOB	1	2	3	4
	PEERS	1	2	3	4
	SUPERVISOR(S)	1	2	3	4
INTERNAL/EXTERNAL GUEST SERVICES ABILITY		1	2	3	4

1 = NEEDS IMPROVEMENT   2 = SATISFACTORY   3 = ABOVE AVERAGE 4 = OUTSTANDING

OVERALL EVALUATION

STRONG POINTS   **WEAK POINTS**

and these can be used more effectively by: and these can be strengthened by:

_____   _____

GOALS FOR THE NEXT EVALUATION PERIOD

_____   _____

This Performance Evaluation has been discussed and I have received a copy.

EMPLOYEE'S SIGNATURE _____   DATE _____

* Valhahha Inn Markham

methods," but some evidence exists showing that "BARS improves evaluator attitudes toward performance appraisal."[39] It takes time, usually in "lengthy job analyses and a considerable amount of the organization's resources,"[40] however, to develop the necessary scales and to identify what is effective and what is ineffective behaviour. A supervisor cannot use one BARS to apply to all jobs; each job will demand a unique BARS all its own. To use a classroom example: if a professor is teaching listening skills for a human relations course, he/she would need to isolate those skills, and then determine what excellent and poor and levels in between looked like for each of the skills. These levels would be on a scale, say, from 1 to 7. Each level would be clearly, behaviourally, identifiable from the others. Obviously this BARS task for the course would take considerable time, but at least students would be more realistic about how well they had learned the skills.

THE ADDICTIVE PROCESS AND PROBLEM EMPLOYEES

CODEPENDENCY AND ADDICTION

Codependency is a disease. It is a behaviour in relationships that includes compulsive caretaking and attempts to control others. It is learned "in dysfunctional families and reinforced in our culture"[41] and has been referred to as "the 'invisible' problem"[42] affecting many people. It is a dysfunctional or sick pattern of living and solving problems that one learns primarily through the behavioural rules of one's family of origin and secondarily through one's cultural environment. It happens most frequently when children's legitimate needs for autonomy and boundaries are crushed or violated. To survive, a child learns to adapt by pleasing and controlling those around him/her so that life becomes bearable.

Codependants are reinforced in their dependency behaviour by being in a relationship with an addict. We can diagram this addictive-codependent relationship with the following diagram:[43]

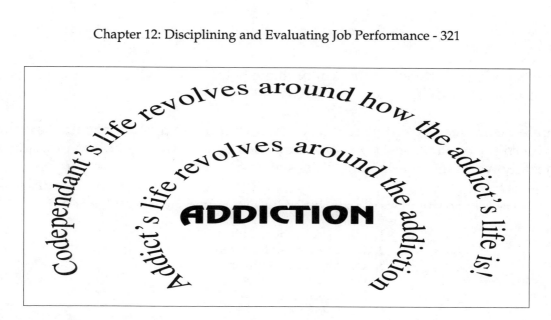

An addiction is mood-altering person, place, or thing that has life-threatening or serious consequences for an individual. Alcohol, for instance, if used unwisely and compulsively -- that is, addictively -- will have life-threatening and serious consequences for an individual. Sometimes an individual is addicted to power as a mood-altering "substance"; some supervisors can easily fall into this addictive pattern. They, in turn, foster codependency in their subordinates. We all have our "addictions," of course; it's just a matter of degree. How many employees are miserable until they have their first cup of coffee! Colleagues tip - toe (a codependent behaviour) around this person so as "not to rock the boat." Addicts, as such, can be quite abusive, therefore, since those around them, if acting codependently, are not themselves, but exist only "in relation to" the addict. Codependants have a good day *only if* the addict is having a good day!

Society is much more aware of its contributing role in fostering the addict - codependant equation.[44] Since organizations also live within this addictive society, it is logical to conclude that organizations can be, and often are, addictive.[45] The core of any addictive system (addict-codependent behaviours) is *denial*: denying that *a* or *the* problem exists. Addictive organizations are often *driven* and extremely compulsive in their objectives. Real feeling is suppressed, denied, ignored, and smothered. The addiction may be supported "at the altar" of persona, profit, power, or prestige (PPPP). But at the core of the experience is *denial*: of the real problem, which usually lies in the realm of people's real feelings.

Supervisors need to recognize and become aware of this dysfunctional behaviour pattern for two reasons: (1) to stop any such behaviours, and (2) to promote a healthy working environment. This is often easier said than done.

In a dysfunctional department or organization, key rules prop up the addictive illusion:[46]

1. Don't discuss the real problem(s).
2. Don't be open with real feelings.
3. Don't be straight in communicating.
4. Don't be less than perfect.
5. Don't count yourself.
6. Don't have fun.
7. Don't make waves.

PSYCHOLOGICAL SCUDS[47]

When supervisors are addicted to being right all the time, we know that they are scared of being wrong. The addict's adage is, "The best defence is offence!" "Judge and blame others for my mistakes, fear, hurt or pain!" -- the SHAME - BLAME syndrome. Addiction creates a mood-altering feeling inside which allows addicts to think they're all right. However, addicts have to become more and more addictive to feel okay! Supervisor-addicts will therefore have to become more judgmental, if their addiction is that of always being right. Employees will learn to become codependent, that is, they will spend their time and energy reacting to the addiction rather than getting the job done. Codependants are always *anticipating, reacting, always on guard*. That is one of the clear signals of codependent behaviour. Addicts feel there is nothing wrong with them; it's others; it's the system. Codependants react to this craziness -- for fear of losing their jobs, or because this reactive behaviour fits with what they learned at home. Codependent employees learn to *perform, to act as if* ... Thus, they are always *pretending*. Authenticity is sacrificed on the altar of fear.

Supervisor-addicts and their codependent subordinates, therefore, create and support what are called dysfunctional working relationships. Codependent employees *enable* supervisor-addicts to continue their abusive behaviour; the addict-supervisor uses *threats*: loss of job, shaming employees, loss of employee self-esteem, loss of competency, and the loss of dignity. Employees never know when or where these "psychological Scuds" are going to land, and so they always work in a defensive manner, a posture that kills freedom, joy, spontaneity, and profits!

ALCOHOL ABUSE

The addiction to alcohol is one of the most illusive and problematic addictions there is. Alcohol is sanctioned by society; it is seen as a social lubricant; we promote alcohol quite extensively. And yet society reacts very negatively to the "alcoholic." In the U.S. it is estimated that 10 per cent of executives struggle with alcohol addiction; 47 per cent of industrial accidents are also caused by the drug![48] It is one of the few illnesses for which the patient resists getting the needed help.[49] In 1991, 15,000 Canadians died as a result of alcohol abuse, with drinking and driving being the number one cause of death in Canada among sixteen- to twenty-four-year-olds.[50] "In Ontario alone in 1987, alcohol cost taxpayers $4.3 billion in extra health care costs, law enforcement, social welfare, and lost productivity."[51] As well, alcohol abuse has many "silent sufferers," those who are directly and indirectly affected by the addict.[52] There are varying estimates of the cost of alcohol-related problems with employees, but it is $1 billion more or less each year. One estimate shows the Department of Health and Welfare claiming $2 million a day at least in lost productivity.[53] In 1977, it was estimated to be $1.7 billion.[54] In 1979 in Canada, work-related expenses caused by alcohol, were estimated to be "$900 million in reduced productivity and $35 million in wages and salaries paid for time off work."[55]

22 days of lost productivity per year! The cost of having a problem-drinking, troubled employee![56]

The most beneficial approach that a supervisor can take when faced with an alcohol- or drug-related employee situation is the following: get the employee immediate counselling, and let the employee know there is no choice in the matter. It's either "get help" or "get out." The supervisor doesn't have to be nasty with the employee, but must definitely be firm: This is the *only* choice: counselling or job loss.[57]

MANDATORY DRUG TESTING

Mandatory drug testing is a controversial issue for many employers and employees. CN Railways in 1986 was the first to use it in Canada when it

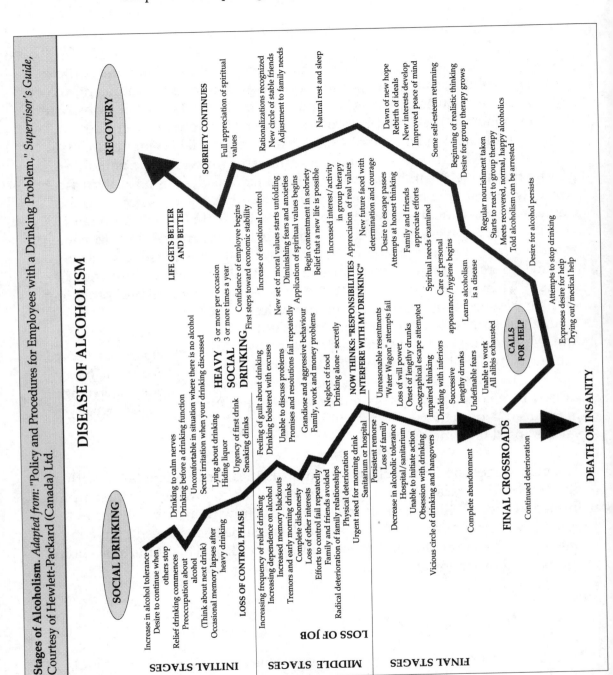

Stages of Alcoholism. *Adapted from:* "Policy and Procedures for Employees with a Drinking Problem," *Supervisor's Guide,* Courtesy of Hewlett-Packard (Canada) Ltd.

required job applicants who were going to work in blue-collar positions to submit to drug tests.[58] In 1991, nearly 75 per cent of 1,200 U.S. companies had a mandatory drug testing policy, compared to only 2% of Canadian companies. Mandatory drug testing is controversial because of the invasion of privacy issue, uncertainty over the reliability of the lab reports,[59] and the fear engendered by the corporate Big Brother who can snoop biochemically.[60]

Some claim that drug abuse among employees is no higher than alcohol abuse, roughly 6 to 10 per cent of employees.[61] On the other hand, employers claim that working on oil rigs, with dangerous substances or in dangerous situations -- high-risk industrial settings -- presents a real problem, to employees and to their colleagues, if employees are on drugs. Imperial Oil's East Coast tanker crews have been required since January 1992 to submit to random alcohol-and-drug testing. This has upset some of the employees; four cases are already before the Ontario Human Rights Commission. William Barnes, the program's implementer, says that employees who refuse to take the random tests will be assigned to other comparable jobs, but if they are then found to be drinking or taking drugs, they will be fired. "The company is basically guaranteeing these people a job."[62] Air Canada has a similar random drug testing policy and some unionized companies are looking to make the issue part of their collective bargaining discussions. Canadian National Railways (CN) claims it saved $5 million when 80 per cent of the 3,000 employees, referred to its employee assistance counsellors for alcohol and drug-related problems, were rehabilitated.[63] *Time* magazine reported an incident showing how an employee of American Airlines who was high on marijuana cost the company $19 million when he failed to load a vital tape into the airline's computer reservation system, which was then out of order for some eight hours. "That was an awfully expensive joint by anybody's standards."[64]

To avoid such costly mistakes, more and more enlightened organizations are informing employees of ways they can seek help for substance abuse and still feel protected. The random mandatory drug testing issue isn't settled yet in Canada: "Proponents of more testing are running into two roadblocks -- a powerful human rights lobby backing an employee's right to privacy and a belief that assistance programs and education are a better answer."[61] Like many policies, random mandatory drug testing may only be resolved by arbitration and the courts. As it stands now, the Canadian Human Rights Commission (CHRC) and the Ontario Human Rights Commission (OHRC) prohibit drug testing, include it under the aegis and policy of a medical examination (i.e., after being employed and necessary for the job), and, for some employers, what may be the most difficult part of all: even if an employee tests positive, the employer still has to find another field of endeavour for the employee.[65]

THE SUPERVISOR AS COUNSELLOR

One thing is certain for the supervisor in view of this chapter's considerations: there are many moments when supervisors must act as counsellors to their employees. "Counselling is preventive discipline, because its effects may never be directly measured or observed. Indirectly, however, counselling may help in creating a positive work atmosphere."[66] Some supervisors may feel that they are not in the business of being psychologists. True. But every supervisor has to be of help, practically and interpersonally.[67] Because employees spend a good portion of their day in a work-related setting, it makes sense that they will approach a supervisor for help, not only with job-related problems, but also with interpersonal problems: colleague - colleague and family - work problems. Some basic counselling "rules" can be very helpful:

Be receptive to the employee
Listen to the employee by showing empathy
Focus on *what* is the problem, not *who*
Affirm the importance of the job
Give encouragement and hope

These counselling "rules" will demonstrate a posture of openness and receptivity on the part of the supervisor, but they will also clearly demonstrate that the focus is still the job. The employee will know that help is available, but that work must still go on. If the employee's problem is more in-depth, then the supervisor must refer the employee to a counselling professional or other qualified personnel.

SUMMARY

Work or *job* performance is the sum of *who* you are and your *abilities* measured against the *energy* you put into doing something which, in turn, is measured against the amount of *backing* your company gives you. Excellent companies *model* excellent performance.

Proactive discipline models behaviour so that employees know what is expected of them. Reactive discipline occurs in order to correct a situation when it is going off track.

A grievance is a formal complaint between a supervisor and an employee and, depending on its complexity, could be resolved with the supervisor, union steward, and employee.

The key step in a performance appraisal is making sure the performance being appraised is job-related. Common rating errors include: halo effect, horn effect, central tendency, recency effect.

The addictive process in organizations involves the addict, the addictive behaviour, and the codependant(s). Substance abuse is a continuing problem for organizations today. Mandatory drug testing is a controversial employment issue.

TERMS/CONCEPTS

work performance
proactive discipline
reactive discipline
mentor - disciple relationship
grievance
corrective disciplinary interview
performance appraisal
halo effect

horn effect
central tendency error
recency effect
codependency
addiction
alcohol abuse
mandatory drug testing
supervisor as counsellor

DISCUSSION QUESTIONS

1. What are the key factors in employee performance?

2. Show how the work performance formula works by using an example from your own work experience.

3. "What's changing, therefore, in the world of business, is not only the concept of *performance* but also the *expectations* suurounding its reality." Discuss this statement with current examples.

4. What does Mr. Knut Brundtland mean by the expression, "Perform or Else!"? Apply it also to your academic experiences.

5. Describe the difference between proactive and reactive discipline.

6. What is discipline?

7. Outline the typical grievance procedure.

8. What are the key questions the supervisor needs to ask in preparing for a corrective disciplinary interview?

9. List and define the most common performance rating errors.

10. What is the addictive process? Define codependency and addiction.

ASSIGNMENT

Performance Management Assessment
A BARS (*behaviourally anchored rating scale*) Exercise

Instructions: listed below is a sample BARS key factor in performance excellence in a business course. Study the example and write your own following instructions below.

Sample	*Your Example*
Performance Dimension: *Course knowledge*	Performance Dimension: *Quality of Work* *Write your examples in dotted line spaces*
Excellent — Very proficient, extensive understanding, and invaluable input	
Superior — Quite knowledgeable about the course; all assignments and readings thoroughly researched and presented	
Satisfactory — Knows adequate amount of course content; still needs supervision with personal commitment and application	
Below standard — Needs extensive follow-through, coaching, and practice; course understanding is only fair; needs consistent supervision	
Totally unacceptable — Almost no understanding of course knowledge and basic principles and applications	

CHAPTER THIRTEEN

WORKING AND
MANAGING WITH THE UNION

> We believe if a union has the right to strike, a business has the right to operate.
>
> -- Stephen Van Houten, president,
> Canadian Manufacturers' Association[1]

LEARNING OBJECTIVES

At the end of this chapter, students will be able to:

- Describe the history of unionism in Canada
- Explain the role of the union in organizations
- Discuss the relationship of supervisor and union steward
- Define the collective bargaining process
- Explain the steps in managing the collective agreement
- Describe the role of unions in the information age

Opening scenario

U nions. Those in favour will argue that in the long run unions are cost-effective; others will argue that they curb productivity and profits too much.[2] While the presence of the union has contributed to higher costs, it has also contributed to a more stable and predictable workforce, thus eliminating the costs associated with high turnover and layoffs. Unionized employees have a collective voice.[3] Only the naive would say that *no* costs are incurred *with* unions and only the naive would say that *no* costs are incurred *without* unions.[4]

In Canada, union activity has a history of being involved in *business* concerns, what is called *business unionism*.[5] There is also what is called *political unionism*, union activity aimed at political objectives. Bob White, the new president of the Canadian Labour Congress, says, "We must have direct political action that gets rid of the governments that advocate the corporate agenda.[6] With the increase of service industries in Canada -- traditionally a non-unionized sector -- there is debate as to whether the union will have as much impact in the future.[7] How the union movement responds to the new knowledge worker and to eight out of ten workers being in the emerging service industries will greatly affect its influence.[8] A new industrial relations model is emerging that stresses productivity, commitment, and an end to "the old, crude workplace ethos and the adversarial relationship it spawns."[9]

A new spirit of co-operation[10] is in the making. The renewed emphasis on quality is difficult to do without the participation of employees. The new rallying cry for the survival of Canadian business is *competitiveness*. Today's system of "management turf" and "worker turf" is obsolete.[11] Perhaps all government legislation should be put to the *competitiveness test*: If the legislation doesn't lead to increased productivity and to the raising of employee skills, then it should be scrapped![12] As Canadians, we'll either stand united -- citizens, as well as workers and management -- or divided we'll fall. Vaclav Havel, playwright and former president of Czechoslovakia, reminds us that it was not force that destroyed communism, but rather, "life, ... thought, ... human dignity." He goes on to say, "there is only one way to strive for decency, reason, responsibility, sincerity, civility, and tolerance, and that is decently, reasonably, responsibly, sincerely, civilly, and tolerantly."[13]

The purpose of this chapter is to examine the history and role of the union in business and the supervisor's response through a proactive and effective labour relations philosophy and approach.

THE HISTORY OF UNIONISM IN CANADA

However the supervisor views the presence of the union, unions are here to stay! Prior to 1920, union membership estimates are not trustworthy. Today, however, roughly 35 per cent of Canadian employees (or nearly 4 million employees) are covered under some form of collective agreement[14] with approximately 60 per cent of these employees represented under the Canadian Labour Congress (CLC). Unlike the United States, especially after 1965, union membership has either stayed even, or increased, although membership has declined almost 4% from a high of 40% in 1983 to 36.2% in 1989.[15] In 1986, Canada had 38% of its workers unionized, the U.S. 19%![16] On Canada's 100th birthday in 1967, 1,921,000, or 24.9%, of the labour force was unionized; in 1990 that figure had climbed to 4,031,000, but still only represented 29.9%![17]

Reflective exercise

Describe your first experience of unions. Did you receive a favourable impression? How have unions shaped your career choices?

_____

_____

_____

_____

Unions are more established in the public service, communications, and transportation sectors; but not as well organized in the retail,[18] wholesale, and real estate sectors. Unions are still considered chauvinistic and male-dominated, with little representation of women on union executive boards, although women's membership did climb to 54 per cent between 1962 and1984.[19] The new changes to British Columbia's and Ontario's new labour

AND AFTER WHAT YOU'VE DONE, YOU WANT LOYALTY?

Perhaps the biggest loser of the 1990 - 1992 recession was the ethic of loyalty. Employers want loyalty from their employees; no business can operate without it. Yet, when "push came to shove" during the recession, did the loyalty ideal of business stand the test? Toronto lawyer Brian Grosman has pointed out that loyalty "is very much in the eye of the beholder."[24] When the harshness of recessionary reality breaks through, will "dehiring" be what management says it is, or is it what employees truly believe it is -- "firing"? How can employees be "members of the family" and yet be fired? How can employees be considered "our company's greatest asset" and yet be expendable? Whose to be trusted any more?

laws leave room for "new organizing powers."[20] Unions will also more easily be able to recruit women and members of minority groups in such sectors as trust companies, building maintenance, and food services. Even the United Steelworkers of America "has developed expertise in pay equity and has taken a hard line against sexual harassment and violence against women,"[21] in its attempt to change its macho image.

With the experience of the 1990 - 1992 recession, and the threat of job insecurity, most probably more white-collar employees and other business sectors will seek unionization.[22] The *expendability factor* -- that employees can be got rid of when times get tough -- has not been lost on employees, and their loyalty has been severely tested. This attitude is only reinforced with the following statement from Wall Street: "In the repulsive words of one Wall Street whiz: 'Loyalty is for losers'."[23]

The latter part of the nineteenth century in Canada saw the formation of the Trades and Labour Congress (TLC, in 1886); the U.S. equivalent was the American Federation of Labour (AFL). Both were conservative organizations[25] made up of *craft*, or skilled, union members. Not to be ignored, unskilled or *industrial* unions were later organized under the Canadian Congress of Labour (CCL) and the American Congress of Industrial Organizations (CIO). From 1935 to 1955, there was intense rivalry between these international Canadian - American union groups: the TLC - AFL and the CCL - CIO. In 1955 the AFL - CIO groups were united and George Meany became president; in 1956, the TCL - CCL came together and formed the Canadian Labour Congress (CLC), of which Bob White, formerly president of the Canadian Auto Workers (CAW), is the current new president.[26] The diagram on page 335 shows these historical union dynamics:

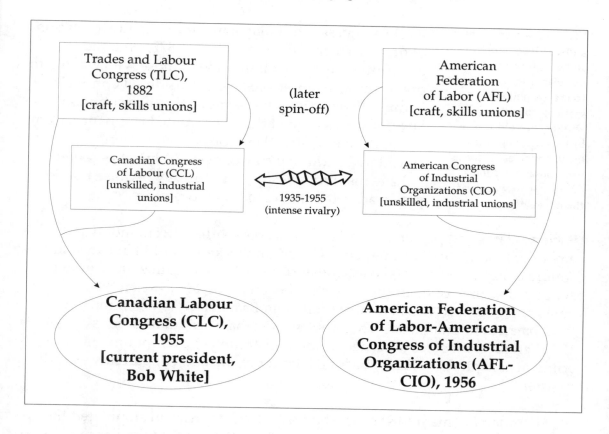

Ten percent of unionized employees in Canada are covered under federal jurisdiction and the remaining 90 percent come under provincial legislation in contrast to the United States which has 90 percent of its unionized workforce under federal legislation and 10 percent under state legislation.

If management had not treated workers poorly, as they did, in terms of wages, working conditions, quality of supervision, etc., unions would have had a more difficult task getting established. But human nature being what it is, the shadow side of management -- its greed and

"In Canada judicial decisions over the years have established that the federal government has jurisdiction in labour relations matters only over the federal public service, crown corporations, airlines, most railways, communication companies, and federal government agencies. The public service accounts for 5 percent and federally regulated industries for approximately 10 percent of the labour force. All other organizations fall under the jurisdiction of the provinces."[27]

"The depression of the mid-1870s to mid-1890s and the growth of manufacturing combined to create inhuman working conditions: workers were disciplined by beatings, imprisonment, and fines; factories were unsanitary; and a 60-hour workweek was the norm."[30]

its abusiveness -- did play a major role in the formation of unions. During the years 1794 - 1872, even the government was not on the side of those who wanted to organize; such employees were considered criminals because their activity was against the then common law, for it was argued that it prevented companies from doing business![28] In other words, unions were considered "criminal conspiracies."[29] Injustice seemed to have institutional support precisely because public policy accepted that reality in those years.

Society's laws and precepts, in other words, reflect the current moral and emotional maturity of its members. Canadian workers would have to wait for a more enlightened societal consciousness in order to organize their union activity. The time of institutional justice began in the 1870s when the government passed legislation, modelled on British law, which removed legal barriers to unionism.[30] The problem was that this Trade Unions Act of 1872 had no clout since it needed union registration to exempt unions from criminal conspiracy charges, but "no labour organization apparently ever did register."[31]

It's an understatement to say that the 1875 - 1895 depression stimulated the growth of unions. Workers needed to band together to fight the oppression. In 1907 the Industrial Disputes Investigation Act (IDI) was passed which forced compulsory conciliation by a tripartite board (a member of labour, a member of management, and an outside chairperson) for disputes. Compulsory conciliation meant that a strike couldn't occur until an investigation first took place, with the hope being that a strike could be avoided. During World War I the IDI Act was also used to prevent employees in industries supporting the war from going on strike.

The *turning-point* for unions came with the Snider case of 1925 which involved the *Toronto Electric Company Commissioners vs. Snider et al.*[32] The Privy Council in England said the Canadian federal government had gone beyond its jurisdictional limits with its continuing application of the IDI Act because civil rights was a provincial jurisdictional matter guaranteed under the 1867 BNA Act. This decision was a turning-point because this was the time when the 10 - 90 per cent factor began: 10 per cent of labour law under federal jurisdiction (the IDI Act was amended to include only this), 90 per cent under provincial jurisdiction. "All the provinces except Prince Edward Island passed such legislation between 1925 and 1932."[33] This factor allowed individual "tailoring" of legislation by particular provinces but also disadvantaged companies who were "multi-provincial" and had to keep track of the differences in provincial legislation. A company that does inter-trade business in Quebec, the Maritimes, and Alberta, for instance, needs to acknowledge and comply with different provincial labour legislation.

The year 1935 was also an important one in the history of the unions. The U.S. Wagner Act was passed giving workers the right to organize and requiring companies to bargain in good faith and not interfere with union organizing, bargaining, or the collective agreement. The Canadian PC 1003 order-in-council of 1944 embodied the main ideas of the Wagner Act, but still kept the "conciliation requirement" of the IDI Act "with its compulsory 'cooling off' period" requirement[34] and became the model for future provincial legislation.

Finally, the 1960s saw the growth of union membership mainly with provincial and federal government employees. The Public Service Staff Relations Act was passed in 1967 allowing government workers a choice: compulsory conciliation (an IDI Act provision) or the right to strike. Certain essential services could not come under this legislation. Even though Saskatchewan and Quebec had had this option since 1944 and 1964 respectively, after the 1967 PSSR Act was passed, save for Ontario and Alberta at the time, all the other provinces followed suit: legitimate public service bargaining units across Canada had the right to strike. Ontario did eventually allow roughly 80 per cent of its 90,000 public servants to unionize, and, in the summer of 1992 this increased to between 90 and 95 per cent.[35] Today the Canada Labour Code protects unionized workers and has labour relations boards (LRBs) in each jurisdiction in Canada to administer that Code. Supervisors and employees have access to mediators and conciliators if needed as well. All collective agreements, with the exception of those in Saskatchewan, have an arbitration provision which stipulates that a final resolution to a dispute *can be* imposed without the interference of a union strike or management lockout.

THE ROLE OF THE UNION IN ORGANIZATIONS

WHY EMPLOYEES JOIN UNIONS

Employees join unions to feel more protection over wages, job security, equity issues, working conditions -- *business unionism objectives* -- and increasingly today, to feel more protection of their social interests, a *political unionism objective.*

Employees join unions because of mistreatment and dissatisfaction.[36] We have stated that if management had treated employees fairly, justly, and humanely from the beginning, unions would have had a much more difficult time getting established. But that was not so. Through the union, workers felt they had support; they could be represented; their issues could be tabled and addressed. With the passage of labour legislation over the years to protect workers, gradually there emerged a labour-management dynamic which exists to today.

Employees join unions to feel more protection over wages, job security, equity issues, working conditions -- business unionism objectives -- and increasingly today, to feel more protection of their social interests, a political unionism objective. Bob White's public statement after becoming head of the CLC aptly illustrates this point: labour's job is to get rid of the Prime Minister and the "business agenda" so that *Canadians* in general can have a more just and equitable society.[37] Of course, management often resists having a union because they fear their costs will go up; they are also afraid and don't want to "have to talk with union types."

When employees want a union to represent them they can take the initiative and invite the union in to help them, or they can go about getting the minimum number of signed-up employees required for union certification. The *minimum* number for union certification can be as low as 25 per cent of employees who support the union drive (Saskatchewan) to a high of 60 per cent (New Brunswick). The percentages for the other provinces are as follows:

The Canada Labour Code protects unionized workers and has labour relations boards (LRBs) in each jurisdiction in Canada to administer that Code.

Newfoundland (50%), Prince Edward Island (50%), Nova Scotia (40%), Quebec (35%), Ontario (45 - 55%), Manitoba (45 - 55%), Alberta (40%), and British Columbia (45%). The federal government requires employee support to be 35 per cent to apply for union certification.

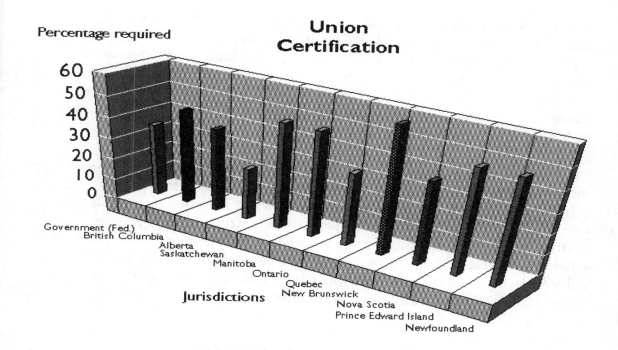

Once the union is certified, the supervisor must learn to live and work within the limits and opportunities of the collective agreement, or negotiated contract. Typical items in the collective agreement for academic employees between the different Colleges and the Employees' Union would include such issues as: recognition of the union, the relationship between management and the union, salaries, workload, vacations, holidays, management functions, seniority, union deduction, union business, and employment stability. When a roadblock occurs in the administration of the collective agreement, the supervisor should take every means to resolve the problem(s). In the same way that management must exhibit good will, so must the union.

An unresolved issue offers the opportunity for conciliation and/or mediation efforts. For instance, in the proposed amendments to Manitoba's Labour Relations Act, an amendment requires "a report from a conciliation officer as a prerequisite to the Labour Board writing a first contract." Labour Minister Darren Praznick wanted this inclusion to make sure that the union and management had in fact reached an impasse or roadblock before first contract provisions were made available.[38] Conciliators provide more of a counselling role in their efforts to get the conflict resolved; mediators make recommendations, not decisions, in the hope that the conflict will be resolved. If the conflict goes to arbitration, both parties have to agree to, and work with, the mandatory decision of an independent third party. Strikes and lockouts are forbidden and illegal at this point.

Even though the compulsory conciliation precondition in the IDI Act of 1907 introduced by William Lyon Mackenzie King -- Canada's first Deputy Minister of Labour and later Prime Minister -- was instituted to be a *stopgap* to prevent a strike or avoid a lockout, sometimes a strike, or lockout, does occur. A strike is the union's main weapon, a lockout, management's. Sometimes what is known as a "wildcat" strike will happen; this is illegal in Canada. In a wildcat strike, employees walk off the job even though their contract has not expired. Legal strikes are allowed in Canada *after* a union - management

---

KEEPING SCORE ON LABOUR UNIONS[39]

Bruce Gajerski
Statistical Analyst, City of Edmonton

The labour movement has been described as being at a crossroad in its history. A conservative political movement emerged during the 1980s promoting the viewpoint that labour unions are outdated and have outlived their relevancy in an era of free-trade markets and global competition.

These sentiments are expressed by the Fraser Institute, a right-wing think-tank on the cutting edge of neo-conservatism, in their 1989 report on the federal government's performance in labour-law reform. The institute notes that employers' rights are "restricted unduly," and the government hasn't yet recognized that "trade unions are anachronistic."

For these reasons, the government is given a failing grade, but earns high marks for trade policy, privatization, foreign investment and energy policy. Passing grades are assigned for its reforms on the universality of social programs (clawback of benefits) and unemployment insurance. These policies are consistent with the philosophy of the new-right agenda in the United States, Canada and Britain.

It is in these conditions that the labour movement has faced an uphill struggle in the drive toward competitiveness which dominates mainstream economic policy. Labour leaders fear the increasing emphasis on competitiveness is essentially a strategy by government and business to lower wages and benefits and dismantle workers' rights while improving our ability to compete in trade markets.

In the United States, more restrictive labour legislation has created low-wage ghettos in many regions. In some states, minimum wages are less than $2 an hour. In others, no minimum wage laws exist. Compounding the situation has been the introduction of right-to-work laws in 21 states. A right-to-work state[40] has laws that prohibit collective-bargaining contracts from requiring union membership as a condition of employment. The resulting availability of cheaper labour has allowed a relocation of industry to old confederacy states.

For example, personal income per capita in Mississippi, Arkansas and Louisiana ranged from $11,724 to $12,921 in 1989. These states have right-to-work laws and their personal income levels were more than 25 per cent below the U.S. average. Of the 20 states with the lowest personal incomes, 15 have right-to-work laws; nine of these 15 have personal income levels more than 22 per cent below the U.S. average. Although average personal income rose by 77.4 per cent between 1980 and 1989, one right-to-work state, Wyoming, experience an increase of only 27.9 per cent.

The growth of right-to-work legislation parallelled a steep decline in unionization rates in the U.S. labour force. Between 1975 and 1989, union membership of employed workers fell from 22.2 million to 16.9 million, a decline from 28.9 per cent to 16.4 per cent. By comparison, in 1988, the unionization rate of employed workers in Canada was 33.7 per cent. Because of Canada's higher rate of unionization, personal income per capita was $20,922 in 1989, compared to $17,596 in the United States.

Median weekly earnings in the United States were $497 for union workers and $372 for non-union workers in 1989, a 34.1 per cent difference. Similar differences in earnings exist here. A Statistics Canada study released in 1991 found average weekly occupational earnings in 1987 to be $508 for union members and $356 for non-union workers.

This is a result of two factors, outlined in a study of unionization by Harvard professors Richard Freeman and James Medoff.[41] They found that unions do not act as a deterrent to productivity. In most sectors, unionized establishments were seen as more productive than non-union firms, due to lower turnover rates, improved managerial performance in response to the union challenge, and generally co-operative labour-management relations at the plant level. It was also concluded that the higher wages in unionized firms reduced profitability, but this was concentrated in highly profitable sectors of the economy.

The overall conclusion to the analysis is that the legislating of right-to-work laws may serve as an incentive to attract investment, but productivity and income levels will be restrained. To achieve earnings, higher unionization rates are necessary.

Despite these favourable findings, public attitudes toward labour unions remain divided. A survey by the Insurance Bureau of Canada in Ontario in 1989 said labour unions had a 43 per cent approval rating. This was significantly higher than insurance companies (28 per cent), Canada Post (36) and oil companies (38). In a 1985 British Columbia survey, 71 per cent of respondents agreed with the statement that employers' power needs to be balanced by unions. Sixty-six per cent agreed that workers would have little protection against management without unions, and 59 per cent felt the growth of unionism has made our democracy stronger.

However, 64 per cent believed that union demands often contribute to unemployment, and only 44 per cent agreed that union leaders usually represent the best interests of their members.

Nevertheless, the weight of evidence suggests that, on balance, unions appear to improve rather than harm the social and economic system. Attacks on the role they have served in society cannot be justified.

contract has expired and management and union cannot agree on a new one. With the threat of a strike, both parties must ask themselves the same question: can we afford this?[42] In difficult recessionary times, this question is an even more pertinent one.

With the new spirit of co-operation emerging in organizations, union and management are each looking for ways to have a win - win relationship. What is known as *preventive mediation* was first introduced into Canada[43] by the Ontario Ministry of Labour in 1978 to promote effective communications in contract disputes in order to minimize the bitterness, negative attitudes, and hostility often associated with union - management conflicts. Preventive mediation has three components: (1) joint action committees, (2) a Relationship by Objectives (RBO) program, and (3) a one-day joint training program.

In effect, a PM approach seeks the following objectives: (1) to get people talking on a regular monthly basis (joint action committees), (2) to get supervisors and union members to experience a three-day relationship training exercise, to be followed up with a progress report in 60 - 90 days (RBO), and (3) to set up a one-day training course on improving attitudes and understanding each other's roles (training program).

THE RELATIONSHIP OF SUPERVISOR AND UNION STEWARD

The new spirit of co-operation needs to be throughout organizations today, but most especially in the supervisor-steward relationship in a unionized environment. In a non-union environment, the supervisor must "sense" the relationship level, the issues and the concerns of employees, acknowledge them, and then act. The British Columbia pulp strike in the summer of 1992 was a good illustration of the tremendous need to sit down and talk! It was costing workers $2 million a day and pulp and paper production losses were valued at $16 million a day! In a seeming spirit of resignation or cynicism, Eric Mitterndorfer, president of the Pulp and Paper Industrial Relations Bureau, said, "It's the same as in any strike. You strike until one party or the other decides they don't want to strike any more."[44] One editorial writer put it this way: "When a settlement is reached, it's usually because both sides become weary of the pain."[45] One would think the lesson in financial costs had been learned in 1991 since it was the worst year for losses in the industry: "$250 million for B.C. market pulp firms and an additional $152 - million for newsprint makers."

How can the supervisor be more proactive, anticipate rumblings of a strike, and stop potential strikes? Often, as we have seen, it may stem from the supervisor's own negative attitude about unions.[46] What we are talking about here is *a balance of power*: any one person or group or nation that feels put down over a long enough period of time will eventually do something to restore a balance of power. Powerlessness breeds anger and that can be explosive. When people's sense of pride and self-worth is violated, trampled on, ignored, or severely abused, a compensatory action begins: to right the injustice.

> "When a settlement is reached, it's usually because both sides become weary of the pain."

This is why the supervisor should first do a personal and departmental "examination of conscience" if there are more than surface "rumblings" and talk of dissatisfaction. Authors George Radwanski and Julia Luttrell, in their book *The Will of a Nation*,[47] pointed out that the Tories in Canada had done inestimable damage by wounding the national psyche because the valuing and nurturance of human resources had been jeopardized and placed on the altar of corporate disposability and layoffs. This union point of view places the objectives of supervisors and unionized employees in sharp relief: supervisors want co-operation, productivity, and competitiveness; the union first and foremost wants protection for its workers, and in today's work environment, that first of all means *survival*. Eastern German economist Rainer Land, in commenting on the fall of the Berlin Wall, points out that the move from communism to capitalism for East Germany is working as it should -- according to the survival of the fittest -- but with one major caution: "The market is doing what the market is always praised for -

> "It would be absurd, after all, to expect workers to co-operate in the introduction of labor-displacing technologies, to learn new skills or to accept the prospect of periodic job changes, unless they can feel certain that society will repay that co-operation by meeting their basic needs if they become displaced."[47]

The union first and foremost wants protection for its workers, and in today's work environment, that first of all means *survival*.

eliminating those who are weak ... The problem is they are all in East Germany."[48] The philosophy of unionism is not that workers can survive by eliminating the weak links, but to provide protection for all, even if it does ironically cost workers $2 million a day, as it did in the 1992 B.C. pulp labour dispute. The union would also argue that it is also costing management $16 million a day!

But will either side win with this kind of adversarial posture? Not likely. That is why the Business Council on National Issues in its summer 1992 report said that this adversarial union attitude and management's lack of good management skills has got to stop. "Canada's economy has been hobbled by 15 years of weak productivity growth that has been the slowest of the seven main industrialized countries."[49] That is a tragedy and it has to stop -- by unions dropping their confrontational stance *and* by managers and supervisors managing better, being more innovative, spending more on research and development, doing more skills training, becoming more involved in high-technology and focusing more on the global marketplace. Companies and unions can cry all they want about North American free trade; but if that is the reality in our world -- and it is -- then crying does not solve the problem. Measuring up to the moment does; and that is done through *strategic strength* and *relationship strength*.

Companies and unions can cry all they want about North American free trade; but if that is the reality in our world -- and it is -- then crying does not solve the problem. Measuring up to the moment does; and that is done through *strategic strength* and *relationship strength*.

The key, then, to the supervisor - steward dynamic, is for both parties to "buy into" the organization's strategic goals *and* corporate culture (relationship) goals. The fault often lies with managers and supervisors inordinately imbalanced in favour of the strategic goals, only to be undone by the impoverished corporate culture/relationship goals, which are lacking or abused. Assuming that strategic goals are in place from senior management levels, the supervisor would do well to establish as positive a relationship with the union steward as possible. There are some basic courtesies here, on both sides: respect for each other *as persons*, respect for each other's time and pressures, and a genuine effort to inform each other of problems so they can be worked out. Thomas d'Aquino, president of the Business Council on National Issues, in its summer 1992 report, chastises management and says they have to do better, not only in relationship matters, but also in skills training and developing a competitive focus *with* employees.

THE COLLECTIVE BARGAINING PROCESS

Collective bargaining is the process by which supervisors/managers *and* unions meet to design a new working agenda and relationship, or employment contract. It not only states *what* each party must do but also *how* each part must conduct itself during the life of the contract. Both parties will have their objectives, of course; but it is through the bargaining process and the negotiations that occur that each party hopefully gets what it wants, or, at least, close to what it wants. Keep in mind that the process historically was to simplify the relationship between two groups, each with representatives. "Both employers and union representatives have a legal obligation to begin collective bargaining in good faith."[50] As well, "most collective bargaining involves agreements between a single plant and a single employer."[51]

Both management and union come to "the bargaining table" with their own demands and requirements. Their objectives are different: productivity, cost effectiveness (management), and job security, good wages, safe working conditions (union). Their demands will each reflect these two different views. The difference between their demands is known as the *bargaining gap*; the area of possibility for each party's demands being met is referred to as the *bargaining zone*. In the initial bargaining stages, with lack of trust between Algoma Steel Corp. Ltd. and the United Steelworkers of America union, both sides came with "impossibly polarized positions," but eventually worked out an agreement because they found common ground: workplace democracy.[52] Similarly, in the summer of 1992, the Toronto Symphony faced a labour dispute, a bargaining gap, and a bargaining zone. Ronald Hurwitz, chairman of the musicians, said that management "should be negotiating, not filing for bankruptcy."[53] Management did, however, return to the bargaining table.[54]

BARGAINING

Table
Gap
Zone
Demands
Offers

For the supervisor and union to bargain in good faith -- genuinely and sincerely communicate and negotiate! -- they must come to the table prepared. This will first of all mean that if any changes are wanted to the old contract, both parties need to notify each other at least 60 days in advance. It's not unlike what is respectful in any relationship. Every now and then there are "issues" to be discussed, changes proposed, areas negotiated, and solutions found. Both parties also have an opportunity to meet and discuss these proposed changes. Realistically, because the changes will usually involve wages, times, benefits, etc., both parties will use computerized problem solving methods and projections to anticipate what the demands of each will cost. In addition, each party has to include areas of concern from the external environment, e.g., new government legislation. When the process has been successfully completed, a new *written* collective agreement is drafted. This can take considerable time given the many different possible interpretations of words and expectations. This becomes the *working* document for the life of the contract. It is not a time for either party "to cry over spilt milk" if they realize there were other issues that could have been covered, or if one party felt they "got the raw end of the deal." Assuming that good faith principles of communication and negotiation presided during the collective bargaining process, the perceived "disadvantaged" party would do well to learn from the experience and become more skilled next time.

"Crying over spilt milk" feelings may have been what happened after the "pattern bargaining"[55] between Caterpillar Inc. (U.S.) - "the earth-moving equivalent of Kleenex"[56] -- and the United Auto Workers union. Joshua Freeman, a labour historian at Columbia University in New York, said the

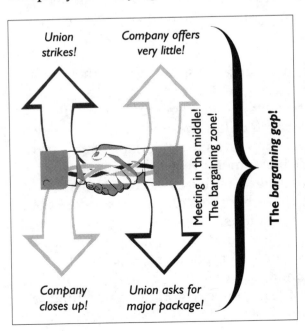

Union strikes!

Company offers very little!

Meeting in the middle! The bargaining zone!

The bargaining gap!

Company closes up!

Union asks for major package!

world may have changed with this labour situation. It typically happens in labour - management bargaining that a supervisor has to know what to do if the union brings up contract items from *another union's* contract with the company. Caterpillar didn't want this type of pattern-setting contract, i.e., that what was good for its biggest competitor, Deere & Co. of Moline, Illinois, should establish the rules for itself as well. It felt that Deere & Co. was a fair comparison and could not realistically pay U.S. wages since it really competed with Komatsu Ltd. of Japan. "From the union's point of view, pattern bargaining had long meant that domestic companies faced similar labour costs and could not play groups of workers off one against another."[57] After a five-month strike, Caterpillar Inc. presented an 8½-day ultimatum to striking workers to get back to work or lose their jobs to new people it would hire, and called the union's bluff by saying that contract terms established in the industry somewhere else in the world didn't apply to the domestic industry. "It was a risky strategy that paid off," said Wall Street analyst Tobias Levkovich. Labour historian Joshua Freeman said, "It's stunning in the sense that the UAW itself drew a line in the sand and then walked across it." In other words, they fell for the bluff. The UAW then had to try to negotiate without the threat or possibility of a strike. Was that fair on management's part? Rudy Kuzel, local UAW president at a Chrysler Corp. engine plant in Kenosha, Wisconsin, indicates revenge is needed: "There's more than one way to be on strike. All you have to do is exactly what the boss tells you and the place will self-destruct."

> "It's stunning in the sense that the UAW itself drew a line in the sand and then walked across it." -- Labour historian Joshua Freeman

Ontario's controversial labour Bill 40 and British Columbia's Bill 84 will outlaw the use of replacement workers as a management tool.[58] The philosophy behind the Ontario proposal is that NDP leader Bob Rae feels that "workers have a proprietary right to their jobs, even when they're on strike."[59] A Federal Court of Appeal, for instance, in Ottawa ruled that the "CBC violated Canada's Labor Code when it forced a broadcaster to either give up his union activities or quit his job."[60] In another case, this time

> "There's more than one way to be on strike. All you have to do is exactly what the boss tells you and the place will self-destruct." -- Rudy Kuzel, local UAW president at a Chrysler Corp. engine plant in Kenosha, Wisconsin

involving Rogers Cable TV Ltd. (Hamilton), the Canada Labour Relations Board found that the company did, in fact, try to get rid of the union. "The federally regulated company was found to have violated sections of the Canada Labour Code that say an employee is free to join the union of his or her choice and that persons acting on behalf of the employer cannot interfere with employees, or threaten, suspend or lay them off."[61] An Ernst & Young study estimated that Ontario's labour changes alone would see 295,000 lost jobs throughout the province.[62] Some employers would rather leave Canada, fire workers, and close shop than have a union. For instance, Bill Nusbaum, president and chief executive officer of Long Manufacturing Ltd., of Oakville, Ontario, is building a new plant in Michigan and hiring 200 workers. In Oakville, 500 employees will be out of work. Nusbaum said, "I could deal with one or two problems, but when you put all the nonsense together -- enough is enough."[58] Hayes-Dana Inc., the auto parts manufacturer, found the proposed NDP Ontario labour legislation chilled its hopes of building a sixth, $8 - million plant in St. Mary's, Ontario. And one firm, Toronto-based DynaTek Automation Systems Inc., lured by government money and a dislike of the New Democrats, set up shop in Nova Scotia. Said president Sam Gur, "I just don't think Toronto today has the best environment to develop business."[63]

NO PLACE FOR CANADA TO HIDE!

The new *information economy* has replaced the old mass-manufacturing economy. Rogers Cantel chairman, George Fierheller, points out that more than 97 per cent of all jobs created in Canada today are in this information economy. "The whole world economy is driving into the Information Age. Trade barriers are falling. There is no place for Canada to hide. Our survival depends on a knowledge-based economy."[65]

On the other hand, however, U.S. Labor Secretary Lynn Martin said hiring replacement workers "is an ineffective management tool."[64] U.S. law has had this replacement provision since 1939; former President George Bush was opposed to a bill blocking replacement workers. Martin concluded a *Good Morning America* interview on ABC by saying, "Hiring replacement workers is an extraordinary thing to do. Collective bargaining isn't necessarily pretty." Bob White said that if this happened in Canada with a major employer, the whole labour movement would be organized around the worker replacement issue. Of concern, therefore, is the realistic fear that union power is being undermined.

The attitude, *now and for the future*, of managers and supervisors will have to be finely tuned to genuineness, credibility, and trust if collective bargaining is to have any semblance of an ethic of fair play. Ordinary employees have been asked to sacrifice a tremendous amount, as the 1990s evolved, due to the grasp, the ambitions, and the greed of many senior managers in the 1980s. The union in its collective bargaining will remember those sacrifices and will ask for its rewards.

PROBLEM-SOLVING NEGOTIATIONS

A win - win attitude and approach to human relations is often sorely tested in the supervisor during labour negotiations, more easily *before* a strike, but definitely *harder* during and right after a strike. If proposals, counterproposals, and mediation have not resolved any impasses in the collective bargaining efforts of management and the union, and if bitterness and suspicion have escalated to unacceptable levels, a strike is usually called.

But there is another option: negotiating with a problem-solving focus *before* matters get out of hand. The Canadian Manufacturers Association points out, "Since 1980, unit labour costs in Canada's manufacturing sector have increased by over 60 per cent. Unit labour costs in the rest of the G7 have also risen, but by only 33 per cent overall."[65] The problem-solving supervisor first of all believes in a relationship ethic that differences, through mutual respect, can be discussed and resolved -- and secondly believes that an adult-adult relationship is the best vehicle for resolving conflict. As such, both management *and* union work together to solve the problem(s). Each has its own bias, but each shares a concern for the agreed-upon problem(s) and seeks ways to resolve the problem(s). The Ford Motor Co. is now reaping many of the benefits of that new spirit of co-operation that it set in motion as early as 1978. UAW Local 420 president Joseph D'Amico saw the handwriting on the wall in 1982: "If we didn't break down some barriers, we'd be history." Formerly known as the Cleveland plant, but now called the Walton Hills plant to reflect the new way of doing things, the plant has seen *quantifiable* differences in their efficiencies: Ford requires a third fewer hours to build its cars than GM, which gives Ford a cost advantage of $795 a vehicle! After visiting a Mazda Motor Corp. plant, D'Amico realized that the Japanese were really not working harder, but doing a better job of working together. "I learned the best way to accomplish anything is to talk."[66]

North American capitalism needs a heart transplant.

David Olive, editor of *The Globe and Mail*, underscored this approach when he said perhaps changes should be made in the executive suites first. It certainly wasn't the ordinary worker who planned the "overzealous expansions and leveraged buyouts" which resulted in thousands being laid off in recessionary times. A forecast released by Wood Gundy Inc. predicted a spectacular recovery for Canada once the recession was over and attributed the validity of that prediction to "the genuine partnership struck between management and workers in recent years."[67] No less than *The Financial Times of Canada* points out in reviewing the new book by Lester Thurow, dean of the Sloan School of Management, that failing to develop community and partnership and take into account all the stakeholders, not just shareholders, will result in companies being increasingly disenfranchised (i.e., owned by offshore conglomerates such as Japan) and "a steady haemorrhaging of well-paid jobs." That is why Thurow says, "[North] American capitalism needs a heart transplant."[68] As pointed out in this chapter, and reiterated by Olive, "workers need ... reassurance that their efforts, at management's urging, to operate in teams, to become obsessed with quality, and suggest improvements to the manufacturing process, have been a worthwhile experiment in labour - management cooperation." At Ford Motor Co. of Canada Ltd., in Windsor, Ontario, the union agreed to teamwork to keep the plant going. Frank McNally, president of Local 200 of the Canadian Auto Workers, still cautions though, "Unions aren't great fans of the team concept. ... But we understand the company's needs. And in today's economic climate, the name of the game is work and jobs."[69] In other words, now that a problem-solving relationship and partnership has been established over the years just prior to the recession, hopefully it will not have been destroyed and employees can proceed into a working future with optimism.

STEPS IN MANAGING THE COLLECTIVE AGREEMENT

Assuming that the supervisor and union, or really the company and the union, have managed to produce a worthwhile collective agreement, voted on favourably by union members, the task for the supervisor now is to live up to the agreement and manage according to the spirit and letter of its content and context.

Like everything else in life, disagreement over what something means, that is, its interpretation, will no doubt occur. That is a normal occurrence in life and in any relationship. What the collective agreement implies is that the need for interpretations of certain or different parts *must* occur in order to clarify their meaning.

As in any healthy relationship, both parties don't agree all the time; they may quarrel; but they "stay in the arena," so to speak, until the matter gets resolved. **Nobody walks out.**

Grievances are a way for both union and management to confront, clarify, interpret, and apply the collective agreement according to the letter and spirit for which it was intended. Of course, grievances can be used as a revenge tactic by employees, with little or no mature justification other than a generalized sense of complaining on their part.[70] In this case, the supervisor would do well to regard the grievance more as a symptom of another problem, possibly the only way employees can get "even" if they feel they are mistreated unfairly. CUPW, Canada Post's union, could be a case example of this. Even with the new agreement in the summer of 1992, there were still 140,000 grievances to be cleared up![71] To put this into perspective, it is important that the supervisor realize that *no grievances* is not necessarily a healthy thing. Everything can't be perfect all of the time with everyone and perhaps employees are just ignoring or living with their discomfort. As we saw earlier, the problem is not the problem; it's what we do with it. Real and perceived problems don't just go away; they get resolved. In a healthy working environment, the supervisor recognizes the value of conflict-as-differences, and, being proactive, anticipates problems, knows the work environment, and is not surprised when conflicts surface. A supervisor needs to be concerned if grievances start becoming "a way of working" for employees, but some conflict is necessary, as in any healthy relationship.

In the summer of 1992, there were still 140,000 grievances to be cleared up within Canada Post!

The collective agreement between the Ontario Council of Regents for the Colleges of Applied Arts and Technology and Ontario Public Service Employees Union (for academic employees)[72] allows for *complaints* -- whereby an employee (faculty member) discusses the matter directly with a supervisor (i.e., chairperson) within 20 days of its occurrence so that it can be

FOUR STEPS IN A TYPICAL GRIEVANCE PROCEDURE.[73]

1. An aggrieved union employee goes to his/her steward with a complaint. The steward may be able to resolve the matter with the employee at this stage. If not, the grievance is put into writing, and both steward and employee present it to the supervisor.

2. The supervisor reads the complaint, understands what the matter is all about, and hopefully, is able to resolve the issue for the employee at this stage. Usually the union steward is with the employee and all three people come to some sort of resolution. The supervisor may reject the employee's claim as well. The employee may or may not accept this decision.

3. If the employee still persists with the grievance, it is then discussed at more senior levels of the company in hopes of finding a resolution. Sometimes this higher level will include the human resource manager (if there is one), or more senior management (e.g., general manager) and union officials.

4. At this point there can be the possibility of a mediator's being brought in to settle the dispute.

5. If no resolution occurs, the grievance is then sent to arbitration. The arbitrator makes a binding decision on the matter. Both management and union at this point have to live and work with that new decision and reality.

resolved as quickly as possible. The supervisor needs to respond to the employee within 7 days. The agreement also allows for *grievances* -- whereby a complaint is taken to the next step within 7 days of the supervisor's reply (above). *Step #1*: The complaint, now in the form of a written grievance, is given to the faculty member's immediate supervisor (i.e., chairperson) in writing. Within 7 days, the chair arranges a meeting with the aggrieved faculty member and the union steward; the Dean also may be present. A decision by the chair and Dean is given to the employee and steward within 7 days. *Step #2:* if the grievor (faculty member) is still not satisfied, a written grievance must be submitted to the president of the College within 15 days of the meeting with the chair and Dean. The president will then convene a meeting within 20 days for the faculty member (grievor) and union steward, and within another 15 days the president will give both of them a written decision. If, at this stage, the complaint-grievance is still not resolved, it is sent in writing by the grievor within 15 days for binding arbitration.

It should be obvious at this point that there may be many points throughout this complaint-grievance-arbitration process for the supervisor to make major contributions, technically, but especially interpersonally. Skilful supervisors can often make the process human and ethical. Perhaps at no other time are the key factors and skills around self-concept and human relations more important. Wise supervisors know this and contribute positively.

THE ROLE OF UNIONS IN THE INFORMATION AGE

Francis Bacon (1561 - 1626) said that "information is wealth."[74] Futurist Frank Feather believes that trade unions "could disappear in the West by 2025 and from the whole world by 2050."[75] This is attributed to enlightened management practices and forms of employee ownership, whether literal or by way of "empowerment," that are becoming more prevalent today. In the short-lived courtship between Canada's largest space company, Spar Aerospace Ltd., and MacDonald Dettwiler and Associates (MDA), one of Canada's leading software companies, one of the factors that complicated the bidding and hoped-for marriage was the fact that MDA employees (roughly 630) owned about 20 per cent of the company stock.[76] At Amdahl Canada, the computer company, president Ronald Smith says that the difference now is the fact that ideas come from employees themselves; they have "ownership."[77] Perhaps the most notable of these "employee-ownership" experiments is what is happening with the 6,000 employees at Algoma Steel Corp. Ltd., which was purchased by Dofasco Inc. in 1988. It is an example of the union bailing out the steel company, responding to economic changes and building a new corporate culture. By 1996, employees (from the steel mill to the executive offices) will own 60 per cent of the company. The trade-off now? Cuts in wages and benefits during the restructuring period (1992 - 96). Will it work? Leo Gerard, outgoing Canadian president of the United Steelworkers of America, thinks so. He says that "it shows what imagination and a willingness to take risks can accomplish."[78]

However, there is still a deeply ingrained resistance -- dating back to the Industrial Revolution of the early 1800s -- by unions to management "wanting more for less," even if it is called "employee ownership" of some kind.

The issue may have more to do with *power and control* than with anything else. If management is too threatened with sharing more power and if the unions continue using a hard-line, adversarial approach, no one will survive.

Survival and economic realities today may change that opposition. The trade-offs for the union have to be higher, with management's strong commitment and joint union - management contributions to the ownership - productivity - profitability equation. The issue may have more to do with *power and control* than with anything else. If management is too threatened with sharing more power and if the unions continue using a hard-line, adversarial approach, no one will survive.[79]

However, as John Emig, field supervisor for Teperman and Sons Inc., says, "There will always be a union. Call it an alliance or a federation. It's the strength of having a collective; it's the unit of one."[80] To highlight this reality, we need only look at the following factors.

THE HISTORICAL EXPERIENCES OF WORKERS

The history of business management and labour relations has not been kind. The Egyptian and Roman "managers," for instance, were often cruel and unjust. What mattered was "efficiency," "productivity," and "economies of scale." For centuries workers were crushed beneath the weight of unjust management practices. The Industrial Revolution of the 1800s brought that reality into modern times. People, often women and children, were exploited; working conditions were unsafe and unhealthy; and attempts by workers to gain a sense of decency, as we have seen, were met by hostility at best, and brutality at worst. Even the Canadian government's common law that business should be able to carry on its practices was interpreted to mean that union activities were illegal because they interfered with that objective. Pierre Berton, in his widely acclaimed book on the depression of 1929 - 1939, shows a systematic attempt by business and politicians to profit at any cost.[81] Reading his book is almost a "déjà-vu" experience when compared with our experience of the 1990 - 93 recession; nothing much seems to have changed. Prime Minister Brian Mulroney told the 1.2 million jobless in 1990 that Ottawa couldn't help because of the $380 billion debt.[82] In June 1992 that number of jobless had increased to some 1.5 million Canadians, with 588,000 in Ontario.[83] In the same way that former Tory finance minister Michael Wilson refused to say the "R" word -- that Canada was in a recession -- so in 1930 the Liberal government of the time said "that there was no real unemployment problem; it was merely a seasonal aberration."[84] In Glace Bay, N.S., in 1931, the coal miners at Dominion Coal were working under "a form of serfdom." Bill McNeil, who grew up there during that time, and who later became a CBC producer, said that "many children died during the Depression in Glace Bay. Nobody said they starved to death, but that was actually the reason."[85] Berton gives many other examples of worker abuse, and then asks, "Is it surprising, then, that with these conditions, and with further cuts in the offing, the miners ... should start to talk about forming a union?"[86]

In the same way that former Tory finance minister Michael Wilson refused to say the "R" work and that Canada was in a recession, so in 1930 the liberal government of the time said "that there was no real unemployment problem; it was merely a seasonal aberration."

CONTEMPORARY ABUSES

One of the most graphic and poignant contemporary descriptions of worker abuse at the hands of management is the recital of abuses -- mostly against children and women -- in factories on "the dark side of Asia's economic trade."[87] Again, we have a sense that we've seen much of this abuse before; and indeed we have, in the child labour abuses of the eighteenth and nineteenth centuries, for instance, which led to legislation outlawing such abuse. Children in Bangkok factories, for instance, work in sweatshops for long hours and little pay and in unsanitary and unsafe conditions. The new world economic order comes from Asia, but on the backs and through the sweat and tears of these little children. "In Bangladesh, children as young as eight spend up to 16 hours a day cutting cloth for shirts and blouses that end up in Canadian department stores. During the first three months, they are paid nothing. After that, wages start at $9 or $10 a month."[88] Or, in Dacca, Bangladesh, "Some factories forced the women to stand on their heads for extended periods as punishment for flaws in their work." What does this cheap labour and abuse bring to us as Canadians? Adult clothing with such

"In Bangladesh, children as young as eight spend up to 16 hours a day cutting cloth for shirts and blouses that end up in Canadian department stores. During the first three months, they are paid nothing. After that, wages start at $9 or $10 a month."

labels as Gitano, Hunt Club, Yves St. Laurent, and children's clothing with such labels as Lemon Drop and Lollytogs. In Bangkok, even a three-year-old little girl was forced to make heroin pellets. She had been chained up to a cellar wall in one of the factories.[89] Child rights activists say *no one really* is doing much to help: neither government, non-governmental organizations, nor even trade unions. Why not? The answer lies in the seduction of profits. Is a mechanism needed to re-balance this ugly and evil situation? The answer is obvious.

Closer to home, there is the impact of high technology on the workforce. While some will claim that this situation also necessitates "high touch,"[90] or the relationship dimension, reality is sometimes different. Thus, while blue-collar issues, such as wages, working conditions, etc., are fairly well established on the whole in much of society, the shift to unionizing white-collar employees is taking place more aggressively. Workers in the 1990s will be mainly in service industries. These workers will be the knowledge, not the industrial, workers, and will "also be more militant on the issues of environmental concerns, flexible working patterns, and shared decision making."[91] "Working conditions" no longer refer as much to the air employees breathe, for instance, but probably to how much exposure a person -- especially a pregnant woman -- has working with a computer[92] and how closely performance is monitored by the computer.

THE NEW UNIONIZED EMPLOYEE

While white-collar and professional workers might feel "less than" if they were union members, the future may be quite different because of the experience of the recession in the early 1990s. We have already given indications in this chapter of instances of management and union sitting down and reconsidering their *common objective*: to serve the customer and their constituents. Traditionally goals for management and union have been different, and while this may not change, *how* these goals are arrived at will probably change substantially. Emphasis will need to be on co-operation, alliances, partnerships, "ownership," and teamwork. The Federal Sector Advisory Council's 83-page report, "Strategy for Growth," recommends that a seriously underfunded industry (for example, the Canadian forest products industry) should look at labour working more co-operatively with management: "Labour, in co-operation with management, should design new work practices with an emphasis on increased flexibility."[93]

> Workers in the 1990s will be mainly in service industries. These workers will be the knowledge, not the industrial, workers, and will "also be more militant on the issues of environmental concerns, flexible working patterns, and shared decision making."

This co-operative environment should be more inviting to white-collar service workers, and, with the experience of the recession behind them, may look quite appealing. But Tom Steers, who is organizing a union drive on behalf of the International Ladies' Garment Workers' Union to unionize the Journey's End motel chain, doubts that when he says, "The service economy is really the sweatshops of the 1990s."[94] Ironically, in Ontario and British Columbia, with their provinces' new labour legislation, especially regarding replacement workers -- traditionally known as scabs -- it is business, in its vocal condemnation, which seems just "... as reactionary, hysterical and ... blindly driven by ideology as is the government itself."[95] Quebec now has historical proof from the last few years that its labour legislation *has* prevented violence on the picket lines!

> Quebec now has historical proof from the last few years that its labour legislation *has* prevented violence on the picket lines!

Would that business would learn the lesson of managerial ethics which would make many of these new labour changes unnecessary precisely because they had been anticipated and implemented. Until that more enlightened group of employers does emerge *en masse*, and come to grips with their shadow side that would want things mainly their way, we will continue to have unions, and necessarily so. As long as the feeling trickles down that the establishment capitalists, and the more recent acquisitor capitalists, who keep flipping properties and using pay phones as their "office outposts"[96] to make deals while on the road, play with people's lives, employees will not feel secure that management has their best interests at heart. The feeling will continue to be that the human factor is still expendable on the altar of another deal, profits only, and the roll of the dice. This perceived and/or actual injustice will need to be confronted.

SUMMARY

Unions are here to stay. While union membership has fluctuated over the years in Canada, with a high of 40 per cent in 1983, it remains consistently around the 30 per cent mark on average.

Unionism is expanding in the white-collar sectors of the business world.

The 10 - 90% Factor refers to 10 per cent of labour law under federal jurisidiction, 90 per cent under provincial jurisdiction, unlike the United States, which has the reverse.

Employees join unions because of mistreatment and dissatisfaction. There are two kinds of objectives: business unionism (wages, job security, equity, working conditions) and political unionism (social interests).

Preventive mediation was first introduced into Canada in 1978 by the Ontario Ministry of Labour to promote effective communications in contract disputes in order to minimize the bitterness, negative attitudes, and hostility often associated with union - management conflicts.

A new spirit of co-operation is developing between union and management, if only for survival economic reasons. Measuring up to the moment is done through *strategic strength* and *relationship strength*.

Collective bargaining is the process whereby supervisors/managers *and* unions meet to design a new working agenda and relationship, or employment contract. It not only states *what* each party must do but also *how* each part must conduct itself during the life of the contract.

In problem-solving negotiations, both management *and* union work together to solve the problem(s). Each has its own bias, but each shares a concern over the agreed-upon problem(s) and seeks ways to resolve the problem(s).

Grievances are a way for both union and management to confront, clarify, interpret, and apply the collective agreement according to the letter and spirit which was intended.

TERMS/CONCEPTS

unionism
craft unions
10 - 90% Factor
business unionism
political unionism
preventive mediation
balance of power
adversarial attitude

strategic strength
relationship strength
collective bargaining process
bargaining: table, gap, zone
collective agreement
problem solving negotiations
complaint
grievance

DISCUSSION QUESTIONS

1. Describe briefly the history of unionism in Canada.

2. How is unionism expanding in Canada?

3. What is the role of the union in organizations?

4. Distinguish between *business unionism* and *political unionism*. Use a contemporary example of each to illustrate your point.

5. What happens when a roadblock occurs in the administration of the collective agreement?

6. Define *preventive mediation* and state its objectives.

7. "Companies and unions can cry all they want about North American free trade; but if that is the reality in our world -- and it is -- then crying does not solve the problem. Measuring up to the moment does; and that is done through *strategic strength* and *relationship strength*." Discuss.

8. Using an example from your own outside reading, describe the collective bargaining process.

9. Why are problem-solving negotiations important?

10. List and describe the steps in managing the collective agreement.

11. What is the role of unions in the information age?

ASSIGNMENT

Instructions: In the appropriate space below, list the **qualities** you have in order to supervise well in a unionized workplace. In the appropriate space below, list the **weaknesses** you have that would prevent you from supervising well in a unionized workplace.

STRENGTHS	WEAKNESSES

THE SHORT LIST

My main strength is

My main weakness is

CHAPTER FOURTEEN

HEALTH AND SAFETY
AND DEALING WITH STRESS

That's the most interesting thing of all. The balance depends on the man's *frame of mind*.

-- Aleksandr Solzhenitsyn[1]

LEARNING OBJECTIVES

At the end of this chapter, students will be able to:

- Discuss the importance of a *healthy* working environment
- Discuss the importance of a *safe* working environment
- Examine the key pieces of legislation
- Define and describe the stress formula
- Know the key signals for workaholism and burnout
- Identify strategies to reduce employee stress

Opening Scenario

W hile drugs of one kind or another have been known since earliest times, except for eighteenth century England, it is only in today's society that "drugs are chic."[2] According to one author, "Economists say that if the flow of cocaine were cut off, the economy of Florida would crumble."[3] But healing and society are more complex because drugs also have a positive and sophisticated contribution to twentieth century ills. There is the psychobiology and mind - body healing revolution as well.[4] Research shows that "mind ultimately does modulate the creation and expression of the molecules of life."[5] Our minds do influence our emotions, which in turn influence our blood pressure and body. Dr. Bernie Siegel says that depression is the net result of living a life that lacks meaning. "Illness then often functions as an escape from a routine that has become meaningless. In this sense it might even be called the Western form of meditation."[6] Science is also showing that the "awfulizing"[7] way of thinking leads directly to illness, does not resolve the perceived negative stress, and contributes to our emotionally polluted environments, at home and at work.

Mindfulness is the skill of being open to the experience of the moment, savouring it just as children do. Children are wholly "into" what they are doing. It's that attentiveness that opens the channel to healing. Norman Cousins gives "undeniable evidence that the human mind can be trained to play an important part both in preventing disease and in overcoming it when it occurs,"[8] what he calls the "intrinsic gifts for self-repair."[9] IBM Canada Ltd. is using the "emotional" component also now in its training courses, says John Denomy, manager of education quality. There is "a decidedly untechnical, human, touchy-feely range of new course offerings that have nothing to do with cold data and everything to do with human emotions."[10] Organizations and supervisors need to pay special attention to these factors as three years of on-going, persistent, negative, and anxious recessionary stress on employees may present a heavier cost than was ever dreamed of. David Olive, editor of *Report on Business*, sums this all up quite nicely: Treating people like economic inputs or raw materials is not the answer. Doing things that way, as is the current widespread belief and practice in business, is "not at all conducive to improving productivity or increasing quality, let alone innovating."[11]

The purpose of this chapter is to study the importance of developing a *healthy* and *safe* working environment. More and more this includes what is referred to as the *psychosocial factors* or the psychological and relationship components in a workplace. These can be negative and unhealthy just as traditional factors, such as physical and chemical components, have caused unhealthy and unsafe working conditions for all concerned.

Reflective Exercise

Think of a time when you felt "really stressed." What was it like? Describe the situation below: how your body felt, what your emotions were like, what you were thinking.

_____

_____

_____

_____

_____

IMPORTANCE OF A HEALTHY WORKING ENVIRONMENT

Developing a healthy working environment is the responsibility of every employee. The supervisor must make this health and safety objective a priority as well. As we shall see in this chapter, health is not only physical health, but includes psychosocial aspects as well, that is, the psychological and social forces present in the work environment.[12] The Department of National Health and Welfare refers to the psychosocial aspects of work as including such factors as the *kind of work* an employee does (working in isolation, the skill level), the work *characteristics* (its complexity, status, responsibility, potential for role conflict), the *kind of organization* an employee works for (its culture and structure), the *backing and support* an employee has (from the supervisor and colleagues), and the *terms of employment* (salary, benefits, pleasantness of the environment).

"Stress in the workplace often stems from paper overload and project deadlines," says Valhalla Markham's general manager Graham Willsher. "I have a sure-fire way of handling both and would recommend the process for all levels of management. Remove each piece of paper from your work area or office, lock yourself in another room where you won't be disturbed, and don't surface until every piece of paper has received action and every project has been advanced a stage. It may take 16 hours, but the feeling of euphoria afterwards is revitalizing."

The first World Health Interdisciplinary Workshop of Psychosocial Factors and Health was held in Stockholm in 1976 and it declared that health was not just the absence of disease but "must include ... variables such as 'quality of life', 'self-actualization' and 'fulfillment'."[13] Since employees spend 60 per cent of their waking hours at work, Health and Welfare Canada has developed what it calls "The Workplace System," a program that addresses three important areas: "personal resources, environment and health practices."[14]

MediPsych Resources Inc. is a company devoted to dealing with work problems that have "medical, psychological, family/social or work related issues" attached to them. Alfred H. Neufeldt, the principal of MediPsych, says that with two similar programs in the United States, direct savings for employers are between $4 and $10 "for every dollar spent."[15] A major turning-point in the psychosocial dimension came in the summer of 1992 when the project "American Business Collaboration for Quality Dependent Care" was announced and scheduled to begin in September 1992. Twelve blue chip organizations[16] -- and a possible further 60 to 80 companies -- established a program for their employees that would help them with daycare and caring for elderly relatives. American Express Co. spokeswoman Audrey Jonckheer said that the "ability of employees to care for dependents is a major workplace problem and a critical business issue."[17] When employees are preoccupied with home responsibilities, they are less productive. The program aims to eliminate that worry.[18] Organizational behaviourists Peter Vaill and Dorothy Marcic describe "spirituality in organizations"[19] as the sense of "spirit" that organizations have which includes such characteristics as vision, integrity, inspiration, and love of work. Supervisors can cultivate, nurture, and enrich such a working environment by employing key principles described in this text, such as treating employees with dignity and respect (Theory Y) and listening empathically, for example.

To Work Or Not To Work!
That Is Another Question![20]

There is a wonderful story about a man who woke up one day and found himself in a place where all his needs were met. He didn't lack for anything. He had all the right food, the great creature comforts of life. Anything he wanted he could have. All went well with him until one day he realized there was something more he wanted. He wanted to do something besides just taking in so much all the time. He was bored being waited upon and served.

Finally, one day when he was really fed up, he called to the head waiter and said, "I am bored. You are very gracious to me here. I have everything I want; I lack for nothing. But I am still bored. I want to do something; I want to work, to feel that I too can contribute something." The waiter replied, "But, sir, we can do everything for you, but we cannot fix it so you can work. That's the way things are around here. You have to be satisfied with having the best of everything and being waited upon day and night and not wanting or craving for anything, except your desire to work."

The man became still, his face fell, and he despaired. "I appreciate everything you're doing for me here, but if I can't contribute by working too, not just being served all the time, that'll just be hell for me."

"But, sir," said the waiter, "you are in hell!"

IMPORTANCE OF A *SAFE* WORKING ENVIRONMENT

In addition to having a healthy working environment, supervisors need to develop one that is *safe* as well. What does that mean? Being safe was, and is, the key human resource, legal, and supervisory issue with the May 9, 1992, Westray Mine explosion in Nova Scotia. Twenty-six miners died. Mine officials were accused of permitting unsafe working conditions.[21] Roger McCabe, one of the rescue workers, described conditions in the mine after the explosion as "two miles the other side of hell."[22] Compensation for the families of the miners has been pegged at $1 million.[23]

Just from a cost point of view, workplace safety is a vitally critical element. It was estimated that the cost of work-related accidents in Canada in 1990 was $14 billion[24] and medical expenses alone were estimated to be $8 billion![25] Supervisors *and* employees carry not only *cost* and *legal* obligations, but also an *ethical responsibility*, to ensure a safe working environment.

In 1986, 446,000 workers were injured on the job, enough to fill Maple Leaf Gardens for 26 consecutive nights.[26] Or, a work injury, involving lost time, occurs every 15 seconds in Canada![27]

Northern Telecom Canada Ltd. is an excellent example of a company that did it "right the first time" with its customized health and safety program. They built it from the ground up, with management kicking it off with "an aggressive commitment to health and safety."[28] When "the quality of executive leadership"[29] is not at its best, the case for organized labour is strengthened because there are still many companies which "simply do not care about the health and safety of their workers."[30] At Northern Telecom, however, health and safety was not left to chance.

About 50 per cent of Northern Telecom's 16,000 employees in 24 locations across Canada are unionized, the largest union being the Canadian Auto Workers (CAW). Even before the current teamwork emphasis, labour and management got together in 1987, and through a consultative development process, conceived, designed, and delivered a model comprehensive health and safety program. They went beyond what the WHMIS (Workplace Hazardous Materials Information System) demanded -- that workers have information and help in handling dangerous substances -- and, while including toxicology in the training, also emphasized the need for awareness and training on environmental protection. Employees in Kingston, Ontario, for instance, got six hours of basic training, and in Calgary, Alberta, the NT plant now includes questions on chemical safety in its bi-monthly safety audits.

THE ISSUE OF DRUG TESTING

Does a safe working environment include testing for drugs? The issue of mandatory drug testing in Canadian companies (e.g., General Motors, Chrysler Canada, Weyerhaeuser Canada Ltd.) to ensure safety in their working environments cannot have a simplistic solution.[31] The October 23, 1987, policy of the Ontario Human Rights Commission (OHRC) placed drug testing under the same rubric as a mandatory medical exam as a condition for employment: it is prohibited.[32] What the OHRC calls "reasonable and bona fide" exceptions to medical examinations (which could include drug testing) have to meet the following criteria: (1) after a written offer of employment, (2) with specific, and necessary, physical abilities to do the job outlined, (3) with the test focused just on those abilities to determine if the candidate can in fact do the *specific* task, and (4) if a candidate fails the test, to provide reasonable accommodation for the candidate. In the mid-1980s, more and more U.S. firms were including drug testing as a precondition to employment because of their fears of developing negative customer and colleague relationships by employees on drugs.[33] In 1991, 75 per cent of U.S. companies polled, versus 2 per cent of Canadian firms, used random drug testing.[34] Canadian Bar Association chairperson Sandra Chapnik said that mandatory drug testing is a serious issue that all Canadians need to take a look at in a free and democratic society because it could violate the basis of Canada's common law: that each Canadian is presumed innocent until proven guilty. According to Chapnik, "Mandatory drug testing reverses the Common Law presumption of innocence and could be viewed as an unreasonable search and seizure."[35]

> Mandatory drug testing could violate the basis of Canada's Common Law: that each Canadian is presumed innocent until proven guilty.

Thus, in Canada no mandatory drug testing can occur as a precondition for employment, only *after* a conditional written job offer is given to the prospective employee and *if* it can be proven to be *essentially* job-related and job-necessary.[36] In unionized workplaces, drug testing "can only be allowed if it's supported by implied or express terms in a collective agreement or where there's 'real and substantial suspicion of misconduct'."[34] Unions aren't against the testing *but* employers must provide drug education and employee assistance. Even then, if the employee does test positive, reasonable accommodation must be made by the employer to fit the employee in somewhere else in the organization.[37] "Essential duties ... refers to the central aspects of the job."[38] For example, a typist doesn't have to be able to lift weights! The dice seem to be loaded in favour of the employee on this issue since the employer, with these human rights constraints, still has "to maintain a safe workplace for employees and the public."[39]

> *What you see is what you get* is a phrase repeatedly used by the Valhalla Markham's general manager whenever he observes a supervisor's personal office or work station. "It may be a harsh observation, but the *state* of that office or station may give an indication of their effectiveness and organizational ability."

PROBLEMS A SUPERVISOR SHOULD CONSIDER AROUND THE MANDATORY
DRUG TESTING ISSUE IN DEVELOPING A SAFE WORKING ENVIRONMENT

1. *Drug testing results are not 100% reliable.* Hence, there is room for abuse, misinterpretation, and misjudgment. The most common EMIT (Enzyme Multiplied Immunoassay Test) urinalysis test reportedly gives a 97% accuracy rating and even then needs a second laboratory opinion for reassurance's sake.[40] Sometimes tests have been known to be 95% accurate, and, if done properly, could be 100% reliable.[41] The Canadian Bar Association report places the accuracy figure at no more than 90%, and even as low as 66%. The U.S. Navy's experience in the early 1980s, after a fatal accident on a ship in the summer of 1981, would challenge all this, of course. Leo Cangianelli, Captain of the U.S.S. *Nimitz*, said, "The single most important factor in bringing down drug use in the Navy has been the urinalysis program." He also goes on to say, "And it has been the ability to take punitive action from a positive urinalysis."[42] The 1987 Canadian Bar Association report, however, showed *no* significant correlation of excessive drinking and drug taking to accidents on the job. Bruce Cunningham, a consultant with the Addiction Research Foundation of Ontario, would substantially agree with this legal conclusion but go a step further and say there is "a high correlation between *heavy* use of alcohol or drugs and health and safety problems in the workplace."[43]

2. *The costs associated with mandatory drug testing can be significant.* U.S. figures for a drug test fluctuate between $25 and $35.[41] In a small company of 300 employees, that could represent between $7,500 and $10,500. In a firm of 1,000 employees, the cost could be between $25,000 and $35,000. In the U.S. Navy's case (above), a sailor testing positive with marijuana, for instance, is tested again in 60 days. Costs go up once more.

3. *There is the fear that abuses will take place.* For instance, what's to stop unethical companies or supervisors from taking a urine sample from a mandatory drug testing requirement and checking for pregnancy, or AIDS, or, given modern genetic engineering breakthroughs, trying to screen, through "biomedical surveillance" for "genetically superresistant workers"?[44] Meanwhile, sincere employees who could benefit from employee assistance programs or be protected from workplace abuse and other safety hazards would be more vulnerable.

4. *The fear of punitive consequences from testing positive is real.* For some employees, mandatory drug testing would be a self-incriminating activity. Others might argue, "If you have nothing to hide, then why be afraid?" The issue comes back to human rights.

5. *There is a real threat to the privacy of individuals.* The Canadian Charter of Rights and Freedoms guarantees each and every Canadian the right and freedom to live, work, and build a responsible life free from unnecessary interference. If the supervisor feels a drug testing program is necessary, then the supervisor must make sure that it is job-related, and argue the case in such a way that it is clearly related to *safely* doing what the job requires.

THE ISSUE OF AIDS IN THE WORKPLACE

In 1988, Halfdan Mahler, director-general for the World Health Organization, pointed out that by 1993, Canada would have 50,000 AIDS cases.[45] AIDS is expensive to treat. In a 1987 *Financial Post* analysis, it was estimated that AIDS treatment would be $200 million by 1991, and AIDS life insurance claims were projected to add 6 per cent to the total claims bill by 1999.[46] The position of the Canadian Human Rights Commission (CHRC) on testing for AIDS is similar to that for drug testing: it is considered a medical exam. And a medical exam is unnecessary and discriminatory unless it is job-related. A written job offer may be made conditional upon passing a medical examination, but all four conditions attached to drug testing (above) are to be applied. Other than that, AIDS is considered a handicap, for instance, by the Ontario Human Rights Commission (OHRC), and doesn't warrant a separate policy since it is a medical illness, not a moral one.

THE ISSUE OF EMPLOYEES WHO SMOKE

If an employee needs to smoke a pack of 20 cigarettes at work, that means 20 breaks a day! Dow Chemical, in Midland, Texas, said smokers cost the company an extra $657,146.73 in wages alone; the United States Steel Corp. found that smokers had more work-loss days than non-smokers; and the fire department in Alexandria, Virginia realized it paid an extra $140,000 in retirement benefits for *every* firefighter who retired with a smoking-related disability.[47] Tobacco companies still claim that their rights are being trampled on and that society wants the "sin tax" from tobacco, but not the tobacco. While governments like the $3 billion that the Canadian tobacco industry contributes, there is also a $5.2 billion annual bill from the costs of smoking! "This figure includes fines, lost work time, hospitalization and early deaths."[48] Professor William Weiss of Seattle University estimated that (in 1981 U.S. dollars) smoking employees who earn $30,000 a year cost their employer an additional $5,620![47]

"According to the Center for Disease Control, 434,000 preventable tobacco-related deaths occur each year in the United States alone. That's the number that would die in a year if three 747 jumbo jets, fully loaded with passengers, crashed every day -- plus two additional crashes on weekends."[49]

HOW MUCH EXTRA AN EMPLOYEE WHO SMOKES COSTS THE COMPANY _THE WEISS RESULTS_	
FACTORS	COSTS
absenteeism	$ 330
medical care	230
disability, early death	770
fire, industrial accidents	90
time on smoking rituals	2,710
property damage, depreciation	500
maintenance	500
damage to two non-smokers	490
	$ 5,620 (1981 U.S. dollars)

The no-smoking rule is policy in most workplaces today. But it did take time to gain acceptance, in spite of the evidence. Part of the resistance has been because of the "cold-turkey" approach that was often foisted upon workers who resented the imposition. To avoid this kind of resistance, Boeing of Canada Ltd. (Winnipeg Division) gradually built up to their July 2, 1984, no-smoking policy date because patience was part of their culture and the union felt that, at first, it was too much too soon. Malcolm Stamper, president of the Boeing Company, said, "The individual's choice of whether to smoke or not has not been infringed upon -- that choice is still there. The choice of whether to smoke within the confines of the Boeing Company, however, will no longer be available."[48]

THE ISSUE OF ERGONOMICS

Another important contribution that a supervisor can make to the health and safety of employees is through ergonomics, "how human beings physically interface with their work"[50] or "the long-term effects of workplace design on employee health and safety."[51] Questions that the supervisor would need to ask could include some of the following:

1. Is the office (or shop) laid out in the most efficient and humane way possible?

2. Is equipment (e.g., tools) easily accessible?

3. Is furniture designed in such a way that it helps employees get their work done?[52] Dr. John P. Kostiuk of Toronto, now director of spinal surgery-orthopedics at John Hopkins, and past president of the North American Spine Society, points out that back problems occur during people's most productive years, ages 35-65. The estimated financial loss in the workplace is $60 billion (U.S.)![53]

4. Are there ways that I can help typists, data entry processors with their keyboard responsibilities?[54]

5. Can repetitive physical tasks that employees do be modified and still allow for efficiency?

6. Are employees easily able to discuss problems with ergonomics?

THE ISSUE OF THE AGING WORKFORCE

The so-called "greying of the population"[55] has become a reality. One company, Northwest Drug Co. Ltd. of Edmonton, is gearing up to meet the increasing demand for prescription drugs and other drugstore products that is anticipated. Because of this aging factor, supervisors who do not plan carefully now will experience an unyielding shortage of skills.[56]

While the obvious problem of not discriminating because of a person's age will still be legislated -- although that is now being challenged -- there will also be other problems that supervisors will need to consider. For instance, Japan is beginning to face this major problem for themselves. While Japan Inc. finds itself on top of the economic ladder, it realized by 1992 that 40 per cent of its population would be at least 50 years old. "Aside from those over 50, virtually the only age groups that will grow in numbers over the next 10 years will be those aged 25 to 34 years, and those under the age of five."[57] Japan may face a severe shortage of mature managers to carry on the economy. Professor Michael Donnelley, of the University of Toronto, postulates the following: "We may see the energy, verve, and vitality of this country disappear over the next 20 years."[58] Of course, the message is clear: with Japan floundering, how will the rest of the industrialized world cope? Tomorrow's supervisors may have to build some important coping skills for this eventuality.

The aging population is also expected to have an impact on the company through their shareholder rights.[59] Hiring job applicants over 40 -- or the "mature candidate range"[60] -- has become an important factor for such companies as McDonald's and American Airlines. Recruiters, for instance, are going after people between 40 and 65 so they will not miss out serving their customers who will be in that age range by 2002. More mature workers are more reliable, generally speaking.

THE HEALTH AND SAFETY NET: LEGISLATION TO WORK BY

Maintaining a healthy and safe working environment in Canada should be a priority objective for every supervisor. Besides the fact that to do so is an ethical requirement of the highest magnitude, a healthy and safe working environment saves a company time, energy, and costs. "A study by the Economic Council of Canada suggests that indirect costs could range from two to ten times the direct costs."[61] Another way to put it is this: "Labour Canada estimates that for every 100 employees, approximately five disabling injuries occur each year."[62] Most employees also have a right to a safe and healthy working environment. As a matter of fact, employees can refuse work they feel is unsafe. Obvious exceptions would be occupations which could essentially involve danger (e.g., police officers and firefighters) and potentially high tension situations (e.g., correctional officers).[63]

The federal Canada Labour Code (Part IV, Safety of Employees) regulates the federal government as well as agencies under its jurisdiction, and is administered by Labour Canada and Health and Welfare Canada. Health and safety bodies in selected provinces, for instance, would include the following: *Manitoba* has its Workplace Saftey and Health Act, 1976, amended in 1983, and administered by the Department of Environment and Workplace Safety and Health; *Ontario* has its 1978 Ontario Occupational Health and Safety Act (OHSA) to guide companies and organizations; OSHA is administered through the Ministry of Labour, Occupational Health and Safety Division; and *Prince Edward Island* has its Workers' Compensation Act, 1974, amended in 1980 (administered through the Workers' Compensation Board), and its Industrial Safety Regulations, 1974.[64] Supervisors need to contact the

The American Experience	The Canadian Experience
In 1970 the United States passed legislation for the Occupational Safety and Health Act (OSHA). OSHA legislation forced companies to comply with federal regulations to keep their work places safe and healthy for employees. Before this Act was passed, "regulation of health and safety was the state's responsibility."[65] However, public concern over unsafe actions, deaths, and injuries forced the federal government to take charge; the public's concern was too great.	Canada doesn't have this national body that companies and organizations have to report to. Rather, the 1982 federal Charter of Rights and Freedoms, a part of the Constitution Act, directs federal organizations and their affiliates, as well as provincial bodies, to make their own health and safety legislation, which tends to be quite similar in intent and content from province to province. Thus, Canada has health and safety regulations and enforcement agencies by province and territory (with commissioners instead of inspectors in the Northwest Territories). As in the United States these health and safety bodies are in response to companies *not* maintaining health and safety as one of their priorities. To enforce the regulations, the provinces have inspectors who go around to the different companies and organizations just to make sure things are in order.

appropriate agencies in their particular province to be fully informed, and companies doing business in several provinces must have their supervisors cross-provincially trained.

ONTARIO'S OHSA (OCCUPATIONAL HEALTH AND SAFETY ACT), 1978

"OHSA covers all workplaces except those of domestic workers, farm workers, teachers, and the academic staff of a university or related institution."[66] This Act, which came into force on October 1, 1979, says (1) employers must inform employees and supervisors about any health or safety hazards on the job; (2) supervisors must model health and safety procedures (e.g., gloves) and advise employees; (3) employees must conform to the health and safety requirements (e.g., protective devices), but can refuse work if they feel that it would endanger them or other workers; (4) joint health and safety commitees must be established (see below); (5) Ministry of Labour inspectors will reinforce the regulations, can come into a workplace unnanounced, identify a problem, and expect it to be fixed. An employer who refuses will be fined or jailed. And finally, (6) an employer must provide information for employees on aspects of health and safety.

BILL 208

This is an updated and revised version of OHSA and has some major changes included. For instance, joint health and safety committees have a lot more power now, being responsible for safety audits and enforcement of the regulations, and if the regulations are ignored or dismissed, the company can be held accountable and fined significantly, as well as any individuals who are in a position to correct the health and safety hazard. These individuals would include such people as directors[67] of the company, managers, and supervisors.

Directors, for instance, are now asking themselves more carefully what their fiduciary and ethical responsibilities are. An interesting situation involves the Westar Mining Ltd., of Vancouver, B.C. In July 1992 six directors quit the board because they felt "they could be on the hook for wages, severance and holiday pay, and pension contributions for about 1,900 Westar miners." Directors in B.C. are caught between two pieces of legislation: the federal Companies Creditors Arrangement Act, which gives them protection from creditors until the company can be reorganized, and the provincial Employment Standards Act, which protects employees so that unscrupulous company officials and owners "don't spirit away funds needed to pay wages and benefits."[68] Perhaps the public is seeing this more in the environmental arena than anywhere else. The Ontario Environment Ministry completed an 84-page study and said that as far as senior corporarte officials are concerned, "the message from the courts is clear ... [they] can no longer hide behind their corporate veil. Individual convictions are likely to continue to increase in coming years."[69]

For computer disk {"Shareware") version of Bill 208, contact: The Industrial Accident Prevention Association, 2 Bloor Street West, 31st Floor, Toronto, Ontario, M4W 3N8 (416) 965-8888; Fax (416) 963-1189; Toll-free Ontario 1-800-387-1210

WHMIS (WORKPLACE HAZARDOUS MATERIALS INFORMATION SYSTEM)

On June 30, 1987, Canadian workers were about to be protected in a way unheard of before, and certainly unlegislated. Through Bill C-70, workers who regularly worked with hazardous materials would now be informed, through their employer, about the materials they were handling. Workers would also be trained to work with these materials and have labels on containers and hazardous materials called a Material Safety Data Sheet (MSDS) with cautions for people handling them. Symbols were designed to let the worker know the *kind* of hazardous material. For instance, any poisonous and infectious material would have the skull and crossbones on it (as in diagram). Thus, workers would have information, education, and help in handling, dangerous materials. WHMIS was introduced gradually between October 1988 and October 1989, allowing companies and organizations the opportunity to make their own provisions.

Example: Gojko Toljagic died when he was 57 years old. He had worked for the Toronto Board of Education for 23 years. What did he die of? His death was ruled asbestos-related.[70]

Example: In Campbell River, British Columbia, the late Sally Giles, nurse, had worked for over 25 years and claimed before she died that her illness was an "occupational disease"[71] since she had often been exposed to cytotoxins, or cancer-producing agents from working with chemotherapy processes with cancer patients. As of August 1992, her appeal to overturn the Workers' Compensation Board rejection of her claim was under way. If the case is won, this will be the first time a court has accepted what many throughout the world believe: workplaces that have such dangerous equipment can produce dangerous effects, even after a long period of time, just as was proven with asbestos workers. In a case which argues for the *who* and *what* of the causes of accidents, "Giles says she was not aware of 1983 compensation board guidelines for handling cancer drugs until 1989 or 1990, at which time she and her co-workers started wearing gloves and taking precautions."[72]

JOINT HEALTH AND SAFETY COMMITTEES

Managers and employees are encouraged to work together to address the important concern of health and safety in the workplace. One of the ways that

In Ontario, the Industrial Accident Prevention Association, begun in 1917, is a member-driven organization dedicated to helping over 71,000 firms in Ontario achieve safe workplaces. The Association operates on a not-for-profit basis and is funded by Ontario's Workplace Health and Safety Agency. Volunteer safety practitioners, from member companies, work with IAPA staff to develop and deliver research, training, education, and consulting services. With 75 years' experience, the Association is a recognized leader in workplace health and safety. Non-members are also entitled to some IAPA services.

the legislation in most provinces encourages this type of co-operation is through mandated joint safety committees whose members comprise both management and workers and whose purpose is to identify and resolve health and safety problems in the work environment. The great value of these committees is that they keep the issue of employee health and safety up front so that any problems are not shuffled under a carpet, but resolved. In Ontario, when a workplace has 20 or more employees, a joint committee is required. With 50 or fewer employees, two members are sufficient; over 50, a minimum of four members are required with one at least being certified by the Workplace Health and Safety Agency. The IAPA sells a "Joint Health and Safety Committee Start Kit" (#LPKA0029109).

WHO WILL HELP YOU?

(1) *CCOHS (Canadian Centre for Occupational Health and Safety)*: This Centre is sponsored by the federal government and is a public corporation. It seeks to promote the physical and mental well-being of working Canadians by gaining allegiances among labour and management concerning health and safety concerns and by being a central statistic gathering place for health and safety information. Assistance is provided to anyone throughout Canada (1-800-263-8276, general inquiries; 1-800-263-8266, information inquiries). (2) *The health and safety act and agency in your province.*[73]

WHO, OR WHAT, CAUSES ACCIDENTS?

Over the last 100 years many theories have been put forward to jutsify why accidents happen. These justifications have ranged from the idea of *accident proneness*, to *unsafe acts* on the part of employees, to the *lifestyle and hypersusceptibility* argument, that is, that an employee is predisposed to accidents, and the *epidemiological* rationalization, that is, there are multiple causes.[74] The argument on the cause comes down to this: does the *worker* cause the accident by unsafe acts, or is the *work environment* the main contributing factor? Is it *who* creates the accident, or is it *what* creates the accident?

Some authors argue that it is the unsafe acts and carelessness of workers that cause accidents. A worker, for instance, leaves a tool lying around and someone gets hurt. These same authors argue that accidents will not be eliminated by removing unsafe working conditions alone and, to date, there is no such thing as an "accident-free employee."[75] Other authors, however, say, "Increasingly, attention is shifting to the work environment," and insist that to blame the worker is to promote the bias of the "dumb worker."[76]

However, often the worker does not have the necessary information for a healthy and safe working environment, or may, because of work pressures, ignore these health and safety constraints.[77] Thus, the answer to *who* or *what* is as follows:

unsafe work conditions **?** unsafe work behaviours

Studies indicating the causes of occupational injuries are split about equally between unsafe work conditions and unsafe work behaviours.[78]

THE STRESS FORMULA

in the last few years the word *stress* has become part of almost every person's daily vocabulary. Stress workshops have been held for individuals as well as managers and supervisors. In 1985 job stress costs were estimated to be in the range of $8 to 10 billion in Canada![79] In the United States, through health insurance disability claims and lost productivity, the cost of stress and its consequences is estimated to be in the neighbourhood of $150 billion a year![80] In comparison to our American counterparts, we are told that Canadians experience more job stress.[81] The noted English psychologist Dr. Hans J. Eysenck through the use of "The Health Personality Test," finds a strong correlation "between certain personalities and specific illnesses."[82] For instance, a noted Bay Street lawyer attributess some of his professional misconduct to inordinate stress demands.[83] Caught in the vicious cycle of needing more and more positive recognition, or "stroking," he did things, under stress and overwork, that caused him to use faulty judgment in his legal practice. And the impact of future shock -- constant and too fast changes -- in people's lives is driving them to break down. Stress is seen as "the culprit."[84] In a most extraordinary experiment, Dr. Shlomo Breznitz, a psychologist at Hebrew University in Jerusalem, found that "stress hormone levels always reflected the ... *estimates* rather than the actual distance"[86] of soldiers he was testing on a grueling 40-kilometre forced march. By giving more or less accurate information on what to expect to different groups of soldiers, he found their stress levels were in direct relation to their estimates or expectations based upon the information they had.

"... two-thirds of all stress-related problems result from 'abusive, unsatisfying, limiting or ill-defined relationships' in the workplace or out of it."[85]

A more technical definition is this: "**Stress** is defined as the physiological and emotional response to demands, constraints, and opportunities that create uncertainty when important outcomes are at stake."[87] Business professor Robert M. Cohen, of Trent University, says, "When actions (stressors) occur within the working environment, the human body counters by reacting based on previous experiences and the perceived magnitude and direction of the outcomes. Depending on the individual, the pendulum will swing between distress (negative stress) and eustress (positive stress)."[88]

Stress creates tension from a "disturbing factor"[89] of some sort in the environment. With too much tension there is burnout and breakdown, with too little, there is boredom and inactivity.

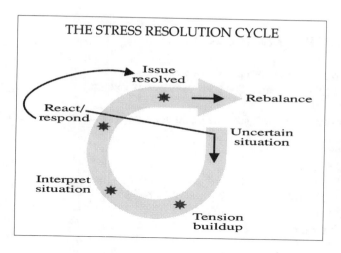

THE STRESS RESOLUTION CYCLE

Issue resolved

Rebalance

React/respond

Uncertain situation

Interpret situation

Tension buildup

WHAT WE INTERPRET IS WHAT WE GET!
The *chemistry of our thinking* is often more important than the actual stress event. What seems to be the difference between health and illness is the meaning we attribute to an uncertain situation and how we respond[90] - - "how we look at a stressful situation, the attitudes and beliefs we bring to the problem, influences what chemical messages the brain sends the body,"[91] which explains American poet Robert Frost's words, "The reason that worry kills more people than work is that more people worry than work."[92]

Since the source of much of our stress comes from factors *outside* the work environment, some authors will say, "In most cases, the person, not the job, creates this tension."[93] Some employees will be more prone to negative, that is, *dis*-stress, rather than positive or *eu*-stress. This doesn't mean that *eu*-stress types don't experience *dis*-stress. If there is enough of an actual or percieved threat, anyone will *react* rather than *respond*. It must be repeated: a *reaction*, that is, taking fight or flight, may be the commonsense thing to do in a situation. It is the *sustaining* of this pattern -- either fleeing (TURTLE posture) or fighting (SKUNK posture) -- that creates the *dis*-ease and eventual illness. The noted researcher Dr. Hans Selye said it is when individuals can't cope any more, when their coping mechanisms fail, that trouble begins. In his research he wrote about GAS or *general adaptation syndrome* (how we manage uncertain situations) with its three phases: **alarm, resistance**, and **exhaustion**.[94] In the first phase, *alarm*, a person is alerted to a threat and gets ready to fight or take flight; in the second phase, *resistance*, the person *adapts* to the stress and threat; and in the third phase, *exhaustion*, coping mechanisms begin to fail and, in some cases, death will occur. Employees who are able to *respond* to threat from their environment are able to cope. Coping and the feeling that one can cope are critical to mental, physical, and spiritual health. It's when an employee feels overloaded (too much and/or too little time), or "underloaded" (not being able to work to one's potential) with little or no options, that stress becomes *dis*-tress.

STRESS QUOTIENT POTENTIAL SCALE (SQPS)

**(1 = to a very little extent, 2 = to a little extent,
3 = to some extent, 4= to a great extent, 5 = to a very great extent)**

Instructions: Think of a job you are doing presently, or your last one if you don't have a current job, and answer the following questions:

On the job

1.	Do you know what your job duties are?	1	2	3	4	5
2.	Do you kow what's expected of you?	1	2	3	4	5
3.	Do you have too much in too little time?	1	2	3	4	5
4.	Do you work to your potential?	1	2	3	4	5
5.	Do you have freedom in what you do?	1	2	3	4	5
6.	Do you feel important doing what you do?	1	2	3	4	5
7.	Do you have variety in your work?	1	2	3	4	5
8.	Do you have a say in what you do?	1	2	3	4	5
9.	Do you find meaning in your work?	1	2	3	4	5
10.	Do you have responsibility at work?	1	2	3	4	5

Personally

11.	Do you turn life into a competition?	1	2	3	4	5
12.	Do you live life as a journey?	1	2	3	4	5
13.	Do you feel in charge of your life?	1	2	3	4	5
14.	Do you need outer reinforcement?	1	2	3	4	5
15.	Do you have major changes in your life?	1	2	3	4	5
16.	Do you have good work relationships?	1	2	3	4	5
17.	Do you experience turmoil in your life?	1	2	3	4	5
18.	Do you have a sense of commitment?	1	2	3	4	5
19.	Do you worry about job security?	1	2	3	4	5
20.	Do you fear burnout?	1	2	3	4	5

Scoring instructions:
1. Add up the score you gave yourself on items 3, 10, 11, 14, 15, 17, 19, 20.
2. Reverse your score on the rest of the items. For example, if you gave yourself a "1," count it as "5"; a "2" becomes a "4"; "3" remains the same; "4" becomes "2"; and "5" becomes "1". Add up all of these item scores.
3. Shade in up to your score on the *Stress Quotient Potential Scale*.

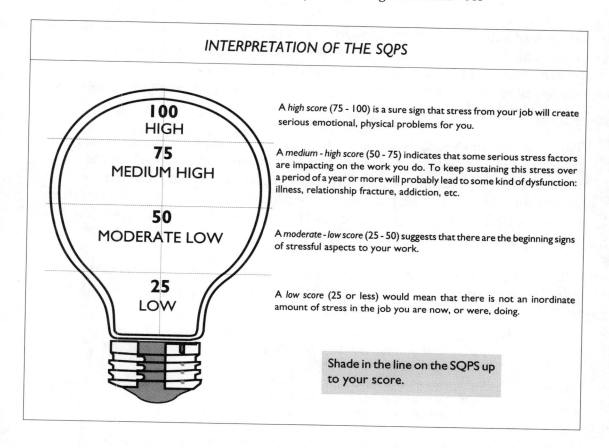

INTERPRETATION OF THE SQPS

100 HIGH

75 MEDIUM HIGH

50 MODERATE LOW

25 LOW

A *high score* (75 - 100) is a sure sign that stress from your job will create serious emotional, physical problems for you.

A *medium - high score* (50 - 75) indicates that some serious stress factors are impacting on the work you do. To keep sustaining this stress over a period of a year or more will probably lead to some kind of dysfunction: illness, relationship fracture, addiction, etc.

A *moderate - low score* (25 - 50) suggests that there are the beginning signs of stressful aspects to your work.

A *low score* (25 or less) would mean that there is not an inordinate amount of stress in the job you are now, or were, doing.

Shade in the line on the SQPS up to your score.

WORKAHOLISM AND BURNOUT

It was predicted before the information age and the coming of the computer revolution that once technology was in place, we would have time to relax! Most people today would agree that it's safe to say that myth has come crashing down! Many today are racing to to keep up and, because of the recession, just to make ends meet.[95] This is a new stress factor in the lives of many people today, and supervisors have to manage employees who feel overworked, anxious, and afraid of what lies ahead. In their efforts just to keep up, or to feel significant in some way or other, they have taken on stress factors that are leading more and more of them to experience job burnout, or, "adverse effects of working conditions where stressors seem unavoidable and sources of satisfaction or relief seem unavailable."[96] High-stress workers like nurses, air traffic controllers, police officers, etc., can experience burnout[97] which brings on physical, emotional, and mental exhaustion.[98] The net result is that employees are not able to cope any more with their work and basically give up trying.

The Japanese have long been noted for their workaholic habits and the price they pay for this work style[99] From our Canadian perspective, it seems peculiar that "the families of the deceased receive compensation from the government"[100] as though this is like one more "work soldier" who has died on the battlefied of corporate honour! The Japanese call this white-collar death from overwork *karoshi*.

When supervisors are aware of job burnout with an employee, they should look for areas to reduce their stress level:

1. Is the employee experiencing too much conflict?
2. Does the employee have major financial problems?
3. Is the employee out of his/her depth?
4. Is the employee acting differently than usual?
5. Does the employee feel isolated and alone?
6. Does the employee have a sense of control in the work environment?

A wise supervisor is able to take appropriate action by providing job variety, if possible a change to a new location, or counselling.

Job stress is not only a workplace health and safety issue; it is also a workplace insurance issue. For instance, in 1991 in Ontario, 400,000 employees made claims with the Workers' Compensation Board of Canada. That's roughly $2,000 paid out on behalf of each employee! Two important questions loom large: (1) When is an employee entitled to such workplace insurance? and (2) Is the "net of entitlement," as it is called, expanding unrealistically so that now compensation might also include "stress" and "burnout."[101]

The pressure is on to include more of the psychosocial factors of stress as deserving compensation. This will mean additional financial burdens for employers, but it might force managers and supervisors to design a more safe and healthy workplace too. In the U.S., a Burroughs Corp. secretary won $7,000 because of her boss's criticism; a General Motors "compulsive perfectionist" received lifetime compensation for mental strain; a state trooper in Maine got a $5,000 stress award when his sex life deteriorated because he was always "on call";[102] a university student in Texas got $30,000 for job stress; a California jury awarded $32.2 million to a family when the father died from a stroke because of the stress of trying to rescue his daughter from a Hare Krishna group.[103] In Canada, at the Craylo (Binney & Smith Canada) crayon plant in Lindsay, Ontario, supervisors receive "exhaustive education in interpersonal skills, problem-solving, conflict management, maintaining self-esteem and providing positive feedback to negative situations."[104] This is b eing proactive in reducing workplace stress.

WHAT THE SUPERVISOR CAN DO

Besides making the work environment more healthy and safe, and implementing a set of core values that promote the dignity and worth of each and every employee, the supervisor can also do other things.

1. Stress relaxation seminars and workshops can be held, or time permitted for employees to attend these.
2. An Employee Assistance Program can be put into place, or employees referred to EAP counsellors for help.
3. Many organizations now have exercise facilities for employees to get fit. Others go to gyms on their own, and take up boxing or martial arts as a way to cope with work stress.[105]
4. Employees can also be taught or encouraged to meditate and to develop a positive mental map for themselves, using inner images of health and equanimity to harness the body's own dynamic for health.
5. Employees can be taught to do simple stress reduction exercises while they're doing their work, even while they're sitting down.
6. In certain circumstances, an employee may be counselled to take a "'mental health day' (instead of absenteeism)."[106]
7. As suggested by Norman Cousins, there could be more laughter in the

work environment.[107]

8. Some employees may be better off to leave the company or organization.
9. All that some supervisors may need to do is acknowledge employees and say, "I'm sorry," concerning a perceived or actual hurt to an employee.
10. Sometimes negotiators use this technique: if someone is stressing them on the phone, they *hang up*, not when they're talking, but when the other person is. They leave the receiver off the hook. The other party assumes there is a bad connection and will often feel apologetic!

SUMMARY

Developing a healthy working environment is the responsibility of every employee. Each of us is a mind-body-spirit person. Only such a holistic approach to developing a healthy working environment meets today's standards. This is achieved by attention, not only to physical factors, but also psychosocial factors on the job.

Drug testing is a controversial topic since it impacts on such issues as human rights, discrimination, and responsibilities. AIDS is considered an illness, not a moral issue, by the Human Rights Commission.

Employees who smoke cost employers almost $6,000 more than non-smoking employees.

Ergonomics refers to the way employees physically interface with their work environment, e.g., how the office is laid out, kinds and shapes of equipment, etc.

Canada's population is aging. It is called the "greying of the population." This aging factor is also reflected in the workplace.

The health and safety net includes such legislation as Canada's Labour Code, health and safety acts, WHMIS (Workplace Hazardous Materials Information System), and joint health and safety committees.

Stress is a disequilibrium in the body's functioning brought about by some perceived environmental threat. Job burnout refers to the adverse effects of working conditions where stressors seem unavoidable and sources of satisfaction or relief seem unavailable.

Additional things a supervisor can do to promote a healthy and safe work environment include: organizing stress relaxation seminars and workshops, putting in place an employee assistance program (EAP), and helping employees develop a positive mental map (PMM) for themselves, physically and psychologically.

TERMS/CONCEPTS

healthy working environment	OHSA
spirituality of work	Bill 208
safe working environment	WHMIS
mandatory drug testing	joint health/safety committees
AIDS in the workplace	CCOHS
employees who smoke	stress formula
ergonomics	workaholism
aging workforce	burnout
health and safety net	karoshi

DISCUSSION QUESTIONS

1. Why is developing a healthy working environment important to today's supervisor?

2. What is *a spirituality of work*?

3. Why is developing a safe working environment important to today's supervisor?

4. What are the main isues that supervisors must consider when it comes to mandatory drug testing?

5. Discuss AIDS in the workplace.

6. Identify the main ideas in the following issues: employees who smoke, ergonomics, the aging workforce.

7. What are the key pieces of legislation that forms the health and safety net?

8. Who, or what, causes accidents?

9. "Stress creates tension from a 'disturbing factor' of some sort in the environment." Discuss.

10. What can supervisors do to maximize positive stress factors in their work environment?

ASSIGNMENT

Instructions: (1) **Step #1:** Review the results from your *Stress Quotient Potential Scale* . Write the five items that give you the most difficulty, and rank order these five (in left column), placing the most difficult problem item as your #1, next most difficult as your #2, etc. Identify a key solution for each problem.

My Stress Reduction Plan

⬇	PROBLEM ITEM	PROPOSED SOLUTION	
1			
2			
3			
4			
5			

Step #2: Rank order your proposed solutions (in the right column) in terms of their difficulty to put into practice.

Step #3: My biggest challenge _____

CHAPTER FIFTEEN

SOCIAL DYNAMICS
AND THE WORKPLACE

I shall cycle!

-- Victorian-era woman[1]

LEARNING OBJECTIVES

At the end of this chapter, students will be able to:

- Discuss the impact of women in the workplace
- Know what employment equity is and its concerns
- Examine the issue of workplace sexual harassment
- Identify the key elements in pay equity legislation
- Explain diversity in the workplace
- Discuss the emphasis on human values

Opening scenario

O n April 20, 1964, Nelson Mandela was sentenced to life imprisonment and gave his last public speech from the dock at the Rivonia Trial, saying, "Political division, based on color, is entirely artificial, and when it disappears, so will the domination of one color group by another."[2] Kathleen Mahoney, a University of Calgary law professor said, "There is no political correctness about justice. Justice is fairness and treating people in such a way before the courts so that no one is disadvantaged by the operation of the law in an unfair way."[3]

The fairness of pay[4] for men and women in the workplace is a justice issue. A study of 373 government-related firms showed that women are paid 70% of what men earn for essentially the same job.[5] Unfairness truly hurts when it is noted that women's unpaid work amounts to 40% of Canada's national product.[6] "Until we succeed in changing attitudes about the ability of women, we can't achieve equality," says Stentor Telecom Policy president Jocelyn Cote-O'Hara.[7] Even in 1988 it was recognized that voluntary affirmative action programs to rebalance unfairness to women did not seem to be working,[8] and in 1990, Dorothy Lipovenko remarked, "As soon as men *perceive* that too many women have infiltrated a job specialty, the job loses sex appeal, the men lose interest ... and presto!, a new pink ghetto is born."[9] Even though there is an employment equity law in Japan, it is not strictly enforced, a fact which allows for widespread abuse and discrimination. Hiroshi Yamada, a former employee of Matsushita Electric Co., described the "harsh" conditions after the layoffs [2,000, mainly women, or "Office Ladies"] occurred: "We suddenly had to make our own tea and open our own mail ... It was a shock ... but we survived."[10]

Doris Anderson, the woman who established the first royal commission on the status of women twenty-five years ago cites peace activist Margarita Papandreou of Greece, "Feminism is ... trying to ... achieve a true revolution -- a revolution of the human spirit." Anderson concludes: "The women's movement has no armies. ... We want liberation for men -- liberation from early heart attacks, from being forced into a strait-jacketed macho role and from a tradition of learned violence that ends in death for so many men at the hands of other men."[11]

The purpose of this chapter is to discuss the main social dynamics that impact on the supervisor in the workplace today. These dynamics include: the significantly increasing role of women, employment and pay equity, sexual harassment, the diverse workforce, and the shift to an emphasis on human values.

THE IMPACT OF WOMEN IN THE WORKPLACE

There are many significant social dynamics in the workplace today, but perhaps the most momentous is the increasing presence of women. In the United States today, 69 percent of women ages 18 to 64 are in the work force, compared to 33 percent in 1950. In 1991, in Canada, women made up 45 per cent of the work force compared to 35 per cent in 1971. "Such societal change is bound to cause upheaval."[12] Attitudes toward women are hopefully changing, given our painful awareness of the 1989 Montreal massacre of the female engineering students.[13] To think, Tyson-like, that a male is innocent of violence against a woman because "there were no black eyes, no broken ribs" is not only intellectually stupid, but also a debasing and unethical relationship position to hold.[12]

Men have traditionally been the breadwinners since the time of the Industrial Revolution and it was at that time, according to physicist Thomas Berry, that the split of work - home occurred: women stayed home to "tend the hearth" and men went to factories all day to work.[14] This split of work and home led to work role definitions whereby men didn't see their family and home for hours on end and women spent their days cooking, looking after the house, and raising the children. But the split has been seen as a male-created entity, that is, separation of work and family "is based on a male-centred view of society."[15]

Of the ten department heads responsible for operations at the Valhalla Inn Markham, five are women, including the assistant general manager. "With that ratio in place, few equity problems seem to arise," says general manager, Graham Willsher. "Tokenism, thankfully, is giving way to the merits of qualification in both traditional and non-traditional positions in terms of female placement."

Today, of course, all that has changed. This traditional work - home dynamic is being challenged to such an extent that companies are offering flexible working arrangements so that the split is not as onerous.[16] Much of this change is due to the women's movement, the increased presence of more women in the workplace, as well as the high proportion of single mothers with children who need these arrangements. In 1990 concern over family issues at work was almost triple that of 1977. Statistics Canada figures showed that for "women with preschool children, absenteeism rose to 25.1 days a year, up from 20.5 days in 1987. The figures include time taken from maternity leaves, which averaged 17 weeks in 1987."[17] Supervisors, because of increased demand, will have to put more effort into finding low-cost solutions to this need.[18] One reference highlights the fact that perhaps 66% of workers are affected by family stresses.[19]

"I don't think society is an end in itself. I think a person is the most important thing. Anything else is there to assist the person to fulfill one's life." -- Chief Justice Antonio Lamer, Supreme Court of Canada[20]

At Levi Strauss & Co. (Canada) work and home and the aging population issues are just two of the concerns being addressed by the person in the newly created position called "organizational effectiveness manager." The "work - family juggling act" is seen not only as a social issue but as an organizational one as well.[21] At the Bank of Montreal there are five different flexible work arrangements for their "People Care Days." According to Johanne Totta, vice-president for workplace equality, this is to facilitate "balancing multiple commitments."[22] The federal Tory "family caucus" would seemingly like to turn the clock back to the good ol' days so that the traditional idea of family stays intact, with its values, metaphors, and life.[23] "Roles are changing so fast that it's hard to keep up," says Beverly King, the director of human resources at the Los Angeles Department of Water and Power, which offers a seminar entitled "Contemporary Men's Issues."[24] Other companies are also following suit: Hewlett-Packard Co. offers a seminar called "Fatherhood in the '90s" and the Aetna Life and Casualty Co. sponsors a father's support group and child-care program.

It is women who are bringing these issues to light. Obviously these realities are changing the tone and expectations of the supervisor's new work environment. For supervisors who still hold more traditional views -- that women should be at home -- but who value children highly, it would be well for them to reflect on the paradox they're in: "History has shown that children's rights often flow from women's rights."[25] Unicef refers to this inequality of women as "the apartheid of gender."[26] Indeed, times are changing; the new supervisor must quickly adapt as well.

Reflective exercise

List below for yourself some of the changes that you think are happening now that the workplace is changing as radically as it is.

_____

_____

_____

_____

_____

THE GLASS CEILING

In 1988 in Ontario, the unconscious barrier, or "velvet ghetto"[27] -- commonly known as the glass ceiling -- that blocks women from being promoted into managerial ranks, was alive and well in the health sector field. This was one of the reasons given by Nancy Myers, Vice-President of Human Resources at Mississauga Hospital, to explain why only 15 per cent of 220 Ontario hospitals had female CEOs, especially when the health care field was traditionally female-dominated.[28]

Male supervisors may often feel threatened by the increased presence of women at work. Stanford University researcher Myra Strober discovered a "15 per cent glass ceiling." That is, after the number of women managers increases above the 15 per cent level, "the occupation becomes segregated as a woman's occupation,"[29] in effect controlling the number and promotability of women. The 1989 Montreal massacre of 14 women, mainly engineering students, highlights dramatically this aspect of control and jealousy, with hate even erupting at the sign of others' success.[30]

676 public and crown corporations were surveyed by accounting professor Leo-Paul Lauzon of the Université du Québec à Montréal. 64 per cent had no female executives and only one in six companies had a female senior executive.

Accounting professor Leo-Paul Lauzon of the Université du Québec à Montréal surveyed 676 public and Crown corporations and found that 64% had no female executives and only one in six companies had a female senior executive. Lauzon said, "Women have no power because they are not represented ... There is no excuse for that. It is shocking."[31] Even though women in the 1980s made significant gains and increased public awareness tremendously, still only 10 per cent of women hold key positions in companies in Canada. At the United Nations, from 1987 to 1990, women executives increased by 0.6 per cent and 0.5 per cent of cabinet positions were filled by

---

WORK AND MONEY

Since 1970 women's share in the workforce has risen. But segregation of jobs and discrimination at work persist and there is a big gap between what women produce and what they earn. Access to training and capital is poor.

TIME

• Women work as much or more than men everywhere in the world - as much as 13 hours a week more in Africa and Asia.

• In developing countries very poor women are now working 60 - 90 hours a week just to maintain the megre living standards of a decade ago.

• Before 1975 women and men in Western Europe worked (paid and unpaid) similar hours. Now women work 6 hours more than men per week. In Eastern Europe they work 7 hours more than men.

• Only in North America and Australia do women work (paid and unpaid) the same number of hours as men. Shopping is more evenly shared but women still do 75 per cent of household chores.

MONEY

• The value of women's unpaid housework as a percentage of GDP is estimated at 23 per cent in the US and 33 per cent in India.

• When women do the same work as men they get paid 30 - 40 per cent less on average worldwide. In Canada women professionals still earn 15 - 20 per cent less than their male counterparts.

• Although women's participation in the informal sector is increasing, returns are decreasing, and there is a bigger gap in earning between women and men than in the formal sector.

POSITION

• Officially measured, 41 per cent of the world's women are economically active. Another 10 - 20 per cent are economically productive but not counted because of inadequate measurement.

• Women hold 10 - 20 per cent of managerial and administrative jobs worldwide and less than 20 per cent of manufacturing jobs. Of the top 1,000 US corporations only two are headed by women.

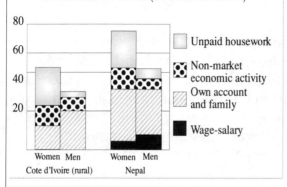

TIME SPENT IN WORK (HOURS PER WEEK)

Unpaid housework
Non-market economic activity
Own account and family
Wage-salary

Women Men
Cote d'Ivoire (rural)

Women Men
Nepal

[*Source:* "Women Today -- The Facts," *New Internationalist*, No. 227, January 1992. Used with permission]

women! 46 per cent of countries that belong to the UN don't have women cabinet ministers at all! "Female and secretary-general are probably a contradiction in terms."[32] The U.S. National Organization of Women (NOW), however, predicts that this artificial ceiling -- "the invisible but real barrier preventing women from advancing beyond a certain level in the work force"[33] -- will be broken in the coming years.[34]

While there are many examples of companies and organizations still holding the glass ceiling in place, so to speak,[35] there are also examples of organizations working to eliminate the glass ceiling, such as the Toronto-Dominion Bank[36] and the Bank of Montreal, with its efforts, as we have seen, in recognizing parents, especially single mothers with children, who have to balance "multiple commitments."[22] President F. Anthony Comper said he would be "delighted to have "a target of 50 per cent women in bank senior management by the end of the century."[37]

MAKING GAINS, SLOWLY, BUT SURELY!

"It's been three years of hell, three years of trying to prove myself, to bust my ass, to out-work everybody. ... It's lots of hard work. It's tough. You've got to have balls and perseverance. Sometimes, you gotta be a bitch. It's not as glamorous as people make it out to be." - Lisa Welch, sports agent[38]

THE REALITY AND EXPERIENCE OF DISCRIMINATION

Discrimination can be (1) direct or intentional, and (2) constructive or "adverse effect." Direct discrimination is blunt: "No Jews allowed!" Systemic discrimination and having an artificial height requirement for employment are examples of adverse effect discrimination because they result from an action or activity which, while it might have been designed not to cause pain or discrimination, does so, however, in its consequences.[39] This kind of discrimination has often created stereotypes.[40] As we saw in chapter 13, **job streaming,** or putting female employees into the lowest paid jobs, is often a way to discriminate against women. Interestingly, China too is catching up on ending discrimination, even if the effort is very weak. Authorities have had to acknowledge that not even 40 years of socialism have eradicated sexism. A draft of a new law declares that women are equal to men at work and at home, but, in reality, "The law simply reaffirms past government pledges of sex equality, has no enforcement mechanism and would not likely have an immediate effect on women. But the government's admission that sex discrimination exists was unusual."[41]

Listed below are selected national and international
examples of actual and alleged work discrimination situations

1. Betty Irwin was a 30-year veteran of the Oshawa (Ontario) Public Utilities Commission. Irwin had earned a CMA (certified management accountant) in 1975, but when a job for secretary-treasurer was posted, she was passed over in favour of a male, who had a CA (chartered accountant). She went to the Ontario Human Rights Commission which voted in her favour. Irwin argued successfully that the new job "was equivalent" to her old one. She got the job and also $45,000, plus a $7,500 contribution to her pension fund from the utilities commission![42]

2. Pam Posterna, of San Clemente, California, always wanted to be an umpire in the major leagues. She worked successfully in the minor leagues for 13 seasons, and in her words, could have had a chance with the majors had she some "outdoor plumbing." She sued major league baseball for sexually discriminating against her. In an angry tone she emphasizes how the macho attitude carried the day: "Almost all of the people in the baseball community don't want anyone interrupting their little male-dominated way of life. They want big, fat male umpires. They want those macho, tobacco-chewing, sleazy sort of borderline alcoholics."[43]

3. On December 21, 1989, Natalie Pollock was fired as a performer on a Winnipeg television show, the *Pollock and Pollock Gossip Show*, for allegedly having too much of a bouncing bust! Pollock exclaimed, "Big feet or big breasts, it shouldn't matter. ... If I dance, I can't stop bouncing." She sued the Winnipeg Videon Public Access station manager, Richard Edwards. The Canadian Human Rights Commission agreed to take her case.[44]

4. In Besancon, France, where dwarf-tossing has been a bar room "sport," Manuel Wackenheim, a 3' 11" dwarf has sued the interior ministry for lost wages and infringement on his freedom to work when it halted the sport, calling it an affront to human dignity and an exploitation of the handicapped. "In dwarf-tossing, participants in bars and elsewhere vie to see who can throw the human projectiles the farthest onto a mattress."[45]

Of special concern to more and more people, especially after the constitutional debates of 1992, is the question whether Canada has gone too far in its acceptance of differences and if what we have is a "tyranny of excess tolerance."[46] If everything is acceptable, then nothing is really acceptable; no choice is made and, therefore, nothing is distinguished from anything else. Sociologist Reginald Bibby at the University of Lethbridge, Alberta, says that if we nurture diversity, we will get diversity, but not unity. In what would be an understatement for many supervisors, Bibby says, "57 per cent of Canadians now acknowledge that 'the overemphasis on individual rights is making social life difficult'."[47] Two authors go even further and wonder if the tyranny of the majority and the collective goal could become a fascist goal[48] and if employment equity legislation, with its emphasis on asking employees "to register their race, gender, ethnic origins and handicap so that promotions, layoffs, part-time work, contract work, terminations and hiring correctly reflect the number of status Indians, non-status Indians, Inuits, blacks, blind people and so on," will make "the Third Reich's Nuremberg laws look benign."[49]

How does a supervisor react to the news that former Justice Minister Kim Campbell made changes to the Human Rights Act to protect gay and lesbian rights, and that British Columbia has already introduced amendments to end discrimination based on sexual orientation,[50] to hear shortly after, in a landmark ruling, that the Ontario Court of Appeal ruled that the Canadian Human Rights Act failed to protect against discrimination on the basis of sexual orientation which opens the door now for gays and lesbians to fight for spousal benefits?[51] The new supervisor has to adjust to these new realities. "The Ruling said that from now on, discrimination against sexual orientation should be treated as though it were covered by law."[52]

More conventional supervisors will find these social dynamics especially challenging. There are people, however, like Terry Thompson, CA, a director and founding chair of the Canadian Centre for Ethics & Corporate Policy, who try to inject some balance: "All the talk these days about 'rights' needs to be put in perspective, and the thinking moved toward communal good and shared needs. We need to think about doing 'the right thing'."[53]

The Canadian Charter of Rights and Freedoms (1982) does not allow for absolute individual rights but balances individual rights in relation to community rights, in effect, placing a "reasonable limit" on the rights of individuals. The trick is for the court systems to discern the often fine line between these two realities.

One way for new and "old school" supervisors to grasp what is happening is to reflect on what Canada really is and the fact that its "Magna Carta" of 1982 -

Canada's social experiment goes something like this: "Suppose there could be a country where people could live freely and to their fullness, irrespective of who they are in any shape or form, literally and figuratively, that people who get off the boat in Halifax, or off the plane in Vancouver, Winnipeg, Toronto, Montreal, St. John's, Nfld., etc., would have the same rights and freedoms as anyone else living in Canada. Suppose we could create a country with this kind of social, spiritual, and emotional expansiveness in the hearts, minds, bodies, and actions of its citizens, what kind of a country would that be? Let's suppose we can do that. Let's suppose that Canada can do that. Let's do it!" No other place in this world is attempting that experiment; Canada is unique. No other country, not even the United States, has this vision of rights and freedoms within its constitution.

the Charter of Rights and Freedoms -- started Canada on a "social experiment"[54] of the greatest magnitude. It is analogous to the "capitalist experiment" begun in 1776 with the United States.[55]

There are some real dangers with this experiment: it could break down and "individualisms" could end up fighting one another with nothing to hold Canadians together. Concerned citizens genuinely raise this possibility when they learn, for instance, that in Ontario, children as young as 12 years of age, if they need medical help, can overrule their parents with the Consent to Treatment legislation, Bill 109. The legislation, originally set up to protect vulnerable, elderly, disabled, and mentally/physically ill people, requires a "rights adviser"[56] to adjudicate between the doctor/ parents and child if treatment (e.g., putting in stitches for a cut) should proceed. Is there a new twist to the old saying, "Children should be seen and not hurt"?[57]

If the social experiment fails, it will mean that the vision of who we are and who we can be as Canadians -- people with a high spiritual, emotional, intellectual vision of dignity and grandeur for everyone -- will have failed. The promise in the Charter would have dissolved, and the courage to make the vision possible would have failed. But there is hope, in spite of the tensions, the uncertainties, the changes. The answer lies in the hearts of each of us as Canadians and the commitment to stretch ourselves to mature. This does not imply being stupid or a doormat, but digging more deeply for mature understanding and acceptance. As the experiment begins to take hold, hopefully we, as Canadians, will portray to ourselves and to the world the "higher road" of enlightened self-interest, decency, dignity, respect, affection, and compassion, and intelligently recognize when to say "no" and mean it.

EMPLOYMENT EQUITY AND ITS CONCERNS

In 1984, the Abella Commission produced for the federal government a document which has become the blueprint for what is known as employment equity, or the elimination of employment practices that would discriminate against potential employees and the provision of meaningful opportunities for employment.[58] "In April 1986 the federal government passed Bill C-62, an act respecting employment equity,"[59] in other words, the federal government's Employment Equity Act, which became law in 1987. The bill also contained the Legislated Employment Equity Program and the Federal Contractors program, which latter made it a condition for potential contractors with 100 employees and $200,000 or more of goods and services with the federal government, to commit themselves to employment equity as a condition of getting a contract. If they fail to do so, employers can be fined up to $50,000.

The key difference with the Abella report is that it addresses the issue of *systemic discrimination*, or discrimination that is indirect, often subtle, long-standing, and part of the "system." That is, the *adverse result* of a policy or employment practice discriminates. If the employer can prove that the practice or policy falls under the *bona fide occupational requirement*, then a possible exemption can be made. It aims to eliminate this kind of systemic discrimination by particularly singling out four target groups that employers must actively *avoid* discriminating against by actively *promoting* women, visible minorities, aboriginals, and the handicapped.[60] Why these four? "The most frequent complaints filed with the Canadian Human Rights Commission relate to disabilities, sex, race/colour, and age, respectively."[61]

> "The bottom line for hiring and promoting anyone should be: May the best qualified *human being* get the job." -- Editorial, *The Financial Post*[62]

AN EMPLOYMENT EQUITY PROGRAM[63] A SET OF POLICIES SUCH AS PAY ADJUSTMENTS, HIRING GOALS, AND PROMOTION TARGETS THAT FAVOUR EMPLOYMENT OPPORTUNITIES WITHIN THE ORGANIZATION FOR A DISADVANTAGED GROUP.

AN AFFIRMATIVE ACTION PROGRAM A PROGRAM TO FAVOUR GROUPS THAT HAVE BEEN UNDERREPRESENTED IN THE WORKPLACE, ORDERED BY A HUMAN RIGHTS TRIBUNAL OR A COURT.

For some people, employment equity legislation feels as though "targets = quotas," especially when it seems clear that if organizations do not have the correct ratio of the targeted people they will be fined and will still have to come up with the "right" numbers for the government.[64] For supervisors and human resource professionals, keeping track of who's who in the organization will be more important than ever. What this will probably mean -- as it did in the United States -- is the development of an HRIS, or human resource information system. "Whether or not an employer uses an HRIS for HRP [human resource planning] purposes, the reporting requirements of this act dictate that employment, pay, and employee mobility data must be available for various race, ethnic, and sex categories of employees."[65] The main question seems to be: are employment *inequities* more damaging than "the greater evil of forcing people to publicly own up to their disability or the hue of their skin color"?[66] Three companies that have done something about employment equity are St. John Shipbuilding Ltd., Warner-Lambert Canada Ltd., and Canadian Standards Association, by making job site modifications in their building designs to accommodate handicapped employees, by offering flexible working hours, job-sharing, and part-time work so that mothers with young families can have some flexibility. Deb Chessell, director of human resources at CSA, an organization that employs 1,500 people, says that employment equity is "just good business."[67]

BUT WHAT ABOUT REVERSE DISCRIMINATION?

The Canadian Civil Liberties Association supports the notion that white males should not be penalized now because of past wrongs, i.e., that women and minorities were held back from top jobs: "Even if whites, and men in general, enjoy a number of advantages because of our society's heritage of discrimination, it is not acceptable for any individual white or man to be made to suffer for the sins committed by other people."[68] It would be untrue to say that preferential treatment is not accorded the four targeted groups. If Section 15(1) of the Canadian Human Rights Act is not violated in spirit, then a preferential bias is permitted. Section 15(1) says that an employer who adopts an affirmative action plan to promote, eliminate, reduce, or prevent discrimination is not discriminating if not to do so would in fact disadvantage a person or group because of factors such as their race, national or ethnic origin, colour, religion, age, sex, marital status, or physical handicap. Philosopher Thomas Hurka of the University of Calgary, points out that equality means that everyone is entitled to fair treatment, but that some individuals and groups face special obstacles, and since we don't live in an ideal world, these people need special help. In Hurka's words: "equality demands an equal chance for all. But sometimes giving that equal chance means treating people differently -- levelling a playing field that would otherwise be full of bumps and hollows."[69]

SEXUAL HARASSMENT

For those who don't think that sexual harassment is "such a big deal," or that it doesn't happen as much as is claimed, the following shocking account is more proof than necessary. Jacqueline Ortiz, of Las Vegas, N.M., was in the U.S. Army during the time of the Persian Gulf war in 1991. She told a Democratic veteran affairs committee that her sergeant forcibly sodomized her right after the war. Said Ortiz, "I'm very proud to serve my country but not to be a sex slave to someone who has a problem with power." Alan Cranston, chairman of the committee, *conservatively* estimated that "60,000 of the present 1.2 million women veterans were raped or assaulted while in the military."[70] An equally shocking example concerns the now-closed Bell Cairn Training centre in Hamilton, Ontario, opened in 1991, which had been a facility to train new recruits to work as guards in the provincial correctional facilities. Premier Bob Rae said a system-wide problem of sexual harassment by colleagues and supervisors had been happening for months;[71] even the male recruits said they had been given a hard time! At a party to mark the end of a seminar women recruits were sexually assaulted, raped, and sodomized.[72] One woman, who later chose not to give her name to the press, but who wanted to tell some of the story, got a call from one of the men who asked her, "if she had 'ever heard the squeal of a rat before it dies'."[73] Sexual harassment was considered just part of the job.

> "Sexual harassment is fundamentally an abuse of power. ... But many women, when in the presence of the harasser, feel powerless. This terrible inequality in perceived power is the most frightening aspect of sexual harassment." -- Bonnie Cornell, Judy Hauserman, human resource professionals[74]

IGNORANCE IS NOT BLISS!

[Edited interview with Diane White, co-ordinator, Human Resources Management Program, and professor, School of Business, Seneca College, Toronto, Ontario, Thursday, June 18, 1992]

To prepare for the future, there needs to be more education than there is at this point on equity issues, such as harassment, because more information is being legislated now than ever before, and students need to know that a lot of actions, courses of conduct -- not just physical, perhaps even a workplace comment -- have serious consequences to them if they are found to be inappropriate. For instance, do they know what constitutes harassment in the workplace? They have to look at their own ownership of such acts and take responsibility. There is a lot going on in terms of equity right now when we talk about the federal Pay Equity Act and the different provincial Employment Equity Acts.

The Canada Labour Code and the Ontario Code have specified that harassment could be any form of vexatious comment or course of action that's proved to be offensive to the individual. The following is a case settled on the basis of gender, but it wasn't your typical form of harassment. A co-worker was harassing a female colleague in the office, not sexual harassment particularly, but because of her female sex. The harasser was making such comments as, "A mother should be home with her children," and when she would walk by, he would say, "Swish! Swish!" because her nylons made a noise, caused apparently by her overweight. It was found that he was harassing her when the case went to court. She left work because of this harassment and because her work environment was poisoned at this point. It was ruled in her favour, "Yes, this constitutes harassment on the basis of sex." Twenty years ago such comments that this harasser made were fairly common and not perceived as that unusual. But today, in our workplaces, we have to be a lot more sensitive to an offensive comment or action or conduct.

Rationalizations

Rationalizations, such as, "But, that's the way I was raised," or, "Can't you take a joke!" don't work any more and can cost supervisors a lot, both personally and professionally. When harassment occurs, employees will lodge a complaint with the Human Rights Commission. It could be the Canadian Human Rights Commission for federally regulated crown corporations or their provincial Human Rights Commission for private or smaller organizations. They will investigate the claim. Usually the ownership and responsibility lies with the corporation or company and the owners, operators, directors for preventing the build-up of a poisoned workplace, and stopping this kind of inappropriate conduct. Sometimes the individual supervisor or co-worker isn't found liable; but there is a clause in the Code which states that *it should have been known that the conduct or comment was unwelcome*. As future supervisors students will have to be *extremely careful and sensitive* to not just ignore those comments or employee conduct and dismiss them by saying, "Well, that's the nature of our workplace," or, "They're just teasing; they're just having fun." *It's no longer a situation where a supervisor can avoid or ignore comments or actions*. Rather, each person in the organization, and in particular the owners, directors, supervisors and managers have a responsibility to be aware of harassment-type conduct and listen to harassment-type comments, and **take action**.

Concerns

Some people are asking, "Am I allowed to do this? Am I allowed to do that? I'm just being friendly; this is my natural way of relating." But if I cross that line where a person begins to feel harassed, then it's important to be sensitive here. There is common sense involved and I do believe that men can pick up on signals. Sometimes they choose to ignore them, but there *are* signals. If one does not wish to be touched or to have a certain comment made around them, they should pick up on signals such as distancing, avoiding the individual, walking away, being ignored, or hearing something, like, "I don't find that funny," or, "I don't appreciate that comment," or, "Don't touch me; I don't like it."

Employees, and especially supervisors, have a responsibility not to have a poisoned workplace. More companies are now taking legal action against individuals because of harassment. Ignorance is not bliss any more!

The Canadian Supreme Court has ruled that sexual harassment is sex discrimination.[75] It's a serious matter. In Toronto alone, sexual harassment cases at the Ontario Human Rights Commission have increased 83 per cent from 1990 to 1992.[76] The Canadian Armed Forces has a "zero tolerance" level now for sexual harassment.[77] The United Steelworkers unions, both in Canada and in the United States have also "taken a hard line against sexual harassment and violence against women."[78] E.I. Du Pont Nemours & Co. (U.S.) developed a program called "A Matter of Respect" in 1988. It has been highly successful, so much so that it is marketed now to other companies. The basis of the program is information, communication, and reminding participants of people's dignity and respect.[79] Harassment leaves emotional scars and losses in the workplace.[80] Susan Webb, president of the Seattle-based training company Pacific Resource Development Group Inc., put the matter this way: "Costs accrue back to the organization in terms of lost productivity, turnover, rehiring, retraining, loss to the victim, and loss to the harasser. ... There are no winners in these suits - they're horrible, just horrible."[81] A 1988 U.S. figure from 160 Fortune 500 companies put the cost of harassment at $7 - million per company annually![82]

know 6 or 7 of these

10 Commandments on Sexual Harassment[83]

List

1. Realize that while a workplace free of any form of sexual harassment is a goal to strive for, it is probably not a situation that exists.
2. Make your company's position on sexual harassment a matter of record.
3. Remember that your policy will be effective only if employees know about it.
4. Ensure that your managers and human resources staff are adequately trained.
5. Educate your employees.
6. Ensure that executives and managers are good role models.
7. Handle complaints with sensitivity to the rights of all concerned.
8. If your company is unionized, get the union involved.
9. Ensure that penalties imposed for sexual harassment are appropriate.
10. Audit to determine compliance.

The Canadian Supreme Court has ruled that sexual harassment is sex discrimination.

KEY ELEMENTS IN PAY EQUITY LEGISLATION

Pay equity is also a part of employment equity and aims to make sure compensation is fair for work of comparable worth between men and women. Historical patterns and experience vividly demonstrate the financial inequities between men and women doing the same or comparable jobs. Pay equity legislation was introduced in 1978 as an amendment to the Canadian Human Rights Act (federal).

At first pay equity meant *equal pay*, that is, paying both men and women the same amount for the same type or similar work. Because change did not happen quickly enough, and women were still in "occupational ghettoes," a new approach was made called *equal pay for work of equal value*. In Canada this is known as *pay equity*, in the U.S., *comparable worth*.[84] The concept of pay equity, therefore, means that employers must "pay equal wages to employees who hold jobs that are substantially different but that have comparable economic value, in order to abolish any sex discrimination in pay that may be inherent in the usual structure of who holds which jobs."[85]

Like employment equity, pay equity has its controversial side. William Watson of McGill University, for instance, argues that fairness is better when it comes out of a labour market dynamic and that's what we should be working for. "As a social and philosophical system pay equity is rooted squarely in the twelfth century, when theologians spent their time trying to decide the 'just wage.' The Ayatollah himself would feel at home in such a world."[86] But are market forces really that fair or is society eager to make things equitable for its citizens? Experience would often argue otherwise.

The "equal pay for work of equal value" concept did not begin with the women's movement, but with a resolution passed by the International Labor Organization in 1963.[87] Canada simply ratified this convention in 1972 in the form of pay equity, and it became part of the Canadian Human Rights Act in 1977 and law in 1978. As of June 1992, pay equity was law for the federal government and in all but three western provinces: Saskatchewan, Alberta, and British Columbia. Sexism does exist quite extensively in Canada,[88] as elsewhere. Between 1986 and 1989, for instance, in Quebec, women's salaries *shrank* from 69.2% of the male average dollar to 62.4%! Violette Trepanier, Status of Women Minister, said, "Women (in Quebec) have gotten poorer."[89]

The cost of pay equity can be phased in over a four-year period at about 1% of payroll costs per year. Of course, on such a sensitive topic -- "Pay equity is a political document"[90] -- different costs will be attributed. Catch-up costs have been projected to be 2% to 6% of a year's wages,[91] and even as high as 14%![92] Whatever the final tally will be when our society "balances out" wages between men and women doing comparable jobs of comparable worth, one thing is for sure: "Your daughters will thank you."[93]

Ontario has developed sophisticated techniques and shown consistent commitment to pay equity in the workplace. In addition to "working a pay equity plan," supervisors, through an unprecedented ruling by the province's pay equity tribunal, must also "ferret out and acknowledge the overlooked 'invisible skills' performed by female employees."[94]

Overlooked and invisible skills
- adjusting to rapid change
- juggling priorities
- co-ordinating schedules
- dealing with upset or irrational people
- providing emotional support to distressed or ill people
- working with constant noise and interruption

What the government is saying with these prescriptions is that women often perform vital and necessary work which goes unrecognized and unrewarded, personally and, especially, financially. That has to stop. Lynne Sullivan, a partner with William Mercer Ltd., says that pay equity can even pay dividends![95] According to Sullivan, employers will reap the benefit of attracting job candidates from many different backgrounds -- a real help because of Canada's aging population, or what F. Anthony Comper, president, Bank of Montreal, calls "a demographic crunch."[96] Because companies with ten or more employees will need to have a pay equity plan -- and this will include most businesses -- they will be able to compete on a more level playing field. A former Ontario labour minister, Gregory Sorbara, said that "pay equity will make it easier for men and women to move into jobs that used to be considered the other's territory and will improve productivity."[97]

Probably the most contentious issue is deciding what *value* a job has so that it can be compared to a man's *comparable* job. While there may be political, personal and "turf" decisions in estimating a value, there are also some government guidelines. How does pay equity work in practice? Whether and when to introduce a pay equity plan in Ontario is determined by the number of employees a company had in 1987. Ontario is the first province to *include* small business -- 10 or more employees. The schedule for posting a pay equity plan in Ontario is below:[98]

WHEN DO YOU NEED TO POST YOUR PLAN?
If your're a

- public sector employer, mandatory date is January 1, 1990
- private sector employer with 500+ employees, mandatory date is January 1, 1990
- private sector employer with 100 - 499 employees, mandatory date is January 1, 1991
- private sector employer with 50 - 99 employees, mandatory date is January 1, 1992*
- private sector employer with 10 - 49 employees, mandatory date is January 1, 1993*

---

*Private sector employers with 100 employees or less need to post, but voluntarily

---

KEY TERMS AND STEPS FOR A SUPERVISOR DOING PAY EQUITY IN ONTARIO:[99]

EMPLOYER: information on which to base the plan. In most cases, employers, employees, and bargaining agents know who the employer is. In defining an "employer," legal decisions are based on answers to the following: (1) who exercises direction and control over the employees? (2) who determines compensation? (3) who hires, disciplines, and dismisses employees? (4) who do the employees perceive to be the employer? (5) was there an intention to create an employer-employee relationship? "How the <u>employer</u> is defined ultimately affects the nature of the relevant establishment(s) and the comparisons that can be made between female-dominated job classes and male-dominated job classes. In addition, the payroll of the employer determines the amount of money that must be spent on pay equity adjustments in any one year."[100] An establishment "is <u>all</u> the employees of an employer who work in a geographic division."[101]

FEMALE/MALE JOB CLASSES: these are "job titles or positions that are building blocks of pay equity."[102] Section 1(1) of the <u>Pay Equity</u>

Act defines job class as "those positions ... that have similar duties and responsibilities and require similar qualifications, are filled by similar recruiting procedures, and have the same compensation schedule, salary grade, or range of salary rates." This is important because the Act requires (Section 4(2) and Section 12) that female job *classes* be compared with male job *classes* in each establishment.[103]

A GENDER-NEUTRAL COMPARISON SYSTEM:

a job evaluation methodology. Gender-neutrality "is the elimination of all bias toward both female-dominated and male-dominated jobs in all phases of valuing jobs, which include gathering job information, selecting a job comparison system, and applying that system to jobs."[104] "The Act does not specify, and the Pay Equity Commission does not endorse, any particular method or system of job evaluation or comparison."[105] However, the system must be free of gender bias and employ the criteria outlined in Section 5(1) of the Act: skill, effort, responsibility, and working conditions.[106]

POTENTIAL COMPARATORS:

this is the evaluation of all female job classes and all male job classes which appear to be potential comparators, or "the criteria we use to compare apples and oranges."[107] Human rights expert Ted Ulch said that while it may involve the apples-oranges metaphor, even though one might not be able to compare for taste, one can compare for nutritional value: "acidity, water content and vitamin content."[108]

COMPARABLE JOBS:

a sequential comparison process to determine which female job class will be compared to which male job class. "If there is no male job class of equal or comparable value in the establishment, look at male job classes that are of lower value but higher paid than the female class under consideration."[109]

COMPENSATION:

the actual comparison of each female job class with that of the male comparator class, adjusting the wage and salaries to a common base (e.g., hourly), sorting the data by male and female job class, value, and job rate, calculating the cost of benefits into the job rate.

ADJUSTMENTS:

the process that determines the adjustment of the female classes. A job rate is the highest rate of pay for a job class and must include both salary and/or wages *and* benefits. Each pay equity plan must determine where to make adjustments, as well as the rate and timetable for these adjustments. Up to 1% of the payroll, or the cost of the plan, if it is less, must go to the adjustments "to close the wage difference between male and female job classes of equal value."[110]

PAY EQUITY DOCUMENT:

the plan completed for each bargaining and/or non-bargaining unit in each establishment.

PAY EQUITY PLAN:

"Pay equity plan documents must be posted prominently where they may be read by all employees in the workplace."[111] A pay equity plan will include the following:

a. *Name and address of the company;*
b. *Date of posting and pay equity adjustments;*
c. *Establishment;*
d. *Jobs covered by the plan;*
e. *Gender-predominant job classes;*
f. *Method of comparison;*
g. *Comparison results;*
h. *Pay equity adjustments;*
i. *Costs of adjustments;*
j. *For further information, contact (e.g., personnel);*

k. Approval (by appropriate company official).

OBJECTIONS/COMPLAINTS: to resolve disputes such as failing to agree on a negotiated plan, objecting to a plan posted by an employer, or complaining about how the plan was implemented. There is a two-part process (with distinct functions and powers):[112] a **Review Services** (to resolve issues at the Pay Equity Office level itself) and a **Pay Equity Hearings Tribunal**, a "quasi-judicial body"[113] that has exclusive powers to determine all questions of fact or law that arise in any manner before it. The dispute resolution process[114] is diagrammed below:

MAKE REQUIRED ADJUSTMENTS: to tie up any loose ends and integrate key suggestions or rulings.

RESOLVING DISPUTES

Even though the implementation of pay equity in Ontario is to be a self-managed process, sometimes disagreements occurr, or there are conflicts over interpretation. Disputes may be resolved at what is called the Review Services stage, or, if this is not satisfactory, a hearing before the Pay Equity Hearings Tribunal is possible. A hearing before the Tribunal happens when parties object to a review officer's determination order. The review officer's role, of course, is to have matters settled quickly and efficiently when a dispute is first presented. The diagram below gives an indication of the dispute process.

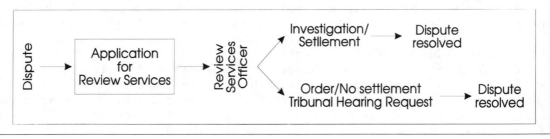

By January 1, 1990, companies in Ontario with 500 or more employees had to have posted their pay equity plan, or "objective ways to measure the value of every job they have."[115] The main contentious issue, of course, is *the fact that, and how,* jobs can be compared. Norman D. Willis and Associates is a Seattle-based consulting company that has designed a way to "compare any two jobs on earth."[116] What is the trick? "The trick is to break the jobs down into the various demands and skills involved, assign a point value in each area, and total the points. The more points a job carries, the more pay it should bring."

Four factors, with accompanying points, are then used to "measure" each job: knowledge and skills (skill), mental demands (effort), accountability (responsibility), and working conditions.

A pay equity process which resulted in annual raises of up to $2,500, at a total cost of $420 million, is the now famous case of the 470 federal government librarians.[108] This is an early instance of the elimination of "the one third to one quarter of the wage gap that has occurred because of traditional undervaluing of women's work."[117] However, in another situation, nurses were in an uproar because they were compared to an assistant pastry chef! For the 104,000 nurses, this was too narrow a comparison based on the government's insistence that comparisons only involve *one* workplace.[118] Diagrammed below is a simple chart to illustrate the "cross-overs" that can happen when points are allocated. In the example, while Julianna has fewer points on (1) skills (job knowledge and people skills) and mental effort (independent judgment and problem solving), Matthew is considerably lower on (2) working conditions (physical effort, hazards, discomfort) than Julianna. (3) In the end, when the points are added up, both are within 2 points of each other. In this case, if Julianna had been receiving $260/month less pay than Matthew, she would now be entitled to equal pay, plus some back pay adjustment benefits because of the closeness of the points.

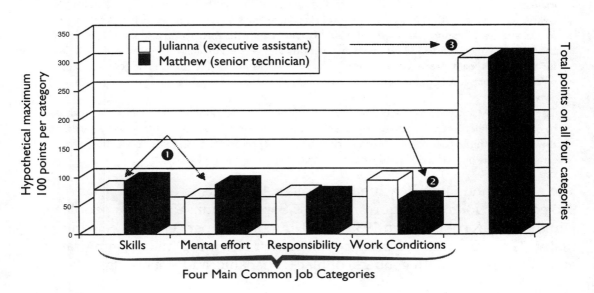

DIVERSITY IN THE WORKPLACE

What was referred to above as the *demographic crunch*, that is, immigration to bolster Canada's population, is upon us. Canada now has 27 million people. If it maintains its current birthrate of 1.7 births, we will drop to 13 million people by the year 2020! The answer to this dilemma is immigration. This also accounts for part of the reason that Canada's workplaces, especially in larger cities, have, and will continue to have, diversity. By the year 2000, Toronto alone is expected to have nearly a 50 per cent multicultural work environment. John Samuel, demographer at Carleton University, Ottawa, says, "We are a nation of minorities."[119] Toronto has citizens speaking more than 100 different languages; one in four persons is a minority. In the early 1960s, minorities were only 3 per cent of Toronto's population. "By the year 2001, visible minorities will make up 45 per cent of the population." For example, in 1991, Metro Toronto kept "on the move" precisely because of working immigrants.[120] It will be more and more critical for supervisors and employees to eliminate racism from their workplaces, but also to have the freedom and skill to speak well without fear of being called racist.[121] Eliminating racism is not only the ethical thing to do, but it also costs not to, financially and from a public image point of view.

> Majestic Electronics Ltd., Canada's largest discount chain, found this out the hard way. A former owner, Curtis Ramsauer, was found guilty of racism: telling staff not to hire "niggers, chinks, skid marks and trash"[122] and was fined $300,000! Robert Lee, who was vice-president of finance for the company, refused to follow these instructions and was accordingly fired. He got $200,000 for lost wages, damages, and losses, for he had to sell his house. He said, "I had four kids and a wife to support, but I couldn't live with the kind of practices that were going on there."[123]

> The Faculty Association of the University of Manitoba in 1990 wanted Dean William Mackness to quit. They felt his remarks on hiring personnel, in letter form, were racist. Mackness wrote that the university hired too many "Third World" staff, and if precautions were not taken, there would be nothing left but "Third World mathematicians" running the university![124]

The now-famous 1987 benchmark study by the Hudson Institute[125] has projected the following figures for the U.S. population: 25 million people will join the workforce between 1985 - 2000, but only 15 per cent will be white males. "The remaining 85 percent will consist of white females; immigrants; and minorities (of both genders) of black, Hispanic, and Asian origins."[126] The most dramatic piece of these projections is the following though: "The Hispanic and Asian populations will each grow by 48 percent; the black population will grow by 28 percent; and the white population by only 5.6 percent." The American experience, unlike Canada's, which is multiculturalism,[127] is built on the idea of the "melting pot." Arthur M. Schlesinger Jr. wonders if the center, in Canada, will hold when there is so much diversity and each group claiming its inviolable identity.[128]

Canada has a *multicultural* mosaic as opposed to the American *melting pot* understanding of diversity, but has similar social and work challenges. Canadian human resource professionals and supervisors need to be prepared. Many in Canada do wonder if the centre will hold, or if we will only be a group of babbling voices. Or is Canada nothing but a "League of provinces,"[129] and "the Great Levelling"?[130] It was Benjamin Disraeli in 1866 who stated that individuals may form communities, but it is institutions alone that create one.

The social experiment continues! Comparison by Employment and Immigration Canada of the 1988-89 immigration figures shows increases among the top ten immigration admissions to Canada of 72.7% from Poland, 36.5% from the Philippines, 36.2% from Viet Nam, 26.3% from Portugal, 94.9% from Lebanon, and 56% from China. T.R. Balakrishnan, of the University of Western Ontario, estimates that, for Metro Toronto alone, comparing census figures from 1986 to projections for 2001, the major increases will involve South Asian (54.5%), Chinese (66.1%), Caribbean (43.2%), and South American (72.3%).[131] Exercising social skills well is not only a smart thing to do, but an ethical imperative as well. The most important supervisory skills may yet be those of communication and human relations! For sure, listening, under-standing, challenging, and accepting diverse viewpoints will be part of every supervisor's future agenda.

The impact of the global economy and Canada's dependence on relationships with the rest of the world

"We've been worried too long about investing in real estate, stock markets and our careers instead of our collective future. It's starting to sink in to our Western ears that the way we live now is rather flawed. One of the ways to ensure that things improve is to work together for a united Canada that, in keeping with our best traditions, is an innovator, a peacekeeper, a compassionate neighbour." -- Elizabeth Renzetti[132]

Authentic citizenship and multiculturalism insist that we see ourselves as Canadians, but also as a people with diverse talents in a world where we are all part of the human family. Citizenship says that we can live and work together because we are all part of the Canadian family. Our Canadian citizenship says that our Canadian family has many colours and tongues, and that it is this plurality of our visions, hopes, and dreams that make us a rich and wonderful nation. The multicultural fabric of Canada gives us not only our breadth of vision but also our depth of perception and integrity as Canadians.[135]

to survive economically and as a country are strong catalysts for nurturing diversity in the workplace. Big U.S. companies even have "diversity managers"![133] Graeme McDonald, president of the Asia Pacific Foundation, says, "By the end of this decade, more than 70 percent of all world trade will be with or among the economies along the western shore of the Pacific. ... We need people with Asian skills and networks, firms with Asian partners and alliances."[134] In other words, if Canada is to compete, Canadian/ Asian immigrants, employees, and employers will be a major key and bridge. It is not, under these circumstances, a question of *whether*, but rather, *how well* a diverse workforce is prepared to compete globally.

THE EMPHASIS ON HUMAN VALUES

A final word needs to be said about the renewed emphasis on human values that is also at work in today's workplace. It may seem strange to indicate this emphasis given all the dehumanizing tasks and work that are apparent in our world today. However, there are some good things as well. Placing importance on new human values is key to success in organizations and an important social dynamic.[136]

For instance, because of the reality and presence of the knowledge worker in today's workplace, more and more employees demand that supervisors treat them with dignity and value them with respect. Long gone are the days when supervisors could just use an employee for the company's purposes and not face the consequences. Some managers have also been "choosing to opt out of traditional work roles rather than agreeing to continue playing by rules that ignore humanity."[136] Today the human resource professional, as well as supervisors, must administer corporate enlightenment. "Organizations ... are moving towards a more civilized society -- one in which the 'basics' of work and love need no longer tear people apart emotionally."[137]

SUMMARY

There are many significant social dynamics in the workplace today, but perhaps the most momentous is the increasing presence of women.

The traditional work - home dynamic is being challenged to such an extent that companies are offering flexible working arrangements so that the split between work and home is not as onerous.

The unconscious barrier, or "velvet ghetto" -- commonly known as the glass ceiling -- blocks women from being promoted into managerial ranks.

Discrimination can be direct or intentional, and constructive or adverse effect in nature. *Job streaming* is a way to discriminate against women on the job by putting female employees into the lowest paid jobs.

Employment equity is the elimination of employment practices that would discriminate against potential employees and the provision of meaningful opportunities for employment.

The Supreme Court has ruled that sexual harassment is sex discrimination.

Pay equity is a part of employment equity and aims to make sure compensation is fair for work of comparable worth between men and women. There are also overlooked and *invisible skills* that must be accounted for.

Probably the most contentious issue in a pay equity plan is deciding what *value* a woman's job has so that it can be compared to a man's *comparable* job.

Canada's workplaces, especially in larger cities, have, and will continue to have, diversity. By the year 2000, Toronto alone is expected to have nearly a 50 per cent multicultural workplace.

Placing importance on new human values is key to success today in organizations and an important social dynamic.

KEY TERMS/CONCEPTS

work - home dynamic
organizational effectiveness manager
apartheid of gender
velvet ghetto
discrimination
stereotypes
job streaming
employment equity
affirmative action
systemic discrimination
bona fide occupational requirement
HRIS
Bill 79
Bill 40
reverse discrimination
sexual harassment

zero tolerance
pay equity
equal pay
occupational ghettoes
equal pay for work of equal value
comparable worth
invisible skills
demographic crunch
pay equity plan
diversity in workplace
multiculturalism
melting pot
racism
multicultural mosaic
diversity manager
corporate enlightenment

DISCUSSION QUESTIONS

1. What are social dynamics and why are they important in today's work environment?

2. Describe key ideas on the impact of women in the workplace.

3. What is the glass ceiling and why is this important?

4. Discuss employment equity and some of the concerns surrounding it.

5. Research three examples of sexual harassment from your local newspaper.

6. What is pay equity?

7. Citing an example, discuss how the overlooked and invisible skills played a part in the inequality.

8. Why is diversity in the workplace such an important issue now?

9. "Organizations ... are moving towards a more civilized society -- one in which the 'basics' of work and love need no longer tear people apart emotionally." Discuss.

ASSIGNMENT

Instructions: Describe in the spaces below your own personal experiences under the topic. Be as detailed as possible, giving date, time, place, circumstances. In the right column, describe what you did to manage yourself in the situation.

TOPIC	WHAT HAPPENED	WHAT I DID
Sex discrimination		
Race discrimination		
Pay discrimination		

Complete the following:

As a result of my experiences, I would recommend to others that _____

_____

_____

ENDNOTES

PREFACE

1. Allan Bloom, "Preface,' in *The Closing of the American Mind*. New York: Simon and Schuster, 1987, p. 19.
2. Roy MacLaren, "Rediscovering the Political Centre," *The Financial Post*, March 2, 1992, s4.
3. In other words, the supervisor must manage both the internal (or employees) and the external (or customers) stakeholders.
4. Jan Carlzon, "Moments of Truth: New Strategies for Today's Customer-Driven Economy," in Jon L. Pierce, John W. Newstrom (Eds.). *The Manager's Bookshelf: A Mosaic of Contemporary Views*. New York: Harper & Row, 1990, 326-333.
5. Geoffrey Rowan, "Xerox Canada First Winner of Federal Government Award for Quality," *The Globe and Mail*, Wednesday, November 8, 1989, B3.
6. Thomas J. Peters, Robert H. Waterman, Jr. *In Search of Excellence*. New York: Warner Books, 1982.

CHAPTER 1

1. John Bachmann, "An Efficient Way to Whip Our Schools into Shape," *The Globe and Mail*, Tuesday, February 4, 1992, A15.
2. Lawrence G. Tap, "If Canada's to be a Winner on the Global Playing Field, it Needs a Decent Game Plan," *The Globe and Mail*, January 30, 1992, D4.
3. Daniel Stoffman, "Brave New Work," *The Globe and Mail, Report on Business Magazine* (September 1991), p. 39.
4. Stan Kossen. *Supervision. A Practical Guide to First-Line Management*. New York: Harper & Row, 1981, 4.
5. John Raymond, "Worth Repeating," *The Globe and Mail*, Friday, February 7, 1992, B6.
6. Margot Gibb-Clark, "In Praise of the Business Hierarchy," *The Globe and Mail*, Thursday, February 27, 1992, B1, 21.
7. S.C. Certo. *Principles of Modern Management: Functions and Systems*. 2nd ed. Dubuque, Iowa: Wm. C. Brown Publishers, 1983.
8. Arthur G. Bedeian. *Management*. 2nd ed. Toronto: The Dryden Press, 1989, 6.
9. Canadian Bible Society. *Good News Bible*, 1986, 71.
10. Frederick Taylor (1856-1915), who believed that there was one best way to do a job and it was management's obligation to discover the method and implement it.
11. Henri Fayol (1841-1925), who is called the father of the five functions and fourteen principles of management.
12. Max Weber (1864-1920), who felt that the bureaucracy was the most efficient form for complex organizations.
13. The Hawthorne Studies, by Elton Mayo, of Harvard University, at the Western Electric Company (1927 -

32), which showed that *human* factors (e.g., employees' social and emotional environment, their attitudes and perceptions about change) are critical variables in getting people to do what *you* want them to do.
14. The Ford Foundation (1951) research grant to study individual behaviour and human relations -- an approach which utilizes scientific procedures to do empirical studies on people's interactions and behaviour.
15. A research-based theory and approach, emerging after World War II, which studies management problems from a quantitative point of view, relying heavily on mathematics, statistics, and economics.
16. A modern development (1970s) from the personnel management approach of the early part of the twentieth century to help companies comply with the every increasing legislation on human rights and employment standards.
17. "Operations management that strives to perfect the entire manufacturing process through improvements in quality and productivity," in Richard L. Daft. *Management*. Second Edition. Toronto: The Dryden Press, 1991, 588.
18. I am making a distinction here between *objectives*, or *specific tasks* to be completed in a certain time period, and *goals*, or end-results or states-of-being, that are more general and philosophic in nature and tied in with the *purpose* of the department, division, or organization.
19. Everett L. Shostrom. *Man, the Manipulator*. Nashville, Tenn.: Abingdon Press, 1972, xii - xiii.
20. A research study involving new supervisors, in 1974, pointed out that **90%** wanted more knowledge of human relations and **60%** said they needed better communication skills! In Lester Bittel. *What Every Supervisor Should Know*. Third Edition. New York: McGraw-Hill, 1974, 18.
21. Leo Tolstoy. *War and Peace*, Book V, Chapter 2. In *The Great Books of the Western World*. Translated by Louise and Aylmer Maude. Robert Maynard, Editor In Chief. Toronto: Encyclopaedia Britannica, Inc., William Benton, Publisher, 1952, p. 197. I am grateful for this reference to: Aaron Q. Sartain, Alton W. Baker. *The Supervisor and His Job*. Second Edition. New York: McGraw-Hill Book Co., 1972, 191.
22. Robert L. Katz, "Skills of an Effective Administrator," in *Business Classics: Fifteen Key Concepts for Managerial Success*, from the *Harvard Business Review*, September-October 1975, 24.
23. Further ideas, see: Bradford B. Boyd. *Management-Minded Supervision*. Third Edition. Toronto: McGraw-Hill Book Company (Gregg Division), 1984, 101-121.

CHAPTER 2

1. Obituary, "Cardinal Leger Served God in Deeds as Well as Words," *The Toronto Star*, Wednesday, November 13, 1991, A2.

2. Cover Story, "IBM Canada Regroups," *Computing Canada*, Volume 18, Number 4, February 17, 1992, p. 1.

3. "Quality: The Soul of Productivity, the Key to Future Business Growth," *Interview*, Inter-City Gas Corporation, vol. 3, Autumn 1988, 3 - 5.

4. John Heinzl, "Canadians Crossing Border at Record Pace," *The Globe and Mail*, Saturday, February 15, 1992, B1, 11.

5. Martin Slofstra (a profile of Bill Etherington), "The New IBM Canada," *Computing Canada*, February 17, 1992, 13.

6. Alanna Mitchell, "Canadians Want Better Service," *The Globe and Mail*, Monday, July 15, 1991, A1, 4.

7. Bruce McDougall, "The Next Battleground," *Canadian Business*, February 1992, 52 - 56.

8. Daniel Girard, "The New Retail Giants," *The Toronto Star*, Sunday, February 9, 1992, H1, 4.

9. Edward Greenspon, "Honk If You Like Your Toyota," *The Globe and Mail*, Friday, January 31, 1992, A11. John

10. Saunders, "Two Very Different Views on Autos," *The Globe and Mail*, Monday, February 24, 1991, B1, 4.

11. Hugh Winsor, "U.S. Honda Ruling 'Low-level Politics,' PM says," *The Globe and Mail*, Friday, February 14, 1992, A1.

12. Howard Armitage, "Quality Pays," *CGA Magazine*, January 1992, 30 - 37.

13. Daniel Girard, *op. cit.*, H4.

14. Madelaine Drohan, "The Brains Behind Braun," *The Globe and Mail*, Friday, February 28, 1992, B4.

15. Jack Kapica, "Fifth Column," *The Globe and Mail*, Wednesday, February 5, 1992, A14, in discussing John Della Costa. *Meditations on Business*. Scarborough, Ontario: Prentice-Hall Canada, 1991.

16. John Raymond, "Worth Repeating," *The Globe and Mail*, Friday, January 24, 1992, B6.

17. "Markham's Alive and Well Entrepreneur Wins Awards," *Weekender* [*Economist & Sun*], December 28, 1991, 3.

18. Ann Walmsley, "Trading Places," *Report on Business Magazine*, March 1992, 17 - 22, 25, 27.

19. *Ibid.*, 17.

20. Jan Carlzon, "Moments of Truth: New Strategies for Today's Customer-Driven Economy," in Jon L. Pierce, John W. Newstrom. *The Manager's Bookshelf: A Mosaic of Contemporary Views*. New York: Harper & Row, 1990, 328.

21. *Ibid.*, 333.

22. William Thorsell, "The Circles of Power Overlapped and Economic Orthodoxy Triumphed. And Everyone, But Everyone, Was Open for Business," *The Globe and Mail*, Saturday, February 15, 1992, D4.

23. Stephan A. Hoeller, "Hermetic vs. Puritan America: Perennial Opposites in Our Society," *The Quest*, Volume 5/Number 1, Spring 1992, 49.

24. He is referring primarily to Americans, but his comments can be applied to Canadians as well. In *The Cry for Myth*. New York: W.W. Norton & Company, 1991, 108.

25. What May is referring to here is the American myth of "John Wayne-riding-into-the-sunset" -- that we can do it by ourselves, that we don't need others.

26. Judith Timson, "Scenes From a Recession," *Report on Business Magazine*, February 1992, 22 - 25, 27, 29 - 30.

27. Peter Cook, "Why Does Capitalism Need to Feed on Greed?" *The Globe and Mail*, Monday, June 5, 1989, B2.

28. Tony Horwitz (*Wall Street Journal*), "The Feeding Frenzy on Fleet Street," *The Globe and Mail*, Saturday, December 14, 1991, D5.

29. Paul Koring, "Maxwell Memorabilia Hits the Auction Block," *The Globe and Mail*, Saturday, February 15, 1992, B1.

30. David Crane, "We Should Heed Japan's Comments," *The Toronto Star*, Sunday, February 9, 1992, H4.

31. David Olive, "Chronicles The Week," *The Globe and Mail*, Saturday, February 15, 1992, D4: "When the going gets tough, the tough bash the Japanese."

32. Howard Armitage, "Quality Pays," *CGA Magazine*, January 1992, 30. Armitage is making reference to "The Quality Imperative," *Business Week* (special issue), October 25, 1991.

33. Barrie McKenna, "Quebec Proposes Big Changes for Industry," *The Globe and Mail*, Wednesday, September 11, 1991, B1.

34. Reginald W. Bibby, "The Lonely Road of Individualism," *The Globe and Mail*, Tuesday, October 23, 1990, A20.

35. Michael Higgins, "The Tyranny of the New Greed is Exacting a High Spiritual Toll," *The Toronto Star*, Saturday, September 21, 1991, G16.

36. Charles Taylor, "The Sources of Authenticity," *Canadian Forum*, Vol. LXX, Number 806, Jan/Feb 1992, 4 - 5.

37. Geoffrey Rowan, "Air Canada, USAir Preparing to Join Forces," *The Globe and Mail*, Tuesday, August 20, 1991, B1, 2.

38. "Stress on Team May Be Wrong, Professor Warns," *The Toronto Star*, Monday, September 9, 1991, D9.

39. Anne McKague, "The Workgroup Vision," *Computing Canada*, December 5, 1991, 13.

40. Murray Campbell, "The Power of Power on Horsepower," *The Globe and Mail*, Wednesday, August 28, 1991, B1, 5.

41. Carolyn Leitch, "Digital, Microsoft Link to Promote Teamwork," *The Globe and Mail*, Tuesday, November

19, 1991, B18.

42. James Daw, "KeepRite Keeps Its Edge With Employee Teamwork," *The Toronto Star*, Friday, November 1, 1991, B1, 8.

43. Lawrence Martin, "Rushed Off His Feet, *The Globe and Mail*, Wednesday, August 21, 1991, A11.

44. James Christie, "Argo Father Knows Best," *The Globe and Mail*, Saturday, November 23, 1991, A21 (before A 20), 20.

45. "Bombardier Praises Boeing for de Havilland Makeover," *The Globe and Mail*, Thursday, January 23, 1992, B1, 20.

46. Gordon Pitts, "Thinking Globally, Acting Locally," *The Financial Post 500*, Summer 1990, 10, 12, 16.

47. John Raymond, "Worth Repeating," *The Globe and Mail*, Thursday, September 26, 1991, B4.

48. Margot Gibb-Clark, "Autonomy or Teams: Which Will Prevail?" *The Globe and Mail*, Monday, February 3, 1992, B4.

49. David Crane, "Politicians Ignoring Ways to Boost Global Economy," *The Toronto Star*, Thursday, February 13, 1992, C2.

50. Pierre Berton. *The Great Depression: 1929-1939*. Toronto: McLelland & Stewart Inc., 1990, quote on title page.

51. Lois Sweet, "Labor Has New Face, New Strength in '90s," *The Toronto Star*, Monday, September 2, 1991, A1, 4.

52. Richard L. Daft. *Management*. Toronto: Dryden Canada, 1991, 492.

53. Stephen G. Green and M. Ann Welsh, "Cybernetics and Dependence: Reframing the Control Concept," *Academy of Management Review* 13 (1988), 287 - 301. And Kenneth A. Merchant. *Control in Business Organizations*. Marshfield, Mass.: Pitman, 1985; cited in Daft, *ibid.*, 699.

54. Howard M. Armitage, "Quality Pays," *CGA Magazine*, January 1992, 33.

55. Howard M. Armitage, *ibid.*, 33 - 34.

56. See also Jim Clemmer. *Firing on All Cylinders: The Service/Quality System for High-Powered Corporate Performance*. Toronto: Macmillan of Canada (A division of Canada Publishing Corporation), 1991.

57. "The Quality Imperative," *Business Week* (special issue), October 25, 1991.

58. Mary Walton. *The Deming Management Method*. New York: McGraw-Hill, 1980; J.M. Juran. *What is Total Quality Control*. Englewood Cliffs, N.J.: Prentice-Hall, 1989.

59. Michael E. Rock, "Excellence Requires Commitment," *Toronto Business Magazine*, Volume 12, Number 4, April - May, 1986, 27 - 28.

60. U.S. General Accounting Office. *Management Pactices: U.S. Companies Improve Performance Through Quality Efforts*. (GAO/NSIAD-91-190 - Wshington, DC: GAO,

1991), located in Howard M. Armitage, *op. cit.*, 35 and 37, footnote #5.

61. John Raymond, "Worth Repeating," *The Globe and Mail*, Tuesday, December 31, 1991, B4.

62. Michael E. Rock, "Corporate Culture," *Rasaneh*, Vol. VIII, Jan. 16 - Feb. 15, 1989, 7 - 10.

63. "TQM and the Search for That Missing Ingredient," *Computing Canada*, January 20, 1992, 44.

64. Peter Farwell, "How Canadian Businesses Can 'Manage' to Succeed," *The Globe and Mail*, Thursday, February 6, 1992, E4.

65. Harvey Enchin, "Canadian Firms Thinking Quality," *The Globe and Mail*, Wednesday, October 2, 1991, B7.

66. Jerry Zeidenberg, "New Focus For Old Strategy," *The Globe and Mail*, Tuesday, October 1, 1991, B28.

67. John Raymond, "Worth Repeating," *The Globe and Mail*, Friday, December 6, 1991, B6.

68. Lawrence Surtees, "A Journey Toward Perfection," *The Globe and Mail*, Tuesday, October 1, 1991, B28.

69. Robert Cohen, "McDonald's Sizzle Is in the Promotions," *Financial Times of Canada*, February 17, 1992, 6.

70. Alastair Dow, "Leon's Should Be Case Study in How to Stay Competitive," *The Toronto Star*, Saturday, November 30, 1991, C2.

71. Howard M. Armitage, "Quality Pays," *CGA Magazine*, January 1992, 36.

72. In *Vanguard Management: Redesigning the Corporate Future*. New York: Berkley Books, 1985, 9.

73. Quoted in O'Toole, *ibid.*, 141.

74. Allan Swift, "To Belarus With Love," *The Toronto Star*, Monday, January 27, 1992, B5.

75. See the case study "Dayton Hudson Corporation," in John B. Matthews, Kenneth E. Goodpaster, Laura L. Nash. *Policies and Persons: A Casebook in Business Ethics*. Toronto: McGraw-Hill Book Company, 1985, 212 - 31.

76. In O'Toole, *op. cit.*, 147.

77. Michael Valpy, "An Executive's View of Corporate Ethics," *The Globe and Mail*, Wednesday, November 29, 1989, A8.

78. John Raymond, "Business Must Not Live By Profit Alone," *The Globe and Mail*, Wednesday, October 17, 1990, B8.

79. Michael E. Rock. *Ethics: To Live By, To Work By*. Toronto: Concept Press (a Division of Holt, Rinehart and Winston of Canada, Limited), 1992, viii.

80. In *Capitalism and Freedom*. Chicago: University of Chicago Press, 1963.

81. Keith Davis, Robert L. Blomstrom. *Business and Its Environment*. New York: McGraw-Hill, 1966, 174 - 75.

82. "In Praise of the Stakeholder Concept," *The Globe and Mail*, Friday, December 28, 1990, B4.

83. Frederick A. Starke, Robert W. Sexty. *Contemporary Management in Canada*. Scarborough, Ontario: Prentice-

Hall Canada Inc., 1992, 668.

84. Drew Fagan, "Union Carbide Fined $1.7-million for Price Fixing," *The Globe and Mail*, Saturday, September 7, 1991, B2.

85. C. Welles, "What Led Beech-Nut Down the Road to Disgrace," *Business Week*, February 22, 1989, 124 - 28.

86. Michael E. Rock. *Ethics: To Live By, To Work By, op. cit.*, 102.

87. Associated Press, "Salomon Forecasts Big Loss," *The Globe and Mail*, Monday, January 20, 1992, B5.

88. William R. Gale, Jo Ann L. Compton, "Minimizing Hiring Risks," *The Human Resource*, Volume 6, Number 1, December/January 1989, 6 - 7.

89. *Corporate Ethics: A Prime Business Asset*. New York: The Business Roundtable, 1988, 8, located in R. Eric Reidenbach, Donald P. Robin. *Ethics and Profits. A Convergence of Corporate America's Economic and Social Responsibilities*. Englewood Cliffs, N.J.: Prentice Hall, 1989, 239.

90. Michael Valpy, "An Executive's View of Corporate Ethics," *The Globe and Mail*, Wednesday, November 29, 1989, A8.

91. "Note on the Corporation as a Moral Environment," in *Ethics in Practice: Managing the Corporation*. Boston, Mass.: Harvard Business School Press, 1989, p. 98, footnote #13; italics mine.

92. John Raymond, "Business Must Not Live by Profit Alone," *The Globe and Mail*, Wednesday, October 17, 1990, B8.

93. Lawrence G. Tap, "If Canada's to Be a Winner, on the Global Playing Field, It Needs a Decent Game Plan," *The Globe and Mail*, January 30, 1992, D4.

94. Canadian Press, "Our Resistance to Change Hurts Growth, Report Says," *The Toronto Star*, Thursday, February 13, 1992, C3. "'The problem is deeply rooted in Canadian society -- we tend to resist change and avoid competition,' Council chairman Judith Maxwell said in Ottawa." We need to rethink our attitudes and invest in skill development, training, counselling, mobility if we want to compete for world markets.

95. Drew Fagan, "Living Standard at Risk," *The Globe and Mail*, Thursday, February 13, 1992, B3.

CHAPTER 3

1. John Raymond, "Worth Repeating," *The Globe and Mail*, Wednesday, February 19, 1992, B4.

2. Patrick Bloomfield, "Small is Newly Beautiful in Corporate Boardrooms," *The Financial Post 500*, Summer 1987, 8 - 10, 13.

3. Margaret Philp, "Camdev Shares End 4-day Freefall," *The Globe and Mail*, Thursday, February 20, 1992, B9.

4. Jan Cienski, "Consumerism: Beginning of the End?" *The Globe and Mail*, Tuesday, February 18, 1992, A20.

5. Mary Jo Leddy, "Where to Draw the Line?" *The Globe and Mail*, Tuesday, July 3, 1990, A18, gives a description of "a culture such as ours, a consumer culture, where every value seems negotiable, every relationship as disposable as a paper cup." *See also* "Are We a 'Gimme Generation'?" *The Wall Street*, Friday, May 13, 1988, Section 3.

6. Hugh Graham, "Machines Meant to Help Us are Doing Harm, Too," *The Globe and Mail*, Monday, February 17, 1992, A13.

7. Edith Terry, "The Workplace as Killing Field," *The Globe and Mail*, Saturday, September 21, 1991, D1, 2.

8. Jade Hemeon, "Capitalism Shouldn't Crow, Economist Says," *The Toronto Star*, Friday, September 13, 1991, B1, 5.

9. Catherine Harris, "Recovery Now in Sight," *The Financial Post*, Monday, February 17, 1992, 8.

10. Christopher Snyder, "A Recession Has Its Advantages," *The Globe and Mail*, Friday, January 31, 1992, B4.

11. Economist Dian Cohen, quoted in John Raymond, "Worth Repeating," *The Globe and Mail*, Monday, February 24, 1992, B8. Cohen's argument is that Canada is riding boldly into the past! She says that economists now understand that the product cycle follows the business cycle. "If you make something the world wants, you will prosper. If you don't, you won't."

12. John Raymond, "Worth Repeating," *The Globe and Mail*, Monday, February 10, 1992, B6.

13. John Raymond, "Worth Repeating," *The Globe and Mail*, Tuesday, January 14, 1992, B8.

14. Peter F. Drucker, "Management and the World of Work," *Harvard Business Review*, September-October 1988, 65-76.

15. Robert M. Fulmer, Stephen G. Franklin. *Supervision: Principles of Professional Management*. New York: Macmillan Publishing Co., Inc., 1982, 162.

16. Virginia Galt, "Low-cost Solutions Eyed in Easing Work-family Pressures," *The Globe and Mail*, Wednesday, January 22, 1992, A5.

17. David Olive, "Fire at Will," *Report on Business Magazine*, March 1992, 9.

18. Robert Williamson, "Cleaning house, Pattison style," *The Globe and Mail*, Saturday, February 22, 1992, B20.

19. Beppi Crosariol, "Olivetti's Springboard Plans for Canada," *Financial Times of Canada*, February 24, 1992, 12.

20. "Inflation Beaten; Analysts Give Few Cheers," *The Toronto Star*, Saturday, February 22, 1992, B1.

21. David Olive, *op. cit.*, 10.

22. Geoffrey York, "Family Life: Not Enough Money, Too Much Stress," *The Globe and Mail*, Friday, January 3, 1992, A1, 5.

23. Leslie Papp, "Chronic Absenteeism Costs Economy

$10 Billion," *The Toronto Star*, Saturday, November 21, 1992, C1.

24. "More Executives Putting Family First," *The York Region Business Journal*, February 1992, 19, 31.

25. An approach, originally a spin-off of the U.S. Navy's and Lockheed Aircraft Corp.'s Polaris Missile project, used in planning and controlling projects is PERT: Program Evaluation and Review Technique. It is a quantitative and mathematical model where alternatives are analyzed and a "best" solution adopted. It is especially relevant when time is important.

26. John Raymond, "Worth Repeating," *The Globe and Mail*, Friday, December 6, 1991, B6.

27. First advocated by Peter F. Drucker. *The Practice of Management*. New York: Harper & Row, 1954.

28. *Adapted from:* D.D. Warrick, Robert A. Zawacki. *Supervisory Management. Understanding Behavior and Measuring for Results*. New York: Harper & Row, 1984, 262.

29. John Raymond, "Worth Repeating," *The Globe and Mail*, Thursday, February 20, 1992, B5.

30. John S. Hodgson, "Management by Objectives: The Experience of a Federal Government Department," *Canadian Public Administration*, 16, no. 4 (1973), 423.

31. D.D. Warrick, Robert A. Zawacki, *op. cit.*, 261.

32. John E. Jones, "Criteria of Effective Goal-Setting: The S-P-I-R-O Model," *The 1972 Annual Handbook for Group Facilitators*. Eds. J. William Pfeiffer, John E. Jones. Iowa City: University Associates, 1972, 133 - 34.

33. *Adapted:* D.D. Warrick, Robert A. Zawacki, *op. cit.*, 261-262 and Arthur G. Bedeian. *Management*. 2nd Edition. Toronto: The Dryden Press, 1989, 151.

34. Ann Walmsley, "Trading Places," *Report on Business Magazine*, March 1992, 17 - 22, 25, 27, esp. 25.

35. William B. Werther, Jr., Keith Davis, Hermann F. Schwind, T.P. Hari Das, Frederick C. Miner, Jr. *Canadian Personnel Management and Human Resources*. Toronto: McGraw-Hill Ryerson Limited, 1985, 440 - 41.

36. Lawrence L. Steinmetz, H. Ralph Todd, Jr. *First-Line Management: Approaching Supervision Effectively*. Fourth Edition. Plano, Texas: Business Publications, Inc., 1986, 197.

37. Margot Gibb-Clark, "Evaluating Work Performance of Employees," *The Globe and Mail*, Wednesday, February 22, 1989, D13.

38. David Olive, *op. cit.*, 9.

39. Harry Levinson, "Appraisal of WHAT Performance?" *Harvard Business Review: On Human Relations*. New York: Harper & Row (1959), 1979, 280 - 92.

40. P.S. Hundel, "Knowledge of Performance as an Incentive in Repetitive Industrial Work," *Journal of Applied Psychology*, 1969, 53, 224 - 26.

41. Daniel R. Ilgen, Cynthia D. Fisher, M. Susan Taylor, "Consequences of Individual Feedback on Behavior in Organizations," *Journal of Applied Psychology*, 1979, 64, No. 4, 349 - 71.

42. Raymond F. Gale. *Developmental Behavior: A Humanistic Approach*. London: The Macmillan Co., 1969, esp. ch. 3, "The Emerging Self, Self-Perception, and Self-Awareness," 49 - 75.

43. Arthur W. Coombs, Donald Snygg. *Individual Behavior: A Perceptual Approach to Behavior*. New York: Harper & Row, 1959.

44. Raymond F. Gale, *op. cit.*, 64.

45. R. Bruce McAfee, Paul J. Champagne. *Organizational Behavior: A Manager's View*. St. Paul, Minn.: West Publishing Company, 1987, 208 - 16. Edwin A. Locke, "Toward a Theory of Task Motivation and Incentives," *Organizational Behavior and Human Performance*, May 1968, 157 - 89. G.P. Latham, G.A. Yuki, "A Review of Research on the Application of Goal Setting in Organizations," *Academy of Management Journal*, 1975, 824 - 845.

46. Les D. Barry, Q.C., "Alert to Change," *The Canadian Manager*, 1980, V, 4 - 5.

47. Pat Johnson, "Looking for Value in Training," *Financial Times of Canada*, February 9, 1981, 31. Also, John Miteff, "Managerial Performance: **You're Good** But you Can Be Better," *The Canadian Manager*, Vol. 7, No. 1, 1982, 5 - 8; "Defying Business Downturn By Improving Performance Effectiveness," *Canadian Manager*, Vol. 7, No. 4, August 1982, 16 - 18.

48. An interesting spin-off of this process is Canada Grocers Ltd. See William B. Werther, Jr., Keith Davis, Hermann F. Schwind, Hari Das. *Canadian Human Resource Management*. Third edition. Toronto: McGraw-Hill Ryerson Limited, 1989, 120.

49. Chris Lee, "Talking Back to the Boss," *Training*, April 1990, Vol. 27, No. 4, 29 - 32, 34 - 35.

50. Arthur G. Bedeian, *op. cit.*, 201 - 23.

51. Joseph White, Gregory A. Patterson, Paul Ingrassia, "A Change Is in the Works," *The Globe and Mail*, Monday, January 13, 1992, B1, 2.

52. E. Scannell. *Communication for Leadership*. New York: McGraw-Hill, 1970, 5.

53. Source unknown. Original idea, with a military application, in *DS Letter* Vol. 1, No. 3 (1971). Copyright 1974 by Didactic Systems, Inc., Crawford, New Jersey 07016, USA.

54. Frederick A. Starke, Robert W. Sexty. *Contemporary Management in Canada*. Scarborough, Ontario: Prentice-Hall Canada Inc., 1992, 256.

55. Joan Woodward. *Management and Technology*. London: Her Majesty's Stationery Office, 1958; *Industrial Organizations: Theory and Practice*. London: Oxford University Press, 1965, 35 - 40.

56. Starke and Sexty, *op. cit.*, 256-57.
57. Richard Daft. *Management*. Second Edition. Chicago: The Dryden Press, 1991, 294.
58. David J. Lawless, "The Manager As Teacher," *Effective Management: Social Psychological Approach*. Englewood Cliffs, New Jersey: Prentice-Hall, Inc., 1972, 333 - 47.
59. Ann Walmsley, *op. cit.*, 18.
60. Patricia Lush, "Goodbye to Neckties and Forklifts," *The Globe and Mail*, Monday, February 18, 1990, B1, 4.
61. John Raymond, "Worth Repeating," *The Globe and Mail*, Tuesday, December 17, 1991, B6.
62. For instance, Bedeian, *op. cit.*, 213, author's italics.
63. Robert Waterman, co-author of *In Search of Excellence*, in Ann R. Dowd, "Learning from Reagan's Debacle," *Fortune*, April 27, 1987, 170.
64. Leslie W. Rue, Lloyd L. Byars. *Supervision: Key Link to Productivity*. Second Edition. Homewood, Illinois: Irwin, 1986, 27.
65. John Raymond, "Worth Repeating," *The Globe and Mail*, Wednesday, November 20, 1991, B4.
66. Drew Fagan, "Getting Off with a Nod and a Wink," *The Globe and Mail*, Monday, December 17, 1990, B1, 4.
67. L. Archer, "I Saw What You Did and I Know Who You Are," *Canadian Business*, November 1985, pp. 70 - 83.

CHAPTER 4

1. Letter to Editor, *The Globe and Mail*, Saturday, February 22, 1992, D7.
2. Barrie McKenna, "A Perfection Reflection," *The Globe and Mail*, Wednesday, January 22, 1992, B1, 3.
3. Thomas Peters, Robert Waterman. *In Search of Excellence*. New York: Warner Books, 1982, 292ff.
4. Dahmar Bottenbruch, auto analyst at Credit First Boston in Milan, in Timothy Aeppel (*Wall Street Journal*), "BMW Shifting Gears to Stay in Fast Lane," *The Globe and Mail*, Thursday, February 20, 1992, B4. BMW sticks to an established path.
5. Thomas Claridge, "Morale Problems Plague Courts," *The Globe and Mail*, Monday, September 9, 1991, A8.
6. Hugh Graham, "Machines Meant to Help Us are Doing Harm, Too," *The Globe and Mail*, Monday, February 17, 1992, A13.
7. For an interesting description and application of this idea, see Dudley Lynch, Paul L. Kordis. *Strategy of the Dolphin: Scoring a Win in a Chaotic World*. New York: Fawcett Columbine, 1988, 17, 111 - 40.
8. Frederick A. Starke, Robert W. Sexty. *Contemporary Management in Canada*. Scarborough, Ontario: Prentice-Hall Canada Inc., 1992, 192.
9. Robert Fulmer. *The New Management*. Third Edition. New York: Macmillan Publishing Co., Inc., 1983, 75.
10. Dunnery Best, "The $250M Cost of Crownx's Silliness," *The Financial Times of Canada*, March 2, 1992, 4.
11. Peter F. Drucker. *Management: Tasks, Responsibilities, Practices*. New York: Harper & Row, Inc., 1974, 467 - 70.
12. Steve Lehr, "Overhauling America's Business Management," *New York Times Magazine*, January 4, 1981, 17; reference located in Roger D'Aprix. *Communicating For Productivity*. New York: Harper & Row, 1982, x.
13. John Raymond, "Worth Repeating," *The Globe and Mail*, Monday, February 24, 1992, B8.
14. Richard L. Bencin, "How to Keep Creative Juices Flowing," *International Management*, July 1983, 26.
15. Video -- "Crazy People: A Comedy About Truth in Advertising," starring Dudley Moore and Daryl Hannah, a Paramount Picture.
16. *See* Stan Kossen. *Supervision: A Practical Guide to First-Line Management*. New York: Harper & Row, 1981, 62.
17. Daniel J. Isenberg, "How Senior Managers Think," *Harvard Business Review*, November - December 1984, 81.
18. Kate Dourian, "Silly Walks Enter the Boardroom," *The Globe and Mail*, Tuesday, November 12, 1991, B23.
19. "Executives Turning to Psychic, Intuitive Power," *The Toronto Star*, Monday, October 1, 1990, B3.
20. John Stackhouse, "Abitibi's Last Stand," *Report on Business Magazine*, October 1991, 23.
21. "CP Shifts Gears to Survive," *Report on Business Magazine*, September 1991, 22.
22. John Stackhouse, "Abitibi's Last Stand," *Report on Business Magazine*, October 1991, 26.
23. Richard L. Daft. *Management*. Second Edition. Chicago: The Dryden Press, 1991, 187.
24. *For further reading see* M. Basadur, G. Graen, S. Gree, "Training in Creative Problem Solving," *Organizational Behavior and Human Performance*, 30, 1982, 41 - 70.
25. Bernard Lonergan. *Insight*. New York: Philosophical Library, 1957.
26. Karen R. Gillespie. *Creative Supervision*. Second Edition. Toronto: Harcourt Brace Jovanovich, 1989, 94 - 95.
27. Jacquie McNish, "Worker Takeover No Miracle Cure," *The Globe and Mail*, Monday, February 24, 1992, B1, 4.
28. Geoffrey York, "Day Care Called Shameful," *The Globe and Mail*, Friday, February 28, 1992, A5.
29. "More Executives Putting Family First," *The York Region Business Journal*, February 1992, 19.
30. Anne McKague, "'Learning Culture' Vital," *Computing Canada*, February 3, 1992, 11.
31. Murray Soupcoff, "CD-ROM Technology Chasing Paper Blues Away," *The Globe and Mail*, Wednesday, January 29, 1992, B6.
32. Associated Press, "Toyota Tries to Add Fun to Winning Recipe," *The Globe and Mail*, Tuesday, February 18, 1992, B1, 2: "Maybe we made a mistake in designing such gloomy factories,' Mr. Jagawa [Tadaaki - Toyota director] said. 'I wish we had used more of our profits

to improve working conditions'" (B2).

33. Margot Gibb-Clark, "The Imperial Way Takes an Abrupt Turn," *The Globe and Mail*, Saturday, February 8, 1992, B21.

34. David Olive, "Move Over, Peter Drucker. Here's Ben Hamper, Straight From the Assembly-line Floor," *The Globe and Mail*, Saturday, August 24, 1991, D4.

35. Mikhail Gorbachev, "Gorbachev's First Column: Will East and West Finally Meet?" *The Toronto Star*, Monday, February 24, 1992, A1.

36. James L. Gibson, John M. Ivancevich, James H. Donnelly, Jr. *Organizations: Structure, Processes, Behavior*. Plano, Texas: Business Publications, 1973, 187.

37. J.T. Burton, Jr., "The Subjective Factor in Decision Making," *Supervisory Management*, 27, July 1982, 11.

38. Lawrence L. Steinmetz, H. Ralph Todd, Jr. *First-Line Management: Approaching Supervision Effectively*. Third Edition. Plano, Texas: Business Publications, 1979, 102.

39. Anthony Robbins. *Unlimited Power*. New York: Fawcett Columbine, 1986, 289.

40. David Olive, "Fire at Will," *Report on Business Magazine*, March 1992, 9.

41. Joseph O'Connor, John Seymour. *Introducing Neuro-Linguistic Programming: The New Psychology of Personal Excellence*. Hammersmith, London: Mandala [An Imprint of HarperCollins Publishers], 1990, 154.

42. Anthony Robbins, *op. cit.*, 293 - 94.

43. Timothy Pritchard, "GM Sends Unions Clear Signal," *The Globe and Mail*, Wednesday, February 26, 1992, B1.

44. Bob McCulloch, "Line Managers Being Forced to Take the Lead in Technology," *The Globe and Mail*, Monday, November 7, 1988, C11.

45. Evan Ramstad, "Arlington Foresaw the Corporate Axe," *The Globe and Mail*, Wednesday, February 26, 1992, B21.

46. Randall Scotland, "How Olivetti Went Back to the Future," *The Financial Post*, March 2, 1992, s24.

47. For instance, there is the Decision Matrix, the mathematical model of Decision Trees, the Delphi technique, Nominal Group Technique (NGT), Operations Research (OR) techniques, such as probability analysis, queuing theory, linear programming, and simulation.

48. *Adapted from:* Lawrence L. Steinmetz, H. Ralph Todd, Jr. *First-Line Management: Approaching Supervision Effectively*. Fourth Edition. Plano, Texas: Business Publications, 1986, 93 - 97.

49. Carolyn Leitch, "Big Blue Staff Let It All Hang Out - - On-line," *The Globe and Mail*, Wednesday, February 26, 1992, B18.

50. Canadian Press, "Pilot Machismo Called Safety Risk," *The Globe and Mail*, Saturday, October 27, 1990, A5.

51. *See* "Case 7.1, NASA's Decision to Launch the Shuttle," in Ricky W. Griffin. *Management*. Second Edition. Boston: Houghton Mifflin Company, 1987, 22 - 26.

52. Leslie Papp, "A Macho Standoff that Hurts Everybody," *The Toronto Star*, Sunday, September 1, 1991, A1, 8.

53. Karen Howlett, "Bought Deals Changing Way Bay Street Works," *The Globe and Mail*, Monday, February 24, 1992, B1, 7.

54. Robert Fabian, "Rough Ride Ahead as Change Rolls On," *The Globe and Mail*, Monday, November 7, 1988, C10.

55. Michael Anderson, Andrew Lamb, "CIO Is Making Presence Felt at Highest Corporate Level," *The Globe and Mail*, Monday, November 7, 1988, C11.

56. Margot Gibb-Clark, "Doing Business Better Requires a Strategy," *The Globe and Mail*, Monday, February 17, 1992, B6.

57. Dan Westell, "Carena Finds 'Structured Partnership' Profitable," *The Globe and Mail*, Tuesday, January 14, 1992, B9.

58. Irving L. Janis, Leon Mann. *Decision Making: A Psychological Analysis of Conflict, Choice and Commitment*. New York: Free Press, 1977.

59. Tom Peters, Nancy Austin, "The Context of Innovation," (ch. 11) in *A Passion For Excellence: The Leadership Difference*. New York: Random House, 1985, 169.

60. Dean Askin, "Not Everyone Is Going Bankrupt," *The York Region Business Journal*, March 1992, 20.

61. I.L. Janis. *Victims of Groupthink: A Psychological Study of Foreign Policy Decisions and fiascos*. Boston: Houghton-Mifflin, 1972.

62. *Adapted from:* Irving L. Janis. *Groupthink*. Second Edition. Boston: Houghton-Mifflin, 1982.

63. John R. Schermerhorn, Jr., James G. Hunt, Richard N. Osborn. *Managing Organizational Behavior*. Fourth Edition. Toronto: John Wiley & Sons, Inc., 1991, 442.

64. Glen Allen, "Politics in the Office," *Maclean's*, July 15, 1985, 32 - 37.

65. Louise Brown, "Office Paranoia," *The Toronto Star*, Saturday, August 30, 1986, L1, 2.

66. Christine Hansen, "Participation: Mandatory," *Toronto Business*, Vol. 11, No. 3, March 1985, 22 - 23.

67. "Canadian Gives Birth on Plane as Passengers Cheer, Applaud," *The Globe and Mail*, Monday, February 20, 1989, A8.

68. Michael E. Rock, "Reflections," *A.C.M.O. Manager*, No. 3, 1987, 34 - 35.

69. Allan R. Cohen, Stephen L. Fink, Herman Gadon, Robin D. Willits. *Effective Behavior in Organizations. Learning from the Interplay of Cases, Concepts, and Student Experiences*. Fourth Edition. Homewood, Illinois: Irwin, 1988, 331.

70. David Climenhaga, "Ford Uses TV to Keep Employees in Touch," *The Globe and Mail*, Monday, May 29, 1989, C6.

71. Carolyn Leitch, "'Killer' Company Crashes," *The Globe and Mail*, Saturday, September 28, 1991, B1, 4.

72. Carolyn Leitch, "Alias Research Makes Hard Drive for More Flexible Management Style," *The Globe and Mail*, Monday, February 17, 1992, B3.

73. Margot Gibb-Clark, "In Praise of the Business Strategy," *The Globe and Mail*, Thursday, February 27, 1992, B1.

74. Randall Scotland, "Anatomy of an Ad Campaign," *The Financial Post*, March 2, 1992, s24.

75 Katherine I. Miller, Peter R. Monge, "Participation, Satisfaction, and Productivity: A Meta-Analytic Review," *Academy of Management Journal*, December 1986, 727 - 53.

CHAPTER 5

1. Peter F. Drucker. *The Effective Executive*. New York: Harper & Row, 1967, 51.

2. F. David Peat. *Synchronicity: The Bridge Between Matter and Mind*. Toronto: Bantam Books, 1987, 41.

3. *See* F. David Peat, *ibid.*, 228.

4. Fritjof Capra. *The Tao of Physics. An Exploration of the Parallels Between Modern Physics and Eastern Mysticism*. Boulder, Colorado: Shambhala, 1975, 163.

5. Stephen W. Hawking. *A Brief History of Time*. New York: Bantam Books, 1988.

6. F. David Peat, *op. cit.*, 228 - 29

7. Ross C.K. Rock, Engineering Science, University of Toronto. Personal communication.

8. F. David Peat, *op. cit.*, 237.

9. Personal communication: a paraphrase of Dr. Tom Janz's idea in his research on corporate culture. Dr. Janz is a psychology professor in the business department at the University of Calgary.

10. A.S. Blinder, "Time Is Not on America's Side," *Business Week*, July 22, 1991.

11. Gerald Graham, "High Achievers Know How to Use Time," *The Toronto Star*, Monday, February 3, 1992, B1.

12. Arden R. Haynes, "Leadership is Needed to Solve Our Society's Ethical Crisis," *The Toronto Star*, Monday, November 28, 1988, B3.

13. Peter F. Drucker, *op. cit.*, 26 - 27.

14. Lawrence L. Steinmetz, H. Ralph Todd, Jr. *First-Line Management: Approaching Supervision Effectively*. Fourth Edition. Plano, Texas: Business Publications, Inc., 1986, 232.

15. Jan P. Muczyk, Eleanor Brantley Schwartz, Ephraim Smith. *Principles of Supervision. First- and Second-Level Management*. Toronto: Charles E. Merrill Publishing Company, 1984, 90.

16. Based upon ideas in Nathaniel Stewart. *The Effective Woman Manager*. New York: John Wiley and Sons, Inc., 1978, 169.

17. D.D. Warrick, Robert A. Zawacki. *Supervisory Management. Understanding Behavior and Managing for Results*. New York: Harper & Row, 1984, 271.

18. *Adaptation from:* Warrick and Zawacki, *ibid.*, 386.

19. Michael Bliss, "Dress Them in Mourning," *Report on Business Magazine*, February 1992, 57 - 58.

20. Jeff Pelline, "The Art and Science of Crisis Management," *The Globe and Mail*, Monday, April 1, 1991, B4.

21. *See also* Adam and Edita Kowalski, "How to Best Plan Your Time," *enRoute*, June 1978, 26-28, 66, 78.

22. Eric Berne. *What Do You Say After You Say Hello?* New York: Grove Press, 1973.

23. Eric Berne. *Games People Play*. New York: Grove Press, 1964, 15.

24. Eric Berne. *What Do You Say After You Say Hello?* New York: Grove Press, 1973, 160 - 65, 318 - 21.

25. J. Orten, "Contributions to Stroke Vocabulary," *Transactional Analysis Journal*, Vol. 2, No. 3, 1972, 104.

26. Ronald B. Adler, Neil Towne. *Looking Out/Looking In. Interpersonal Communication*. Fourth Edition. Toronto: Holt, Rinehart and Winston, 1984, 7.

27. Peter Goodspeed, "North Korean 'Paradise' a Vision of Hell," *The Toronto Star*, Sunday, March 1, 1992, A15.

28. Hedges Capers, Glen Holland, "Stroke Survival Quotient," *Transactional Analysis Journal*, Vol. 1, No. 3, 1971, 40.

29. *See* "A Fuzzy Tale," in Claude Steiner. *Scripts People Live*. New York: Grove Press, 1974, 127ff.

30. Jut Meininger. *Success Through Transactional Analysis*. New York: Grosset & Dunlap, 1973, 61.

31. Tom Harpur, "Towards a New Dawn," *The Toronto Star*, December 29, 1991, B1, 5.

32. Deborah Jones, "Seagull Flies Into Culture Clash," *The Globe and Mail*, Monday, December 2, 1991, B3; *also*, Arthur Johnson, "Mind Cults Invade the Boardroom," *Canadian Business*, January 1992, 38 - 42.

33. Sherod Miller, Ph.D., Daniel B. Wackman, Ph.D., Dallas R. Demmitt, Ph.D., Nancy J. Demmitt, M.C. *Working Together: Productive Communication On The Job*. Interpersonal Communication Programs, Inc., 715 Florida Avenue South, Suite 209, Minneapolis, Minnesota 55426.

34. Robert A. Zawacki, Peter E. LaSota, "The Supervisor as Counselor," *The 1975 Annual Handbook for Group Facilitators*. John E. Jones and J. William Pfeiffer, Editors. La Jolla, California: University Associates, Inc., 135 - 37.

35. Muriel James, Dorothy Jongeward. *Born To Win: Transactional Analysis With Gestalt Experiments*. Reading, Mass.: Addison-Wesley, 1971, 58.

36. Anne Wilson Schaef, Diane Fassel. *The Addictive Organization*. San Francisco: Harper & Row, 1988, 59 - 60.
37. Muriel James, Dorothy Jongeward, *op. cit.*, 59.
38. Keith Crim (Ed.). *Abingdon Dictionary of Living Religions*. Nashville: Abingdon, 1981, 738ff.
39. Interview with Beppi Crosariol, "Encounter: Rod Canion," *Financial Times of Canada*, November 19, 1990, 37.
40. R. Bruce McAfee, Paul J. Champagne. *Organizational Behavior: A Manager's View*. St. Paul: West Publishing Company, 1987, 216.
41. Peter F. Drucker. *Management: Tasks, Responsibilities, Practices*. New York: Harper & Row, 1973, 548.
42. Judith Rosenfield, "Making the Most Out of Meetings," *Marketing Communications*, November 1984, 20 - 22.
43. Peter F. Drucker, *op. cit.*, 408.
44. Anthony Jay, "How to Run a Meeting," *Harvard Business Review*, March-April 1976, 44.
45. B.W. Tuckman, "Developmental Sequence in Small Groups," *Psychological Bulletin*, No. 63, November 1965, 384 - 99.
46. Keith Davis, John W. Newstrom. *Human Behavior At Work*. New York: McGraw-Hill Book Company, 1989, 268-69.
47. This discussion is an adaptation of the well-developed Participation Training group discussion model at Indiana University. *See* Paul Bergevin, John McKinley. *Participation Training for Adult Education*. St. Louis, Missouri: The Bethany Press, 1965. Also, Michael E. Rock, "Participation Training: A Task-Oriented Human Relations Design," *Training 75* (Public Service Commission), September 1975, 16 - 18.

CHAPTER 6
1. J. Watson Wilson, "The Growth of a Company: A Psychological Case Study," *Advanced Management Journal*, January 1966, 43, author's italics.
2. Alanna Mitchell, "Affair With Divorce Shows Signs of Cooling," *The Globe and Mail*, Monday, March 23, 1992, A1, 2.
3. Peter Trueman, "Successfully Downwardly Mobile," *Pathways*. Vol. 1, No. 3, April/May 1992, 28.
4. Vaclav Havel, "Forget the Machines, Cut the Clichés and Get Humanity Back Into Politics," *The Globe and Mail*, Monday, March 16, 1992, A11.
5. John A. Sanford. *Healing and Wholeness*. Toronto: Paulist Press, 1977, 20.
6. Quoted in Bill M.'s article, "Straight Up," *Pathways*, Vol. 1 No. 3, April/May 1992, 21.
7. *Adaptation from: Strange Stories, Amazing Facts*. Montreal: The Reader's Digest Association, Inc., 1976, 41.

8. *Ibid.*, 14.
9. Ronald B. Adler, Lawrence B. Rosenfeld, Neil Towne. *Interplay. The Process of Interpersonal Communication*. Fifth Edition. Toronto: Harcourt Brace Jovanovich College Publishers, 1992, 35.
10. Jean Illsley Clarke. *Self-Esteem: A Family Affair*. Minneapolis, MN.: Winston Press, 1978.
11. Carl Jung, M.D., "Introduction to Wickes's 'Analyse Der Kinderseele'," *The Development of Personality*. Bollingen Series XX. Princeton, New Jersey: Princeton University Press, Fourth Printing, 1974, 39.
12. Alvin Toffler. *Future Shock*. New York: Bantam Books, 1971.
13. Jean Monty, Bell Canada chairman, in John Raymond, "Worth Repeating," *The Globe and Mail*, Monday, March 23, 1992, B6.
14. Margot Gibb-Clark, "Fear More Apt to Paralyze Than Motivate," *The Globe and Mail*, Monday, March 23, 1992, B6.
15. Gerald Utting, "The Japanese Way," *The Toronto Star*, Sunday, March 22, 1992, H6.
16. *Adaptation from:* Raymond F. Gale. *Developmental Behavior: A Humanistic Approach*. Toronto, Ontario: Collier-Macmillan Canada, Ltd., 1969, 21.
17. David Olive, "The Knowledge Gap," *Report on Business Magazine*, The Globe and Mail, Friday, March 20, 1992, 12.
18. John Raymond, "Worth Repeating," *The Globe and Mail*, Tuesday, March 3, 1992, B8.
19. Diane Francis, "Parrot's Postal Union Must Be Out To Lunch," *The Financial Post*, Tuesday, August 27, 1991, 11.
20. Virginia Galt, "Postal Rancour Has Roots in Past," *The Globe and Mail*, Thursday, September 5, 1991, A9.
21. Thomas Verny, M.D., John Kelly. *The Secret Life of the Unborn Child*. New York: Summit Books, 1981.
22. C.G. Jung. *Memories, Dreams, Reflections*. New York: Vintage Books (a Division of Random House), 1965, 150, 158.
23. Henri F. Ellenberger. *The Discovery of the Unconscious*. New York: Basic Books, Inc., 1969, 669.
24. C.G. Jung. *Modern Man in Search of a Soul*. New York: Harcourt, Brace & World, Inc. (a Harvest Book), 1933, 229.
25. Robert Bly, "The Human Shadow," recorded by Sound Horizons Audio Video, Inc., 250 West 54th. Street, Suite 1527, New York, N.Y. 10107.
26. See the editorial cartoon in *The Financial Times of Canada*, January 20, 1992, 20, on De Havilland and Bombardier Inc.
27. Christopher Donville, "Dark Side of Prosperity Revealed by Task Force," *The Globe and Mail*, Wednesday, October 31, 1990, A9.
28. Edward C. Whitmont, M.D. *The Symbolic Quest*.

Princeton, New Jersey: Princeton University Press, 1978, 162.

29. Stephen McHale, "Tilley Fighting to Hang on to His Hats," *The Globe and Mail*, Wednesday, February 12, 1992, B1, 7.

30. Shakespeare, *Hamlet*, Act III, Scene 2, line 240.

31. Michael Rock, "The Shadow Knows," *Travelling on Business*, 1987, 9 - 10.

32. Paul Quinn-Judge, "The KGB's Dark Past Sees the Light of Day," *The Christian Science Monitor*, October 31 - November 6, 1988, 5.

33. Tyra Arraj, James Arraj. *Tracking the Elusive Human. Volume 1. A Practical Guide to C.G. Jung's Psychological Types, W.H. Sheldon's Body and Temperament Types and their Integration*. Chiloquin, Oregon: Inner Growth Books, 1988, 70.

34. Thought du jour, *The Globe and Mail*, Friday, March 6, 1992, A14.

35. In Ronald B. Adler, Neil Towne. *Looking Out/Looking In. Interpersonal Communication*. Fourth Edition. Toronto: Holt, Rinehart and Winston, 1984, 175.

36. Alan Toulin, "Cynicism Dogs Prosperity Initiative," *The Financial Post*, April 6, 1992, s6.

37. Tom McCormack, "Get Ready Canada For Next Boom," *The Toronto Star*, Sunday, April 5, 1992, H4.

38. John Raymond, "Worth Repeating," *The Globe and Mail*, Monday, April 6, 1992, B4.

39. Ken Wilbur, "Taking Responsibility for Your Shadow," in Jeremiah Abrams, Connie Zweig (Eds.). *Meeting the Shadow: The Hidden Power of the Dark Side of Human Nature*. Los Angeles: Jeremy P. Tarcher, Inc., 1991, 274.

40. Ronald B. Adler, Neil Towne. *Looking Out/Looking In. Interpersonal Communication*. Fourth Edition. Toronto: Holt, Rinehart and Winston, 73.

41. Michael E. Rock, "Psychological Scuds," *Rasaneh*, March 1991, 3.

42. "Warspeak," *The Toronto Star*, Friday, January 25, 1991, A1.

43. Michael E. Rock, "Magnanimity," *Rasaneh*, January 1991, 11.

CHAPTER 7

1. Jon Winokur (Ed.). *The Portable Curmudgeon*. Scarborough, Ontario: NA: Books (New American Library), 1987, 74.

2. *The Wall Street Journal*, November 2, 1979.

3. Ronald B. Adler, Neil Towne. *Looking Out/Looking In*. Fourth Edition. New York: Holt, Rinehart and Winston, 1984, 138 - 140.

4. Thanks are due to Prof. Marvin Karlins for this term *worthplace*: "Making the Workplace a Worthplace: The Role of Behavioral Science and the Plus-Plus Relationship" (ch. 3), in *The Human Use of Human Resources*. New York: McGraw-Hill Book Company, 1981, 15ff.

5. *Slightly adapted from The Newsletter*, The Christophers, New York, 1980.

6. Terry Kellogg. *Broken Toys Broken Dreams. Understanding & Healing Codependency, Compulsive Behaviors & Family*. Amherst, MA: BRAT Publishing, 1990, 51.

7. *Located in:* John Bradshaw. *Bradshaw on The Family: A Revolutionary Way of Self-Discovery*. Deerfield Beach, Florida: Health Communications, Inc., 1988, 41.

8. Blair Justice, Ph.D. *Who Gets Sick*. Los Angeles: Jeremy P. Tarcher, Inc., 1988, 127.

9. *Discussion adapted from:* Ronald B. Adler, Neil Towne. *Looking Out/Looking In: Interpersonal Communication*. Sixth Edition. Toronto: Holt, Rinehart and Winston, 1990, 7 - 11.

10. R. Narem, "Try a Little TLC," research reported in *Science*, Vol. 80, No. 1, 1980, 15.

11. Dawson Church, Dr. Alan Sherr. *The Heart of the Healer*. New York: Aslan Publishing, 1987.

12. J. Lynch. *The Broken Heart: The Medical Consequences of Loneliness*. New York: Basic Books, 1977, 239 - 242.

13. E. A. Liljefors, R.H. Rahe, "Psychosocial Characteristics of Subjects with Myocardial Infarction in Stockholm," in E. K. Gunderson, R.H. Rahe (Eds.). *Life Stress Illness*. Springfield, Ill. Charles C. Thomas, 1974, 90 - 104.

14. W. D. Rees, S.G. Lutkins, "Mortality of Bereavement," *British Medical Journal*, No. 4, 1967, 13.

15. *Adapted from:* Michael E. Rock, "Justice in the WORTHPLACE: Creating a Healthy and Ethical Working Environment," *Rasaneh*, April-May 1990, 7 - 8.

16. Dorothy Lipovenko, "Fifth Column," *The Globe and Mail*, Monday, September 24, 1990, A16.

17. Gordon Pape, "Future Shock: The Soaring Cost of CPP," *The Globe and Mail*, Friday, January 3, 1992, B4.

18. Jacquie McNish, "Corporate Dinosaurs Leaving Some Fossils Behind," *The Globe and Mail*, Monday, December 23, 1991, B1.

19. Gwynne Dyer, "Has the World Undergone a Fundamental Shift?" *The Toronto Star*, Thursday, December 26, 1991, A31.

20. Martin Goldfarb, "In Today's Economic World Value Is the New Bottom Line," *The Toronto Star*, Monday, December 2, 1991, B6.

21. Carolyn Van Brussel, "Software Skills in Crisis: Study," *Computing Canada*, March 30, 1992, 4.

22. David Olive, "The Knowledge Gap," *Report on Business Magazine, The Globe and Mail*, Friday, March 20, 1992, 12.

23. Michael Harrison, "How to Recognize Your Crazy Boss," *The Financial Post*, Monday, February 17, 1992, S12.

24. Roger D'Aprix. *Communicating For Productivity*. New York: Harper & Row, 1982, 11.

25. Nattalia Lea, "CMA Course Puts Emphasis on People Skills," *The Globe and Mail*, Tuesday, October 1, 1991, B26.

26. It is estimated that "people costs" account for roughly 75% of corporate net profit before taxes! J. Rosnow, "Solving the Human Equation in the Productivity Puzzle," *Management Review*, August 1977, 40 - 43. Reference located in Marvin Karlins. *The Human Use of Human Resources*. New York: McGraw-Hill Book Company, 1981, 6.

27. David Shoalts, "Season Has Ended, NHL Says," *The Globe and Mail*, Wednesday, April 8, 1992, A2.

28. First Column,, "NHL Strike Hurting CBC," *The Globe and Mail*, Thursday, April 9, 1991, A1.

29. *Cited in* David G. Myers. *The Inflated Self: Human Illusions and the Biblical Call to Hope.* New York: Seabury Press, 1980, iv.

30. Damien Cox, "They're Back! NHL Strike Ends," *The Toronto Star*, Saturday, April 11, 1992, A1.

31. Robert Williamson, "B.C. Pulp Strike Drags On, Losses Mount," *The Globe and Mail*, Monday, July 6, 1992, B3.

32. Jack McArthur, "On the Downside, It Can Be a Risky World Out There," *The Toronto Star*, Monday, June 29, 1992, B1.

33. Paul R. Timm, Brent D. Peterson, Jackson C. Stevens. *People At Work: Human Relations in Organizations*. St. Paul, Minn.: West Publishing Co., 1990, 14, and citing research from Kate Ludeman, *Executive Excellence*, April 1987, 3.

34. Cathryn Motherwell, "How to Win the Rubber Match," *The Globe & Mail*, November 3, 1992, B28.

35. David Pyette, "Worth Repeating," *The Globe and Mail*, Thursday, November 23, 1989, B2.

36. John Holusha, "Soothing and Slaps From on High," *The Globe and Mail*, Thursday, March 5, 1992, B1.

37. Bruce McDougall, "The Next battleground," *Canadian Business*, February 1992, 52 - 56.

38. Mark Stevenson, "Hamburger Heaven," *Financial Times of Canada*, March 30, 1992, 12, 13.

39. *See* The Royal Bank of Canada Monthly Letter, "The Act of Listening," Vol. 60, No. 1, January 1979, 1 - 4.

40. Sheldon E. Gordon, "Pricking Corporate Consciences," *Report on Business Magazine, The Globe and Mail* (July/August 1985), pp. 38 - 42.

41. "Criticism at Work Can Be Constructive If Your Self-image Is Good, Expert Says," *The Toronto Star*, Thursday, November 9, 1989, L8.

42. Margot Gibb-Clark, "Working on Expressing Emotions," *The Globe and Mail*, Thursday, November 15, 1990, B8; Deirdre Fanning, "A Place for Feelings," *The Globe and Mail*, Wednesday, January 2, 1991, B4.

43. Jim Murray, "Handling Anger Key to Controlling Your Work Relationships," *Marketing*, September 9, 1991, 20.

44. From studies summarized by Dr. Ralph Nichols. *Are You Listening?* New York: McGraw-Hill, 1957; reference located in Madelyn Burley-Allen. *Listening: The Forgotten Skill*. Toronto: John Wiley & Sons, Inc., 1982, 1 - 2.

45. Interview, "Northrop Frye Talks About the Role of the Humanities," *Columns*, University of Toronto, Fall 1985, 7.

46. Nicholas Bradbury, "Cross Current," *The Globe and Mail*, Tuesday, January 28, 1992, C1.

47. William Lutz. *Doublespeak*. New York: HarperPerennial (a Division of HarperCollinsPublishers), 1989, 4. *Also*, Susan Gittins, "Digging Into Firms' Footnotes," *The Financial Post*, April 6, 1992, 22: "Companies Like to Put Their Best Foot Forward in the Letter to Shareholders"; Jerry Trites, "Annual Reports Need a New Openness," *The Financial Post*, April 6, 1992, s5.

48. William Lutz, *op. cit.*, 15.

49. Douglas Goold, "The Doublespeak of Annual Reports," *The Globe and Mail*, Saturday, March 28, 1992, B23.

50. Grace Casselman, "Piracy Fighters Turn up Heat in Bid to Nab Violators," *Computing Canada*, March 16, 1992, 7.

51. Geoffrey Rowan, "New Air Canada President Welcomed With Record Loss," *The Globe and Mail*, Friday, February 21, 1992, B1, 7.

52. Alan Gathright, "L-word Proves Taboo in Flood of 'Focused Reductions'," *The Toronto Star*, Sunday, February 16, 1992, H1, 4.

53. *Adapted from:* Michael E. Rock, "The Crisis of Being Right," *The Condominium Manager*, Vol. 12, No. 4, Winter 1991, 37 - 38.

54. David Crane, "Study Slams Low-tech Canada," *The Toronto Star*, Friday, October 25, 1991, A1, A22, A23.

55. Lynda Hurst, "Can (*not!*) lit," *The Toronto Star*, Saturday, April 11, 1992, H1, 11.

56. Erna Paris, "A Letter to the Thought Police," *The Globe and Mail*, Tuesday, March 31, 1992, A16.

57. Bob Papoe, "Big Brother Attitude Curtails Advertising, Agency Official Says," *The Toronto Star*, Tuesday, March 31, 1992, C16.

58. October 14, 1991.

59. Lynne Ainsworth, "Intellectual Freedom Hurt by Feminists, Professor Says," *The Toronto Star*, Friday, September 13, 1991, A2.

60. Thought du jour, Michael Kesterton, "Social Studies," *The Globe and Mail*, Monday, April 6, 1992, A11.

CHAPTER 8

1. Jon Winokur (Ed.). *The Portable Curmudgeon*.

Scarborough, Ontario: NAL Books (New American Library), 1987, 197.

2. John Raymond, "Worth Repeating," *The Globe and Mail*, Monday, March 23, 1992, B6.

3. Joseph White, Gregory A. Patterson, Paul Ingrassia, "A Change Is in the Works," *The Globe and Mail*, Monday, January 13, 1992, B1, 2.

4. Alison Eastwood, "Apple, IBM Level in PC Race," *Computing Canada*, February 3, 1992, 19.

5. Curt Suplee, "IBM-Apple Deal Anticipates New PC Era," *The Toronto Star*, Sunday, July 14, 1991, F1, 2.

6. "Apple, Sharp Enter Partnership," *The Globe and Mail*, Wednesday, April 1, 1992, B5.

7. Grace Casselman, "Deal With Bull Gives IBM European Partner," *Computing Canada*, March 2, 1992, 11.

8. John Heinzl, "Retailer Hammers Home Message to Suppliers," *The Globe and Mail*, Tuesday, March 31, 1992, B1, 17.

9. Lawrence Surtees, "BCE, Systemhouse Seek Partnership Approval," *The Globe and Mail*, Wednesday, February 26, 1992, B3.

10. Lawrence Surtees, "Northern Telecom, Motorola Connect on Cellular Market," *The Globe and Mail*, Tuesday, February 11, 1992, B1, 17.

11. Reuter News Agency, "Unisys, Motorola Form Technology Partnership," *The Financial Post*, Thursday, January 30, 1992, 9.

12. Marina Strauss, "Baker's Brassy Style May Rub Off on McKim, *The Globe and Mail*, Monday, January 27, 1992, B1, 6.

13. "Volvo Merger Worth $6.6-billion," *The Globe and Mail*, Monday, January 27, 1992, B5.

14. Adrian Bradley, "Four Seasons Poised to be No. 1," *The Financial Post*, Wednesday, March 18, 1992, 3.

15. Leslie Papp, "Bridging the Gap," *The Toronto Star*, Saturday, March 7, 1992, D1.

16. Virginia Galt, "Labour Gaining Political Clout," *The Globe and Mail*, Wednesday, March 4, 1992, A8.

17. Timothy Pritchard, "Who's Where in Battle for GM Survival," *The Globe and Mail*, Friday, April 4, 1992, B1, B4.

18. Gordon Simpson, "Managers Must Give People as Much Emphasis as Financial Results," *The Globe and Mail*, Saturday, January 13, 1990, B2.

19. Harvey Enchin, "Bata Puts Million-dollar Boot to Bland Style," *The Globe and Mail*, Tuesday, July 9, 1991, B2.

20. Allan Swift, "Saving Air Canada $25 Million," *The Toronto Star*, Sunday, December 15, 1991, H2.

21. "Salaries Seldom Cause Quitting," *The Globe and Mail*, Tuesday, June 28, 1988, B3.

22. Margot Gibb-Clark, "Frustrated Workers Seek Goals," *The Globe and Mail*, Thursday, May 2, 1991, B7.

23. Arthur G. Bedeian. *Management*. Second Edition. Toronto: The Dryden Press, 1989, 394.

24. Raymond F. Gale. *Developmental Behavior: A Humanistic Approach*. Toronto: Collier-Macmillan Canada, Ltd., 1969, 96.

25. Richard L. Daft. *Management*. Second Edition. Toronto: The Dryden Press, 1991, 402.

26. John R. Schermerhorn, Jr., James G. Hunt, Richard N. Osborn. *Managing Organizational Behavior*. Fourth Edition. Toronto: John Wiley & Sons, Inc., 1991, 134.

27. John Raymond, "Worth Repeating," *The Globe and Mail*, Tuesday, December 31, 1991, B4.

28. Victor E. Frankl. *Man's Search for Meaning. An Introduction to Logotherapy*. 26th printing. New York: Pocket Books (a Kangaroo Book), 1977, 127.

29. Nicholas Bradbury, "When Life at the Top Hits Bottom," *The Toronto Star*, Friday, October 4, 1991, A23.

30. Jackie McNish, "Women Can Grab Brass Ring, But It's Costly," *The Globe and Mail*, Tuesday, November 28, 1989, B25, 26.

31. Tom Peters, Nancy Austin. *A Passion for Excellence*. New York: Random House, 1985, 218.

32. From *Federal News Clip Sheet*, June 1979; located in George T. Milkovich, Jerry M. Neuman. *Compensation*. Plano, Texas: Business Publications, 1984, 265 - 66.

33. L. Lindahl, "What Makes A Good Job?" *Personnel*, Vol. 25, 1949, 263 - 66.

34. Richard Turner, "Trouble in Dreamland," *The Globe and Mail*, Saturday, November 30, 1991, B18.

35. Celia Brady, "Fear and Loathing in Hollywood," *Spy*, Vol. 6, No. 6, April 1992, 14.

36. John Crudele, "Here's How Wall St. Assesses the Value of Top Executives," *The Toronto Star*, Tuesday, February 16, 1988, F3.

37. Margot Gibb-Clark, "Workers Feel Uniformed, Researcher Finds," *The Globe and Mail*, Friday, March 16, 1990, B3.

38. Margot Gibb-Clark, "Switching to Work-team Arrangement Leaves Some Concerned for Their Future," *The Globe and Mail*, Monday, April 9, 1990, B6.

39. George Brett, "Canadians Satisfied With Their Jobs, But Down on Bosses, Survey Finds," *The Toronto Star*, Thursday, September 19, 1991, C1, 5. *See also* Margot Gibb-Clark, "Canadian Workers Need Some Respect," *The Globe and Mail*, Wednesday, September 4, 1991, B1, 6.

40. Tim Friend, "Kindness is the Best Motivator," *USA Today*, Tuesday, February 16, 1988, 1D.

41. Claudia H. Deutsch, "Good Corporate Citizenship Now Beginning to Count," *The Globe and Mail*, Wednesday, May 23, 1990, B2.

42. Tom Peters, Nancy Austin. *A Passion for Excellence*. New York: Random House, 1985, 50.

43. John Crudele, "Here's How Wall St. Assesses the Value of Top Executives," *The Toronto Star*, Tuesday,

February 16, 1988, F3.

44. Associated Press, "Bonanza for Coke Chief," *The Globe and Mail*, Friday, March 20, 1992, B16.

45. Martin Dickson, "A Check on the Boss's Cheque," *The Financial Post*, Wednesday, April 1, 1992, 43.

46. Wendell L. French, Fremont E. Kast, James E. Rosenzweig. *Understanding Human Behavior in Organizations*. New York: Harper & Row, 1985, 100.

47. Bill Saporito, "Allegheny Ludlum Has Steel Figured Out," *Fortune*, June 25, 1984, 40 - 44

48. "When It Comes to Management, Less Is More," *The Globe and Mail*, February 1, 1988, A7.

49. *Located in:* Tom Peters, Nancy Austin. *A Passion for Excellence*. New York: Random House, 1985, 219.

50. Carolyn Leitch, "Cognos Learns Lesson," *The Globe and Mail*, Monday, January 20, 1992, B1, 2.

51. *Adapted from:* Craig R. Hickman. *Mind of a Manager, Soul of a Leader*. Toronto: John Wiley & Sons, Inc., 1990, 262 - 63.

52. W.C. Langer. *Psychology and Human Living*. New York: Appleton-Century-Crofts, 1937.

53. Abraham H. Maslow, "A Theory of Human Motivation," *Psychological Review*, Vol. 50, 1943, 370 - 96; Abraham H. Maslow. *Motivation and Personality*. New York: Harper & Row, 1954.

54. Gregory B. Northcraft, Margaret A. Neale. *Organizational Behavior: A Management Challenge*. Toronto: The Dryden Press, 1990, 137.

55. Arthur G. Bedeian. *Management*. Second Edition. Toronto: The Dryden Press, 1989, 397.

56. Abraham Maslow, "A Theory of Human Motivation," *Psychological Review*, 50, 1943, 370 - 96.

57. M.A. Wahba, G. Bridwell, "Maslow Reconsidered: A Review of the Research on the Need Hierarchy Theory," *Organizational Behavior and Human Performance*, Vol. 15, 1976, 212 - 240.

58. Allan R. Cohen, Stephen L. Fink, Herman Gadon, Robin D. Willits. *Effective Behavior in Organizations*. Fourth Edition. Homewood, Illinois: Irwin, 1988, 178. *See also* E.E. Lawler, J.L. Suttle, "A Causal Correlational Test of the Need Hierarchy Concept," *Organizational Behavior and Human Performance*, 7, 1972, 265 - 287.

59. Douglas M. McGregor, "The Human Side of Enterprise," *Management Review*, Vol. 56, November 1957, 22 - 28, 88 - 92. Also, Douglas McGregor. *The Human Side of Enterprise*. New York: McGraw-Hill, 1960.

60. Arthur G. Bedeian, *op. cit.*, 397.

61. *See* D. Hellreigel, J.W. Slocum. *Management*. Reading, Mass.: Addison-Wesley, 1989, 433 - 34.

62. A.H. Maslow, "Deficiency Motivation and Growth Motivation," in M.R. Jones (Ed.). *Nebraska Symposium on Motivation*. Lincoln, Nebraska: University of Nebraska Press, 1955.

63. Ricky W. Griffin. *Management*. Second Edition. Boston: Houghton Mifflin Company, 1987, 393.

64. Lyman W. Porter, "Job Attitudes in Management: II. Perceived Importance of Needs as a Function of Job Level," *Journal of Applied Psychology*, Vol. 47, April 1963, 141 - 48.

65. Marilyn B. Gilbert, Thomas E. Gilbert, "What Skinner Gave Us," *Training*, Vol. 28, No. 9, September 1991, 42 - 48.

66. B.F. Skinner. *Science and Human Behavior*. New York: Free Press, 1953.

67. E.L. Thorndike. *Animal Intelligence*. New York: Macmillan, 1911, 244.

68. J.B. Watson. *Psychology, From the Standpoint of a Behaviorist*. Philadelphia: Lippincott, 1919.

69. *The Wall Street Journal*, February 4, 1977, 6.

70. Frederick Herzberg, Bernard Mausner, Barbara B. Snyderman. *Work and the Nature of Man*. New York: Wiley, 1959; Frederick Herzberg. *The Managerial Choice*. Second Edition. Salt Lake City, Utah: Olympus, 1982; Frederick Herzberg, "Workers' Needs: The Same Around the World," *Industry Week*, September 21, 1987, 29 - 32.

71. John Raymond, "Worth Repeating," *The Globe and Mail*, Thursday, April 2, 1992, B4.

72. D.C. McClelland, et al. *The Achievement Motive*. New York: Appleton-Century-Crofts, 1953; D.C. McClelland. *The Achieving Society*. Princeton, N.J.: Van Nostrand, 1961; D.C. McClelland, D.G. Winter. *Motivating Economic Achievement*. New York: Free Press, 1971.

73. R.M. Steers, N.D. Braunstein, "A Behaviorally Based Measure of Manifest Needs in Work Settings," *Journal of Vocational Behavior*, Vol. 9, 1976, 251 - 266.

74. Victor Vroom. *Work and Motivation*. New York: Wiley, 1964.

75. Carol Kleiman, "Even Companies Laying Off Workers are Looking for Middle Managers," *The Toronto Star*, Monday, March 30, 1992, B1.

76. E.E. Lawler. *Pay and Organizational Effectiveness*. New York: McGraw-Hill, 1971.

77. Virginia Galt, "White Sees Salvation in Holding the Line," *The Globe and Mail*, Thursday, March 26, 1992, B1.

78. Virginia Galt, "CAW Settlement on Overtime No Guarantee for Oshawa's Future," *The Globe and Mail*, Thursday, April 3, 1992, A1, 6.

79. "GM Willing to Meet With Bob White to Settle Oshawa Overtime Dispute," *The Toronto Star*, Saturday, March 21, 1992, C3.

80. Virginia Galt, "Low-cost Solutions Eyed in Easing Work-Family Pressures," *The Globe and Mail*, Wednesday, January 22, 1992, A5.

81. Catherine Dunphy, "Make the Job Fit the Worker,

Author Says," *The Toronto Star*, Monday, April 11, 1988, C1; Virginia Galt, "Helping People Juggle Work, family," *The Globe and Mail*, Tuesday, January 21, 1992, B1, 4.

82. Jerry Zeidenberg, "Telecommuters Keep in Touch With Computers," *The Globe and Mail*, Tuesday, March 24, 1992, B24.

83. Elizabeth Harris, "A Guide to Creating a Home Office," *The Globe and Mail*, Monday, March 9, 1992, B6.

84. Carey French, "Home Is Where the Work Is," *The Globe and Mail*, Tuesday, March 24, 1992, B24.

85. Jerry Zeinberg, "All in the Family," *Human Resources Professional*, July/August 1991, 10-11, 13; "Workers at Home Making Their Mark," *The Toronto Star*, Monday, October 7, 1991, D1.

86. Carey French, "Home Is Where the Work Is," *The Globe and Mail*, Tuesday, March 24, 1992, B24.

87. Jerry Zeidenberg, "Telecommuters Keep in Touch With Computers," *The Globe and Mail*, Tuesday, March 24, 1992, B24.

88. Lawrence Surtees, "Northern Telecom Posts Record Profit," *The Globe and Mail*, Wednesday, January 22, 1992, B2.

89. Gregory B. Northcraft, Margaret A. Neale, *op. cit.*, 493.

90. Madeleine Drohan, "Rover's British Style Seeks a Japanese Edge," *The Globe and Mail*, Monday, September 23, 1991, B1.

91. Norm Alster, "What Flexible Workers Can Do," *Fortune*, February 13, 1989, 62 - 66.

92. Thomas H. Stone, Noah M. Meltz. *Human Resource Management in Canada*. Second Edition. Toronto: Holt, Rinehart and Winston of Canada, 1988, 402.

93. Information based on personal experience teaching in the senior executive development program, Tourraine, P.Q.

94. H.E. Meyer, "Personnel Directors Are the New Corporate Heroes," *Fortune*, February 1976, Vol. 93. 84-88; cited in Stone and Meltz, *ibid.*, 403.

95. Editorial, "A New Blueprint for Skills Training," *The Toronto Star*, Friday, July 27, 1990, A18.

96. Gordon Simpson, "Training Canada's Competitive Edge," *The Globe and Mail*, Saturday, February 2, 1991, B4.

97. Los Angeles Times, "Billionaire Sam Walton was founder of Wal-Mart," *The Toronto Star*, Monday, April 6, 1992, A5.

98. Associated Press, "Wal-Mart Founder Built Success on Service," *The Globe and Mail*, Monday, April 6, 1992, B4.

99. Margot Gibb-Clark, "Most Companies Refuse to Invest a Cent in Training," *The Globe and Mail*, Monday, October 30, 1989, B3.

100. Pat Johnson, "Looking for Value in Training," *Financial Times of Canada*, February 9, 1981, 31.

101. Margot Gibb-Clark, "IBM Measures Up in Employee Training," *The Globe and Mail*, Thursday, January 25, 1990, B1, 5.

102. Margot Gibb-Clark, "IBM Budgets Millions for its Employees' Skills Training," *The Globe and Mail*, Wednesday, January 24, 1990, B1, 4.

103. Beppi Crosariol, "IBM Canada's New Gold Mine: Education," *Financial Times of Canada*, March 30, 1992, 9.

104. Timothy Pritchard, "Ontario Firm Gears up for $40-million Rockwell Deal," *The Globe and Mail*, Monday, March 30, 1992, B1.

105. John Heinzl, "Retailer Hammers Home Message to Suppliers," *The Globe and Mail*, Tuesday, March 31, 1992, B1, 17.

CHAPTER 9

1. *The York Region Business Journal*, April 1992, 22.

2. Timothy Pritchard, "GM Canada Management in Despair Over Union Vote," *The Globe and Mail*, Thursday, March 19, 1992, B1.

3. Mark Stevenson, "Schneider Is On a Roll," *Financial Times of Canada*, April 6, 1992, 8.

4. The consumer products division of Crayola is part of Binney and Smith International Inc., which considers this Lindsay plant the "pearl" of its three plants in North America. Each year "it turns out 100 million crayons, 22 million markers, 1 million jars of paint and more than 135,000 kilograms (about 300,000 pounds) of clay." Canadian Press, "Crayola Plant in Lindsay Scores Top Marks," *The Toronto Star*, Sunday, April 5, 1992, H4.

5. Michael E. Rock, "Reflections," *The Condominium Manager*, Vol. 12, No. 2, Summer 1991, 26 - 27.

6. John Stackhouse, "Abitibi's Last Stand," *Report on Business Magazine*, October 1991, 23 - 28, 30, 32, 34.

7. John Stackhouse, *ibid.*, 25.

8. John Stackhouse, *ibid.*, 34.

9. Craig R. Hickman. *Mind of a Manager, Soul of a Leader*. Toronto: John Wiley & Sons, Inc., 1990, 14 - 18, 283.

10. Anne Kingston, "Power to the People," *Report on Business Magazine*, July 1992, 15 - 22.

11. Edward Shevardnadze, "The Other Side of the Wall," *The Globe and Mail*, Thursday, April 2, 1992, A19.

12. Michael Stern, "Cranky Managers Mean Trouble," *The Globe and Mail*, Monday, April 6, 1992, B4.

13. Warren Bennis. *On Becoming a Leader*. Don Mills, Ontario: Addison-Wesley, 1989, 39 - 41.

14. Warren Bennis, *ibid.*, 44.

15. William A. Dimma, "Real Industry Leaders Are Made Under Pressure as They Gradually Grow Into The Challenging Job," *The Toronto Star*, Monday, December 19, 1988, D3.

16. Craig Hickman, *op. cit.*, 45-51.

17. Robert Kent, "You Can't Lead Without Managing," *The Globe and Mail*, Saturday, July 14, 1990, B2.

18. John Raymond, "Worth Repeating," *The Globe and Mail*, Tuesday, April 7, 1992, B6.

19. Morgan W. McCall, Jr., Michael M. Lombardo, "Off the Track: Why and How Successful Executives Get Derailed" (Technical Report No. 21); Carol Hymowitz, "Five Main Reasons Why Managers Fail," *The Wall Street Journal*, May 2, 1988, 21.

20. Peter Kizilos, "Fixing Fatal Flaws," *Training*, Vol. 28, No. 9, September 1991, 68.

21. Fred Luthans, "Successful vs. Effective Real Managers," *Academy of Management Executive*, May 2, 1988, 127 - 32.

22. Peter Kizilos, *op. cit.*, 66.

23. *Ibid.*, 68.

24. Ken Romain, "Deal Moves Bombardier Into Aerospace Elite," *The Globe and Mail*, Friday, January 24, 1992, B1.

25. "Canadian Couple Carve Niche as Trade Finance Consultants," *The Financial Post*, Thursday, August 22, 1991, 17.

26. Patrick Sullivan, "OHIP Quirk Opened Private-clinic Niche," *The Globe and Mail*, Tuesday, March 13, 1990, C6.

27. Thomas J. Peters, Robert H. Waterman, Jr. *In Search of Excellence*. New York: Warner Books, 1982, 280.

28. Peters and Waterman, *ibid.*, 281 - 82.

29. Peters and Waterman, *ibid.*, 287.

30. Office of the President, "A Personal Vision For a Preferred Future," Inter Office Memorandum to all employees, March 10, 1992, Appendix C, 1 - 2.

31. Douglas M. McGregor, "The Human Side of Enterprise," *Management Review*, Vol. 56, November 1957, 22 - 28, 88 - 92.

32. Albert J. Robinson, "McGregor's Theory X-Theory Y Model," in *The 1972 Annual Handbook For Group Facilitators*. Eds. J. William Pfeiffer, John E. Jones. Iowa City, Iowa: University Associates, 121 - 23.

33. Louis A. Allen, "M for Management: Theory Y Updated," *Personnel Journal*, December 1973, 1061 - 67, esp. 1066 - 67.

34. Robert MacLeod, "No-show Workers Plague City," *The Globe and Mail*, Friday, April 10, 1992, A1, 17.

35. Donn Downey, "McKenna Attacks Education System," *The Globe and Mail*, Thursday, April 8, 1992, A1.

36. John Raymond, "Worth Repeating," *The Globe and Mail*, Thursday, April 9, 1992, B8.

37. Ralph M. Stogdill. *Handbook of Leadership*. New York: Free Press, 1974.

38. Associated Press, "Wal-Mart Founder Built Success On Service," *The Globe and Mail*, Monday, April 6, 1992, B4.

39. "Domino's Pizza Owner Resumes Firm Leadership," *The Toronto Star*, Monday, November 9, 1991, B6.

40. Bettijane Levine, "The New Boss," *The Ottawa Citizen*, Saturday, December 1, 1990, J1.

41. Renis Likert. *New Patterns of Management*. New York: McGraw-Hill, 1961.

42. Paul Hersey, Kenneth H. Blanchard. *Management of Organizational Behaviour*. Englewood Cliffs, N.J.: Prentice-Hall, 1988.

43. Developed by Michael E. Rock, John Miteff, professors, School of Business, Seneca College, Toronto, 1983.

44. Michael. E. Rock, "Reflections," *ACMO Manager*, Vol. 7, No. 2, July 1986, 24 - 25.

45. Description by Janice E. Rock, B.A., M.A., Jungian relationship therapist, personal communication.

46. Jack Miller, "Why Bosses Live Longer," *The Toronto Star*, Saturday, December 8, 1990, D4.

47. What follows is a compilation from: Richard L. Daft. *Management*. Second Edition. Toronto: The Dryden Press, 1991, 372-73; John R. Schermerhorn, Jr., Andrew J. Templer, R. Julian Cattaneo, James G. Hunt, Richard N. Osborn. *Managing Organizational Behaviour*. First Canadian Edition. Toronto: John Wiley & Sons, 1992, 495-96; and Frederick A. Starke, Robert W. Sexty. *Contemporary Management in Canada*. Scarborough, Ontario: Prentice-Hall Canada Inc., 1992, 295 - 97.

48. Michael E. Rock, "Reflections," *ACMO Manager*, Vol. 8, No. 4, July/August 1987, 29 - 30.

49. Richard L. Daft, *op. cit.*, 461.

50. Ann Walmsley, "Trading Places," *The Globe and Mail, Report on Business Magazine*, March 1992, 17 - 22, 25, 27.

51. Margot Gibb-Clark, "Autonomy Or Teams: Which Will Prevail?" *The Globe and Mail*, Monday, February 3, 1992, B4.

52. Arthur G. Bedeian. *Management*. Second Edition. Toronto: The Dryden Press, 1989, 459.

53. Marina Strauss, "Cossette Gets More Than Burger and Fries," *The Globe and Mail*, Thursday, November 7, 1991, B4.

54. Virginia Corner, "A Revolution in the Workplace," *The Toronto Star*, Saturday, May 21, 1988, G1, 14.

55. Eric Sundstrum, Kenneth P. De Meuse, David Futrell, "Work Teams," *American Psychologist*, Vol. 45, February 1990, 120 - 23.

56. Richard L. Daft, *op. cit.*, 473.

57. Richard L. Daft, *op. cit.*, 480 - 81.

58. J.E. Newall, "Firms Must Help Employees Strive for Excellence," *The Toronto Star*, Monday, November 2, 1987, B3; Cathryn Motherwell, "Appointments Pave Way for Nova Restructuring," *The Globe and Mail*, Wednesday, August 14, 1991, B1.

59. Walter Kiechell III, "A Hard Look at Executive Vision," *Fortune*, October 23, 1989, 207 - 11; Allan Cox, "Focus on Teamwork, Vision, and Values," *The New York Times*, February 26, 1989, F3.

60. N.M. Tichy, D.O. Ulrich, "The Leadership Challenge -- A Call for the Transformational Leader," *Sloan Management Review*, Fall, 1984, 59 - 68; B.M. Bass, "From Transactional to Transformational Leadership: Learning to Share the Vision," *Organizational Dynamics*, Winter, 1990, 19 - 31.

61. Jay A. Conger, R.N. Kanungo (Eds.). *Charismatic Leadership: The Elusive Factor in Organizational Effectiveness*. San Francisco: Jossey-Bass, 1988.

62. Bob Papoe, "Soft Drink Chief Plays Hard To Win," *The Toronto Star*, Sunday, July 14, 1991, F1 - 2.

CHAPTER 10

1. Herb Cohen. *You Can Negotiate Anything*. Secaucus, N.J.: Lyle Stuart Inc., 1980, 31.

2. Konrad Yakabuski, "Raising the Veil of Reichmann Secrecy," *The Toronto Star*, Sunday, April 12, 1992, H1, 4.

3. Dianne Maley, "The Philosopher King," *Report on Business Magazine*, December 1988, Cover, 58 - 59, 61, 63.

4. Margaret Philp, Jacquie McNish, Brian Milner, Alan Freeman, "O&Y's New Boss Having Second Thoughts," *The Globe and Mail*, Thursday, April 9, 1991, B1, 10.

5. Konrad Yakabuski, "Bankers Dissatisfied As O&Y Withholds Vital Data," *The Toronto Star*, Saturday, April 18, 1992, C1.

6. Konrad Takabuski, *op. cit.*, H1, 4.

7. 1018 Finch Avenue West, Suite 201, North York, Ontario M3J 2E1. Tel: (416) 650-5645; Fax: (416) 650-5649.

8. Herb Cohen, *op. cit.*, 18.

9. Joan Wester Anderson, "Childhood Conflicts Tax Adults," *The Toronto Star*, Tuesday, August 14, 1990, B1.

10. Robert Townsend. *Up the Organization*. New York: Alfred Knopf, 1970, 39.

11. Timothy Pritchard, "Steering Toward the Future," *The Globe and Mail*, Saturday, April 18, 1992, A1.

12. Catheryn Motherwell, "Novatel 'Fire Sale' Possible," *The Globe and Mail*, Saturday, April 4, 1992, B7.

13. Vera J. Elleson, "Competition: A Cultural Imperative?" *The Personnel and Guidance Journal*, December 1983, 195 - 98.

14. Catherine Dunphy, "What Your Boss Can Do for You," *The Toronto Star*, Tuesday, December 20, 1988, F1, 3.

15. Robert R. Blake, Jane S. Mouton, "Overcoming Group Warfare," *Harvard Business Review*, November-December 1984, 98 - 108.

16. Deborah Jones, "Seagull Flies Into Culture Clash," *The Globe and Mail*, Monday, December 2, 1991, B3.

17. Rebecca Sisco, "De-Escalating Workplace Wars," *Training*, Vol. 29, No. 2, February 1992, 75.

18. M. Deutsch, "An Experimental Study of the Effects of Cooperation and Competition Upon Group Process," *Human Relations*, Vol. 2, 1949, 199 - 232.

19. L.K. Hammond, M. Goldman, "Competition and Noncompetition and Its Relationship to Individual and Group Productivity," *Sociometry*, Vol. 24, 1961, 46 - 60.

20. Associated Press, "Texaco Pays Penzoil $3 Billion (U.S.) to End Bitter Feud," *The Globe and Mail*, Friday, April 6, 1988, B15.

21. Mikhail Gorbachev, "Was This a War to End All Wars?" *The Toronto Star*, Monday, March 2, 1992, A11.

22. Adam Smith. *An Inquiry Into the Nature and Causes of the Wealth of Nations*. Toronto: Encyclopaedia Britannica, Inc., 1952, 194b.

23. Harold W. Berkman, Linda L. Neider. *The Human Relations of Organizations*. Boston, Mass.: Kent Publishing Co., 1987, 314.

24. Kevyn D.I. Nightingale, "Why Being 'Correct' Isn't Right," *The Globe and Mail*, Monday, January 20, 1992, A16.

25. Editorial, "Message from Chairman Adam," *The Financial Post*, Thursday, April 16, 1992, 14.

26. Roy MacLaren, "Preparing Canadians to Cope With Change is Principle Challenge," *The Toronto Star*, Sunday, February 16, 1992, B4.

27. A. Paul Gill, "Junk-food Economy Unhealthy for Youth," *The Globe and Mail*, Monday, September 2, 1991, A11.

28. T. Janz, D. Tjosvold, "Costing Effective *vs.* Ineffective Work Relationships," *Canadian Journal of Administrative Sciences*, Vol. 2, 1985, 43-51.

29. S. Robbins. *Managing Organizational Conflict: A Nontraditional Approach*. Englewood Cliffs, New Jersey: Prentice-Hall, 1974, 11 - 14.

30. R. Adler, N. Towne. *Looking Out/Looking In*. Fort Worth, Texas: Holt, Rinehart and Winston, 1990, 357.

31. E. Boulding, "Further Reflections on Conflict Management," R. Kahn, E. Boulding (Eds.). *Power and Conflict in Organizations*. New York: Basic Books, 1964, 146 - 50.

32. Hugh J. Arnold, Daniel C. Feldman, Gerry Hunt. *Organizational Behaviour: A Canadian Perspective*. Toronto: McGraw-Hill Ryerson Limited, 1992, 683.

33. Leslie Papp, "A Macho Standoff That Hurts Everybody," *The Toronto Star*, Sunday, September 1, 1991, A1, 8.

34. *Adapted from:* Richard L. Daft. *Management*. Second Edition. Toronto: The Dryden Press, 1991, 477 - 78.

35. Janis Foord Kirk, "Disappointment Is the Affliction of this Decade," *The Toronto Star*, Saturday, April 11, 1992, J1.

36. Margaret Philp, Jacquie McNish, Brian Milner, Alan Freeman, "O&Y's New Boss Having Second Thoughts," *The Globe and Mail*, Thursday, April 9, 1991, B1, 10.

37. "Johnson Absent," *The Globe and Mail*, Monday, April 13, 1992, B2.

38. Dianne Daniel, "Enthnocultural Course Helps Professional Break Barriers," *Computing Canada*, March 15, 1990, 16.

39. John Holusha, "Soothing and Slaps From on High," *The Globe and Mail*, Thursday, March 5, 1992, B6.

40. Robert Meinbardis, "The Apprenticeship of Pierre-Karl Peladeau," *Financial Times of Canada*, February 24, 1992, 11.

41. Hugh Prather. *Note To Myself*. Moab Utah: Real People Press, 1970, no page numbers in book, but near end.

42. Virginia Galt, "Pay Equity Decision Enrages Rights Panel," *The Globe and Mail*, Thursday, February 27, 1992, A7.

43. Joan Skelton, "Terms of Endearment That Aren't," *The Globe and Mail*, Friday, December 27, 1991, A14.

44. John Heinzl, "Burger King Makes It His Way, Right Away," *The Globe and Mail*, Friday, April 17, 1992, B1.

45. Richard Julien, "Downsizing Trend Breeds New Genre of Service," *Computing Canada*, February 17, 1992, 40.

46. Daniel Girard, "Beaver Canoe Sinks Tossing 180 Out of Work," *The Toronto Star*, Wednesday, April 15, 1992, F1.

47. Marina Strauss, "Levi Aims to Fit With Conservative Clientele," *The Globe and Mail*, Thursday, July 18, 1991, B4.

48. Marina Strauss, "First, You Have to Get the Attention of Teens," *The Globe and Mail*, Friday, July 12, 1991, B3.

49. Anne Wilson Schaef, Diane Fassel. *The Addictive Organization*. San Francisco: Harper & Row 1988, 172.

50. Ronald B. Adler, Lawrence B. Rosenfeld, Neil Towne. *Interplay: The Process of Interpersonal Communication*. Fifth Edition. Toronto: Harcourt Brace Jovanovich College Publishers, 1992, 362. The following discussion is a summary of some of their ideas on functional and dysfunctional conflicts.

51. Hugh Prather, *op. cit.*, no page reference, but near end.

52. Harold W. Berkman, Linda L. Neider. *The Human Relations of Organizations*. Boston, Mass.: Kent Publishing Co., 1987, 331.

53. W.G. Stephan, "Intergroup Relations," in G. Lindzey, E. Aronson (Eds.). *The Handbook of Social Psychology*. Third Edition. New York: Random House, 1985, Vol. 2, 599 - 658.

54. *See* "Creating Strategies For Win/Win Solutions," in Sherod Miller, Daniel B. Wackman, Dallas R. Demmitt, Nancy J. Dimmitt. *Working Together. Productive Communication On The Job*. Minneapolis, Minn.: Interpersonal Communication Programs, Inc., 1985, Section 6:1 - 6.

55. Karen Howlett, "Moysey Says He Was Fired," *The Globe and Mail*, Wednesday, April 15, 1992, B1, 23.

56. *Slightly adapted from:* Susan R. Glaser. *Toward Communication Competency: Developing Interpersonal Skills*. Toronto: Holt, Rinehart and Winston, 1980, 211 - 12.

57. Kenneth Thomas, "Conflict and Conflict Management," in M.D. Dunnett, ed. *Handbook of Industrial and Organizational Behavior*. Chicago: Rand McNally, 1976, 889 - 935; T. Ruble, K.W. Thomas, "Support for a Two-Dimensional Model of Conflict Behavior," *Organizational Behavior and Human Performance*, 1976, Vol. 16, 145.

58. Found in Jon Winokur (Ed.). *The Portable Curmudgeon*. Scarborough, Ontario: NA: Books (New American Library), 1987, 73.

59. Maggie Scarf, "Images That Heal," *Psychology Today*, September 1980, 39.

60. Hans J. Eysenck, "Health's Character," *Psychology Today*, December 1988, 28.

61. "Criticism At Work Can Be Constructive If Your Self-image is Good, Expert Says," *The Toronto Star*, Thursday, November 9, 1989, L8.

62. Leslie Smith, "Investing in the Right Image," *The Financial Times of Canada*, March 2, 1992, 19.

63. Michael Stern, "Forget Your Abilities -- Make Sure of Fit," *The Globe and Mail*, Monday, August 12, 1991, B1, 4.

64. Morden Shapiro, "Image Management," *The Bottom Line*, April 1986, 12.

65. Dr. Diane Sacks, Dr. Saul Levine, "It's Not Unusual for a Teenager to be Embarrassed About Body," *The Toronto Star*, Tuesday, September 24, 1991, F7.

66. Suzanne Alexander, "Teen-age Cosmetic Surgery Fad Dismays Experts," *The Globe and Mail*, Wednesday, September 26, 1990, D8.

67. Gary Oakes, "Man Gets Life Term in 'Macho' Killing," *The Toronto Star*, Thursday, April 16, 1992, A30.

68. Robert F. Allen, Charlotte Kraft. *The Organizational Unconscious. How To Create the Corporate Culture You Want and Need*. Englewood Cliffs, N.J.: Prentice-Hall, Inc., 1982.

69. Michael E. Rock, "Creating Excellence," *Canadian Manager*, Vol. 11, No. 3, Fall (October) 1986, 24 - 25, 28.

70. Mikhail Gorbachev, "Gorbachev's First Column: Will East and West Finally Meet?" *The Toronto Star*, Monday, February 24, 1992, A1.

71. John Naisbitt, Patricia Aburdene. *Megatrends 2000: Ten New Directions for the 1990s*. New York: William Morrow and Company, Inc., 1990, 16.

72. *Found in* Ronald B. Adler, Neil Towne. *Looking Out/ Looking In. Interpersonal Communication*. Fourth Edition. Toronto: Holt, Rinehart and Winston, 1984, 337.

73. *Adapted from:* Ronald B. Adler, Neil Towne, *op. cit.,* 337 - 43.

74. John Geddes, "Canada Is World's Best Place to Live," *The Financial Post,* Thursday, April 16, 1992, 7.

75. Len Bolger, Fraser Mustard, Gordon MacNabb, "'Clusters' Could be an Answer to Wealth-Creation," *The Financial Post,* Thursday, April 16, 1992, 17.

76. Steven L. McShane. *Canadian Organizational Behaviour.* Homewood, IL.: Irwin, 1992, 498ff.

77. John R. Schermerhorn, Jr., Andrew J. Templer, R. Julian Cattaneo, James G. Hunt, Richard N. Osborn. *Managing Organizational Behaviour.* First Canadian Edition. Toronto: John Wiley & Sons, 1992, 482ff.

78. Arthur G. Bedeian. *Management.* Second Edition. Toronto: The Dryden Press, 1989, 262.

79. Henry Mintzberg. *The Nature of Managerial Work.* New York: Harper & Row, 1973, 92 - 93.

80. Don Hellriegel, John W. Slocum, Jr., Richard W. Woodman. *Organizational Behavior.* Fifth Edition. St. Paul: West Publishing Co., 1989, 463.

81. M. Dale Beckman, David L. Kurtz, Louise E. Boone. *Foundations of Marketing.* Fifth Canadian Edition. Toronto: Dryden (a Division of Holt, Rinehart and Winston of Canada, Limited), 1992, 373.

82. Susan Gittins, "O&Y Lenders Clamor for More Information," *The Financial Post,* Thursday, April 16, 1992, 5.

83. R. Stagner, H. Rosen. *Psychology of Union-Management Relations.* Belmont, Calif.: Wadsworth, 1965, 95-96, 108 - 110.

84. In George Seldes. *The Great Thoughts.* New York: Ballantine Books, 1985, 225.

85. James Bagnall, "Trouble On The Line," *Financial Times of Canada,* April 20-26, 1992, 13.

86. John Heinzl, "Burger King Makes It His Way, Right Away," *The Globe and Mail,* Friday, April 17, 1992, B2.

87. *Adapted from:* Virgina Galt, "Algoma Workers Take Pay Cut to Own the Mill," *The Globe and Mail,* Thursday, April 16, 1992, A1, 2.

88. Terence Corcoran, "Algoma Is No Panacea for the 1990s," *The Globe and Mail,* Saturday, April 18, 1992, B2.

89. Also known as *distributive negotiation* and based on equity theory. See Jeffrey Gandz, "Justice At Work," in Kalburghi M. Scrinivas (Ed.). *Human Resource Management: Contemporary Perspectives in Canada.* Toronto: McGraw-Hill Ryerson Limited, 1984, 499 - 523, esp. 500 - 01.

90. Also known as *integrative bargaining* or *negotiation.* See Gregory B. Northcraft, Margaret A. Neale. *Organizational Behavior. A Management Challenge.* Toronto: The Dryden Press, 1990, 246.

91. *See* R. Fisher, W. Ury. *Getting to Yes.* New York: Houghton-Mifflin, 1981, 10 - 14.

92. *Adaptation of* R. Fisher, W. Ury, *op. cit.;* Gregory B. Northcraft, Margaret A. Neale, *op. cit.,* 247 - 48.

93. Damien Cox, "They're Back! NHL Strike Ends," *The Toronto Star,* Saturday, April 11, 1992, A1, 24.

94. Allen L. Appell. *A Practical Approach to Human Behavior in Business.* Columbus, Ohio: Charles E. Merrill, 1984, 92.

95. Drew Fagan, "Trade Teams Toe Common Ground," *The Globe and Mail,* Saturday, April 18, 1992, B3.

96. Herb Cohen, *op. cit.,* 161.

97. *Adapted from:* Herb Cohen, *ibid.,* 163.

98. *See* Peter F. Drucker, "The Coming of the New Organization," *Harvard Business Review,* January-February 1988, 45 - 53.

99. Paul Bernstein, "The Trust Culture," *SAM Advanced Management Journal,* Summer 1988, 6.

100. Denis D. Umstot. *Understanding Organizational Behavior.* Second Edition. St. Paul: West Publishing Co., 1988, 276.

101. Denis D. Umstot, *op. cit.,* 280. The questions below are an adaptation.

102. Mary Ormsby, "Elizabeth Manley Sharing the Story of Past Depression," *The Toronto Star,* Saturday, April 18, 1992, B6.

103. Jean Monty, Bell Canada chairman, in John Raymond, "Worth Repeating," *The Globe and Mail,* Thursday, April 16, 1992, B6.

104. Susan Delacourt, "Steady Hand On Unity Helm," *The Globe and Mail,* Saturday, April 18, 1992, A4.

CHAPTER 11

1. Rosalie Abella, "History Is a Tutor, and She Is Its Awestruck Student," *The Globe and Mail,* Friday, May 15, 1992, A14.

2. Alan Freeman, "The Department That Counts," *The Globe and Mail,* Monday, June 1, 1992, A5.

3. Editorial, "Keep Hiring Practices Fair," *The Financial Post,* Wednesday, June 3, 1992, 10.

4. Editorial, "Job Losses Waste Efficiency Gains," *The Toronto Star,* Saturday, May 30, 1992, C2.

5. Edmund Faltermayer, "Is This Layoff Necessary?" *Fortune,* June 1, 1992, 71.

6. Steven B. Kaufman, "Tough Times Mean Demoralized Workers," *Training,* Vol. 29, No. 2, February 1992, 12 - 13.

7. H. Jackson Brown, Jr. (compiler). *A Father's Book of Wisdom.* Nashville, Tennessee: Rutledge Hill Press, 1990, 143.

8. Thomas H. Stone, Noah M. Meltz. *Human Resource Management in Canada.* Second Edition. Toronto: Holt, Rinehart and Winston of Canada, 1988, 13.

9. Michael Stern, "HR Losing Goody-Two-Shoes Image," *The Globe and Mail,* Monday, May 18, 1992, B4.

10. John Raymond, "Worth Repeating," *The Globe and Mail*, Monday, July 20, 1992, B3.

11. Margot Gibb-Clark, "Give Employees More Say in Pensions," *The Globe and Mail*, Monday, June 15, 1992, B4.

12. R. M. Steers. *Organizational Effectiveness: A Behavioral View*. Santa Monica, Calif.: Goodyear Publishing Co., Inc., 1977, 5.

13. The Supreme Court of Canada has established 65 years of age as the required age for retirement. There have been unsuccessful challenges to this mandatory requirement. "Supreme Court Upholds Mandatory Retirement," *Human Resources Management in Canada*, Report Bulletin No. 95, January 1991, 1 - 2. However, there are proposed changes to the Canadian Human Rights Act now before the House of Commons. "Bill C-108 would amend the act to eliminate the automatic exemption which now applies to mandatory retirement policies, requiring employers to prove the policies are a bona fide occupational requirement," in "Federal Human Rights law to be Changed," *Canadian HR Reporter*, January 15, 1993, 4.

14. Richard Worzel, "Aging Work Force Worries Japan Inc.," *The Globe and Mail*, Tuesday, June 9, 1992, B24.

15. Richard L. Daft, Patricia A. Fitzgerald. *Management*. First Canadian Edition. Toronto: Dryden Canada, 1992, 380.

16. Royal Bank Letter, "The Civilized Workplace," Vol. 73, No. 2, March/April 1992, 4.

17. Robert W. Sexty. *Canadian Business: Issues and Stakeholders*. Scarborough, Ontario: Prentice-Hall Canada Inc., 1991, 125.

18. Sexty, *ibid.*, 128.

19. George T. Milkovich, William F. Glueck, Richard T. Barth, Steven L. McShane. *Canadian Personnel/Human Resource Management: A Diagnostic Approach*. Plano, Texas: Business Publications, Inc., 1988, 19.

20. Michael Stern, "HR Losing Goody-Two-Shoes Image," *The Globe and Mail*, Monday, May 18, 1992, B4.

21. Thomas H. Stone, Noah M. Meltz, *op. cit.*, 134.

22. George T. Milkovich, et al., *op. cit.*, 154.

23. Karen R. Gillespie. *Creative Supervision*. Second Edition. San Diego: Harcourt Brace Jovanovich, 1989, 211.

24. Robert P. Gephart, Jr., Larry Charach, "Human Resource Planning: Balancing Supply and Demand," in Kalburghi M. Srinivas (Ed.). *Human Resource Management: Contemporary Perspectives in Canada*. Toronto: McGraw-Hill Ryerson Limited, 1984, 146.

25. See *Singh vs. Security and Investigated Services Ltd.*, Ontario Board of Inquiry, May 30, 1977; cited in Gary Dessler, Alvin Turner. *Human Resource Management in Canada*. Canadian Fifth Edition. Scarborough, Ontario: Prentice-Hall Canada Inc., 1992, 55, 72.

26. *CCDO Guide*. 6th. ed. Ottawa: Employment and Immigration Canada, 1986. Catalogue No. MP53-8/1986E.

27. John R. Schermerhorn, Jr., Andrew J. Templer, R. Julian Cattaneo, James G. Hunt, Richard N. Osborn. *Managing Organizational Behaviour*. First Canadian Edition. Toronto: John Wiley & Sons, 1992, 204.

28. George T. Milkovich, Jerry M. Newman. *Compensation*. Plano, Texas: Business Publications, Inc., 1984, 60.

29. Priti Yelaja, "Woman's Complaint of Job 'Streaming' May Set Precedent," *The Toronto Star*, Friday, May 22, 1992, A8.

30. "Virgin Attendants Tough to Find, Chinese Airline Says," *The Toronto Star*, Tuesday, April 21, 1992, B1.

31. Drusilla Menaker, "Women Need Not Apply in Former Workers' State," *The Globe and Mail*, Monday, June 15, 1992, A10.

32. Royal Bank Letter, "The Civilized Workplace," Vol. 73, No. 2, March/April 1992, 2.

33. Royal Bank Letter, *ibid.*, 3.

34. Herbert J. Sweeney, Kenneth S. Teel, "A New Look at Promotion From Within," *Personnel Journal*, August 1979, 535.

35. Michael Stern, "Your Résumé Can Open or Close Doors," *The Globe and Mail*, Monday, June 8, 1992, B4.

36. Employment and Immigration Canada. *Employment Programs and Services for Canadians*. Catalogue No. WH-7-092. Ottawa: Minister of Supply and Services Canada, 1981. *See also* Employment and Immigration Canada. *People Planning*. Cat. No. MP 43-74/1979; *The National Job Bank*. Cat. No. 1090, February, 1980.

37. *Slightly adapted from:* Jac Fitz-enz, Ph.D. *How to Measure Human Resources Management*. New York: McGraw-Hill Book Company, 1984, 54 - 55.

38. William Owens, "Background Data," *Handbook of Industrial and Organizational Psychology*. Ed. M. Dunnette. Chicago: Rand McNally, 1976.

39. Thomas H. Stone, Noah M. Meltz , *op. cit.*, 224.

40. Hari Das, "Organizational Engagement: Recruitment, Selection and Orientation," in Kalburghi M. Srinivas (Ed.). *Human Resource Management: Contemporary Perspectives in Canada*. Toronto: McGraw-Hill Ryerson Limited, 1984, 173.

41. Tom Janz, Lowell Hellervik, David G. Gilmore. *Behavior Description Interviewing*. Boston: Allyn and Bacon, Inc., 1986, 14.

42. Tom Janz et al., *op. cit.*, 15. *See also* N. Schmidt, "Social and Situational Determinants of Interview Decisions: Implications for the Employment Interview," *Personnel Psychology*, Vol. 29, No. 1, 1976, 79 - 101.

43. L. Ulrich, D. Trumbo, "The Selection Interview Since 1949," *Psychological Bulletin*, Vol. 63, 1965, 100 - 116.

44. Richard D. Arvey, James E. Campion, "The Employment Interview: A Summary and Review of Recent Research," *Personnel psychology*, Vol. 35, 1982,

282 - 322.

45. Ernest J. McCormick, Daniel R. Ilgen. *Industrial Psychology*. Seventh Edition. Englewood Cliffs, New Jersey: Prentice-Hall, Inc., 1980, 192.

46. *Summarized and adapted from:* Joseph P. Zima, "Distorting Influences in the Interview," in *Interviewing: Key to Effective Management*. Toronto: SRA (Science Research Associates, Inc.), 1983, 17 - 32. *Also,* William C. Donaghy. *The Interview: Skills and Applications*. Dallas, Texas: Scott, Foresman and Company, 1984, *passim,* but especially for purposes here, 39 - 73.

47. Richard D. Arvey, James E. Campion, "The Employment Interview: A Summary and Review of Recent Research," in Craig Eric Schneier, Richard W. Beatty, Glenn M. McEvoy. *Personnel/Human Resource Management Today: Readings and Commentary*. Second Edition. Reading, Mass.: Addison-Wesley Publishing Company, 1986, 256 - 58.

48. An excellent and enjoyable reference for the supervisor is the following book: "The Canadian Human Rights Act: A Guide," Canadian Human Rights Commission, Minister of Supply and Services Canada, 1985, Cat. No. HR21-18/1984.

49. Stephen Bindman, "Gays Win New Rights Under Planned law," *The Toronto Star*, Saturday, June 13, 1992, A8.

50. Canadian Press, "Top Court Ponders Gay 'Family' Question," *The Globe and Mail*, Thursday, June 4, 1992, A4. *See also* Stephen Bindman, "Gay Lovers Forced to Split," *The Toronto Star*, Monday, June 9, 1992, D2: "Although neither federal nor provincial laws in Canada explicitly prohibit same-sex marriages, judges have traditionally recognized that marriage is 'the union of a man and a woman'."

51. Canadian Press, "Canada Watch," *The Globe and Mail*, Tuesday, June 16, 1992, A7. "gay couples have been asking the courts for a definition of the family that would include them too," Gerald Hannon, "How Gay Society Is Blazing a Trail for the Future," *The Globe and Mail*, Saturday, June 27, 1992, D4.

52. Margot Gibb-Clark, "'Family' Feud Over Gay Couples," *The Globe and Mail*, Monday, June 8, 1992, B2. *See also* Sean Fine, "Top Court Rejects Gay Man's Claim," *The Globe and Mail*, Friday, February 26, 1993, A1, 2; David Vienneau, "Top Court Denies Family Benefits to Gay Couples," *The Toronto Star*, Friday, February 26, 1993, A1, 14; Quotes, "What Exactly Is a Canadian Family?" *The Globe and Mail*, Tuesday, March 2, 1993, B21.

53. Thomas Claridge, "Ontario Court Uses Power to 'Read In' Words Not in Law," *The Globe and Mail*, August 8, 1992, A1, 5.

54. Thomas H. Stone, Noah M. Meltz, *op. cit.*, 72.

55. William B. Werther Jr., Keith Davis, Hermann F. Schwind, Hari Das. *Canadian Human Resource Management*. Third Edition. Toronto: McGraw-Hill Ryerson Limited, 1990, 76.

56. Material from Thomas H. Stone, Noah M. Meltz, *op. cit.*, 232ff.

57. George T. Milkovich et al., *op. cit.*, 295.

58. "Baby Formula Maker Faces Pricing Charges," *The Toronto Star*, Sunday, June 14, 1992, B6.

59. Erik Heinrich, "Canadian Retailers Pummelled by Theft," *The Financial Post*, Wednesday, May 13, 1992, 6.

60. Ron Zemke, "Employee Theft" How to Cut Your Losses," *Training*, May 1986, 74.

61. Hazel de Burgh, CA, "MONEYCARE: Is Your Business Being Defrauded?" *The Markham Board of Trade Reporter*, June 1992, 4.

62. "Compensation Board Worker Is Charged with Fraud," *The Toronto Star*, Saturday, June 13, 1992, A5.

63. Abby Brown, "Employment Tests: Issues Without Clear Answers," *Personnel Administrator*, September 1985, 52; Gary Dessler, Alvin Turner, *op. cit.*, 200.

64. "Phony Academic Degrees Held by Federal Workers," *Iowa City (Iowa) Press Citizen*, March 10, 1986.

65. Howard Levitt, "Should Companies Be Hesitant to Give Ex-Employees References?" *The Toronto Star*, Monday, July 20, 1992, C3.

66. Steven L. McShane, Trudy Baal, "Rediscovering the Employee Orientation Process," *The Human Resource*, Vol. 4, No. 6, December/January 1988, 11-14.

67. C.D. Fisher, "Organizational Socialization: An Integrative View," *Research in Personnel and Human Resources Management*, Vol. 4, 1986, 132 - 137.

68. R.T. Mowday, L.M. Porter, R.M. Steers. *Employee-Organization Linkages: The Psychology of Commitment, Absenteeism, and Turnover*. New York: Academic Press, 1982, 56.

69. Karen Gillespie, *op. cit.*, 244. *See also* R.L. Klein, "Welcoming New Employees the Right Way," *Administrative Management*, July 1987, 14 - 15.

70. "More than 20 percent of new hires do not last a full year, usually because of unacceptable performance or an inability to adapt to the work culture," Claudine Kapel, "The Skills Shortage," *Human Resources Professional*, February 1992, 11.

71. E.R. Gomersall, M.S. Myer, "Breakthrough in On-the-Job Training," *Harvard Business Review*, Vol. 44, 1966, 62 - 72.

72. E.J. McGarrell, Jr., "An Orientation System That Builds Productivity," *Personnel*, November-December 1983, 32-41.

73. *See* E.H. Schein. *Career Dynamics: Matching Individual and Organizational Needs*. Reading, Mass.: Addison-Wesley Publishing Co., 1978.

74. R. Pascale, "Fitting New Employees into the Company Culture," *Fortune*, May 28, 1984, 28 - 43.

75. Ron Wolf, "What's a Great Company?" *The Toronto Star*, Sunday, May 24, 1992, F2. *See also* Thomas J. Peters, Robert H. Waterman, Jr. *In Search of Excellence*. New York: Warner Books, 1982, 243 - 44.

76. Anne Kingston, "Power to the People," *The Globe and Mail, Report on Business Magazine*, July 1992, 20.

77. Janis Foord Kirk, "Training and Retraining Are Vital to Your Career," *The Toronto Star*, Saturday, April 18, 1992, G1.

78. Barrie McKenna, "How a Megaproject Became a Millstone," *The Globe and Mail*, Tuesday, December 22, 1992, B18.

79. Thomas H. Stone, Noah M. Meltz, *op. cit.*, 277.

80. Thomas H. Stone, Noah M. Meltz, *op. cit.*, 278.

81. Ronald L. Crawford, "Employee Development," in Kalburghi M. Srinivas (Ed.). *Human Resource Management: Contemporary Perspectives in Canada*. Toronto: McGraw-Hill Ryerson Limited, 1984, 196. *Also*, Dr. Roosevelt Thomas, founder of the American Institute for Managing Diversity, says that what is needed to impliment cultural change to include diversity sensitivity in an organization is *education* and not so much *training*, that, employees have a long way to go before learning "techniques" to manage diversity, in Margot Gibb-Clark, "Attitudes to Being Different Are Changing," *The Globe and Mail*, Monday, March 1, 1993, B4.

82. Paul Solman, "Polishing the Brass," *The Globe and Mail*, Tuesday, April 28, 1992, B24.

83. Anne Kingston, "Power to the People," *The Globe and Mail, Report on Business Magazine*, July 1992, 18.

84. Jane Gadd, "IBM Centre Focuses on New Age," *The Globe and Mail*, Tuesday, April 28, 1992, B23.

85. Anne Kingston, "Power to the People," *The Globe and Mail, Report on Business Magazine*, July 1992, 20.

86. "New Worker Power at Chrysler Called Sure-Fire Way to Deliver," *The Toronto Star*, Saturday, June 6, 1992, C1.

87. Edmund Faltermayer, "Is This Layoff Necessary?" *Fortune*, June 1, 1992, 71, 72.

88. Harvey Enchin, "Canada Loves Quality, in Theory," *The Globe and Mail*, Friday, May 15, 1992, B1, 2. Enchin opens the article with the following sentence: "Canadian companies missed the quality train when it left the station years ago. Finally on board, they have no idea where they are going."

89. Arthur G. Bedeian. *Management*. Second Edition. Chicago: The Dryden Press, 1989, 306.

90. John Raymond, "Worth Repeating," *The Globe and Mail*, Wednesday, April 22, 1992, B6.

91. John Raymond, "Worth Repeating," *The Globe and Mail*, Wednesday, June 17, 1992, B12.

92. Michael Salter, "Makeovers, Executive-Style, Back in Business," *The Financial Post*, September 1, 1984, 19.

93. *Human Resource Planning: A Guide for Employers*. Ottawa: Minister of Supply and Services Canada, 1983, Cat. No. MP43-146/1983, 8.

94. Jane Gadd, *op. cit.*, B23.

95. Timothy Pritchard, "Blood, Sweat and Gears: GM Reinvents the Factory," *The Globe and Mail*, Tuesday, June 16, 1992, B28.

96. John Raymond, "Worth Repeating," *The Globe and Mail*, Tuesday, June 16, 1992, B10.

97. *Rasaneh* (The First Persian/Iranian Publication in Canada), Vol. 5, No. 3, May 1986, 12.

98. "Toronto's Face Reflects the World," *The Toronto Star*, The Toronto Star, Sunday, June 7, 1992, A1, 12 - 13.

99. Margot Gibb-Clark, "Racists Bring Their Biases to Work," *The Globe and Mail*, Monday, May 11, 1992, B4.

100. Stephen M. Panko. *Martin Buber*. Waco, Texas: Word Books, Publishers, 1976, 119.

101. Linda Diebel, "Soul-destroying Racism Sparked L.A. Riots," *The Toronto Star*, Sunday, May 3, 1992, A1.

102. Craig McInnes, Martin Mittelstaedt, Lila Sarick, "Discrimination Pervasive, Lewis Says," *The Globe and Mail*, Wednesday, June 10, 1992, A13.

103. Michael E. Rock, "Paths to Dialogue: Multiculturalism in Canada," *Rasaneh* (The First Persian-English Publication in Canada), Vol. 7, No. 7, November 16-December 15, 1988, 7. Dr. Roosevelt Thomas, founder of the American Institute for Managing Diversity, points out the goal of diversity is to have everybody "accept the mix" which means that supervisors will have to learn to manage employees who are not like them and also change their way of life, in Margot Gibb-Clark, "Attitudes to Being Different Are Changing," *The Globe and Mail*, Monday, March 1, 1993, B4.

104. William B. Werther, Jr., et al., *op. cit.*, 300 - 01.

105. John Raymond, "Worth Repeating," *The Globe and Mail*, Wednesday, May 13, 1992, B8.

106. Canadian Press, "Government Hiring of Natives Declining," *The Globe and Mail*, Monday, June 15, 1992, A4.

107. "'Drifter' Found a Puzzling Life as Crown Attorney in the North," *The Toronto Star*, Sunday, June 14, 1992, B10.

CHAPTER 12

1. Vaclav Havel, "The Honest Politician," *Saturday Night*, June 1992, 64. *See also* Vaclav Havel. *Summer Meditations*. Toronto: Knopf Canada, 1992.

2. Brian S. Tracy, "I Can't, I Can't," *Management World*, Volume 15, Number 4, April-May 1986, 1, 8, Administrative Management Society, Washington, D.C.

3. Bob Papoe, "A Souper Effort," *The Toronto Star*, Sunday, April 19, 1992, H1, 4.

4. Jo-el Glenn Brenner, "The Universe of Mars Inc.," *The Toronto Star*, Sunday, May 10, 1992, H5.

5. Barbara Aarsteinsen, "Crayola Staff Tickled Pink by Surge in U.S. Demand," *The Toronto Star*, Saturday, May 16, 1992, F1.

6. Harvey Enchin, "Competitiveness Not New to Canadians," *The Globe and Mail*, Thursday, May 7, 1992, B4.

7. Katherine Gay, "Performance Appraisal a Two-Way Street," *The Financial Post*, July 20, 1992, S19.

8. John R. Schermerhorn, Jr., Andrew J. Templer, R. Julian Cattaneo, James G. Hunt, Richard N. Osborn. *Managing Organizational Behaviour*. First Canadian Edition. Toronto: John Wiley & Sons, 1992, 107.

9. Richard L. Daft, Patricia A. Fitzgerald. *Management*. First Canadian Edition. Toronto: Dryden Canada, 1992, 12.

10. Arthur Bedeian. *Management*. Second Edition. Chicago: The Dryden Press, 1989, 22.

11. Michael H. Mescon, Timothy S. Mescon, "Cold Storage: Not a Winning Strategy," *Sky*, Vol. 15, February 1986, 100.

12. Harold Geneen with Alvin Moscow. *Managing*. Garden City, New York: Doubleday, 1984, 285.

13. Ron Wolf, "What's a Great Company?" *The Toronto Star*, Sunday, May 24, 1992, F2.

14. Virginia Galt, "Union's Macho Image Undergoes Transformation," *The Globe and Mail*, Saturday, May 30, 1992, A8.

15. Patricia Pitcher, "Directors Under Fire," *Report on Business Magazine*, May 1992, 22 - 23.

16. Bert Hill, "Managers Feel Overworked, Study Finds," *The Toronto Star*, Thursday, June 18, 1992, A18.

17. Anne Kingston, "Power to the People," *The Globe and Mail, Report on Business Magazine*, July 1992, 22.

18. John Heinzl, "Crayon Plant a Brighter Place," *The Globe and Mail*, Thursday, June 18, 1992, B2. *See also* Jennifer Wells, "Winning Colours," *The Globe and Mail, Report on Business*, July 1992, 26 - 27, 29 - 30, 32, 34 - 35.

19. Michael A. Silva. *Creating Excellence: Managing Corporate Culture, Strategy, and Change in the New Age*. Scarborough, Ontario: New American Library (a Plume Book), 1984.

20. "The mark of a true mentor is the power to influence a career," in Leslie Goodson, "The Mentor Model," *Human Resources Professional*, March 1992, 19. Selected organizations with mentor-protegé programs in place include the Ontario Public Service, Imperial Oil Ltd., Products Division, and Canada Mortgage and Housing Corporation.

21. Paul Barker, "Regrouping of Compaq," *Computing Canada*, June 22, 1992, 4.

22. Lawrence Surtees, "Bill and Ted's Adventure Will be a Tough Journey," *The Globe and Mail*, Monday, June 15, 1992, B1.

23. Martin Levin, "Scan," *Financial Times of Canada*, April 20, 1992, 27.

24. Claudine Kapel, "Widening the Pool," *The Human Resources Professional*, May 1992, 13.

25. *Adapted from:* Karen R. Gillespie. *Creative Supervision*. Second Edition. San Diego: HBJ: Harcourt Brace Jovanovich, Publishers, 1989, 393.

26. O. Jeff Harris, Sandra J. Hartman. *Human Behavior at Work*. Saint Paul: West Publishing Company, 1992, 186, 474; citing research from Edwin A. Locke, "Toward a Theory of Task Motivation and Incentives," *Organizational Behavior and Human Performance*, Volume 3, Number 1, February 1968, 157 - 189; Gary P. Latham, Gary A. Yukl, "A Review of Research on the Application of Goal Setting in Organization," *Academy of Management Journal*, Volume 18, Number 4, December 1975, 824 - 845.

27. For a more through discussion, see Thomas H. Stone, Noah M. Meltz. *Human Resource Management in Canada*. Second Edition. Toronto: Holt, Rinehart and Winston of Canada, Limited., 1988, 55.

28. Maria Leonard, "Challenges to the Termination-at-Will Doctrine," *Personnel Administrator*, February 1983, 49-56.

29. Wendell L. French. *The Personnel Management Process*. Boston: Houghton Mifflin Company, 1978, 522.

30. David Shoalts, "Lindros 'Trade' a Tale of Two Cities," *The Globe and Mail*, Monday, June 22, 1992, A1.

31. Virgina Galt, "Algoma Workers Take Pay Cut to Own the Mill," *The Globe and Mail*, Thursday, April 16, 1992, A1, 2.

32. Thomas H. Stone, Noah M. Meltz, *op. cit.*, 571.

33. Thomas H. Stone, Noah M. Meltz, *op. cit.*, 332.

34. G.P. Latham, K.N. Wexley, E.D. Pursell, "Training Managers to Minimize Rating Errors in the Observation of Behavior," *Journal of Applied Psychology*, Volume 60, 1975, 550 - 555.

35. Arthur G. Bedeian, *op. cit.*, 311.

36. Thomas H. Stone, Noah M. Meltz, *op. cit.*, 344.

37. Thomas H. Stone, Noah M. Meltz, *op. cit.*, 351.

38. Gary Dessler, Alvin Turner, *op. cit.*, 300.

39. Thomas H. Stone, Noah M. Meltz, *op. cit.*, 354.

40. Gregory B. Northcraft, Margaret A. Neale. *Organizational Behavior: A Management Challenge*. Chicago: The Dryden Press, 1990, 561.

41. Judith A. Pfeiffer, "Codependence: Learned Dysfunctional Behavior," *The 1991 Annual: Developing Human Resources*. 4190 Fairview Street, Burlington, Ontario L7L 4Y8: University Associates of Canada, J. William Pfeiffer, Editor, San Diego, California: University Associates 1991, 215.

42. In *Solutions for Your Workshops, Programs, & Training Needs* advertising by Pfeiffer & Company, 4190

Fairview Street, Burlington, Ontario L7L 4Y8.

43. As suggested by Terry Kellogg in his video, "Co-Dependency," from Lifeworks Communications, 20300 Excelsior Blvd., Minneapolis, Minn. 55331 -- (612) 529-9187.

44. Anne Wilson Schaef. *When Society becomes an Addict.* San Francisco: Harper & Row, 1987.

45. Anne Wilson Schaef. *The Addictive Organization.* San Francisco: Harper & Row, 1988.

46. *Adapted from:* Judith A. Pfeiffer, *op. cit.,* 216. While Dr. Pfeiffer's context is that of the family, these "rules" are easily applied to organizations.

47. Michael E. Rock, "Psychological Scuds," *Rasaneh,* March 1991, 3-6.

48. *Business Week - The Globe and Mail,* Wednesday, March 27, 1991, A20.

49. Ross A. Won Wiegand, "Advances in Secondary Prevention of Alcoholism through the Cooperation Efforts of Labor and Management in Employer Organizations," *Preventive Medicine,* Vol. 3, No. 3, 1977, 80 - 85.

50. "Alcohol - A Deadly Drug," *Pathways,* June/July 1992, 12 - 13.

51. *Pathways, op. cit.,* 13.

52. Wendy Trainor, "The Silent Victims of Alcohol," *The Globe and Mail,* Monday, May 4, 1992, B4.

53. Glenn Thede, "Employee Assistance Programs: How They Began and Where They Stand," *CTM: The Human Element,* August-September 1983, 14.

54. Kalburghi M. Scrinivas, Harish C. Jain, "Management of Human Resources and Organizational productivity," in Kalburghi M. Srinivas (Ed.). *Human Resource Management: Contemporary Perspectives in Canada.* Toronto: McGraw-Hill Ryerson Limited, 1984, 83, note 13.

55. Keith Thompson, "Alcoholism and Drug Abuse in the Workplace," *IR Research Reports,* January-February 1980, Vol. 4, 11.

56. C.A. Filipowicz, "The Troubled Employee: Whose Responsibility?" *The Personnel Administrator,* June 1979, 18.

57. Rosanne Bonanno, "Managing Codependency in the Workplace," *Canadian HR Reporter,* June 18, 1992, 16 - 17.

58. Colin Languedoc, "Battle Lines Forming over Worker Drug Tests," *The Financial Post,* April 13, 1987, 1, 4.

59. Carsten Stroud, "Do What's Fair," *Canadian Business,* April 1987, 68, 70, 101.

60. Carsten Stroud, "Rights May Be Violated by Random Drug Testing," *COSHL Monthly Report,* June 1987, 5.

61. Michael Crawford, "Storm Over Drug Testing," *The Financial Post,* Tuesday, April 21, 1992, 19.

62. Kevin Cox, "Mandatory Drug Tests Irk Crews," *The Globe and Mail,* Wednesday, May 6, 1992, A1, 2.

63. Peter Silverman, "United Effort to Beat Alcoholism," *The Financial Post,* Mat 23, 1981, 25.

64. An estimate by the Research Triangle Institute, North Carolina, reported in J. Castro, "Battling the Enemy Within," *Time,* March 17, 1986, 52 - 61.

65. Canadian Human Rights Commission, "Drug Testing," Policy 88-1, Ottawa, January 1988.

66. Paul Preston, Thomas W. Zimmerer. *Management for Supervisors.* Second Edition. Englewood Cliffs, New Jersey: Prentice-Hall, Inc., 1983, 250.

67. Robert A. Zawacki, Peter E. LaSota, "The Supervisor as Counsellor," *The 1975 Annual Handbook for Group Facilitators.* La Jolla, California: University Associates, 1975, 135 - 137.

CHAPTER 13

1. POINT and COUNTERPOINT -- Stephen Van Houten, "Changes to Labor Law Will Damage the Economy," *The Financial Post,* April 6, 1992, s4.

2. Milton Friedman, Rose Friedman. *Free to Choose.* New York: Harcourt Brace Jovanovich, 1980.

3. Albert O. Hirschman. *Exit, Voice, and Loyalty.* Cambridge, Mass.: Harvard University Press, 1971.

4. Morely Gunderson, "Union Impact on Wages, Fringe Benefits, and Productivity," in John Anderson, Morely Gunderson (Eds). *Union - Management Relations in Canada.* Don Mills, Ontario: Addison-Wesley Publishers, 1982, 247 - 268.

5. Samuel Gompers. *Labour and the Common Welfare.* In E. Wright Bakke, Clarke Kerr, Charles Amrod (Eds.). *Unions, Management and the Public.* Third Edition. New York: Harcourt, Brace & World, 1967, 42.

6. David Crane, "Big Business Fires 1st Salvo in New War with Big Labor," *The Toronto Star,* Tuesday, July 14, 1992, C1.

7. Madeline Drohan, "Internationals Lead Unions on Government Holdings," *The Globe and Mail,* September 1989, B6.

8. Steven H. Appelbaum, M. Dale Beckman, Louis E. Boone, David L. Kurtz. *Contemporary Canadian Business.* Third Edition. Toronto: Holt, Rinehart and Winston of Canada, 1990, 275.

9. Thomas A. Kochan, Thomas A. Barocci. *Human Resource Management and Industrial Relations. Text, Readings, and Cases.* Toronto: Little, Brown and Company, 1985, 15.

10. Royal Bank of Canada Letter, "About Building Morale," Vol. 58, No. 7, July 1973, 1-4.

11. Thomas A. Kochan, Thomas A. Barocci, *op. cit.,* 19.

12. John Raymond, "Worth Repeating," *The Globe and Mail,* Wednesday, July 1, 1992, B6.

13. Vaclav Havel, "The Honest Politician," *Saturday Night,* June 1992, 64.

14. Richard L. Daft, Patricia A. Fitzgerald. *Management.*

First Canadian Edition. Toronto: Dryden Canada, 1992, 386.

15. Labour Canada. *Directory of Labour Organizations in Canada, 1989*. Ottawa: Supply and Services Canada, 1989. This is "union membership as percentage of non-agricultural paid workers."

16. Thomas H. Stone, Noah M. Meltz. *Human Resource Management in Canada*. Second Edition. Toronto: Holt, Rinehart and Winston of Canada, Limited, 1988, 544.

17. Rick Cash, Alexandra Eadie, Rose Gdzodinski, "Canada: That Was Then, This is Now," *The Globe and Mail*, Wednesday, July 1, 1992, A6, citing Statistics Canada. The 29.9% figure is "union membership as percentage of civilian labour force."

18. Scott Feschuk, "How Ontario's New Rules Would Change 3 Strikes," *The Globe and Mail*, Saturday, June 20, 1992, B4. *See also* Frances Phillips, "Union Claims Second Eaton's Store," *The Financial Post*, April 21, 1984, 4.

19. *Work Life Report*, Vol. 5, No. 3, 1987, 8.

20. Richard Mackie, "Unions Target Retail Chains for Ontario Membership Drive," *The Globe and Mail*, Saturday, June 6, 1992, B1, 8.

21. Virginia Galt, "Union's Macho Image Undergoes Transformation," *The Globe and Mail*, Saturday, May 30, 1992, A8.

22. Alton Craig. *The System of Industrial Relations in Canada*. Toronto: Prentice-Hall Canada Inc., 1991, 52 - 53.

23. Richard Worzel, "Building Little Boxes for Ourselves," *The Globe and Mail*, Wednesday, June 24, 1992, A18.

24. Brian Grosman, "The Future of Loyalty," *The Globe and Mail*, Thursday, December 8, 1988, B13. These are notes from a speech he gave to the Centre for Ethics and Corporate Policy, Toronto, Ontario.

25. Steven H. Applebaum, et al., *op. cit.*, 258.

26. Brent Jang, "Labor's Job 'To Get Rid' of Mulroney White Says," *The Toronto Star*, Friday, June 12, 1992, A1, 7. After thirty-three years outside of the mainstream Canadian labour modvement, the Canadian Teamsters union finally "teamed up" with Bob White and CLC. They had been expelled "in 1960 for raiding members from other unions -- historically regarded by the labour movement as an unpardonable, although not uncommon act, between rival unions," Virginia Galt, "Canadian Teamsters, CLC Plan to Affiliate," *The Globe and Mail*, Monday, March 1, 1993, A1, 2.

27. Steven H. Applebaum et al., *op. cit.*, 260.

28. Alton W. Craig, *op. cit.*, 36-37.

29. Thomas H. Stone, Noah M. Meltz, *op. cit.*, 541.

30. Steven H. Applebaum et al., *op. cit.*, 257.

31. Thomas H. Stone, Noah M. Meltz, *op. cit.*, 541.

32. *Toronto Electric Power Commission vs. Snider* (1923) OLR at p. 455 (S.C.), rev'd OLR. loc. cit. p. 454 (1924) 2 ALR 761 (S.C. App. Div.); reference cited in Gary

33. Thomas H. Stone, Noah M. Meltz, *op. cit.*, 542.

34. Thomas H. Stone, Noah M. Meltz, *op. cit.*, 543, 568. This "cooling" or compulsory conciliation was instituted by W.L. Mackenzie King, Canada's first deputy minister of labour (and later prime minister) as part of the Industrial Disputes Investigation Act of 1907.

35. Leslie Papp, "13,500 Civil Servants May Be Unionized," *The Toronto Star*, Friday, July 17, 1992, A1.

36. Bert Spector, "Note on Why Employees Join Unions," Michael Beer, Bert Spector (Eds.). *Readings in Human Resource Management*. New York: The Free Press (A Division of Macmillan, Inc.), 1985, 153 - 162.

37. Brent Jang, *op. cit.*, A1, 7.

38. "Manitoba Introduces Labour Relations Amendments," *Canadian HR Reporter*, June 4, 1992, 6.

39. Bruce Gajerski, "Keeping Score on Labour Unions," *The Globe and Mail*, Thursday, July 2, 1992, B4. Reproduced with permission.

40. Rosemary Brown, of Calgary, Alberta, in a letter to the editor, writes: "We should not be fooled by the of working people in the U.S., where many states have such legislation [right-to-work], that the 'right to work' means the right to work for low wages, few or no benefits and in appalling working and safety conditions," Rosemary Brown, "Unions Worth Fighting For," *Calgary Herald*, July 4, 1992, A6.

41. See R.B. Freeman, J.L. Medoff. *What Do Unions Do?* New York: Basic Books, 1984.

42. The videotape, "Anatomy of a Strike," Centre for Industrial Relations and the media Centre, University of Toronto, 1983, is an excellent portrayal of what to expect in a strike situation.

43. Originally developed by the Federal Mediation Service in the United States; cited in and adapted from Thomas H. Stone, Noah M. Meltz, *op. cit.*, 575 and originally based on Ontario Ministry of labour, "Ontario Initiatives with Respect to Preventive Mediation and Quality of Working Life," W. Craig Riddell, Research Co-ordinator. *Labour-Management Co-operation in Canada*. Toronto: University of Toronto Press, 1986, 57 - 71.

44. Robert Williamson, "B.C. Pulp Strike Drags On, Losses Mount," *The Globe and Mail*, Monday, July 6, 1992, B3.

45. Editorial, "A Sure-Fire Way of Killing Jobs," *The Toronto Star*, Thursday, April 30, 1992, A28.

46. Joseph Tomkiewicz, Otto Brenner, "Union Attitudes and the 'Manager of the Future'," *The Personnel Administrator*, October 1979, 67 - 70, 72.

47. George Radwanski, Julia Luttrell. *The Will of a Nation*. Toronto: Stoddart Publishing Company, 1992, in "Combatting Canada's Crisis of Will," *The Toronto*

Star, Friday, May 8, 1992, A25.

48. Madelaine Drohan, "Unification Woes Worsen for the Weak," *The Globe and Mail*, Tuesday, June 23, 1992, B1.

49. "Labour's Extremism 'Out of Step'," *The Globe and Mail*, Monday, July 6, 1992, B4.

50. Thomas H. Stone, Noah M. Meltz, *op. cit.*, 566.

51. Steven H. Applebaum et al., *op. cit.*, 265.

52. Marian Stinson, "Algoma Suits, Boots Find Common Ground," *The Globe and Mail*, Tuesday, July 14, 1992, B5.

53. Kate Taylor, "TS Rejected Pay-Cut Offer, Musicians Reveal," *The Globe and Mail*, Tuesday, June 30, 1992, D1.

54. Kate Taylor, "TS and Musicians resume Bargaining," *The Globe and Mail*, Wednesday, July 1, 1992, C2.

55. Audrey Freedman, William E. Fullmer, "Last Rights for Pattern Bargaining," *Harvard Business Review*, March-April 1982, 30 - 48.

56. John Saunders, "Bulldozing a Union," *The Globe and Mail*, Saturday, April 18, 1992, B6.

57. John Saunders, *ibid.*, B1.

58. Scott Peschuk, "Labour Law Feared Chilling Ontario," *The Globe and Mail*, Friday, June 5, 1992, B1, 2; Deborah Wilson, "B.C.'s Labour Bill Faces Easier Ride Than Ontario's," *The Globe and Mail*, Thursday, October 29, 1992, A4; Deborah Wilson, "B.C. Labour Code Called Threat to Investment," *The Globe and Mail*, Wednesday, December 16, 1992, A4; Rosanne Bonanno, "What to Expect in Workplace Legislation in 1993," *Canadian HR Reporter*, December 17, 1992, 6 - 7, 22.

59. Editorial, "A Sure-Fire Way of Killing Jobs," *The Toronto Star*, Thursday, April 30, 1992, A28.

60. "CBC Violated Labor Code, Court Rules," *The Toronto Star*, Friday, May 15, 1992, A24.

61. Margot Gibb-Clark, "Bid to End Union at Cable Firm Rejected," *The Globe and Mail*, Thursday, July 16, 1992, B5.

62. Editorial, "Consolation Prize for Labor Unions," *The Toronto Star*, Sunday, July 22, 1992, A16.

63. Canadian Press, "Ontario Computer Firm Defects to N.S.," *The Globe and Mail*, Monday, December 28, 1992, B9.

64. Reuters News Agency, "Hiring Replacements Criticized," *The Globe and Mail*, Saturday, April 18, 1992, B6.

65. John Raymond, "Worth Repeating," *The Globe and Mail*, Monday, December 28, 1992, B4.

66. Neal Templin, "Ford Giving Every Worker 'A Purpose'," *The Globe and Mail*, Monday, December 28, 1992, B6.

67. David Olive, "Chronicles the Week," *The Globe and Mail*, Saturday, May 2, 1992, D4.

68. Ian McGugan, "Why North American Capitalism Is Facing a Day of Reckoning," *Financial Times of Canada*, July 6, 1992, 23.

69. Timothy Pritchard, "Team Concept Keeps Plant Humming," *The Globe and Mail*, Wednesday, July 13, 1992, B4.

70. Virginia Galt, "Star, Strikers Reach Tentative Agreement," *The Globe and Mail*, Wednesday, July 8, 1992, A13.

71. Drew Fagan, "Postal Deal Sign of Labour Thaw," *The Globe and Mail*, Wednesday, July 8, 1992, B1, 10.

72. A copy of this agreement can be obtained from OPSEU, 1901 Yonge Street, Toronto, Ontario M4S 2Z5.

73. *Adapted from:* Thomas H. Stone, Noah M. Meltz, *op. cit.*, 571.

74. Frank Feather, "G-Force E-4: Building the Planetary Information Economy (PIE), in *G-Forces: Reinventing the World. The 35 Global Forces Restructuring our World.* Toronto: Summerhill Press Ltd., 1989, 213.

75. Frank Feather, *ibid.*, 64.

76. Robert Williamson, "Spar Aborts Takeover Bid for MacDonald Dettwiler," *The Globe and Mail*, Thursday, July 9, 1992, B1.

77. Anne Kingston, "Power to the People," *Report on Business Magazine*, July 1992, 16.

78. Marian Stinson, "Algoma Redesigns the Workplace," *The Globe and Mail*, Monday, June 1, 1992, B1.

79. Rosanne Bonanno, "Declining the Carrot: Are Canada's Unions Still Nixing Performance Pay?" *Canadian HR Reporter*, June 4, 1992, 10 - 11.

80. Personal communication, Monday, June 29, 1992.

81. Pierre Berton. *The Great Depression: 1929-1939.* Toronto: McLelland & Stewart Inc., 1990.

82. Pierre Burton, "Will History Repeat Itself?" *The Toronto Star*, Saturday, December 29, 1990, A1.

83. Shawn McCarthy, "Jobless Rate Hits Highest Level in 8 Years," *The Toronto Star*, Saturday, July 11, 1992, A1.

84. Pierre Berton. *The Great Depression: 1929 - 1939*, 50.

85. Pierre Berton, *ibid.*, 105, 106.

86. Pierre Berton, *ibid.,*, 111.

87. Dave Todd, "From the Cradle to the Factory," *Calgary Herald*, Sunday, July 5, 1992, B1. See also the three-part series by *The Toronto Star*, Saturday-Monday, July 4 - 6, 1992.

88. Dave Todd, "Companies Keep Firm Grip on Workers," *Calgary Herald*, Sunday, July 5, 1992, B1.

89. Dave Todd, "Children Pine For Better Life," *Calgary Herald*, Sunday, July 5, 1992, B2.

90. Patrick Doyle, Jerry Zabel, "Career Planning and the Fallacy of the Future," *The 1992 Annual: Developing Human Resources.* San Diego: California: Pfeiffer & Co., 1992, 208.

91. Steven H. Applebaum et al., *op. cit.*, 275.

92. "San Francisco Law Gets Tough on VDT Regulation," *The Globe and Mail*, Tuesday, January 1, 1991, B6; *also,*

Jane Coutts, "Study links use of VDTs to menstrual problems," *The Globe and Mail*, Wednesday, September 13, 1989, A3.

93. "Overhaul Urged for Forest Sector," *The Globe and Mail*, Saturday, July 17, 1992, B1.

94. Virgina Galt, "Unions Court Service Industry," *The Globe and Mail*, Saturday, July 17, 1992, A1.

95. Editorial, "Business Misses the Boat on Labour Act Reform," *Canadian HR Reports*, June 18, 1992, 4.

96. Peter C. Newman. *The Canadian Establishment. Volume Two: The Acquisitors*.Toronto: McLelland & Stewart Inc. (An M&S Paperback), 1990, 194. See also Gerald Caplan, a former national secretary of the New Democratic Party and a public affairs consultant, who critiques capitalism, greed, and the free market by saying, "For a dozen years in the United States and eight and one-half here, unashamed conservatives have controlled government and unleashed upon us unfettered capitalist values and capitalist economics. ... Aren't those right-wing guys supposed to be such fabulous managers? Are they the ones obsessed with cutting deficits? So how come Ronald Reagan and George Bush managed the unparalled feat of saddling their coubtry with a debt of almost *$4 trillion*?" Gerald Caplan, "Unfettered Capitalism Put our Economy in Chains," *The Toronto Star*, Tuesday, March 2, 1993, A17.

CHAPTER 14

1. Bernie S. Siegel, M.D., "The Physiology of Love, Joy and Optimism," *Peace, Love & Healing. BodyMind Communication and the Path to Self-Healing: An Exploration*. New York: Harper & Row, Publishers, 1989, 7.

2. Derrick Elkin, "Slaying the Serpent of Drug Addiction," *The Globe and Mail*, Monday, July 13, 1992, A15.

3. Quoted in Derrick Elkin, *ibid.*, A15.

4. Meaning "the study of the relationship between emotions and health," June Callwood. *Emotions*. Toronto: Doubleday Canada Limited, 1986, 37.

5. Ernest lawrence Rossi. *The Psychobiology of Mind-Body Healing: New Concepts of Therapeutic Hypnosis*. New York: W.W. Norton & Company, 1986, xiv. *See also* Jay A Seitz, "I Move ... Therefore I Am," *Psychology Today*, March/April 1993, Volume 26, No. 1, 50 - 55.

6. Bernie S. Siegel, M.D. *Love, Medicine & Miracles. Lessons Learned About Self-Healing from a Surgeon's Experience with Exceptional Patients*. New York: Harper & Row, Publishers, 1986, 76 - 77.

7. Joan Borysenko, Ph.D. *Minding the Body, Mending the Mind*. Don Mills, Ontario: Addison-Wesley Publishing Company, Inc., 1987, 59.

8. Norman Cousins. *Anatomy of an Illness as Perceived by the Patient*. Toronto: Bantam Books, 1979, 118.

9. Norman Cousins. *The Healing Heart. Antidotes to Panic and Helplessness*. New York: W.W. Norton & Company, 1983, 13.

10. Jane Gadd, "IBM Centre Focuses on New Age," *The Globe and Mail*, Tuesday, April 28, 1992, B23.

11. David Olive, "Fire at Will," *Report on Business Magazine*, March 1992, 9.

12. Peter Clutterbuck, "Health in the Workplace," *The Human Resource*, Vol. 6, No. 5, 10 - 11. Figure 1 is a chart outlining this paradigm shift. *Also*, R. Sass, "The Social in the Technical: Effects on Workplace Health and Safety," *Alternatives: Perspectives on Society, Technology and Environment*, Vol. 9, No. 1, Winter 1980, 45.

13. Robert M. Cohen, "Pink Collar Stress," *The Human Resource*, April - May 1984, 14.

14. Diane Jacovella, "A Healthier Workplace: Making It Happen!" *Toronto Business*, November 1989, 32.

15. Aldred H. Neufeldt, "In Sickness and in Health," *The Human Resource*, December 1985/January 1986, 16, 17.

16. IBM, American Express, Xerox Corp., Exxon Corp., Eastman Kodak Corp., Travelers Corp., Johnson & Johnson, Amoco Corp., NationsBank Corp., the Allstate unit of Sears Roebuck and Co., Motorola and AT&T.

17. "U.S. Firms Focusing on Families," *The Globe and Mail*, Friday, July 17, 1992, B1.

18. "U.S. Firms Join Forces to Build Daycare Centres," *The Toronto Star*, Friday, July 10, 1992, D1.

19. Dorothy Marcic. *Organizational Behavior: Experiences and Cases*. Second Edition. St. Paul: West Publishing Company, 1989, 34.

20. The idea for the following tale came from Rick Fields, Peggy Taylor, Rex Weyler, Rick Ingrasci. *Chop Wood, Carry Water*. Los Angeles: Jeremy P. Tarcher, Inc., 1984, 105.

21. Kevin Cox, "Westray Rejects Allegations That Worker Safety Ignored," *The Globe and Mail*, Tuesday, May 12, 1992, A1, 5.

22. David Olive, "Chronicles The Week," *The Globe and Mail*, Saturday, May 16, 1992, D4.

23. "Dead Miners' Families Given $1 Million of Relief," *The Toronto Star*, Sunday, June 28, 1992, A8.

24. Headline, *The Globe and Mail*, Friday, October 14, 1990, B3.

25. David Olive, "Chronicles The Week," *The Globe and Mail*, Saturday, May 16, 1992, D4.

26. Peter Edwards, "New Safety Bill: Praise for All," *The Toronto Star*, Saturday, January 28, 1989, A2.

27. David Olive, "Chronicles The Week," *The Globe and Mail*, Saturday, May 16, 1992, D4.

28. Lucille Blainey, "Winners: Chemical Safety Training at Northern Telecom," *The Human Resource*, February/ March 1989, 7.

29. John Raymond, "Worth Repeating," *The Globe and*

Mail, Wednesday, July 13, 1992, B5.

30. Barry Sheehy, "Safety and Organized Labour," *The Human Resource*, February/March 1988, 12.

31. Colin Languedoc, "Battle Lines Forming Over Worker Drug Tests," *The Financial Post*, April 13, 1987, 1, 4; "Rights May Be Violated by Random Drug Testing," *COSHL Monthly Report*, June 1987, 5; Abby Brown, "Employment Test: Issues Without Clear Answers: Today's tests Screen Well, But Raise Some Tough Issues as Well," *Personnel Administrator*, Vol. 30, No. 9, September 1985, 58 - 65.

32. Documentation on this is found in Dilys Robertson, "Occupational Health and Safety," *Human Resource Management in Canada*. Scarborough, Ontario: Prentice Hall, 1987, 60,028 - 60,030.

33. Fern Schumer Chapman, "The Ruckus Over Medical Testing," *Fortune*, August 19, 1985, 57 - 58, 60 - 63.

34. Michael Crawford, "Storm Over Drug Testing," *The Financial Post*, Tuesday, April 21, 1992, 19.

35. Peter Edwards, "Ban Mandatory Drug Tests at Work, Law Group Demands," *The Toronto Star*, Wednesday, July 29, 1987, A1.

36. In a macabre sort of way, could some employees argue that there may be jobs, or job duties, which do not require abstinence from alcohol or drugs to perform the job or duty, and therefore, are all right for consumption? What's implied here, of course, is the case of an employee who has, on occasion, "too much to drink" the night before and, while "slow" at his/her job the next day, can still perform it more or less adequately without endangering another employee. Michael Crawford, *op. cit.*, 19.

37. Canadian Human Rights Commission, "Drug Testing," Policy 88-1, Ottawa, January 1988.

38. Ontario Human Rights Commission, "Human Rights In Employment," 5. Handicap.

39. Peter Edwards, *op. cit.*, A4.

40. Thomas H. Stone, Noah M. Meltz. *Human Resource Management in Canada*. Second Edition. Toronto: Holt, Rinehart and Winston of Canada, Limited, 1988, 239. *Also*, Margot Gibb-Clark, "Alcohol Tops List for On-the-job Abuse," *The Globe and Mail*, Friday, August 14, 1992, B4.

41. Eric Rolfe Greenberg, "Workplace Testing: The 1990 AMA Survey, Part 2," *Personnel*, Vol. 67, No. 7, July 1990, 26 - 29.

42. *Chemical Engineering News*, Vol. 64, No. 22, June 2, 1986, 8.

43. "Health and Safety Aspects of Alcohol and Drug Use," *The Worklife Report*, 1988, Vol. 6, No. 2, 4 (italics added).

44. Stephanie Yanchinski, "Employees Under a Microscope," *The Globe and Mail*, Saturday, February 3, 1990, D1, 3. *Also*, Canadian Press, "Genetic Testing Under Fire," *The Globe and Mail*, Thursday, May 21, 1992, A4.

45. "AIDS," *The Bulletin*, William M. Mercer Meidinger Hansen, Inc., June 1988, No. 156.

46. Philip Mathias, "The High Cost of Treating AIDS," *The Financial Post*, Inside Business, July 13, 1987, 11.

47. Martin Sewey, "Counting the Costs," *The Human Resource*, August/September 1988, 17.

48. Karen Sprenger, "Case History: Towards a Smokeless Work Environment," *The Human Resource*, June/July 1985, 15.

49. Charles Scriven, "Controlling Tobacco-Industry 'Child Abuse'," *Sojourners*, June 1992, 7.

50. William B. Werther, Jr. Keith Davis, Hermann F. Schwind, Hari Das. *Canadian Human Resource Management*. Third Edition. Toronto: McGraw-Hill Ryerson Limited, 1990, 164.

51. George T. Milkovich, William T. Glueck, Richard T. Barth, Steven L. McShane. *Canadian Personnel/Human Resource Management: A Diagnostic Approach*. Plano, Texas: Business Publications, Inc., 1988, 579.

52. Lois Sweet, "When Work Is a Pain," *The Toronto Star*, Friday, January 17, 1992, F1, 2. *Also*, Moira Farr, "Work That Wounds and How to Cure It," *Canadian Business*, December 1991, 84 - 86, 88, 90.

53. Marvin Ross, "Putting Titanium in Our Backbones," *The Globe and Mail*, Saturday, August 1, 1992, D8.

54. See Dilys Robertson, "Occupational Health and Safety," *Human Resources Management in Canada*. Toronto: Prentice-Hall Canada Inc., 1980, 60,086 - 60-087.

55. Edward Clifford, "Aging Trends a Plus for Northwest," *The Globe and Mail*, Tuesday, July 14, 1992, B11.

56. Claudine Kapel, "The Skills Shortage," *Human Resources Professional*, February 1992, 9, 11 - 12.

57. Richard Worzel, "Aging Work Force Worries Japan Inc.," *The Globe and Mail*, Tuesday, June 9, 1992, B24.

58. Richard Worzel, *ibid.*, B23.

59. Sheila Arnott, "Gray 'Panthers' Strike Back," *The Financial Post*, August 14, 1987, 17.

60. "Over-40s Recruited as Flight Attendants," *The Toronto Star*, Monday, August 5, 1991, B3. *See also* "Federal Human Rights Law to be Changed," *Canadian HR Reporter*, January 15, 1993, 4; "GM Extends Retirement Plan," *The Globe and Mail*, Saturday, November 7, 1992, B8.

61. Thomas H. Stone, Noah M. Meltz. *Human Resource Management in Canada*. Second Edition. Toronto: Holt, Rinehart and Winston of Canada, Limited, 1988, 502, citing P. Manga et al.. *Occupational Health and Safety: Issues and Alternatives*. Technical Report Series No. 6. Ottawa: Economic Council of Canada, 1981.

62. Werther et al., *op. cit.*, 439.

63. Dilys Robertson, "Occupational Health and Safety," *Human Resource Management in Canada*. Toronto: Prentice-Hall Canada Inc., 1990, 60,053 - 60,600.

64. Robertson Dilys, *ibid.*, 60,028 - 60,030.

65. Jan P. Muczyk, Eleanor Brantley Schwartz, Ephraim Smith. *Principles of Supervision: First- and Second Level Management*. Toronto: Charles E. Merrill Publishing Company, 1984, 450.

66. Thomas H. Stone, Noah M. Meltz, *op. cit.*, 510.

67. Patricia Pitcher, "Directors Under Fire," *Report on Business Magazine*, May 1992, 22 - 23.

68. Patricia Lush, "Six Westar Directors Resign," *The Globe and Mail*, Wednesday, July 22, 1992, B1, 6.

69. Robert Fulford, "Making Boards of Directors More Than Rubber-Stamp Committees," *Financial Times of Canada*, May 25, 1992, 23.

70. Peter Edwards, Lynne Ainsworth, "'Few Boards' Obeying Laws on Asbestos in Schools," *The Toronto Star*, Tuesday, January 30, 1990, A20.

71. Deborah Wilson, "Lifesaving Drugs That Can Kill," *The Globe and Mail*, Tuesday, July 7, 1992, A5.

72. "Nurse Claims Exposure to Drugs Led to Cancer That is Killing Her," *The Toronto Star*, Thursday, June 11, 1992, A6.

73. For information and a chart on the different provincial Acts and Agencies, see Dilys Robertson, "Occupational Health and Safety," *Human Resource Management in Canada*. Scarborough, Ontario: Prentice-Hall Canada Inc., 1987, 60,028 - 60,030.

74. Charles E. Reasons, "Occupational Health: Material and Chemical Aspects," Kalburghi M. Scrinivas. *Human Resource Management. Contemporary Perspectives in Canada*. Toronto: McGraw-Hill Ryerson Limited, 1984, 471 - 476.

75. Gary Dessler, Alvin Turner. *Human Resource Managemen in Canada*. Canadian Fifth Edition. Scarborough, Ontario: Prentice-Hall Canada Inc., 1992, 560.

76. George T. Milkovich, et al., *op. cit.*, 579. *Also*, Margot Gibb-Clark, "Working Conditions Cause Most Stress Among Managers," *The Globe and Mail*, Wednesday, November 9, 1988, B11.

77. Charles E. Reasons, *op. cit.*, 483 - 484.

78. J. F. Follman, Jr. *The Economics of Industrial Health*. New York: AMACOM, 1976; and N.A. Ashford. *Crisis in the Workplace: Occupational Disease and Injury*. Cambridge, Mass.: MIT Press, 1976.

79. B. Shein, "Bright Lights that Fail," *Canadian Business*, July 1985, 61 - 64, 69 - 72.

80. "Stress: The Test Americans Are Flunking," *Business Week*, April 18, 1988, 74 - 78.

81. "Job Stress Growing, Firms Say," *The Toronto Star*, Wednesday, June 3, 1992, F3.

82. Hans J. Eysenck, "Health's Character," *Psychology Today*, December 1988, 28.

83. Margot Gibb-Clark, "18-Month Suspension Recommended for Lawyer," *The Globe and Mail*, Friday, May 22, 1992, B4

84. Clarke Wallace, "Why Everything Goes Wrong," *The Financial Post Magazine*, May 1980, 22.

85. Keith Travis, Ph.D., "How to Manage Stress That's Caused by Faulty Interpersonal Relationships," *CTM: The Human Element*, April-May 1983, 14.

86. Shlomo Breznitz (Ed.). *The Denial of Stress*. New York: International Universities Press, 1984; cited in Bernie S. Siegel, M.D. *Love, Medicine & Miracles*. New York: Harper & Row, 1986, 29.

87. Richard L. Daft, Patricia A. Fitzgerald. *Management*. First Canadian Edition. Toronto: Dryden Canada (a Division of Holt, Rinehart and Winston of Canada), 1992, 699; referencing T.A. Beehr, R.S. Bhagat. *Human Stress and Cognition in Organizations: An Integrated Perspective*. New York: Wiley, 1985.

88. Robert M. Cohen, "Pink Collar Stress," *The Human Resource*, April-May 1984, 14.

89. Jerry L. Gray, Frederick A. Starke. *Organizational Behavior: Concepts and Applications*. Toronto: Merrill Publishing Company, 1988, 89.

90. Blair Justice. *Who Gets Sick: How Beliefs, Moods, and Thoughts Affect Your Health*. Los Angeles: Jeremy P. Tarcher, Inc., 1988, 43.

91. Blair Justice, *ibid.*, 55.

92. Michael Kesterton, "Social Studies," *The Globe and Mail*, Tuesday, July 7, 1992, A15.

93. Jack Halloran, Douglas Benton. *Applied Human Relations: An Organizational Approach*. Englewood Cliffs, New Jersey: Prentice-Hall, Inc., 1987, 29.

94. Hans Selye. *The Stress of Life*. New York: McGraw-Hill, 1976.

95. Janis Foord Kirk, "Disappointment is the Affliction of this Decade," *The Toronto Star*, Saturday, April 11, 1992, J1.

96. Don Hellriegel, John W. Slocum, Richard W. Woodman. *Organizational Behavior*. Fourth Edition. St. Paul: West Publishing Company, 1986, 530; citing L. Moss. *Management Stress*. Reading, Mass.: Addison-Wesley, 1981, 66.

97. Jerry E. Bishop, "The Personal and Business Costs of 'Job Burnout'," *The Wall Street Journal*, November 11, 1980, 31.

98. D. Etzion, "Moderating Effect of Social Support on the Stress-Burnout Relationship," *Journal of Applied Psychology*, Vol. 69, 1984, 615 - 622.

99. "Japanese Are Worked to Death," *The Toronto Sun*, Monday, March 12, 1990, 43.

100. "Tokyo Rules Executive Died of Too Much Work," *The Toronto Star*, Thursday, July 16, 1992, F2.

101. Alastair Dow, "Compensating Injured Workers No Simple Issue," *The Toronto Star*, Saturday, May 2, 1992, D2.

102. Joann S. Lublin, "On-the-Job Stress Leads Many Workers to File - and Win - Compensation Awards,"

The Wall Street Journal, September 17, 1990.

103. L. Sutton, "Worker's Stress Claim Setback for Employers," *Austin-American Statesman*, March 2, 1978; *also*, "Hare Krishnas Ordered to Pay $32.3 Million in Damages to Women," *Houston Post*, June 18, 1983, 9C.

104. John Heinzl, "Crayon Plant a Brighter Place," *The Globe and Mail*, Thursday, June 18, 1992, B1.

105. Howard Akler, "Executives Fight For Fitness," *Financial Times of Canada*, April 27, 1992, 20.

106. Richard M. Steers. *Introduction to Organizational Behavior*. Third Edition. Glenview, Illinois: Scott, Foresman and Company, 1988, 518.

107. "Laughter: The Best Medicine for Burnout?" *Arizona Daily Star*, March 22, 1987, A5

CHAPTER 15

1. Patricia Owen, "The Fight for Dignity," *The Toronto Star*, Tuesday, February 25, 1992, A19.

2. "Mandela: Now and Then," *The Globe and Mail*, Monday, February 12, 1990, A7.

3. David Vienneau, "Gender Push Is Paying Off, Women Told," *The Toronto Star*, Sunday, February 16, 1992, A11.

4. Tom Villemarie, "A Search For Fairness," *The News*, January 31, 1988, 8.

5. Catherine Dunphy, "Workplace Equality," *The Toronto Star*, Monday, January 2, 1989, C1

6. Sean Fine, "Women's Unpaid Work 40% of National Product, Author Says," *The Globe and Mail*, Tuesday, March 13, 1990, A4.

7. John Raymond, "Worth Repeating," *The Globe and Mail*, Monday, July 13, 1992, B4.

8. Ann Rauhala, "An Uphill Battle," *The Globe and Mail*, Saturday, August 20, 1988, D1, 2.

9. Dorothy Lipovenko, "Fifth Column," *The Globe and Mail*, Monday, September 24, 1990, A16.

10. Donald E. Yates, "Japanese-style Layoffs Put Women First," *The Toronto Star*, Monday, July 20, 1992, C5.

11. Doris Anderson, "Finishing the Unfinished Revolution," *Canadian Forum*, Vol. LXX, Number 806, January/February 1992, 6.

12. Joyce Hollyday, "Trials and Triumphs for Feminism," *Sojourners*, June 1992, 4. *See also* Alanna Mitchell, "Working Women Gaining Equality," *The Globe and Mail*, Wednesday, March 3, 1993, A1, 6.

13. Michele Landsberg, "Killer's Rage Too Familiar to Canadians," *The Toronto Star*, Friday, December 8, 1989, A1, 16.

14. Jay Kinney, "Imagination and the Sacred," *Gnosis*, Spring, 1992, 55.

15. Colleen Dudgeon, "Trying to Keep Work and Home Life Separate," *The Toronto Star*, Monday, January 20, 1992, B1.

16. Chris Lee, "Balancing Work & Family," *Training*, Vol. 28, No. 9, September 1991, 23 - 28.

17. Margot Gibb-Clark, "Time Taken Off for Family Soars," *The Globe and Mail*, Wednesday, March 4, 1992, A1.

18. Virginia Galt, "Low-cost Solutions Eyed in Easing Work-family Pressures," *The Globe and Mail*, Wednesday, January 22, 1992, A5.

19. Margot Gibb-Clark, "Family Stress Affecting Two-thirds of Workers, Study Finds," *The Globe and Mail*, Friday, September 22, 1989, B3.

20. Jeff Sallot [interview of Chief Justice Antonio Lamer of the Supreme Court of Canada], "How the Charter Changes Justice," *The Globe and Mail*, Friday, April 17, 1992, A11.

21. Margot Gibb-Clark, "Stitching Together the Family Fabric," *The Globe and Mail*, Tuesday, July 28, 1992, B20.

22. Margot Gibb-Clark, "'People Care Days' at Bank of Montreal," *The Globe and Mail*, Monday, June 29, 1992, B4.

23. Canadian Press, "Canada Watch," *The Globe and Mail*, Tuesday, June 16, 1992, A7.

24. Sue Shellenbarger, "Firms help Men Adapt to Changing Roles," *The Globe and Mail*, Monday, August 3, 1992, B4.

25. Ruth Miller, "Fifth Column," *The Globe and Mail*, Tuesday, April 14, 1992, A16.

26. Sean Fine, "Unicef Report Links Child Welfare to Women's Rights," *The Globe and Mail*, Friday, December 13, 1991, A1.

27. Sarah Jane Growe, "The Glass Ceiling," *The Toronto Star*, Friday, June 11, 1986, B1. *See also* Diane Francis, "Women Are Closer to Breaking the 'Glass Ceiling'," *The Financial Post*, Tuesday, March 9, 1993, 19.

28. Carol Thomas, "Still Trying to Close the Gap for Women," *Hospital News*, August 1988, 20.

29. Margot Gibb-Clark, "Give Employees More Say in Pensions," *The Globe and Mail*, Monday, June 15, 1992, B4.

30. Clarence Page, "Hate Erupts When Others Start Doing Well," *The Toronto Star*, Thursday, December 14, 1989, A25.

31. Barrie McKenna, "Women Face Closed Door to Boardrooms," *The Globe and Mail*, Tuesday, June 30, 1992, B14.

32. Olivia Ward, "Women's Interests Still Take Back Seat," *The Toronto Star*, October 21, 1991, A11.

33. Reuters News Agency, "Women Will Shatter 'Glass Ceiling' of Congress, NOW President Says," *The Globe and Mail*, Saturday, June 27, 1992, A6.

34. Anne B. Fisher, "Where Women Are Succeeding," *Fortune*, August 3, 1987, 78 - 81, 84; *also*, "Women Executives" in *Macleans*, September 3, 1990, Vol. 103, No. 36 and "Women at the Top," *Report on Business Magazine*, October 1990.

35. Orland French, "Top Jobs Still Elude Women Teachers," *The Globe and Mail*, Wednesday, August 15, 1990, A6.

36. Peter Gorrie, "TD Bank Paves Way to Employment Equity," *The Toronto Star*, Wednesday, September 5, 1990, B1, 6.

37. Margot Gibb-Clark, "Bank Mulls Quotas for Women," *The Globe and Mail*, Thursday, October 25, 1990, B1.

38. Danny Gallagher, "Agent Works Hard to Dispel Myth," *The Globe and Mail*, Tuesday, February 25, 1992, C10.

39. Carole Hoglund, "Discriminating Behaviour," *The Human Resources Professional*, February 1992, 7.

40. "Manager Study Raises Controversy," *The Globe and Mail*, Monday, December 10, 1990, B4.

41. "China Ponders Equality for Women," *The Globe and Mail*, Saturday, March 28, 1992, A11.

42. "Woman Wins 4-Year Fight for Better Job," *The Globe and Mail*, Thursday, April 30, 1992, A7.

43. Mary Jollimore, "Female Umpires Need Not Apply," *The Globe and Mail*, Friday, July 3, 1992, C12.

44. "Bouncing Bust Got Her Fired TV Host Says," *The Toronto Star*, Tuesday, March 13, 1990, D7.

45. "Dwarf to Sue French Government for Lost Wages," *The Globe and Mail*, Saturday, January 18, 1992, A12.

46. Diane Francis, "Canada Is a Tyranny of Excess Tolerance," *Maclean's*, July 27, 1992, 13.

47. Reginald Bibby, "Canadians Left Out on a Limb," *The Globe and Mail*, Thursday, June 27, 1991, A18.

48. Michael Posner, "The Individual in Retreat," *The Globe and Mail*, Saturday, August 17, 1991, D1.

49. Barbara Amiel, "Another Threat to Freedom in Ontario," *Maclean's*, July 20, 1992, 11.

50. Jack Kapica, "Fifth Column," *The Globe and Mail*, Wednesday, August 5, 1992, A14.

51. Tony Wong, "Rights Law Ruled Unfair to Lesbians, Gays," *The Toronto Star*, Friday, August 7, 1992, A1.

52. Canadian Press and Staff, "Rights Act Discriminates Against Gays, Court Rules," *The Globe and Mail*, Friday, August 7, 1992, A4.

53. Terry Thompson, "Rhetoric and Reality," *CA Magazine*, August 1992, 56.

54. Richard Gwyn, "Canada's 'Rights Revolution'," *The Toronto Star*, Sunday, July 19, 1992, B1, 7. *Also*, Richard Gwyn, "Is Multiculturalism Becoming Multi-nationalism?" *The Toronto Star*, Sunday, February 28, 1993, B3.

55. Michael Novak. *The Spirit of Democratic Capitalism*. New York: An American Enterprise Institute/Simon & Schuster Publication, 1982.

56. "Doctors Question Consent Legislation," *The Globe and Mail*, Thursday, August 6, 1992, A8.

57. Andrew Mair, "Bill 109 on Health Care Is a Serious Misdiagnosis," *The Weekender (Markham Economist & Sun)*, August 8, 1992, 8.

58. Judge Rosalie Silberman Abella, Royal Commission on Equality in Employment (Abella Commission). *Equality in Employment*. Ottawa: Minister of Supply and Services Canada, 1984, 7.

59. Thomas H. Stone, Noah M. Meltz. *Human Resource Management in Canada*. Second Edition. Toronto: Holt, Rinehart and Winston of Canada, Limited, 1988, 40.

60. "Hiring Law Remedies Past Error, BDP Says," *The Toronto Star*, Friday, June 26, 1992, A8.

61. George T. Milkovich, William F. Glueck, Richard T. Barth, Steven L. McShane. *Canadian Personnel/Human Resource management: A Diagnostic Approach*. Plano, Texas: Business Publications, Inc., 1988, 280. *See also* Canadian Human Rights Commission. *1986 Annual Report*. Ottawa: Minister of Supply and Services Canada, 1987, 24; Warren Gerard, "Workplace Equality Law Just Around the Corner," *The Toronto Star*, Saturday, February 8, 1992, D5; Craig McInnes, Martin Mittelstaedt, Lila Sarick, "Discrimination Pervasive, Lewis Says," *The Globe and Mail*, Wednesday, June 10, 1992, A13.

62. Editorial, "Keep Hiring Practices Fair," *The Financial Post*, Wednesday, June 3, 1992, 10.

63. Richard L. Daft, Patricia A. Fitzgerald. *Management*. First Canadian Edition. Toronto: Dryden Canada (a Division of Holt, Rinehart and Winston of Canada), 1992, 385. There is a debate as to whether employment equity is the same or not as affirmative action. The Cross Cultural Communication Centre of Toronto says "affirmative action" *before* the Abella report (1984) and "employment equity" *after* the Abella report (1984 on): Jane Allan. *Employment Equity: How We Can Use It To Fight Workplace Racism*. Toronto: Cross Cultural Communication Centre, 1988, 6. *See also* Marjorie Cohen, "Employment Equity is Not Affirmative Action," *Canadian Women's Studies*, Vol. 6, No. 4, Winter 1984, 38 (in Jane Allan, *ibid.*, 24).

64. Editorial, "Equity Law Adds Another Burden," *The Financial Post*, Friday, June 26, 1992, 44. *Also*, Editorial, "The Arithmetic of Race and Pay," *The Globe and Mail*, Thursday, November 21, 1991, A20; Editorial, "Affirmative Action Without the Quotas," *The Globe and Mail*, Wednesday, May 20, 1992, A12; Editorial, "When Is a Quota Not a Quota?" *The Globe and Mail*, Saturday, June 27, 1992, D6.

65. Thomas H. Stone, Noah M. Meltz, *op. cit.*, 101. *See also* Linda Gutri, "Training for Equity," *Human Resources Professional*, February 1993, 13 - 14, 16.

66. Helen Hendersen, "Job Equity Commissioner Battles Misconceptions," *The Toronto Star*, Saturday, August 8, 1992, H5.

67. Trish Crawford, "Creating Opportunities," *The Toronto Star*, Sunday, February 23, 1992, H4.

68. Paula Todd, "Don't Make White Males Suffer for Past, NDP Urged," *The Toronto Star*, Thursday,

November 21, 1991, A2.

69. Thomas Hurka, "Fifth Column," *The Globe and Mail*, Tuesday, December 3, 1991, A20.

70. Reuters News Agency, "Veterans Tell of Sex Assaults by Colleagues," *The Globe and Mail*, Wednesday, July 1, 1992, A10.

71. Paula Todd, "NDP Closes School for Prison Workers," *The Toronto Star*, Friday, July 17, 1992, A32.

72. Martin Mittelstaedt, "Abuse Began Early at Guard School," *The Globe and Mail*, The Globe and Mail, Saturday, July 17, 1992, A3.

73. Kelly Toughill, "Harassment Part of Job for Female Jail Guards," *The Toronto Star*, Saturday, August 1, 1992, A18.

74. Bonnie Cornell, Judy Hauserman, "Working It Out," *Pathways*, January/February 1993, Volume 2, No. 1, 20.

75. Linda Hossie, "Men Often Deny Harassment Charges," *The Globe and Mail*, Wednesday, October 16, 1991, A10.

76. Robert Macleod, "Toronto Life," *The Globe and Mail*, Thursday, June 18, 1992, A19. Also, Geoffrey York, "Rights Panel Reports Rise in Harassment Complaints," *The Globe and Mail*, Friday, March 19, 1993, A3.

77. "Female Corporal Files Sex Harassment Charge," *The Toronto Star*, Sunday, June 28, 1992, A8.

78. Virginia Galt, "Union's Macho Image Undergoes Transformation," *The Globe and Mail*, Saturday, May 30, 1992, A8.

79. Chris Lee, "Sexual Harassment: After the Headlines," *Training*, Vol. 29, No. 3, March 1992, 29.

80. Wilfred List, "Sexual Harassment Leaves Emotional Scars, Disrupts the Workplace," *The Globe and Mail*, Thursday, December 8, 1988, B13.

81. Chris Lee, *op. cit.*, 25.

82. Lynne Sullivan, "10 Commandments on Sexual Harassment," *The Globe and Mail*, Monday, November 4, 1991, B4.

83. Lynne Sullivan, *op. cit.*, B4.

84. Thomas Flanagan, "Equal Pay for Work of Equal Value: Some Theoretical Criticisms," *Canadian Public Policy*, Vol. 13, No. 4, December 1987, 435 - 444.

85. Thomas H. Stone, Noah Meltz. *Personnel Management in Canada*. Toronto: Holt, Rinehart and Winston, 1983, 307.

86. William Watson, "Pay Equity: Idea Whose Time Has Passed," *The Financial Post*, April 12, 1986, 8.

87. Walter McLean, MP Waterloo, "Pay Equity Cost Need Not Be High," *The Financial Post*, March 15, 1986, 8.

88. Jane Coutts, "'Sexism Runs Deeper than Greed'," *The Globe and Mail*, Saturday, December 16, 1989, D1, 8.

89. "Pay Equity Gap Widens in Quebec," *The Toronto Star*, Friday, November 22, 1991, A13.

90. Susan Pigg, "Nurses and Pay Equity," *The Toronto Star*, Tuesday, August 28, 1990, E2.

91. Margot Gibb-Clark, "Pay Equity Catch-up Costs Put at 2 to 6% of Year's Wages," *The Globe and Mail*, Friday, May 25, 1990, B5.

92. Gene Allen, "Ontario Wage Bill to Grow by 14%," *The Globe and Mail*, Saturday, August 31, 1991, A5.

93. Martin Harts, *op. cit.*, B8.

94. Virginia Galt, "Ontario Pay-equity Ruling Sets Precedent for Women," *The Globe and Mail*, Wednesday, June 26, 1991, A4.

95. Bon Papoe, "Pay Equity Can be Profitable, Consultant Advises Employers," *The Toronto Star*, Friday, March 22, 1991, B3.

96. John Raymond, "Worth Repeating," *The Globe and Mail*, Thursday, November 1, 1990, B8.

97. Carolyn Adolph, "Pay Equity Law Will Be Good for Business, Sorbara Says," *The Toronto Star*, Saturday, January 14, 1989, C2.

98. *Implementing Pay Equity in the Workplace*, prepared by the Pay Equity Commission, 150 Eglinton Avenue East, 5th. Floor, Toronto, Ontario M4P 1E8. Telephone: 1-800-387-8813 or 481-3314.

99. Key terms and steps found in "Implementation Checklist," Pay Equity Commission. Accompanying discussion for each term comes from author's research.

100. The Pay Equity Commission, "Pay Equity Implementation Series #2," March 1988, 1.

101. The Pay Equity Commission, "Pay Equity Implementation Series #4," March 1988, 1.

102. The Pay Equity Commission, "How To Read Your Pay Equity Plan: An Information Package For Employees," 3.

103. The Pay Equity Commission, "Pay Equity Implementation Series #5," May 1988, 1.

104. The Pay Equity Commission, "Principles of Gender Neutrality," Vol. 1, No. 7, September 1989, 1.

105. The Pay Equity Commission, "Pay Equity Implementation Series #9," July 1988, 1.

106. The Pay Equity Commission, "How To Ensure Gender Neutrality in Job Comparisons."

107. The Pay Equity Commission, "How To Read Your Pay Equity Plan: An Information Package For Employees," 6.

108. Joel Ruimy, "In Ottawa: How 470 Librarians Rated Annual Raises up to $2,500," *The Toronto Star*, Sunday, February 3, 1985, F5.

109. The Pay Equity Commission, "Pay Equity Implementation Series #10," July 1988, 4.

110. The Pay Equity Commission, "How To Read Your Pay Equity Plan: An Information Package For Employees," 8.

111. The Pay Equity Commission, "Pay Equity Implementation Series #15," January 1989, 1. The contents of the plan below are on 12 - 14.

Implementation Series #10," July 1988, 4.

110. The Pay Equity Commission, "How To Read Your Pay Equity Plan: An Information Package For Employees," 8.

111. The Pay Equity Commission, "Pay Equity Implementation Series #15," January 1989, 1. The contents of the plan below are on 12 - 14.

112. The Pay Equity Commission, "Pay Equity Implementation Series #16," July 1989, 1.

113. The Pay Equity Commission, "Pay Equity Implementation Series #17," July 1989, 1.

114. The Pay Equity Commission, "Pay Equity Implementation Series #16," July 1989, 6.

115. Carolyn Adolph, "Pay Equity: A Scramble Under Way to Decide Job Values," *The Toronto Star*, Saturday, January 14, 1989, C1.

116. Dan Smith, "Who Should Be Paid More - A Carpenter or a Secretary?" *The Toronto Star*, Sunday, February 3, 1985, F1.

117. Tom Villemarie, "A Search For Fairness," *The [Richmond Hill, Ontario] News*, January 31, 1988, 8.

118. Gene Allen, "Pay-equity Process Rejected by Nurses," *The Globe and Mail*, Thursday, April 19, 1990, A, 2.

119. "Toronto's Face Reflects the World," *The Toronto Star*, The Toronto Star, Sunday, June 7, 1992, A1.

120. Paul Watson, "Foreign-born Workers Keep Metro Moving," *The Toronto Star*, Saturday, September 21, 1991, A1, 8.

121. Erna Paris, "Unsaid Words on Racism," *The Globe and Mail*, Tuesday, July 21, 1992, A14.

122. Matthew Ingram, "The Fight to Exorcise Majestic's Bad Image," *Financial Times of Canada*, March 30, 1992, 5.

123. Deborah Wilson, "Hiring Policy 'Racist,' Firm to Pay $300,000," *The Globe and Mail*, Saturday, January 7, 1989, A2.

124. "Dean Urged to Quit for Racist Remark," *The Toronto Star*, Sunday, September 2, 1990, A14.

125. W.B. Johnston, A.E. Packer. *Workforce 2000: Work & Workers for the Twenty-first century*. Washington, D.C.: Hudson Institute, 1987.

126. S. Kanu Kogood, "Managing Diversity in the Workplace," in J. William Pfeiffer (Ed.). *The 1992 Annual: Developing Human Resources*. San Diego, California: Pfeiffer & Company, 1992, 241.

127. Alanna Mitchell, "63 Per Cent Like Multicultural Canada," *The Globe and Mail*, Tuesday, November 5, 1991, A1, 2.

128. "The national ideal had once been *e pluribus unum*. Are we now to belittle *unum* and glorify *pluribus*? Will the center hold? Or will the melting pot yield to the Tower of Babel?" Arthur M. Schlesinger Jr., The Disuniting of America, 1991," in Jack Gordon, "Rethinking Diversity," *Training*, Vol. 29, No. 1, January 1992, 23.

129. Randall Litchfield, "The Deconstitution of Canada," *Canadian Business*, August 1992, 23.

130. Michael Posner, "The Individual in Retreat," *The Globe and Mail*, Saturday, August 17, 1991, D1, 4.

131. Paul Watson, "But Immigration Surge Could Challenge Us All," *The Toronto Star*, Saturday, June 30, 1990, A2.

132. Elizabeth Renzetti, "The View of a Second Century Canadian," *The Globe and Mail*, Wednesday, July 1, 1992, A1.

133. "Equity Issues," *The Globe and Mail*, Tuesday, August 18, 1992, B18.

134. John Raymond, "Worth Repeating," *The Globe and Mail*, Wednesday, May 13, 1992, B8.

135. Michael E. Rock, "Paths to Dialogue: Multiculturalism in Canada," *Rasaneh*, November 16 - December 15, 1988, 9.

136. Janis Foord, "New Human Values Key to Company's Success in Future," *The Toronto Star*, Saturday, February 18, 1989, F6.

137. Royal Bank Letter, "The Civilized Workplace," Vol. 73, No. 2, March/April 1992, 4.

READER REPLY CARD

We are interested in your reaction to *The Dynamics of Supervision*. You can help us to improve this book in future editions by completing this questionnaire.

1. What was your reason for using this book?

   ☐ university course   ☐ college course   ☐ continuing education course
   ☐ professional   ☐ personal   ☐ other _____
     development   interest   _____

2. If you are a student, please identify your school and the course in which you used this book.

3. Which chapters or parts of this book did you use? Which did you omit?

4. What did you like best about this book? What did you like least?

5. Please identify any topics you think should be added to future editions.

6. Please add any comments or suggestions.

7. May we contact you for further information?

   Name: _____

   Address: _____

   _____

   _____

   Phone: _____

(fold here and tape shut)

MAIL ➤ POSTE

Canada Post Corporation / Société canadienne des postes

Postage paid
If mailed in Canada

Port payé
si posté au Canada

**Business
Reply**

**Réponse
d'affaires**

0116870399   01

0116870399-M8Z4X6-BR01

Scott Duncan
Publisher, College Division
HOLT, RINEHART AND WINSTON OF CANADA, LIMITED
55 HORNER AVENUE
TORONTO, ONTARIO
M8Z 9Z9